European Union and its Neighbours in a Globalized World

Volume 6

The series "The European Union and its Neighbours in a Globalized World" will publish monographs and edited volumes in the field of European and International Law and Policy. A special focus will be put on the European Neighbourhood Policy, current problems in European and International Law and Policy as well as the role of the European Union as a global actor. The series will support the cross-border publishing and distribution of research results of cross-border research consortia. Besides renowned scientists the series will also be open for publication projects of young academics. The series will emphasize the interplay of the European Union and its neighbouring countries as well as the important role of the European Union as a key player in the international context of law, economics and politics.

Unique Selling Points:

• Deals with a wide range of topics in regard of European and International Law but is also open to topics which are connected to economic or political science

• Brings together authors from the European Union as well as from accession candidate or neighbouring countries who examine current problems from different perspectives

• Draws on a broad network of excellent scholars in Europe promoted by the SEE | EU Cluster of Excellence, the Europa-Institut of Saarland University as well as in the South East European Law School Network

Derya Nur Kayacan

The Right to Die with Dignity

How Far Do Human Rights Extend?

Springer

Derya Nur Kayacan
Istanbul, Turkey

ISSN 2524-8928 ISSN 2524-8936 (electronic)
European Union and its Neighbours in a Globalized World
ISBN 978-3-031-04515-8 ISBN 978-3-031-04516-5 (eBook)
https://doi.org/10.1007/978-3-031-04516-5

Dissertation presented to the Doctoral Committee of the Faculty of Law, Saarland University in partial fulfilment of the requirements for the degree of Doctor of Law Supervised by Prof. Dr. Thomas Giegerich.

This Springer imprint is published by the registered company Springer Nature Switzerland AG
The registered company address is: Gewerbestrasse 11, 6330 Cham, Switzerland

Acknowledgments

I would like to express my sincere gratitude to my supervisor Prof. Dr. Thomas Giegerich for his continuous support, invaluable guidance, genuine kindness, and patience. He has been a great role model, one who I will always look up to in my academic career. I would also like to thank Prof. Dr. Torsten Stein for his evaluation of my dissertation and insightful comments. I am grateful to Prof. Dr. Ibrahim Kaya, who has encouraged and mentored me during my Master's and PhD.

My gratitude extends to the Turkish Ministry of National Education for funding my graduate studies and giving me the honour of being a scholarship holder.

I wish to express my heartfelt thanks to Katrin Lück, the Head of the Europa-Institut Library, who has made me feel comfortable all those hours spent at the library and helped me find any resource I needed for this work. I would also like to express how lucky I feel to be part of the Europa-Institut family of Saarland University.

I am forever grateful to all my friends, who have kept me company, picked me up when I needed, and cheered me on when I succeeded. A special thank you to Regi Salataj, who has witnessed this entire journey from the beginning to the end, for being the best friend anyone could ever hope to have.

I am also thankful to the city of Saarbrücken that has been home to me during my studies and will always be 'Dahemm'.

No amount of thank you is sufficient to express how deeply grateful I am to my family. My parents Ramazan and Zeliha, my siblings Osman, Sueda, and Sertaç have been my ultimate source of encouragement and self-confidence. They have helped me through all the hardship that comes alongside a PhD process. I am blessed to have such an amazing support system. I hope that I have made them proud.

March 2022

Derya Nur Kayacan

Contents

List of Abbreviations

ACB	Belgian Advisory Committee on Bioethics
ADMD	*Association pour le droit de mourir dans la dignité* (Association for the Right to Die with Dignity)
AGEAS	*Arbeitsgemeinschaft Evangelischer Ärztinnen und Ärzte der Schweiz* (The Association of Protestant Physicians of Switzerland)
AJP/PJA	*Aktuelle Juristische Praxis/Pratique Juridique Actuelle*
ALfA	*Aktions Lebensrecht für Alle e V* (Right to Life for All Action)
Alta L Rev	Alberta Law Review
Am J Sociol	American Journal of Sociology
Annals Health L	Annals of Health Law
Arch Intern Med	Archives of Internal Medicine
Arch Pediatr Adolesc Med	Archives of Pediatrics & Adolescent Medicine
Ariz L Rev	Arizona Law Review
B C Int'l & Comp L Rev	Boston College International and Comparative Law Review
BCCA	British Columbia Court of Appeal
BCCLA	British Columbia Civil Liberties Association
BCSC	British Columbia Supreme Court
Berk J Int L	Berkeley Journal of International Law
BGer	*Bundesgericht* (Swiss Federal Supreme Court)
BMA	British Medical Association
BMC Health Serv Res	BMC Health Services Research
BMJ	British Medical Journal
Br Med Bull	British Medical Bulletin
BR-Dr	*Bundesrats-Drucksache* (Printed Documents of the German Federal Council)

BT-Dr	*Bundestags-Drucksache* (Printed Documents of the German Federal Parliament)
BVerfG	*Bundesverfassungsgericht* (German Federal Constitutional Court)
BVerwG	*Bundesverwaltungsgericht* (German Federal Administrative Court)
CA	Court of Appeal
Camb Q Healthc Ethics	Cambridge Quarterly of Healthcare Ethics
CD&V	*Christen-Democratisch en Vlaams* (Christian Democratic and Flemish)
CDA	Christian Democratic Appeal Party
CEC	Central Ethics Committee of SAMS
CFCEE	*Commission fédérale de contrôle et d'évaluation de l'euthanasie* (Federal Commission for Control and Evaluation of Euthanasia)
CHF	Swiss franc
CJ	Chief Justice
col	column
cols	columns
Comm L World Rev	Common Law World Review
CPS	Crown Prosecution Service
Crit Care	Critical Care
D66	Democrats 66
Dalhousie L J	Dalhousie Law Journal
DAS	Demedicalized assisted suicide
DPP	Director of Public Prosecutions
ECHR	European Convention on Human Rights
ECtHR	European Court of Human Rights
ERAS	*Echtes Recht auf Selbstbestimmung* (Association for Real Right of Self-Determination)
EU	European Union
Eur J Health L	European Journal of Health Law
Eur J Public Health	European Journal of Public Health
EXIT ADMD	EXIT – Association pour le Droit de mourir dans la Dignité/Suisse Romande
EXIT	EXIT – *Deutsche Schweiz*
Fam Prac	Family Practice
FDHA	Federal Department of Home Affairs
FDJP	Federal Department of Justice and Police
FDP	*Freie Demokratische Partei* (Free Democratic Party)
FMH	*Foederatio Medicorum Helveticorum* (Swiss Medical Association)
FPZV	*Federatie Palliatieve Zorg Vlaanderen* (Flemish Palliative Care Federation)

Front Psychol	Frontiers in Psychology
GC	Grand Chamber
GesG-Aargau	*Gesundheitsgesetz des Kantons Aargau* (Aargau Cantonal Health Act)
GesG-Zürich	*Gesundheitsgesetz des Kantons Zürich* (Zurich Cantonal Health Act)
GH	*Gerechtshof* (Court of Appeal – the Netherlands)
GMC	General Medical Council
Hastings Cent Rep	Hastings Center Report
HC	House of Commons
HL	House of Lords
HR	*Hoge Raad* (Supreme Court of the Netherlands)
ICCPR	International Covenant on Civil and Political Rights
Issues L & Med	Issues in Law & Medicine
J Am Med Dir Assoc	Journal of the American Medical Directors Association
J Hosp Tour Res	Journal of Hospitality & Tourism Research
J Med Ethics	Journal of Medical Ethics
J Med Philos	Journal of Medicine and Philosophy
J Neurol	Journal of Neurology
J Pain Symptom Manage	Journal of Pain and Symptom Management
J Palliat Med	Journal of Palliative Medicine
J Soc Christ Ethics	Journal of the Society of Christian Ethics
J	Justice
JAMA Intern Med	JAMA Internal Medicine
KNMG	*De Koninklijke Nederlandsche Maatschappij tot bevordering der Geneeskunst* (Royal Dutch Medical Association)
LEIF	*LevensEinde InformatieForum* (End of Life Information Forum)
MAID	Medical assistance in dying
MDEL	Medical decisions at the end of life
Med L Rev	Medical Law Review
Med Law	Medicine and Law
Mich St U J Med & L	Michigan State University Journal of Medicine and Law
Minn L Rev	Minnesota Law Review
Mod L Rev	Modern Law Review
MP	Member of Parliament
MschKrim	*Monatsschrift für Kriminologie und Strafrechtsreform*
N Eng J Med	New England Journal of Medicine
NaP	Sodium Pentobarbital

NarcA	812.121 Swiss Federal Act on Narcotics and Psychotropic Substances of 3 October 1951 (1 February 2020)/Narcotics Act
NCE	Swiss National Advisory Commission on Biomedical Ethics
NHS	National Health Service
NJB	Nederlands Juristenblad
NRP 67	National Research Programme 'End of Life'
NVK	*Nederlandse Vereniging voor Kindergeneeskunde* (Dutch Association for Pediatrics)
NVVE	*Nederlandse Vereniging voor een Vrijwillig Levenseinde* (Dutch Association for Voluntary End of Life)
NVvP	*Nederlandse Vereniging voor Psychiatrie* (Dutch Association for Psychiatry)
Ordomedic	Ordre des médecins (Order of Physicians)
Ottawa L R	Ottawa Law Review
Oxf J Leg Stud	Oxford Journal of Legal Studies
Parl	Parliament
PAS	Physician-assisted suicide
PvdA	*Partij van de Arbeid* (Labour Party)
QIL	Questions of International Law
Queen's L J	Queen's Law Journal
QUT L Rev	QUT Law Review
RB	*Rechtbank* (Court of first instance)
RCP	Royal College of Physicians
Rev Esp Sanid Penit	*Revista Española de Sanidad Penitenciaria*
RTE	Regional Euthanasia Review Committees
RWS	*Recht op Waardig Sterven* (Right to Die with Dignity)
SAMS	Swiss Academy of Medical Science
SCC	Supreme Court of Canada
SCEN	*Steun en Consultatie bij Euthanasie in Nederland* (Support and Consultation on Euthanasia in the Netherlands)
Schweiz Ärzteztg	*Schweizerische Ärztezeitung*
sec	section
sess	session
Singapore Med J	Singapore Medical Journal
Statut Law Rev	Statute Law Review
Swiss Med Wkly	Swiss Medical Weekly
Swissmedic	Swiss Agency for Therapeutic Products
TPA	812.21 Swiss Federal Act on Medicinal Products and Medical Devices of 15 December 2000 (1 August 2020)/Therapeutic Products Act

UKSC	Supreme Court of the United Kingdom
Vill L Rev	Villanova Law Review
vol	volume
VVD	*Volkspartij voor Vrijheid* (People's Party for Freedom and Democracy)
VVP	*Vlaamse Vereniging voor Psychiatrie* (Flemish Association for Psychiatry)

Chapter 1
Introduction

Throughout time, the law has adapted itself to society's and individual's needs, aiming to achieve a balance for harmony. A need to recalibrate this balance most often occurs after introducing an innovation that affects the lives of all humankind. The Internet, one of the greatest inventions of the twentieth century, presented several new aspects of social life that required the attention of the legislatures, such as data protection and cyber-security. It has also introduced new dimensions of human rights, especially in freedom of expression and the right to privacy. It has been for the law to reconcile the conflicting interests of individuals with each other and with society. Another area in need of recalibration has emerged due to medical advancements.

Over the past century, and mainly since the 1950s, medicine has gone through tremendous developments that have changed many aspects of human life.[1] The capabilities of medicine are enhancing. Vaccines cure once-incurable diseases, and machines support failing organs that can also be replaced by transplantation. Constant research is being done to find new ways to respond to diseases. Developments in medical science and technology transformed life expectancies and the outlook on death. Medicine, which has concentrated solely on saving lives, has started to perceive death as a sign of failure that ran against its raison d'être.[2] However, over time, the focus has shifted from preserving life at all costs to the quality of life that includes more considerations of the patient's expectations from his or her own life. The once paternalistic approach of medicine, where the physician was perceived as 'the guardian who uses his specialised knowledge and training to benefit patients, including deciding unilaterally what constitutes benefit', has been challenged.[3] In light of the greater significance given to patients' wishes, the physician-patient

[1] Player (2018), p. 121.

[2] Ball (2017), p. 15.

[3] Chin (2002), p. 152; See also Glick (1992), pp. 17–18; Meulenbergs and Schotsmans (2005), pp. 125–126.

D. N. Kayacan, *The Right to Die with Dignity*, European Union and its Neighbours in a Globalized World 6, https://doi.org/10.1007/978-3-031-04516-5_1

relationship has been and continues to be redefined as personal autonomy moves towards the center of medical decision-making.[4] One can see this shift in the development of patients' rights, for example, the concept of informed consent or the right to refuse treatment.[5]

Despite the significant developments, there comes the point where medicine can no longer provide satisfying solutions to the patient's problems. Nowadays, the most common cause of death is chronic conditions such as cancer, diabetes, Alzheimer's, or heart disease.[6] While the symptoms of chronic illnesses, which have slower progress, can be managed, a complete recovery is often not achievable. That is why death has become a medical event, which takes place in healthcare institutions surrounded by machines more often than ever.[7] While symptoms can be managed and life can be prolonged, it is not always possible to guarantee a quality of life acceptable to the patient.

On some occasions, despite all the capabilities of medicine, some patients might find themselves in a situation where they are no longer satisfied with their quality of life and would prefer an earlier death. Several reasons could motivate such a preference. There could be a medical condition that causes severe suffering, making life unbearable. Alternatively, a prognosis might indicate a painful end that one would rather wish to avoid, or perhaps it could feel like life has been stripped of its dignity and is no longer worth living. Whatever the reason might be, some patients ask their physicians to help end their lives. With the enhancement of medicine on the one hand and the growing emphasis on personal autonomy on the other hand, whether such a wish from a patient ought to be granted is a question with great complexity. Which decisions can be made at the end of one's life and to what extent one could demand these decisions to be respected has been one of the most controversial debates over the past few decades. With several intertwined aspects of ethics, law, medicine, psychology, and sociology, the question is: Does one have the right to choose the time and manner of one's own death? Is there a right to a dignified death? Does the respect for personal autonomy, namely the right to self-determination, gain sufficient weight to grant a request to end one's life at one's discretion?

This topic is surrounded by subjective notions. When does the suffering reach a point where life becomes unbearable? What qualifies a good death to a specific individual? Under what circumstances would one define one's life to have lost its dignity? Even though these determinations are highly personal and dependent on many subjective circumstances, there are highly critical societal interests that must

---

[4] Nessa and Malterud (1998), p. 394; Tan (2002), p. 149.

[5] Channick (1999), pp. 586–587.

[6] Chronic illnesses cause %71 of all deaths globally. (2018) Noncommunicable Diseases. In: World Health Organization. https://www.who.int/news-room/fact-sheets/detail/noncommunicable-diseases.

[7] Warraich (2017), pp. 51–66; Whiting (2002), pp. 11–12; Otlowski (1997), p. 1; For an interesting approach to the difficulties of expressing personal autonomy at the end of life and how death has become a medicalized event, see Simmons (2017), pp. 95ff.

be considered as well. Protection of life is the strongest argument that stands against the right to die.

The right to life is protected under Article 2 of the European Convention on Human Rights (ECHR or the Convention)[8] and is 'one of the most fundamental provisions in the Convention'.[9] In addition to a negative obligation imposed on the member States not to deliberately take an individual's life, Article 2 also imposes a positive obligation that requires States 'to take appropriate steps to safeguard the lives of those within its jurisdiction'.[10] This positive obligation applies to the medical sphere and assures that appropriate measures and safeguards are adopted to protect patients' lives, who are under the care of the medical profession.[11] Within the right to die debate, the State's positive obligation to protect life, especially of the vulnerable, embedded within the right to life can be divided into two lines of argument. First, the right to die is contrary to the sanctity of life and, therefore, should not be acknowledged at all. Second, even if such a right were to be acknowledged, its practice should not be allowed due to the risk of abuse inherent in its application, namely the 'slippery slope'.

The slippery slope argument is described as the case when 'a proposal is made to accept A, which is not agreed to be morally objectionable, it should nevertheless be rejected because it would lead to B, which is agreed to be morally objectionable'.[12] Within this line of argument, it is suggested that acknowledging and regulating the right to die will ultimately cause a logical or practical slippery slope or both, where the practice will either intentionally or unintentionally extend beyond its initially drawn lines. The logical slippery slope refers to the arguments in favor of the right to die being used to support other morally unacceptable practices. For example, if one defends the right to die for patients with terminal illnesses awaiting death in agony based on reasons of compassion, one must also accept the right to die for patients who are not terminally ill but suffer under extreme pain. In time, one will eventually start approving ending the lives of mentally incompetent patients, who suffer unbearably, which can ultimately cause considering such lives 'unworthy'. Alternatively, if one argues that the right to die stems from the mere respect for personal autonomy, one must be willing to eliminate all other requirements in practice except for the person's autonomous request and allow death on demand. The practical slippery slope focuses on concerns over the insufficiency of safeguards, for example, physician errors, incorrect determination of capacity, or overly broad interpretation of the rules. These concerns also include the fear of societal normalization of the

---

[8] Council of Europe, European Convention for the Protection of Human Rights and Fundamental Freedoms, as amended by Protocols Nos 11 and 14, 4 November 1950, ETS 5 (ECHR).

[9] *McCann and Others v the United Kingdom* 27 September 1995 Ser A no 324, [147].

[10] Centre for Legal Resources on behalf of Valentin Câmpeanu v Romania [GC] App no 47848/08 ECHR 2014 [130].

[11] *Calvelli and Ciglio v Italy* [GC] App no 32967/96 ECHR 2002-I [49].

[12] Keown (2018), p. 68.

right to die practice, eventually leading to the acceptance of more questionable practices.[13]

The debate on the right to die is a search for reconciliation between personal interests, which are based on the right to self-determination, and societal interests, which are embedded in the right to life and find expression as the State's duty to protect the vulnerable. Notions of human dignity, personal autonomy, and sanctity of life seek a refreshed interpretation. These notions also shape the boundaries of medical ethics, determining to which extent the involvement of the medical profession in end-of-life decisions is appropriate. Despite the common understanding of the importance of these notions, their role in the right-to-die debate depends on their interpretation, reflecting elements from society's legal and historical, cultural, and religious backgrounds. How did the European Court of Human Rights (ECtHR or the Court), which has 47 member States with various backgrounds, interpret these notions within the right-to-die context?

After a short description of the terminology, the exemplary jurisdictions of Switzerland, the Netherlands, and Belgium will be examined to understand how and in which manner the right to die has evolved. The ever-increasing respect for personal autonomy and its expanding boundaries will be analyzed by further examining the United Kingdom, Germany, and Canada. Afterward, a study of the Court's case law will present the development of the right to die under the realm of the Convention. In the concluding remarks, an answer will be sought to the question, what is to be expected from the future of this controversial right?

References

(2018) Noncommunicable Diseases. In: World Health Organization. https://www.who.int/news-room/fact-sheets/detail/noncommunicable-diseases

Ball H (2017) The right to die: a reference handbook. ABC-CLIO, Santa Barbara, CA

Channick SA (1999) The myth of autonomy at the end-of-life: questioning the paradigm of rights. Vill L Rev 44(4):577–642

Chin J (2002) Doctor-patient relationship: from medical paternalism to enhanced autonomy. Singapore Med J 43(3):152–155

Glick HR (1992) The right to die: policy innovation and its consequences. Columbia University Press, New York

Kamisar Y (1958) Some non-religious views against proposed mercy-killing legislation. Minn L Rev 42(6):969–1042

Keown J (2018) Euthanasia, ethics and public policy: an argument against legalisation, 2nd edn. Cambridge University Press, Cambridge

Meulenbergs T, Schotsmans P (2005) The sanctity of autonomy? Transcending the opposition between a quality of life and a sanctity of life ethic. In: Schotsmans P, Meulenbergs T (eds) Euthanasia and palliative care in the low countries. Peeters, Leuven

Nessa J, Malterud K (1998) Tell me what's wrong with me: a discourse analysis approach to the concept of patient autonomy. J Med Ethics 24:394–400. https://doi.org/10.1136/jme.24.6.394

[13] Keown (2018), pp. 71–88; Rachels (1986), pp. 173–174; See also Kamisar (1958), pp. 969ff.

Otlowski M (1997) Voluntary euthanasia and the common law. Oxford University Press, New York

Player CT (2018) Death with dignity and mental disorder. Ariz L Rev 60:115–161

Rachels J (1986) The end of life: euthanasia and morality. Oxford University Press, New York

Simmons J (2017) The continental perspective on assisted suicide and euthanasia. In: Cholbi MJ (ed) Euthanasia and assisted suicide: global views on choosing to end life. Praeger, Santa Barbara, CA, pp 95–120

Tan NHSS (2002) Deconstructing paternalism – what serves the patient best? Singapore Med J 43(3):148–151

Warraich H (2017) Modern death: how medicine changed the end of life. St Martin's Press, New York

Whiting R (2002) A natural right to die: twenty-three centuries of debate. Greenwood Press, Westport, CT

Chapter 2
Definitions

Euthanasia is derived from the Greek words εὐ (good) and θάνατος (death), and refers to a 'gentle and easy death'.[1] There are several descriptions of euthanasia in the literature, and the only element common to all is the fact that there is no consistency.

Euthanasia has been divided into subcategories: active/passive euthanasia and voluntary/involuntary/non-voluntary euthanasia. Active euthanasia entails a deliberate action that causes death, whereas, in passive euthanasia, death results from a deliberate omission. The omission of an act that defines passive euthanasia translates to withdrawing or withholding life-sustaining or possibly life-saving treatment.[2] Although the decision to withhold or withdraw treatment could be based on several different reasons (the patient's wishes or if the patient is not able to communicate his or her wishes, medical futility, or the best interest of the patient), what is often required for this omission to qualify as 'passive euthanasia' is the intent to hasten death.[3] The presence of a request to die is the differential element for the second group of subcategories. If euthanasia is carried out upon the autonomous request of the person killed, this is called voluntary euthanasia.[4] Involuntary euthanasia is when the person has not consented to the termination of his or her life, although he or she *was* competent to do so at the time of the killing. If the person *was not* competent to make such a request, this is referred to as non-voluntary euthanasia.[5] Another distinction made in the literature is direct and indirect euthanasia. Direct euthanasia refers to an action carried out with the express intention to terminate life. In contrast, indirect euthanasia is used for cases when causing death is not the intention but

[1] Focarelli (2020), para. 1.

[2] Lewis (2007), p. 5.

[3] Otlowski (1997), p. 5.

[4] Singer (2011), p. 157; Focarelli (2020), para. 7.

[5] Singer (2011), p. 158; Focarelli (2020), para. 7.

D. N. Kayacan, *The Right to Die with Dignity*, European Union and its Neighbours in a Globalized World 6, https://doi.org/10.1007/978-3-031-04516-5_2

occurs as a known side effect (administering pain medication in increasing dosages to relieve suffering).[6]

Euthanasia has been used as a general term to refer to medical decisions that have the effect of shortening life. However, subcategorizing euthanasia has been recently considered to be 'outdated',[7] confusing, and unnecessary.[8] For the purposes of this study, which focuses on the right to die based on the notion of personal autonomy, euthanasia is the act of terminating the life of a person upon that person's explicit and autonomous request. Other forms described in the previous paragraph that fall outside this definition will not be referred to as euthanasia. Admittedly, the right to refuse treatment and withdrawing or withholding life-sustaining treatment are crucial topics that represent a big part of end-of-life decisions and require a detailed analysis of their own. However, these medical decisions, whether made by the patient or by third parties when the patient is not competent to make such a decision, fall outside the scope of the present study, which focuses on active termination of life.[9] The fact that an explicit and autonomous request to die is an integral component of the euthanasia definition renders the subcategories based on voluntariness substantially flawed. Additionally, death is the primary goal of euthanasia, which makes the direct and indirect classification irrational. Therefore, such adjectives (active, passive, voluntary, involuntary, non-voluntary, direct, indirect) will not be used unless necessary for emphasis.

While being in a terminal phase or the existence of an incurable illness or unbearable suffering has been included in some definitions,[10] it is better to place these concepts as prerequisites for the practice of euthanasia and not as part of its definition. The person requesting euthanasia only makes such a request if he or she has concluded that death is the better option under his or her own specific circumstances. This side of the scale is the realization of personal autonomy. To what extent a euthanasia request ought to be granted, if at all, is determined against the other side of the scale, which holds concerns like respect for human life, medical ethics, and the protection of the vulnerable. Prerequisites such as incurable illness or unbearable suffering answer the question, 'under which circumstances will both sides of the

---

[6]Focarelli (2020), para. 9.

[7]Griffiths et al. (2008), p. 76.

[8]Lewis (2007), p. 5; Radbruch et al. (2016), p. 108; According to Leenen, some life-shortening medical decisions, which can be referred to as a form of euthanasia, such as termination of medically futile treatment, administration of pain medication, or decisions based on the patient's right to refuse treatment are 'distorted silhouettes of euthanasia'. Leenen (1984), pp. 335–337.

[9]The Lambert Case, which will be analysed under Sect. 4.1.7 'The Lambert Case', will touch upon the ECtHR's approach to withdrawal of treatment. However, the inclusion of this judgment in this study does not aim to capture or comment on the legal issues surrounding these topics. It only aims to complement the analysis of the member States' positive obligation under Article 2 of the Convention regarding the process of end-of-life decision-making.

[10]Beauchamp and Davidson's definition requires the person asking to be killed to be in a state of 'acute suffering or irreversibly comatoseness' in order for the act to qualify as euthanasia. Beauchamp and Davidson (1979), p. 304; Editors of Encyclopaedia Britannica (2021) Euthanasia. In: Encyclopædia Britannica. https://www.britannica.com/topic/euthanasia.

scale find balance?' They are tools to identify the limits of personal autonomy and justify *the practice of euthanasia* rather than defining *the act of euthanasia*.

Furthermore, whether someone is terminally ill or whether an illness is truly incurable are medical considerations that cannot always be precisely determined. On the other hand, unbearable suffering is a subjective state that could mean different things to each person. Including these concepts in the definition of euthanasia carries the disputes on its justifiability to its definition.[11]

Assisted suicide takes place when a person ends his or her own life with another person's assistance, and when a physician acting in a professional capacity provides this assistance, it is specified as physician-assisted suicide.[12] What differentiates assisted suicide from euthanasia is by whom the final act is performed. In assisted suicide, the person wishing to die performs the final act that causes death. However, in euthanasia, the final act is performed by another person. It will be seen in Chapter C that assistance is commonly provided in the form of prescribing lethal medication. Some people prefer to avoid using the word 'suicide' in this context due to the negative connotation it entails and choose to call it assisted dying instead. This argument is usually based on the moral stigma attached to the term 'suicide', which is considered a preventable incident often committed in a mentally unstable state. Suicide in this sense is different from what is referred to as 'assisted suicide' because, in the context of the right to die as discussed here, the person wishing to end his or her life has come to this decision for different reasons.[13] Such phrases like 'death with dignity' or 'aid in dying' have also been preferred by proponents of the right to die.[14] Although recognizing the reasons behind the choice to use words free from negative implications that the word 'suicide' might carry, it will be more practical to use the phrase 'assisted-suicide' for this study. Furthermore, the phrase 'assisted dying' will cover both practices of euthanasia and assisted suicide.

---

[11] Leenen (1984), p. 334.

[12] Radbruch et al. (2016), pp. 108–109.

[13] Friesen evaluates the grounds to avoid using the term 'suicide' when talking about assisted dying and concludes that there is more harm than good in concentrating on the differences between the two terms. Friesen (2020), pp. 32ff.

[14] Death with Dignity National Center, which is a nonprofit organization in the USA that promotes legislation for assisted dying, considers the use of 'assisted suicide' within the context of the right to die to be 'politicized language deployed with the intent of reducing support for the issue' and recommend using 'value-neutral language' such as death with dignity, assisted dying or aid in dying. Death with Dignity, Terminology of Assisted Dying. https://www.deathwithdignity.org/terminology/; Compassion & Choices, which is also a nonprofit organization working for the promotion of end-of-life choices in the USA, prefers the term 'medical aid in dying'. Compassion & Choices, Understanding Medical Aid in Dying. https://compassionandchoices.org/end-of-life-planning/learn/understanding-medical-aid-dying/; However, Feltz's study results indicate that there is only a minor decrease in acceptability when the term 'physician-assisted suicide' is used instead of 'assisted dying'. The negative connotation of the word 'suicide' might not have the impact one thinks it does. Feltz (2015), pp. 217ff.

References

Beauchamp TL, Davidson AI (1979) The definition of euthanasia. J Med Philos 4(3):294–312
Compassion & Choices, Understanding Medical Aid in Dying. https://compassionandchoices.org/end-of-life-planning/learn/understanding-medical-aid-dying/
Death with Dignity, Terminology of Assisted Dying. https://www.deathwithdignity.org/terminology/
Editors of Encyclopaedia Britannica (2021) Euthanasia. In: Encyclopædia Britannica. https://www.britannica.com/topic/euthanasia
Feltz A (2015) Everyday attitudes about euthanasia and the slippery slope argument. In: Cholbi M, Varelius J (eds) New directions in the ethics of assisted suicide and euthanasia. Springer, Cham
Focarelli C (2020) Euthanasia. Max Planck Encyclopedia of Public International Law. https://opil.ouplaw.com/view/10.1093/law:epil/9780199231690/law-9780199231690-e793?prd=EPIL
Friesen P (2020) Medically assisted dying and suicide: how are they different, and how are they similar? Hastings Cent Rep 50(1):32–43
Griffiths J, Weyers H, Adams M (2008) Euthanasia and law in Europe. Hart Publishing, Oxford
Leenen HJJ (1984) The definition of euthanasia. Med Law 3(4):333–338
Lewis P (2007) Assisted dying and legal change. Oxford University Press, Oxford
Otlowski M (1997) Voluntary euthanasia and the common law. Oxford University Press, New York
Radbruch L, Leget C, Bahr P et al (2016) Euthanasia and physician-assisted suicide: a White Paper from the European Association for Palliative Care. Palliative Medicine 30(2):104–116. https://doi.org/10.1177/0269216315616524
Singer P (2011) Practical ethics, 3rd edn. Cambridge University Press, New York

Chapter 3
The Right to Die in Practice

Personal autonomy in end-of-life decisions is perceived differently worldwide and receives various levels of interpretation depending on the jurisdiction. The weight given to personal autonomy reflects elements from society's historical, cultural, religious, and legal backgrounds. Today, several jurisdictions interpret personal autonomy in a permissive way of the decision to end one's own life, namely the right to die. Although sharing some common features, the right to die is practiced in various ways. While some only allow physician-assisted suicide, others have chosen to legalize euthanasia. The requirements for assisted dying might be different as well.

Several non-European States have regulated the right to die. The Constitutional Court of Colombia had accepted the right to die with dignity in 1997, and the Ministry of Health and Social Protection adopted a Resolution providing guidelines for the practice of euthanasia in 2015.[1] In 2018, Colombia became the third ever State, after the Netherlands and Belgium, to regulate euthanasia for minors subject to strict requirements.[2] The State of Victoria, Australia, passed a bill in 2017 that legalized assisted dying for terminal patients as of 19 June 2019.[3] Western

[1] In 1997, the Constitutional Court of Colombia had ruled that 'denying a terminal patient the right to die with dignity violated equality and imposed a discriminatory burden against those seriously ill or impaired.' The Government did not take any steps to regulate the right to die until 2015, and the Court's decision did not find any implementation. Upon another judgment from the Constitutional Court in 2014, the Ministry of Health adopted a resolution in 2015 that provided guidelines for the practice euthanasia. The choice is only available for terminal patients with unbearable suffering and who are competent to make a decision to end their life. Only a physician is authorized to carry out the procedure. [1997] Colombian Constitutional Court Decision C-239/1997; [2014] Colombian Constitutional Court Decision T-970/2014; See also Palomino (2017), pp. 51ff.

[2] [2017] Colombian Constitutional Court Decision T-544/2017; Triviño (2018) Colombia Has Regulated Euthanasia for Children and Adolescents. In: LatinAmerican Post. https://latinamericanpost.com/20090-colombia-has-regulated-euthanasia-for-children-and-adolescents.

[3] The physician will administer the medication only if the patient is not physically capable of doing so himself or herself. Therefore, the rule is physician-assisted suicide with an exception for

D. N. Kayacan, *The Right to Die with Dignity*, European Union and its Neighbours in a Globalized World 6, https://doi.org/10.1007/978-3-031-04516-5_3

Australia passed a similar bill in December 2019 that has come into effect on 1st of July, 2021 after an 18-month implementation period.[4] In a referendum held in October 2020, 65.1% of the New Zealanders voted in favour of the assisted dying legislation, which came into force on 7 November 2020.[5] Oregon was the first State to legalize physician-assisted suicide in the United States in 1997. Since then, Montana, Washington, Vermont, California, Colorado, the District of Columbia, Hawaii, New Jersey, and Maine have followed Oregon's example. Physician-assisted dying is legal in Canada, following the Supreme Court's ruling in the Carter Case in 2015. The Council of Europe member States of Switzerland, the Netherlands, Belgium, and Luxembourg have legal systems permissive to assisted dying.

This chapter aims to bring a factual perspective. The most crucial argument, which stands against the right to die, is the protection of life. More accurately, the State must protect its citizens from unwarranted third-party interventions. Within the right-to-die debate, this duty formulates as the protection of the vulnerable. Apart from weakening the value of human life, what is most feared is the possibility of ending one's life without that person's honest and sincere request, meaning that assisted dying will open a door that puts the lives of vulnerable people in danger. Based on the State's duty to protect the vulnerable, any argument made favouring the right to die must be balanced against the risk of abuse. Whether such a risk exists will remain a theoretical question unless one analyses the States that have already permitted assisted dying. How was the legalization of assisted dying enacted in these permissive jurisdictions? What was the path taken and points discussed along the way? As it has been stated, 'the best guide to what *could* happen is what *has* happened'.[6] Famous for its assisted suicide organizations, Switzerland will be analysed first. Following will be an examination of the Dutch and Belgian experiences with their respective legislation on euthanasia. Some crucial developments from the United Kingdom and Germany will be mentioned for comparison. Finally, two landmark cases from the Canadian Supreme Court will contribute by portraying a change of perspective over time.

---

euthanasia only when the circumstances do not allow otherwise. Victoria, Australia, Voluntary Assisted Dying Act 2017, No 61 of 2017 (19 June 2020).

[4]Western Australia, Australia, Voluntary Assisted Dying Act 2019, No 027 of 2019 (19 December 2019).

[5]New Zealand, End of Life Choice Act 2019, 2019 No 67 (7 November 2020); Official Referendum Results Released. In: Electoral Commission. https://elections.nz/media-and-news/2020/official-referendum-results-released/.

[6]Jones et al. (2017), p. 1.

3.1 Switzerland

Switzerland has become famous for its liberal practice of assisted suicide and its assisted suicide organizations. Many people from around the world have travelled to Switzerland to end their lives through the services provided by these assisted suicide organizations, which introduced the term 'suicide tourism' or 'death tourism'.[7] According to one of the two organizations that provide suicide assistance to foreigners, over 3.200 people have travelled to Switzerland between 1999 and 2020 to end their lives.[8] Around 46% of the people seeking assistance from this organization were German nationals. In 2018, an Australian scientist David Goodall chose Switzerland to end his life at the age of 104, causing an intense public debate and drawing attention worldwide.[9] Kay Carter, after whom the Canadian Supreme Court case that legalized assisted dying is named, had also sought assistance in Switzerland.[10] A British citizen, Debbie Purdy, had brought a case before the British courts to guarantee that her husband would not be prosecuted for helping her travel to Switzerland, where she would end her life. The case caused public debate in the UK, and the outcome was defined as a victory for assisted suicide.[11] These are only a few examples illustrating the cross-border effects of the Swiss practice of assisted suicide.

Switzerland, one of the most liberal states on the subject, does not have a legal framework for assisted suicide. The Swiss model of assisted suicide emerged from the omission of a Criminal Code article, which will be mentioned next, and developed over time through informal customs and cases, with the irrefutable influence of the assisted suicide organizations.[12]

After analysing the foundations of assisted suicide, examining the Swiss model and how it became the practice it is today will be approached from four complementary aspects: organizational, medical, judicial, and administrative.

[7] Due to the frequent public debates on the matter, the phrase *Sterbetourismus*, which translates to death tourism, was chosen as the Word of the Year in 2007 in Switzerland. (2007) Death Tourism Tops Swiss Word List. In: SWI swissinfo.ch. https://www.swissinfo.ch/eng/death-tourism-tops-swiss-word-list/6299814; See also Srinivas (2009), pp. 91ff; Yu et al. (2020), pp. 694ff.

[8] Dignitas, Accompanied Suicide of Members of Dignitas, by Year and by Country of Residency 1998–2020. http://www.dignitas.ch/index.php?option=com_content&view=article&id=32&Itemid=72&lang=en.

[9] Oltermann (2018) David Goodall, Australia's oldest scientist, ends his own life aged 104. In: The Guardian. https://www.theguardian.com/society/2018/may/10/david-goodall-australias-oldest-scientist-ends-his-own-life-at-104.

[10] *Carter v Canada (Attorney General)* 2015 SCC 5, [2015] 1 SCR 331; Todd (2015) The Story at the Heart of Friday's Supreme Court Ruling on Assisted Suicide. In: Vancouver Sun. https://vancouversun.com/news/staff-blogs/b-c-woman-chooses-a-dignified-death-in-switzerland.

[11] *R (Purdy) v the Director of Public Prosecutions* [2009] UKHL 45, [2010] 1 AC 345; Hirsch (2009) Debbie Purdy wins "significant legal victory" on assisted suicide. In: The Guardian. https://www.theguardian.com/society/2009/jul/30/debbie-purdy-assisted-suicide-legal-victory.

[12] Hurst and Mauron (2017), p. 203.

3.1.1 Foundation of the Swiss Model

Like many other European States, Switzerland decriminalized suicide in the early twentieth century.[13] Committing suicide for reasons of honour was not unheard of in Switzerland and was even culturally accepted.[14]

Before the Swiss Criminal Code entered into force in 1942, criminal law was within the competency of the Cantons. Attempts for a unified criminal code had started towards the end of the nineteenth century. Carl Stooss, a criminal law professor, was appointed to conduct a comparative analysis of the Cantonal criminal codes.[15] In his report, he pointed out the futility of criminalizing suicide.[16] Since assisting someone with an action that is not a crime does not constitute a crime on its own, it was necessary to include a provision that prohibited suicide assistance in order to prevent any abuse.[17] While the necessity of such a provision was never disputed, the conditions punishing suicide assistance were discussed at large. Article 102 of the 1918 draft added the element of 'selfish motives' as a requirement.[18] Inciting or assisting someone to commit suicide would only be illegal if the act was carried out with selfish motives.

The drafters of the Criminal Code did not necessarily have an outcome as remarkable as organized assisted suicide in mind. The 'selfish motives' requirement was rather 'inspired by romantic stories about people committing suicide in defence of their own, or their family's, honour and about suicides committed by rejected lovers'.[19] This approach can be seen in the commentary of the Federal Council's report on the draft Criminal Code, accepting that assistance with suicide could sometimes be a 'friendly deed'.[20] Interestingly, the report mentions an example of

---

[13] Bondolfi (2020) Why assisted suicide is "normal" in Switzerland. In: *SWI swissinfo.ch*. https://www.swissinfo.ch/eng/why-assisted-suicide-is%2D%2Dnormal%2D%2Din-switzerland-/45924614.

[14] Bondolfi (2004), p. 89.

[15] Thommen (2018), p. 373.

[16] 'Eine Bestrafung des Selbstmörders, dessen Versuch misslungen ist, sehen die schweizerischen Gesetze mit Recht nicht vor; in den meisten Fällen liegt der That Geistesstörung zu Grunde, in allen ein Zustand, der Mitleid und nicht Strafe herausfordert.' Stooss (1893), p. 15.

[17] Art 52 'Wer jemanden vorsätzlich zum Selbstmord bestimmt oder ihm dazu Hülfe leistet, wird mit Gefängnis von 3 Monaten bis zu 1 Jahr bestraft.' Stooss (1894), p. 38.

[18] Art 102 'Wer aus selbstsüchtigen Beweggründen jemanden zum Selbstmord verleitet oder ihm dazu Hülfe leistet, wird, wenn der Selbstmord ausgeführt oder versucht wurde, mit Zuchthaus bis zu fünf Jahren oder mit Gefängnis bestraft.' Bundesblatt (1918) Schweizerisches Strafgesetzbuch, Entwurf des Bundesrates an die Bundesversammlung (BBI 1918 IV 103) p. 137.

[19] Guillod and Schmidt (2005), p. 29.

[20] 'Die Selbsttötung ist im modernen Strafrecht kein Vergehen und es liegt keine Veranlassung vor, etwa aus bevölkerungspolitischen Gesichtspunkten auf das frühere Recht zurückzukommen. Aber auch die Überredung zum Selbstmord und die Beihülfe bei einem solchen kann eine Freundestat sein, weshalb hier nur die eigennützige Verleitung und Beihülfe mit Strafe bedroht wird, so z. B. die Überredung einer Person zum Selbstmord, die der Täter zu unterstützen hat oder die er zu beerben hofft (Art. 102).' (The term 'Freundestat' has been translated as 'friendly-deed' by the author.)

mutual assisted suicide of two unhappy lovers who want to end their lives by mutually killing each other.[21] The drafters had acknowledged the motive to end suffering as an acceptable motive for suicide assistance. Ernst Hafter, a criminal law professor with influence over the discussions[22] and who had argued in favour of adding the 'selfish motives' requirement, gave the example of helping an irretrievably ill person commit suicide.[23] However, in 1918, this was hardly the main idea behind Article 102.[24]

Today's concept of assisted suicide is associated with medicine as a solution to unbearable suffering, a way to end a life that has become a burden due to medical complications.[25] Although one might find it difficult to relate with the 'romantic approach' of the early 1900s, it is not difficult to see that it was an approach based on an understanding of respect for human dignity and self-determination of that time period. The contexts of these terms have changed over time, and the suicide decision of a 'rejected lover' would perhaps receive a much different response today. Nevertheless, the crafting of the assisted suicide article sheds light on the origins of Switzerland's liberal approach.

The Swiss Criminal Code was finalized by the end of 1937 and came into force in 1942. The article on 'inciting and assisting suicide' remained the same throughout the debates and found a place under Article 115 of the Swiss Criminal Code that reads:

> Any person who for selfish motives incites or assists another to commit or attempt to commit suicide is, if that other person thereafter commits or attempts to commit suicide, liable to a custodial sentence not exceeding five years or to a monetary penalty.[26]

Article 115 criminalizes selfish suicide assistance, whereas it omits selfless assistance. The Swiss model is based on this deliberate omission.

There are three major requirements for an act of suicide assistance not to constitute a crime. First of all, the decision to commit suicide must be made by a competent adult who is 18 years old or over and can fully understand the consequences of his or her decision. Secondly, the assistant must act without selfish motives. Eventually, the person who wishes to die must carry out the final act that

---

Bundesblatt (1918) Botschaft des Bundesrates an die Bundesversammlung zu einem Gesetzesentwurf enthaltend das schweizerische Strafgesetzbuch (BBI 1918 IV 1), p. 32.

[21] Bundesblatt (1918) Botschaft des Bundesrates an die Bundesversammlung zu einem Gesetzesentwurf enthaltend das schweizerische Strafgesetzbuch (BBI 1918 IV 1), p. 32.

[22] Guillod and Schmidt (2005), p. 29.

[23] Hafter (1912), p. 399.

[24] Mathwig (2010), p. 145.

[25] Within the debate on the right to die, the predominant perception of assisted suicide is still within a medical framework. However, relatively newer concepts, such as 'existential suffering' or 'tiredness of life', pull the debate away from the medical sphere. This will be mentioned in further detail in Sect. 3.2 'The Netherlands'.

[26] 311.0 Swiss Criminal Code of 21 December 1937 (1 July 2020).

leads to his or her death; otherwise, the act would be punishable under other articles of the Criminal Code.

Article 115 does not require the person assisting with suicide to be a physician and the person wishing to commit suicide to suffer from any medical condition. These two points make the practice of assisted suicide in Switzerland 'unique' and different from other permissive states.[27]

Euthanasia is illegal in Switzerland according to Article 114 of the Criminal Code that states:

> Any person who for commendable motives, and in particular out of compassion for the victim, causes the death of a person at that person's own genuine and insistent request is liable to a custodial sentence not exceeding three years or a monetary penalty.

The administration of pain-relieving medication that might have the side effect of hastening death and withholding or withdrawing life-sustaining or prolonging treatments are both acceptable medical practices that are also not explicitly regulated under Swiss law.[28] However, there are medical-ethical guidelines regarding these practices as well as assisted suicide, which will be covered under the role of physicians.

3.1.2 Organizational Aspect of the Swiss Model

According to Article 115, anyone can lend suicide assistance as long as the action is not selfishly motivated. This situation provided grounds for the establishment of assisted suicide organizations, which, in principle, are not selfishly motivated due to their non-profit character.

3.1.2.1 EXIT – Deutsche Schweiz

The largest assisted suicide organization in Switzerland, EXIT – *Deutsche Schweiz* (EXIT), was established in 1982 by Hedwig Zürcher and Walter Baechi, just a few months after EXIT-ADMD. EXIT has been providing suicide assistance since 1990 alongside advance directives services.

EXIT has faced some internal complications that affected the organization's reputation. The executive director Rolf Sigg (1984–97) and the president Dr Meinrad Schär (1992–98) were strong supporters of the absolute right to self-determination. The next executive director Peter Holenstein (1997–98), contrary to his predecessor, argued in favour of more control over the organization's activities and additional training for the suicide companions, who provide suicide assistance.

[27] Hurst and Mauron (2017), p. 199.

[28] Andorno (2013), p. 246.

Holenstein's 'less liberal' views cost him the executive director position, but his criticism about the organization continued to affect its members. Within the same year, Dr Schär's prescription rights were suspended due to a criminal investigation against him for prescribing sodium pentobarbital (NaP) to a mentally ill member without performing a complete medical examination.[29] Criticism was raised again after board member Andreas Blum resigned in 2007, claiming that EXIT lacked transparency and seriousness in its activities and saw itself above the law. He believed that the Government should regulate assisted suicide organizations.[30]

Although EXIT has been subject to many public debates, it is one of the largest assisted suicide organizations with a membership count of over 120.000. Swiss citizens or people with permanent residence in Switzerland, who are fully competent and over 18-years-old, can become a member of EXIT. Membership of EXIT costs an annual amount of CHF 45 or a one-time amount of CHF 1.100. To receive suicide assistance free of charge, one must be a member for a minimum of three years. Otherwise, the cost of services can range from CHF 1.100 to 3.700.[31] EXIT has over 40 suicide companions called *Freitodbegleiter*, who work as volunteers and are only compensated for their expenses. A suicide companion is in close contact with the member wishing to end his or her life. Apart from providing moral support and assistance, the companion will inform the member of other alternatives and assess whether or not the prerequisites for assisted suicide are fulfilled. Suicide companions are not required to have training in medicine or psychiatry, making it questionable whether they are qualified to assess someone's eligibility for assisted suicide or to provide adequate assistance.[32] EXIT states that their suicide companions go through a one-year funded internal training, after which they must successfully pass a test at the University of Basel.[33] However, there is no information on the contents of this training.

In addition to the three requirements derived from Article 115, EXIT requires the member to have either 'an irremediable prognosis or unbearable suffering or an unendurable disability' to receive suicide assistance.[34] To this end, the member should provide documents regarding his or her current state of diagnosis and competency.[35] EXIT's sole method for suicide assistance is a lethal dose of NaP,

---

[29] Lewy (2011), pp. 89–90.

[30] (2007) Es gibt ein Leben vor dem Tod. In: Neue Zürcher Zeitung. https://www.nzz.ch/es_gibt_ein_leben_vor_dem_tod-1.587887.

[31] EXIT - Deutsche Schweiz, Werden Sie Mitglied. https://pv.exit.ch/register.

[32] A doctor, who is a specialist in palliative care, did not only criticize the fact that the suicide companions were incompetent, but also the fact that the EXIT-affiliated physicians were neither psychiatrists nor specialists in palliative care. Borasio (2015), p. 1736.

[33] EXIT - Deutsche Schweiz (2021) EXIT Haupt-Infobroschüre "Selbstbestimmt bis ans Lebensende", 3rd edn. EXIT – (Deutsche Schweiz), Zurich. https://exit.ch/downloads/, p. 20.

[34] EXIT - Deutsche Schweiz, Statuten. https://exit.ch/verein/der-verein/statuten/, Art 2.

[35] EXIT - Deutsche Schweiz (2021) EXIT Haupt-Infobroschüre "Selbstbestimmt bis ans Lebensende", pp. 18–19.

which is available only with a prescription. Members can obtain a prescription from their own physician or an EXIT-affiliated physician.[36]

After the criminal investigation into Dr Schär's actions in 1998, EXIT decided to suspend suicide assistance to mentally ill members. The decision was criticized for being discriminatory. After an expert assessment in 2004, EXIT relaxed its practice for mentally ill members and would no longer automatically reject their applications.[37] Members, who have been suffering from a severe mental illness for an extended time, can request suicide assistance if they are competent to make an end-of-life decision. EXIT requires two independent expert opinions on the member's decision-making capacity and, if necessary, a positive assessment from its own Ethics Committee.[38]

3.1.2.2 EXIT – Association pour le Droit de mourir dans la Dignité/Suisse Romande

EXIT – Suisse Romande, also known as EXIT-ADMD, was founded in 1982. Located in Geneva, it operates in the French-speaking part of Switzerland. Although independent from the German branch, they are known as sister organizations that share the same ideals.[39] EXIT-ADMD accepts members who are residents in Switzerland and over 18-years-old. With an annual fee of CHF 40, the organization has reached more than 31.000 members by the end of 2020.[40]

Among the 542 applications made for suicide assistance in 2019, EXIT-ADMD refused only two. In 2019, a total of 968 members of the organization had died, but only 352 of those members ended their lives with the assistance of EXIT-ADMD. The most cited reason for suicide assistance was comorbidity (multiple illnesses) or cancer. Only two of the cases were solely related to psychiatric problems.[41] In 2020, the organization accepted 507 requests and assisted the suicide of 369 members. Four cases were based on psychiatric complaints.[42]

---

[36] EXIT - Deutsche Schweiz (2021) EXIT Haupt-Infobroschüre "Selbstbestimmt bis ans Lebensende", p. 20.

[37] (2004) Exit lockert Moratorium für Sterbebegleitung. In: SWI swissinfo.ch. https://www.swissinfo.ch/ger/exit-lockert-moratorium-fuer-sterbebegleitung/4194608.

[38] EXIT - Deutsche Schweiz (2021) EXIT Haupt-Infobroschüre "Selbstbestimmt bis ans Lebensende", p. 21.

[39] Suter D (2012) EXIT (Deutsche Schweiz) 1982–2012: Ein Überblick: 30 Jahre Einsatz für Selbstbestimmung. Sutter B (ed) EXIT (Deutsche Schweiz), Zurich. https://exit.ch/fileadmin/user_upload/download/broschueren/exit_30-Jahre-Broschuere_DE.pdf, p. 9.

[40] EXIT - Suisse Romande (2021) Bulletin EXIT No 74. https://www.exit-romandie.ch/nos-bulletins-fr1263.html, p. 13.

[41] EXIT - Suisse Romande (2020) Bulletin EXIT No 72. https://www.exit-romandie.ch/nos-bulletins-fr1263.html, pp. 11, 15.

[42] EXIT - Suisse Romande (2021) Bulletin EXIT No 74, pp. 11–12.

Despite the organization's annual reports, there is still a problem of transparency with EXIT-ADMD's practice. A study published in 2007 analysed the organization's activities between 2001 and 2005. The study showed that in 31% of the files that contained a physician's letter, the physician had not supported the request for suicide assistance.[43] However, EXIT-ADMD had the highest rate of acceptance (95%) during this time period.[44] Providing suicide assistance despite the objection of the physician brings the value that is given to the physician's opinion into question. Why did the physicians oppose assisted suicide in these cases? Were they of the opinion that there were other possible remedies to the member's suffering, or were they not convinced of the member's competency to make an end-of-life decision? Unfortunately, the files did not include enough information to make a proper analysis.

3.1.2.3 Dignitas

A group of EXIT members, who did not appreciate the constant internal complications, left the organization and founded Dignitas under the leadership of the human rights lawyer Ludwig A Minelli in 1998 in Zurich.[45] Dignitas opened a German branch in Hannover in 2005 to pursue its objectives; nevertheless, German citizens have to travel to Switzerland for assisted suicide.[46] By the end of 2020, Dignitas had 10.382 members from 102 different countries.[47] Being the largest organization that accepts foreign members, Dignitas played a significant role in the creation of the term 'suicide tourism'.

As of January 2020, the membership fee of Dignitas costs a one-time payment of CHF 200 in addition to an annual fee of a minimum of CHF 80. Members, who request suicide assistance from Dignitas, should also pay 'additional membership contributions', which include preparation fees (CHF 4.000), physician consultation fees (CHF 1.000), costs for carrying out suicide assistance (CHF 2.500), and, if preferred, funeral arrangement costs (approximately CHF 2.500).[48] Dignitas can make a waiver or an exemption for members who cannot afford these costs. In 2020,

---

[43] Burkhardt (2011) L'assistance au décès à l'aube du XXIème siècle. Privatdozent Thesis, University of Geneva, doi: 10.13097/archive-ouverte/unige:14584, p. 111.

[44] Lewy (2011), p. 103.

[45] Lewy (2011), p. 105.

[46] See Sect. 3.5 'Germany' for recent developments that might change this situation.

[47] Dignitas (2020) Members of DIGNITAS by Country of Residency. http://www.dignitas.ch/images/stories/pdf/statistik-mitglieder-wohnsitzstaat-31122020.pdf.

[48] These amounts do not include taxes and are subject to changes. A member requesting suicide assistance is provided with an invoice including all expenses, and payment is accepted upfront. Dignitas, Information-Brochure. http://www.dignitas.ch/images/stories/pdf/informations-broschuere-dignitas-e.pdf.

CHF 122.500 was spent from the budget to support members with less financial means.[49]

To receive assistance with suicide, Dignitas requires members to have 'a terminal illness and/or an unendurable incapacitating disability and/or unbearable and uncontrollable pain' in addition to the elements of legally acceptable assisted suicide under Article 115 of the Criminal Code.[50] Most of Dignitas's members do not reside in Switzerland, and they need to travel long distances to receive suicide assistance. To make the procedure more practical for members abroad, Dignitas sends the medical documents of the member to a physician for a preliminary evaluation of suitability for a prescription of NaP. The affirmative response of the physician is called a 'provisional green light', which means that the physician is willing to prescribe NaP based on the preliminary examination of the medical documents. The 'provisional green light' is neither a guarantee that assisted suicide will occur nor a promise by the physician to write a prescription.[51] Once the member arrives in Switzerland, a minimum of two in-person medical examinations is required.[52]

For a brief moment in 2008, Dignitas pursued an alternative method to ease the assisted suicide procedures and be free from the medical requirements. Oxygen deficiency by inhaling helium through a mask was used for four assisted suicide cases.[53] Many did not welcome this new method, which drew much negative attention towards Dignitas and the assisted suicide practice in general.[54] Dignitas has stopped using the helium method, and the only available method now is obtaining a prescription of NaP.

In its brochure on 'How Dignitas Works', a detailed step-by-step explanation of the procedure is provided. The importance of member-initiation is repeated continuously to make sure that no pressure is felt throughout the procedure. Emphasis is given to alternative methods, such as improvement of therapy or palliative care options. Dignitas states that most of its members are unaware of the options available to them, and once they have been informed, they often change their minds about going through with assisted suicide. Dignitas also mentions the benefits of having 'good contacts' abroad, which often work like liaison officers by securing necessary

---

[49] Dignitas (2021) Rückblick 2020 und Ausblick 2021. http://www.dignitas.ch/images/stories/pdf/medienmitteilung-29012020.pdf, p. 3.

[50] Identical requirements to those of EXIT; Dignitas, Information-Brochure, p. 6.

[51] Dignitas (2014) How Dignitas Works. http://www.dignitas.ch/images/stories/pdf/so-funktioniert-dignitas-e.pdf, p. 12.

[52] After a letter written by cantonal physician Dr Ulrich Gabathuler (head of the cantonal office of public health) to Dignitas, informing that 'he would consider any prescription for NaP after only one doctor's consultation to be violation of good medical practice. . .[and] he would take disciplinary action against any doctor who wrote such a prescription after only one consultation', Dignitas changed its practice as of 1 February 2008. Dignitas (2014) How Dignitas Works, p. 15.

[53] For a descriptive explanation of these four cases, see Ogden et al. (2010), pp. 174ff.

[54] (2008) Mit Luftballon-Gas in den Tod. In: Neue Zürcher Zeitung. https://www.nzz.ch/mit_luftballon-gas_in_den_tod-1.691954.

documents or recommending possible medical alternatives in the member's home country.

Since its establishment in 1998, Dignitas assisted with the suicides of 3.248 members. In 2020, 221 members, mostly from Germany, the UK, and France, travelled to Switzerland to end their lives.[55]

Dignitas has faced much criticism for accepting foreign members and for its high costs.[56] Establishing a close physician-patient relationship between the foreign member and the prescribing physician is nearly impossible. With Dignitas, most of the communication is done over paper as the physician examines the medical records to assess the suitability for a prescription of NaP during the 'provisional green light' phase. After the member arrives in Switzerland, two in-person consultations with two different physicians are required. It is arguable if the authenticity of someone's wish to die could be adequately evaluated in such a short period of time. There have been cases in which members have ended their lives within the same day of their arrival in Switzerland.[57] However, an argument of empathy could be made by pointing out the hurdles of travelling to another country while suffering from a severe illness. Willing to travel under such circumstances to end one's own life signals a level of determination that cannot be ignored. Most of these members plan their trip to Switzerland at the latest possible time, i.e., when the illness has advanced towards the final stages. To make someone who has already reached an unbearable level of suffering wait in a foreign environment would probably serve against the relief that the person is seeking.

The main concern regarding the hasty consultation process is about the assessment of capacity to make end-of-life decisions. While this concern will force the exclusion of psychiatric cases from the practice of assisted suicide, it can perhaps be eased in the face of the sympathy argument for cases with somatic illnesses. A proper assessment of the decision-making capacity of a mentally ill patient in only two consultations is highly unlikely. However, an experienced physician can deduce the torment caused by a somatic illness by looking at the medical files. The purpose of a consultation is to make sure that the decision to end one's own life is well thought, genuine and independent from any outside influence. Although not independent from the patient's subjective characteristics, somatic illnesses have objective criteria that can be assessed and analyzed, making them understandable for third parties.

On the other hand, mental illnesses depend heavily on subjective elements that make it difficult to assess from afar. From this point of view, the criticism about the short time period might not necessarily be valid in all cases. What would constitute a sufficient amount of time for a physician to properly assess capacity and prescribe

---

[55] Dignitas, Accompanied Suicide of Members of Dignitas, by Year and by Country of Residency 1998–2020.

[56] Sperling discusses the 'social attitudes within Switzerland towards suicide tourism' that reveals different attitudes towards EXIT and Dignitas. While EXIT is respected more, Dignitas is perceived to be 'fanatic'. However, Sperling also states that Dignitas' reputation has been improving recently. Sperling (2019), pp. 146–158.

[57] Lewy (2011), p. 107.

NaP would depend on each patient's circumstances. While a rushed decision might be defendable in extreme situations, for example, when a terminally ill patient is in excruciating pain with absolutely no relief, it would be challenging to justify such a decision in other situations.

The performance of due diligence by Dignitas on this matter has been questionable. Statements reveal that many foreign members who travel for Dignitas's assistance die within a few days, sometimes even within 24 h. In 2005, a German woman with a history of mental illness ended her life with Dignitas's assistance in Switzerland. She had provided Dignitas with a false medical report that diagnosed her with terminal liver cirrhosis, which she had obtained from her physician in Germany with the false pretext to take some days off from work. The incident was discovered after the German authorities carried out an autopsy. The Swiss physician, who had prescribed the NaP, committed suicide after finding out the woman was not terminally ill.[58]

A British couple, none of whom were terminally ill, travelled to Switzerland in 2003 for Dignitas's assistance. Robert Stokes, 59, had epilepsy with up to three severe episodes a week. Jennifer Stokes, 53, had diabetes and suffered from inoperable spinal injuries due to a traffic accident. Although the couple was under constant pain caused by their chronic illnesses, they both had a history of depression and suicide attempts.[59] It has been reported that once the couple arrived in Switzerland, Mrs Stokes faked paralyses by appearing in a wheelchair and claiming she could not use her arms.[60] According to another report, Mrs Stokes's medical records showed that she had multiple sclerosis.[61] Despite the contradicting facts presented, assisted suicides were carried out the day after the couple arrived in Switzerland.

These two examples illustrate that it is possible to falsify medical reports and that there is a lack of due diligence on behalf of Dignitas. Even if Dignitas was somehow 'tricked' into assisting the members in these cases, the short period of time required for in-person consultations makes it rather difficult to argue that proper due diligence was performed. Another report from 2008 about a Spanish man, who was 39-years-old and had paranoid schizophrenia, reiterates the worries about the lack of due diligence. The required in-depth psychiatric assessment was only half a page, and NaP was prescribed by a gynaecologist without an expert opinion on the patient's competency to make an end-of-life decision.[62]

[58]Leidig (2005), p. 1160.

[59]Frith (2004) Couple who died after suicide clinic visit "not terminally ill". In: The Independent. https://www.independent.co.uk/news/world/europe/couple-who-died-after-suicide-clinic-visit-not-terminally-ill-733208.html.

[60]Cox (2009) The Report - Dignitas: Assisted Suicide in Switzerland. In: BBC. https://www.bbc.co.uk/sounds/play/b00jdnsl.

[61](2009) Sterbehilfe für kerngesunde Frau. In: Der Bund. https://www.derbund.ch/zeitungen/schweiz/sterbehilfe%2D%2Dfuer-kerngesunde-frau/story/24525418.

[62](2010) Dignitas schickte Schizophrenen in den Tod. In: Tages Anzeiger. https://m.tagesanzeiger.ch/articles/20026089.

The cost of Dignitas's services ranges from CHF 7.500 to 11.000. Despite being a non-profit organization, high costs and the lack of financial transparency have shadowed Dignitas's reputation. Mr Minelli has been reluctant to provide transparency into the organization's finances.[63] In 2005, some accusations of profiteering were made by former staff members Mr and Mrs Wernli. Mrs Wernli was a suicide companion, and Mr Wernli was the director alongside his long-time friend Mr Minelli. After three years of working with Dignitas, Mr and Mrs Wernli left the organization claiming that Mr Minelli's operation was money-oriented and he had violated the organization's guidelines by rushing the assisted suicide procedures. Mrs Wernli, who continued to work undercover for a couple of months to gather information for the police, claimed that there had been few incidents when the suicide companion or Mr Minelli himself have administered the lethal dose of NaP to the member wishing to die, which is strictly forbidden under the Swiss Criminal Code.[64]

In 2010, several urns filled with human ashes were discovered in Lake Zurich. The urns carried the logo of a crematorium that Dignitas uses. This type of disposal of human remains without a permit is illegal under Swiss law. No criminal charges were pursued despite previous Dignitas employees' statements and Mr Minelli's comments on how he was throwing urns into the lake.[65] It is unclear if the members had wished for their remains to be thrown into Lake Zurich in all these cases. Martha H, an 81-year-old German woman who ended her life with Dignitas's assistance in 2003, had wished her remains to be sent back to Kiel, Germany. However, Mr Minelli threw her urn into Lake Zurich, claiming that Martha H had changed her mind based on a handwritten note in her file that only said *'Urne in See'* (urn in lake), which was conflicting with Martha H's original request. Her donation of over CHF 200.000 to Dignitas and the fact that her family was unaware of her travel to Switzerland fuelled the suspicions towards Dignitas's practice.[66]

Before settling in its facility, called the 'Blue Oasis' in July 2009, Dignitas struggled to find a proper location for its services.[67] The organization has been

---

[63] Lewy (2011), p. 108.

[64] Strebel (2007) Eine Insiderin klagt an. In: Beobachter. https://www.beobachter.ch/gesellschaft/sterbehilfe-eine-insiderin-klagt.

[65] In an interview to the Atlantic, Mr Minelli said that he stores the urns in the trunk of his car and then disposes of them by throwing them into the lake. Former employees, including Mrs Wernli, stated that this was a usual practice at Dignitas. (2010) Dozens of Urns with Human Ashes Found in Lake Zurich. In: HeraldNet. https://www.heraldnet.com/news/dozens-of-urns-with-human-ashes-found-in-lake-zurich/.

[66] Bütikofer (2010) Dignitas-Mitglied: Mehrere 100000 Franken für Freitod bezahlt. In: Aargauer Zeitung. https://www.aargauerzeitung.ch/panorama/vermischtes/dignitas-mitglied-mehrere-100000-franken-fuer-freitod-bezahlt-8663015.

[67] The Zurich Administrative Court found no obstacles for Dignitas to carry out suicide assistance services in an industrial zone. The Court stated that the public interest in enforcing an authorization requirement did not outweigh the private interests of Dignitas and its members, especially considering that assisted suicide cannot be carried out in hotels or cars. *Case on the Blue Oasis* [2007] Verwaltungsgericht des Kantons Zürich VB.2007.00472.

evicted from several apartments, and some of the municipalities even restricted assisted suicide services to be carried out within their residential areas. In some cases, suicide assistance was carried out in vehicles parked in remote areas, which do not seem to be following Dignitas's motto—to Live with Dignity, to Die with Dignity—and these incidences have raised robust criticism.[68] After finding the Blue Oasis, the location problem was mostly resolved. The Blue Oasis is a prefabricated building in an industrial zone located in Pfäffikon, 20 km from Zurich.

In 2018, charges were brought against Mr Minelli for profiteering from three cases of assisted suicides. The first member was an 80-year-old German woman who did not have a terminal illness but felt tired from life. To obtain a prescription for her, Mr Minelli had pursued four physicians. The prosecutor interpreted the motives behind Mr Minelli's insistence for a prescription as selfish when considering it together with the CHF 100.000 donation the member would make to Dignitas. The second and third members were a mother and her daughter from Germany, who were allegedly overcharged with CHF 10.000 each for their assisted suicides.[69] The District Court of Uster decided that there was not enough evidence to prove a case of profiteering. The Court did not find Mr Minelli's yearly salary of CHF 130.000 excessive either. It is reported that the Judge advised Mr Minelli for more financial transparency.[70] The Court emphasized that the acquittal of Mr Minelli should not be interpreted as a 'free-pass' for assisted suicide organizations and that the decision was solely based on the three instances brought before the Court. Therefore, the authorities were urged to continue carefully investigating cases of assisted suicide.[71]

Since 2016, Dignitas has been hiring an accounting firm and publishing its reviews on the website. Although this is a positive step towards financial transparency, the reviews contain only a short statement that no discrepancies have been found. Dignitas still does not provide financial transparency as much as EXIT does.

Dignitas has strong critics as well as devoted supporters. Due to the contradicting tone of news reports on the same events and especially the evasiveness of Dignitas in allowing access to their documents, it is challenging to obtain impartial studies on their practice. However, the lack of transparency is not the only reason for Dignitas's ill reputation. There have been a few controversial statements by Mr Minelli that drew negative attention. In support of assisted suicide, he commented to the BBC about how failed suicide attempts were a financial burden to the UK's National

[68] Sillgitt (2007) Letzte Ausfahrt Parkplatz. In: Der Spiegel. https://www.spiegel.de/panorama/sterbehilfe-letzte-ausfahrt-parkplatz-a-516121.html.

[69] (2018) Dignitas-Gründer Minelli vor Bezirksgericht Uster. In: Top Online. https://www.toponline.ch/news/zuerich/detail/news/dignitas-gruender-minelli-vor-bezirksgericht-uster-0088378/.

[70] (2018) Freispruch für Minelli - aber kein Freipass. In: Zürcher Oberländer. https://zueriost.ch/bezirk-pfaffikon/pfaffikon/freispruch-fuer-minelli-aber-kein-freipass/1063802.

[71] Hasler (2018) Er hat sich nicht bereichert: Dignitas-Gründer freigesprochen. In: Tages Anzeiger. https://www.tagesanzeiger.ch/zuerich/region/er-hat-sich-nicht-bereichert-dignitasgruender-freigesprochen/story/23093108.

Health Service (NHS). Expressing his economic worries on suicide was strongly criticized by the British media.[72] Believing in an absolute right to self-determination, Mr Minelli advocates for an unconditional right to assisted suicide, providing the option also to people without a medical condition. He emphasizes the importance and benefits of an open discussion by stating:

> To be open to a person's genuine feelings of committing suicide and to strive to urge that person to go on living is often a decisive action in preventing a suicide. Imagine that you are standing in front of a heated steam boiler and the pressure just keeps on rising. By being open to a discussion about a risk-free and painless suicide we achieve two things: first we take away the fire and then the pressure. Only after taking away the pressure, we have a chance of helping the person towards life.[73]

He states that 80% of Dignitas members, who wish to receive assistance with suicide, never contact the organization again after receiving the 'provisional green light'. According to Mr Minelli, this percentage illustrates that the availability of assisted suicide as an option is sufficient relief to most people.[74] Nevertheless, his views have caused worry not only among his critics but also among the supporters of assisted suicide. His approach is often perceived as too radical and endangering to the Swiss model that might ultimately motivate the Government to adopt stricter regulations.[75] Although there have been some attempts to regulate the organized practice of assisted suicide, the existing legislation was found sufficient, which will be discussed later.[76]

3.1.3 Medical Aspect of the Swiss Model

Article 115 of the Criminal Code does not stipulate for the person performing suicide assistance to possess any specific qualifications, and it certainly does not require a physician to be involved. It also does not provide a particular method of assisted suicide. Therefore, the term 'physician-assisted suicide' (*ärtzliche Beihilfe zum Suizid*) is unusual in Switzerland.[77] However, the Swiss model of assisted suicide

---

[72] Betty (2009) Call Dignitas to Account. In: The Guardian. https://www.theguardian.com/commentisfree/2009/apr/03/assisted-suicide-mental-health. Mr Minelli had made the same point in the memorandum to the Select Committee of the Assisted Dying for the Terminally Ill Bill, which was appointed by the House of Lords to prepare a report on the matter. Select Committee of the Assisted Dying for the Terminally Ill Bill, *Assisted Dying for the Terminally Ill Bill* (HL 2004-05, 86-I, II, III) Voll II: Evidence, p. 635.

[73] Minelli (2008), p. 155.

[74] Minelli (2008), p. 155.

[75] Falconer (2010) Death Becomes Him. In: The Atlantic. https://www.theatlantic.com/magazine/archive/2010/03/death-becomes-him/307916/.

[76] Cook (2011) Swiss Back off Restrictions on Assisted Suicide. In: BioEdge. https://www.bioedge.org/bioethics/bioethics_article/swiss_back_off_restrictions_on_assisted_suicide.

[77] Bosshard (2008), p. 464.

has developed primarily through the practice of assisted suicide organizations. The only method of suicide assistance provided by these organizations is a lethal dose of NaP, which requires a prescription.[78] The regulations on NaP make the involvement of physicians unavoidable and bring the Swiss model closer to physician-assisted suicide.[79]

3.1.3.1 Regulation on Sodium Pentobarbital

In accordance with the 1971 Convention on Psychotropic Substances,[80] to which Switzerland acceded on 22 April 1996, NaP is regulated under the Therapeutic Products Act and the Narcotics Act.[81] Under the Ordinance on Narcotics Control, NaP is a partially controlled class b substance only available through a medical prescription.[82] Article 26(1) of TPA and Article 11(1) of NarcA both stipulate that physicians must respect the 'recognised rules of medical science' while writing a prescription. Before prescribing any controlled substances, physicians must personally examine the patient[83] and be aware of the patient's 'state of health'.[84]

Despite its acceptance in practice, none of these acts mention NaP in relation to assisted suicide, resulting in 'a legally unregulated area'.[85] One might try to argue that prescribing NaP for assisted suicide purposes contradicts the recognised rules of medical science. However, that argument has already been rendered invalid in the face of the Swiss approach to assisted suicide. The medical institutions, the Swiss Courts, and government authorities have all accepted NaP as the lethal drug used in assisted suicide.

---

[78] Although there were some cases, in which other methods were used to assist with suicide, they drew negative attention from the public and were strictly investigated. NaP is officially the only method used by the assisted suicide organizations and it seems as though it is the only method that has general public approval.

[79] Schwarzenegger (2007), p. 7.

[80] Pentobarbital is listed under Schedule III of the Convention as a substance that requires a licence for its distribution (Art 8) and is only available with prescription, which is 'issued in accordance with sound medical practice' (Art 9). UN General Assembly, Convention on Psychotropic Substances of 1971, 9 December 1975, A/RES/3443.

[81] 812.21 Swiss Federal Act on Medicinal Products and Medical Devices of 15 December 2000 (1 August 2020) (Therapeutic Products Act, TPA); 812.121 Swiss Federal Act on Narcotics and Psychotropic Substances of 3 October 1951 (1 February 2020) (Narcotics Act, NarcA).

[82] Switzerland, 812.121.1 Ordinance on Narcotics Control of 25 May 2011 (1 January 2013) Art 3(2)(b). The list of controlled substances is prepared by the Federal Department of Home Affairs (FDHA) under: Switzerland, 812.121.11 Ordinance of the FDHA on the Lists of Narcotics, Psychotropic Substances, Precursors and Auxiliary Chemicals of 30 May 2011 (15 December 2020) Annex I.

[83] Ordinance on Narcotics Control Art 46(1).

[84] TPA Art 26(2).

[85] Petermann (2008), p. 1416.

3.1.3.2 SAMS Guidelines

The Swiss Academy of Medical Science (SAMS) was founded in 1943 as a research funding institution, and it is highly influential and respected within the medical sphere in Switzerland.[86] The Central Ethics Committee of SAMS (CEC) prepares and publishes guidelines, manuals, opinions, and recommendations on ethical issues in medicine. These medical-ethical guidelines carry great importance for medical professionals in Switzerland and have mostly been incorporated into the Code of Professional Conduct by the Swiss Medical Association (FMH).[87] Although the Guidelines lack binding legal character, they have been frequently referred to by the Swiss Courts and have affected cantonal health laws.[88]

The first SAMS guideline on end-of-life care was published in 1976.[89] While the unacceptability of active euthanasia was explicitly stated, passive euthanasia in the form of withdrawing or withholding treatment was considered acceptable medical practice based on the respect for patients' wishes. The Guideline'76 did not mention assisted suicide or any physician involvement in hastening the death of a patient other than withdrawing or withholding treatment. Although there was a citation of Article 114 of the Criminal Code on mercy killing, there was no referral to Article 115, which indicates that physician-assisted suicide was not a topic at the time.

In 1981, the revised guideline included the nursing staff and gave greater importance to advance directives than Guideline'76.[90] While the Guideline'76 accepted advance directives only as a non-binding indicative tool for the patient's will, the Guideline'81 held them binding as long as the formal conditions were met.

The establishment of the first assisted suicide organization in 1982 ignited the debates on the compatibility of suicide assistance with medical ethics. Assisted suicide was explicitly rejected from being a part of the medical profession under the 1995 Medical-ethical Guidelines for the Medical Care of the Dying and Patients with Chronic Severe Brain Damage, which was based on the physicians' duty to 'alleviate the physical and mental suffering that can lead a patient to suicidal thoughts.'[91] Advance directives were declared binding, except for wishes that would require an illegal act by the physician or wishes to remove life-sustaining

---

[86] SAMS, Portrait. https://www.samw.ch/en/Portrait.html.

[87] *Foederatio Medicorum Helveticorum* is the professional association for Swiss physicians. The Code of Professional Conduct lists under Annex 1 all the SAMS Guidelines that are binding for its members. FMH (1997, last updated 2020) Standesordnung Der FMH. https://www.fmh.ch/ueber-die-fmh/statuten-reglemente.cfm#i112408.

[88] Bosshard (2008), pp. 464–465.

[89] SAMS (1976) Medizinisch-ethische Richtlinien für die Sterbehilfe. All SAMS Medical-ethical Guidelines can be found under https://www.samw.ch/de/Ethik/Richtlinien.html.

[90] SAMS (1981) Medizinisch-ethische Richtlinien für die Sterbehilfe.

[91] SAMS (1995) Medizinisch-ethische Richtlinien für die ärztliche Betreuung sterbender und zerebral schwerst geschädigter Patienten, s. 2.2.

treatment if recovery to a communicative state and renewed will to live were foreseeable.[92]

Medical aspects of assisted suicide continued to be a topic of debate in the following years. Article 115 alone neither requires the person being assisted with suicide to suffer from any illness nor prohibits physicians from assisting. The question remained, to which extent suicide assistance was compatible with the ethics of medicine. In 2004, a separate guideline that dealt with end-of-life questions was published. The Medical-ethical Guidelines on Care of Patients in the End of Life covered only patients in a terminal phase and whose death was foreseeable within the next few days or weeks.[93] The respect for patients' wishes was central in the Guideline'04. Therefore, the right to self-determination was explicitly set out as the first principle.[94] Although rejecting assisted suicide as part of the medical profession, the Guideline'04 acknowledged the dilemma a physician might face in cases of suffering patients at the end of life.

> On the one hand assisted suicide is not part of a doctor's task, because this contradicts the aims of medicine. On the other hand, consideration of the patient's wishes is fundamental for the doctor-patient relationship. This dilemma requires a personal decision of conscience on the part of the doctor. The decision to provide assistance in suicide must be respected as such. In any case, the doctor has the right to refuse help in committing suicide.[95]

While healing was the sole focus of medicine, the growing importance given to personal autonomy was reflected in the change of approach. This change was also reflected in the approach towards advance directives by strengthening their binding nature.[96] The right to self-determination of patients realises itself in a wide range of areas, from advance directives to the right to refuse treatment or even to the right to decide on the time and manner of one's own death. To what extent these rights are practised, depends on the weight given to the right to self-determination in the face of other rights or interests. In 2004, SAMS was ready to give the right to self-determination enough weight to balance the ethics of medicine with patients' wishes. The subcommittee, appointed by CEC to prepare the Guideline'04, pointed out the risks of accepting physician-assisted suicide, which included the risk of interfering with suicide prevention, unwanted broadening of the practice, and potential disturbance to the physician-patient relationship. Although suicide assistance was not accepted as a part of the medical profession, it was recognized that 'human empathy' could not ignore the patient's wishes under certain circumstances.[97] Therefore, according to the Guidelines'04, if a physician decided to assist a patient with suicide,

[92] SAMS Guideline'95, s. 3.4.

[93] SAMS (2004, updated 2013) Medizinisch-ethische Richtlinien - Betreuung von Patientinnen und Patienten am Lebensende, s. 1; the Guideline'04 was updated in 2013, but paragraphs related to assisted suicide remained the same.

[94] SAMS Guideline'04, s. 2; Ruth (2011), p. 45.

[95] SAMS Guideline'04, s. 4.1.

[96] SAMS Guideline'04, s. 2.2.1.

[97] Ruth (2011), p. 50.

three conditions must have been fulfilled. First, the patient must be approaching the end of life. Second, all alternatives must be discussed, and if desired by the patient, implemented. Third, the patient must have the decision-making capacity, and this must be confirmed by a third person that did not necessarily have to be a physician.[98]

Intense public debates on end-of-life issues led to the appointment of another subcommittee by CEC in 2015. Based on the subcommittee's work, which took into consideration the approach of the Swiss physicians[99] and the study by the National Research Programme 'End of Life' (NRP 67),[100] the new Medical-ethical Guidelines for Management of Dying and Death was adopted in 2018.[101] The Guideline'18 covers a broader area and addresses patients close to the end of life and patients without any terminal illness.

The Guideline'18 emphasizes the quality of life and its subjective meaning for each individual. It is seen that the right to self-determination found a broader scope and more weight in this guideline by accepting the personal dimensions of the quality of life.[102] Personal and environmental elements are taken into account for the description of suffering. Unbearable (SAMS uses the phrase intolerable) suffering, which is a term used frequently in association with assisted suicide, is defined by the Guideline'18 as the following:

> [I]f severe suffering is perceived as chronic or progressive and any hope of alleviation or resolution has been lost, it is often described as intolerable. Intolerable suffering need not be persistent and can, thanks to palliative care or spontaneously, give way to improvement and new hope. However, it is also possible that patients' suffering will be felt to be intolerable permanently, until their death. No objective criteria exist for suffering in general or for intolerable suffering in particular. Intolerability can only be designated as such by sufferers themselves; it is not ascribable by others. It may, however, be more or less comprehensible to others.[103]

Overall, the focus on subjectivity and the emphasis on open dialogue about end-of-life decisions are noteworthy in the patient-oriented Guideline'18.

---

[98] SAMS Guideline'04, s. 4.1.

[99] According to the study, Swiss physicians were generally accepting of assisted suicide, especially in cases of severely suffering terminal patients (78%). In cases of patients with severe pain caused by a chronic illness, acceptance remained around 60%. In the absence of any somatic illness, mentally ill patients and otherwise healthy advance-aged patients, the level of acceptance dropped remarkably (30% and 20% respectively). Overall the study reveals that individual circumstances of the patient and a formerly established physician-patient relationship affect the ethical acceptability of assisted suicide. Brauer et al. (2015), pp. 1–8.

[100] Swiss National Science Foundation & NRP 67 (2017) Synthesis Report NRP 67: End of Life. http://www.nfp67.ch/en/News/Pages/11121-news-nfp67-synthesis-report.aspx, p. 33. NRP 67 started in 2011 and consisted of 33 separate projects examining end-of-life aspects in Switzerland. The report shines light on different aspects of dying with dignity and problematic areas, providing policy recommendations.

[101] SAMS (2018) Medizin-ethische Richtlinien - Umgang mit Sterben und Tod.

[102] SAMS Guideline'18, s. 2.3.

[103] SAMS Guideline'18, s. 2.4.

There are five requirements for physician-assisted suicide set out by the Guideline'18. First of all, the patient must possess the 'capacity in relation to assisted suicide', which differs from the capacity of making everyday decisions. According to the SAMS Guidelines for Assessment of Capacity, factors that might affect capacity, such as mental illness, should be taken into account. It must also be ensured that the patient has a realistic view of the prognosis and is aware of other options.[104] Having a mental illness does not automatically dismiss the possibility of having the capacity to make end-of-life decisions. However, a detailed psychiatric assessment is necessary. Physicians must document their reasons for excluding incapacity. Secondly, the decision to end life through assisted suicide must be well-considered and free from any outside influence. An independent third party, who is not required to be a physician, must confirm these first two requirements. Thirdly, intolerable suffering caused by 'symptoms of disease and/or functional impairment' should be present. Fourth, other alternatives should be explored as long as they are acceptable for the patient. Finally, the patient's decision for assisted suicide should be understandable for the physician based on their previously established relationship and repeated discussions.[105] This final requirement puts the practice of assisted suicide for foreigners into question since building a physician-patient relationship in this sense would not be possible after only one short meeting.

After SAMS had published the Guideline'18, FMH announced that it would not incorporate the new guidelines into its Code of Professional Conduct.[106] FMH criticized extending the scope of assisted suicide from terminally ill patients to patients with intolerable suffering. Because intolerable suffering was a subjective and indefinite term, assisted suicide should have remained limited to patients with terminal illnesses and close to the end of life. The Guideline'18 was also criticized for not laying out standards for the third party person, who is supposed to confirm the capacity of the patient and the authenticity of the wish to die. FMH suggested removing the phrase 'who need not be a physician' and adding the phrase 'independent, qualified'. Although not perfectly clear, this could be interpreted as someone who has the legal qualifications to judge a person's capacity, namely a psychiatrist. Another point was that the Guideline'18 should have clarified the criteria for the capacity for end-of-life decisions since it was differentiated from the capacity for everyday decisions.[107]

According to Dr. Barnikol, who is a lawyer with the legal department of FMH, the term intolerable suffering would cause a conundrum for the physicians, who were responsible for checking the requirements for assisted suicide. Intolerable

[104] SAMS (2019) Medizin-ethische Richtlinien - Urteilsfähigkeit in der medizinischen Praxis, s. 3.9.

[105] SAMS Guideline'18, s. 6.2.1.

[106] FMH (2018) Medienmitteilung: Ärztekammer befürwortet eine partnerschaftliche Tarifrevision. https://www.fmh.ch/files/pdf21/medienmitteilung_aerztekammer_befuerwortet_eine_partnerschaftliche_tarifrevision.pdf.

[107] FMH (2018) Stellungnahme: Richtlinien "Umgang mit Sterben und Tod". https://www.fmh.ch/files/pdf20/Stellungnahme_der_FMH_Richtlinien_Umgang_mit_Sterben_und_Tod.pdf.

suffering was a state that was dependent on the patient's perspective. By nature of the physician-patient relationship, the decision to end life could be conceivable to the physician. However, due to the lack of sufficient objective criteria, supervision of the decisions to assist with suicide would be difficult. Thus, it should be replaced with a more precise requirement that could be assessed with sufficient certainty. In addition to the subjectivity, the vagueness of the term intolerable suffering would be counterproductive to suicide prevention, and the term also contradicted with physicians' duty to treat and alleviate pain in cases of curable diseases.[108]

Since FMH refused to incorporate the Guideline'18 into the Code of Professional Conduct, FMH-member physicians are obliged to follow the Guideline'04. If an FMH-member physician would assist with a patient's suicide following the Guideline'18 but in contrast with the Guideline'04 (for example, a non-terminal patient under chronic pain), the physician could face sanctions within the association.

FMH's refusal of the Guideline'18 received both support and criticism from a divided community of medical professionals. The Association of Protestant Physicians of Switzerland, with approximately 330 members, had urged FMH not to incorporate the new guidelines, as they contradicted the duties of physicians and carried the risk of causing unintended pressure on vulnerable patients to consider suicide. Extending the practice of assisted suicide for non-terminal patients would alter the 'life-affirming medical attitude'.[109] Some physicians argued against accepting assisted suicide as part of the medical profession,[110] finding it incompatible with the Hippocratic oath.[111] A physician suggested FMH to suspend its cooperation with SAMS as he found the new guidelines simply 'outrageous'.[112] While some groups supported the refusal, others interpreted it as FMH's mistrust in its members to make judgments in their patients' best interests.[113] One physician claimed that a false understanding of the Hippocratic oath, which had changed over time under the Christian belief influence, affected this decision. Apart from the Hippocratic oath, physicians were obliged to follow the law, and the right to decide the time and manner of one's death was a reflection of self-autonomy, which was a widely accepted concept in Swiss society.[114] Another physician objected to the basis of FMH's refusal. Even if suffering was subjective and had non-medical elements contributing to it, it remained a matter of medicine. Indeed, the medical practice was based on patient complaints, and restricting pain measurement only to numbers did not reflect the reality of human life.[115] However, the new guidelines included the element of subjectivity and adopted a more personalized approach. The Association

---

108 Barnikol (2018), pp. 1392–1396.

109 AGEAS (2018), p. 1451 (author's translation).

110 Kaiser (2018), p. 1363.

111 Vuilleumier-Koch (2019), p. 419.

112 Aeschlimann (2018), p. 1452 (author's translation).

113 Säuberli (2019), p. 202.

114 Achermann (2018), p. 1614.

115 Stalder (2019), p. 66; Supported by Bär et al. (2019), p. 202.

of General Practitioners and Pediatricians defined this development as a shift from a 'paternalistic "allowing"' to a '"supporting" partnership'.[116]

The drafting process of the new guidelines was based on comprehensive research and input from several groups. Represented on the executive board of SAMS, FMH had also contributed to the drafting process. The rejection of the Guideline'18 that was drafted by a highly respected organization within the medical profession surprised many. The president of SAMS responded to the rejection by stating that they acknowledge the reasoning behind it and will 'carefully analyse the consequences of this decision' through constructive debates with all relevant bodies.[117] Perhaps FMH will change its approach later or perhaps the Swiss Courts will legitimize the new guidelines through a reference.

3.1.3.3 Assisted Suicide in Healthcare Institutions

Before the 2000s, although there were no regulations against it, the generally accepted practice was that there would be no assisted suicide within healthcare institutions since it was seen as contrary to medical ethics and fundamentally opposite to the purpose of healing and caring.[118] Over time, the approach towards assisted suicide changed, and it continues changing. The Swiss model of assisted suicide carries medical elements, such as the prescription of NaP or examination of the person's decision-making capacity. The SAMS Guidelines have come to accept assisted suicide as part of voluntary medical activity. The question arose of whether assisted suicide could be carried out within healthcare institutions.

The discussions on access to assisted suicide in healthcare institutions were focused on the idea of non-discrimination rather than the relationship between assisted suicide and medicine. On a cantonal level, Zurich had banned assisted suicide organizations from entering the premises of hospitals and nursing homes in 1987. The Zurich City Council decided to partially lift the ban as of January 2001, allowing assisted suicide organizations to accompany residents of long-term care institutions, such as retirement homes. The reason behind lifting the ban for long-term care institutions was the fact that they are the only domiciles of most of their residents. As long as the resident has no other place to go, he or she can have access to assisted suicide within the institution.[119]

In its report from 2005, the Swiss National Advisory Commission on Biomedical Ethics (NCE) evaluated the situation of assisted suicide in healthcare organizations. According to the NCE, assisted suicide should be accessible for residents of long-term care institutions with no other domicile. Private long-term institutions can reject assisted suicide on their premises but should inform their residents of this decision at

---

[116]Luchsinger (2018), p. 1399 (author's translation).

[117]Scheidegger (2018), p. 1613 (author's translation).

[118]Bosshard (2008), p. 474.

[119]Ernst (2001), pp. 293–295.

the time of admission. Each hospital should decide if it would allow assisted suicide on its premises and make this decision known to its patients.[120]

The notion of non-discrimination was behind the directive adopted by the University Hospital of Lausanne in January 2006, which is the first Swiss hospital allowing assisted suicide on its premises. The initial criteria are (1) a persistent request to die, (2) the capacity of discernment, and (3) exhausting, if possible, all alternative treatments. Assisted suicide in the hospital will only come into question if the patient does not have a home or is under no condition for transportation. A commission will evaluate the request. The patient will have to contact an assisted suicide organization or an external physician to obtain a prescription for NaP. Hospital staff cannot be forced to participate.[121] The University Hospital of Geneva followed Lausanne in September 2006 and adopted a very similar directive.[122]

After the University Hospital of Lausanne's directive, SAMS published its opinion on the roles of healthcare institutions in assisted suicide.[123] The report does not disapprove of assisted suicide in nursing homes, but due to the delicate nature, advises extra caution towards other residents and the staff. SAMS stated that each hospital should decide whether or not assisted suicide would be allowed on its premises. If allowed, the hospital should lay out clear guidelines on the requirements and procedures. In a report from the following year, CEC advised against the involvement of the healthcare institution staff in assisted suicides, finding it problematic and conflicting.[124]

The University Hospital of Zurich issued a short directive in 2007 that reflects the effort to maintain the line between physicians' role of preserving life and patients' right to self-determination. Physicians of the hospital are prohibited from prescribing NaP for assisted suicide purposes. Hospital staff cannot support a decision of assisted suicide; however, they also cannot prevent it. If there are suspicions related to the decision-making capacity of the patient, who is intending for an assisted suicide, the staff must notify the necessary authorities. In principle, assisted suicide is not permitted on hospital premises. If a patient is not able to leave the hospital, a solution will be sought on an individual basis.[125]

Although the wording seems more restrictive, Zurich's approach is similar to those of Lausanne and Geneva's. They all accept the patient's right to self-determination while refusing to take part in assisted suicide. They also acknowledge

---

[120]NCE (2005) Beihilfe zum Suizid. Stellungnahme Nr. 9/2005. Reports of the NCE can be found under https://www.nek-cne.admin.ch/de/publikationen/stellungnahmen/.

[121]Centre Hospitalier Universitaire Vaudois (CHUV) (2007), pp. 14–19.

[122]Hôpitaux Universitaires de Genève (HUG) (2007), pp. 21–23.

[123]SAMS (2006) Zur Praxis der Suizidbeihilfe in Akutspitälern: die Position der SAMW. https://www.samw.ch/de/Ethik/Themen-A-bis-Z/Sterben-und-Tod/Hintergrund-Sterben-Tod.html.

[124]CEC (2007) Suizidbeihilfe in Akutspitälern: die Haltung der Zentralen Ethikkommission der SAMW. https://www.samw.ch/de/Ethik/Themen-A-bis-Z/Sterben-und-Tod/Hintergrund-Sterben-Tod.html.

[125]Universitätsspital Zürich (2007), pp. 28–29.

that certain circumstances might render the patient's right ineffective, which would need to be remedied.

3.1.4 Judicial Aspect of the Swiss Model

Considering the legal vagueness of the Swiss model, one might expect to see several cases before the courts that have focused on resolving disputed areas in the practice of assisted suicide. However, there are only a few cases related to assisted suicide and they do not necessarily provide sufficient clarification.

3.1.4.1 The Zurich Case

In 1998, the former president of EXIT, Dr Meinrad Schär, had prescribed NaP to a 29-year-old mentally ill woman who wanted to commit suicide with the assistance of EXIT. After meeting with the patient for only half an hour and looking at her medical files, Dr Schär reached a different diagnosis from the patient's psychiatrist. After being notified of the situation, the *Kantonsarzt*[126] of Basel intervened by filing a complaint against Dr Schär after admitting the patient to a psychiatric clinic. The Zurich Department of Health suspended Dr Schär's licence to prescribe controlled substances and restricted his practice to preventive medicine until the criminal investigation was finalized.[127] It was known that Dr Schär had prescribed NaP to several patients without prior examination, for which he had been reprimanded and reminded of the necessity of a personal examination before prescribing any medication. Dr Schär appealed the suspension of his licence to prescribe controlled substances before the Zurich Administrative Court.[128]

The Department of Health argued that prescribing medication was part of the medical activity, which should be in accordance with the recognized rules of medical science and only done after a personal examination of the patient. The purpose of the prescription of NaP in lethal dosage was neither curative nor palliative. Therefore it was not in accordance with the recognized rules of medical science.[129]

The Court agreed with the Department of Health on the necessity of a personal examination before writing a prescription. Referring to the SAMS Guideline'95, the Court stated that exceptions to the medical obligation to preserve human life would

[126] Although the duties of the Kantonsarzt (cantonal physician) vary in each canton, their main responsibility is to serve public health, including enforcement of legislation on narcotics. Hauri, Aufgaben der Kantonsärzte. In: VKS/AMCS. https://www.vks-amcs.ch/de/home/merkblaetter/aufgaben-der-kantonsaerzte.

[127] Bosshard (2008), p. 475; Lewy (2011), p. 90.

[128] *Zurich Case* [1999] Verwaltungsgericht des Kantons Zürich VB.99.00145, (2000) AJP 474.

[129] *Zurich Case*, 475.

only exist under certain circumstances: cases of 'terminal patients whose illness had taken an inevitable turn and patients with severe cerebral injuries'. The exception could only be in the form of withdrawing life-sustaining treatment. The Guideline'95 explicitly excluded suicide assistance from being a medical activity. Although suicide assistance without selfish motives was not punishable and complying with the final wish of a suffering patient might have been a selfless act out of compassion, there were strong reservations mainly out of concern for the risk of abuse from a medical point of view.[130]

The Court stated that the patient's wish to end his or her life could only ever be considered if the physician was convinced of the patient's decision-making capacity, which would require particular caution in cases of mental illness. The Court also drew attention to the lack of consensus within EXIT on the approach towards this matter.[131]

According to the Department of Health and the Court, prescription of a lethal drug required a personal examination of the patient and a proper diagnosis done under the recognized rules of medical science.[132] Considering their responsibilities, physicians should only prescribe medication necessary from a medical point of view. Just as the mere demand of a patient for medication did not suffice for a prescription, the mere wish to die of a patient did not, by itself, suffice for a prescription of NaP. There needed to be a medical indication that justified the prescription. Within the recognized rules of medical science, a prescription of NaP could only be justified if there was a condition that would inevitably lead to death within the meaning of the SAMS Guidelines. On the one hand, the Court found it highly questionable if mental illness alone could classify as an illness 'inevitably leading to death'. On the other hand, the Court acknowledged that a mental illness, just like somatic illnesses, could cause unbearable suffering to a point where the patient perceived life not worth living. Further evaluation of this subject was not found necessary since it was already established that Dr Schär had failed to show due care.[133]

By stating that a prescription of NaP could only be acceptable in cases of terminally ill patients, this judgment does not exclude assisted suicide from being part of the medical profession like the SAMS Guideline'95 explicitly did. The Court was relatively flexible in its approach.

---

[130] *Zurich Case*, 475.

[131] *Zurich Case*, 476.

[132] This was a comment made by the Court in reference to the 'recognized rules of medical science' under NarCA Art 11. At the time of this decision, TPA and the Ordinance on Narcotics Control were not in force, both of which explicitly require personal examination and awareness of the state of the patient before writing a prescription for controlled substances. See footnotes no. 81 and 82.

[133] *Zurich Case*, 476–477.

3.1.4.2 The Aargau Case

Another case was brought before the Aargau Administrative Court by Dr M, who had also appealed against the suspension of his licence to prescribe controlled substances.[134] Dr M was a general practitioner, and he was being accused of assisting several suicides (especially of Dignitas members) without proper due care and keeping insufficient documentation. The Department of Health suspended Dr M's licence to prescribe controlled substances because his behaviour violated medical due diligence, a decision that was approved by the governing council.

Dr M opposed state supervision over his expert activities as a physician. Because assisted suicide was not part of the medical profession, there was no legal ground for control by the Department of Health. The Court rejected this argument. Although assisting suicide was not, in the narrow sense, part of the medical profession, prescribing controlled substances was a medical activity subject to supervision. The assessment of a prescription's justification required previous examinations and documentation, which was also a reason why physicians were obliged to keep records of their professional activities.[135]

Referring to Article 8 of the ECHR and the Pretty Case,[136] Dr M argued that the right to private life included the right to choose the time and manner of one's own death, which was unconditional and independent from any medical indication. Since NaP was the safest method to end one's own life, not providing the possibility to obtain NaP would render this right illusionary. The Court rejected this argument as well. First of all, the ECtHR had not explicitly included the right to choose the time and manner of one's own death within the right to privacy. It had only stated that it was not ready to exclude such a right from the ambit of Article 8. Secondly, even in the case of such an inclusion, the second paragraph of Article 8 justified restrictions that were serving a legitimate aim. The impunity of a selfless act of suicide assistance did not entail an automatic right to a prescription of NaP. No regulation allowed physicians to prescribe NaP outside of their medical profession, namely for assisted suicide without a medical indication. The lack of any regulation thereof was a 'deliberate negative response' rather than a legislative loophole. Regulations on the prescription of controlled substances were based on physicians' duty to act in accordance with the recognized rules of medical science and professional ethics.[137] These regulations pursued a legitimate aim under Article 8(2) of the Convention, foremost preventing abuse of narcotic drugs.[138]

---

[134] *Aargau Case* [2005] Verwaltungsgericht des Kantons Aargau BE 2003.00354-K3.

[135] 301.100 Aargau Cantonal Health Act of 10 November 1987 (before the amendment of 20 January 2009) (GesG-Aargau) Art 23(3).

[136] *Pretty v the United Kingdom* App no 2346/02 ECHR 2002-III; For an analysis of the Pretty Case, see Sect. 4.1.3 'The Pretty Case'.

[137] NarcA Art 11(1); GesG-Aargau Art 22(1).

[138] *Aargau Case*, 310–315.

The nature of the legal concepts of 'recognized rules of medical science', 'principles of medical science', and 'professional ethics' was discussed. Although the Aargau Cantonal Health Act did not make an explicit reference, the SAMS Guidelines were essential tools for interpreting these legal concepts. The Guideline'04 set the prerequisites for assisted suicide as the existence of a decision-making capacity on end-of-life matters and a medical indication undoubtedly leading to death.[139]

After these considerations, the Court evaluated instances in which Dr M had provided suicide assistance. During the trial, Dr M seemed to have trouble remembering patients and their individual situations, which the Court did not appreciate. On several occasions, he had made a differential diagnosis of mentally ill patients than of the psychiatrists on the case and had not consulted an expert while doing so. The Court found it 'simply unthinkable' that Dr M would make a differential diagnosis of a patient only after a short conversation and without performing a medical examination, especially in an area that he had no expertise.[140] Dr M had also neglected to keep proper documentation of his patients. Some of his reports did not include a capacity assessment of the patient. On two occasions, after EXIT had refused to provide suicide assistance, Dr M had personally handed over an antiemetic drug and NaP to two patients, providing detailed instructions on how to use them. Some of Dr M's patients were in hospice and had serious somatic illnesses. These cases lacked due diligence as well since examinations usually took place right before the suicide, and NaP was already available even though the prescription was not yet issued. The Court ruled that the unlimited suspension of Dr M's licence to prescribe controlled substances was justified, considering the 'serious lack of due diligence and the carefree handling of NaP' on his part.[141]

3.1.4.3 The Dr X Case

A decision from the Federal Supreme Court in 2005 directly addressed the question of whether assisted suicide was part of the medical profession. As of July 2002, Dr X's licence to practice medicine was limited to the care of female patients only. The appeal made against this decision was dismissed in November 2002. In February 2004, the Zurich Department of Health gave Dr X a warning after prescribing NaP to a male patient in association with an assisted suicide organization. Dr X's licence to practice medicine was ultimately revoked. He had applied to extend his licence to cover the care of male patients who wanted suicide assistance from the assisted suicide organization. This application was rejected. The Zurich Administrative Court

[139] *Aargau Case*, 316–318.

[140] *Aargau Case*, 320.

[141] *Aargau Case*, 327.

dismissed Dr X's appeal in September 2004, and the case came before the Federal Supreme Court.[142]

Dr X argued that his freedom to exercise his profession was infringed, and since suicide assistance was not a medical activity, the decision to revoke his licence could not have been based on the Zurich Cantonal Health Act.[143] However, both the Administrative Court and the Federal Supreme Court believed that a 'rethinking' process had started regarding the nature of assisted suicide. Although traditionally not perceived as part of a physician's task, there was a shift towards accepting assisted suicide as a voluntary medical activity, which was also reflected in the SAMS Guidelines. It was also clear to the Court that an ethically acceptable 'correct' assisted suicide required a level of medical knowledge. The prescribing of NaP, the examination of the patient, the assessment of the medical records, and whether alternative treatment options had been exhausted were all medical activities that required a licence to practice medicine. Therefore, Dr X's involvement in assisting with suicide was, in fact, a medical activity that would be supervised under the Health Act.[144]

3.1.4.4 The Dr Y Case

In a later decision, the Court repeated the importance of the medical nature of assisted suicide.[145] Physicians, who have reached the age of 70, were required to submit a medical certificate attesting to their mental and physical capacities to continue their medical practice. If they chose not to, they could opt for a senior citizens' permit, which was limited to the care of close relatives and friends and to giving expert opinions.[146] In the Canton of Zürich, this permit was subject to renewal upon the request of the retired physician every three years. The applicant, Dr Y, did not submit a medical certificate and opted for the senior citizens' permit, which was renewed in November 2003. In July 2007, the Zurich Department of Health refused to renew Dr Y's senior citizens' permit and rejected his application for the licence to practice medicine. According to the Zurich Cantonal Health Act, physicians must hold a medical diploma, be trustworthy and not suffer from any mental or physical impairment that would prevent them from practising medicine.[147] The Department of Health claimed that Dr Y did not meet the condition of

---

142 *Dr X* [2005] BGer 2P.310/2004.

143 *Dr X Case*, [4.3].

144 *Dr X Case*, [4.3.2]-[4.3.3].

145 *Dr Y* [2008] BGer 2C_191/2008.

146 The Zurich Department of Health discontinued the Senior citizens' permit (*Seniorenbewilligung*) authorization as of 2018. Physicians over the age of 70 will have to apply for a regular license to practice medicine and comply with all requirements. The decision has been strongly criticized. See Kuhn (2019), pp. 663–665.

147 810.1 Zurich Cantonal Health Act of 4 November 1962 (before the amendment of 2 April 2007) (GesG-Zürich) Art 8(1).

trustworthiness on the grounds that he had prescribed NaP to persons outside the limits of his senior citizen's permit and had breached the duty of care by prescribing NaP after only one consultation.[148] After the Administrative Court of Zurich had dismissed his appeal, Dr Y brought the case before the Federal Supreme Court, requesting that he would be the license to practice medicine.

Dr Y argued that he was wrongfully accused, and the refusal by the Department of Health was disproportionate. Although he did not dispute the facts that he had violated the conditions of his senior citizens' permit, he argued that those conditions were void since he was nevertheless capable of qualifying for a license to practice medicine. The Court rejected Dr Y's argument, stating that he had knowingly acted outside the limits of his permit by prescribing NaP to people other than his close relatives or friends, ultimately breaching the requirement of trustworthiness. The conditions of the senior citizens' permit were explained to and accepted by Dr Y, which was evident from the correspondence with the Department of Health. Referring to its previous judgment in the Haas Case,[149] the Court also emphasized the vital function of the prescription requirement, which was to protect patients from hasty irreversible decisions. In addition, compliance with the law became even more critical in a senstive area like assisted suicide.[150]

Unfortunately, neither the Administrative Court nor the Federal Supreme Court elaborated on whether prescribing NaP after only one consultation breached the duty of care.

3.1.4.5 The Baumann Case

In 2003, a psychiatrist was arrested in Basel for negligent homicide on two accounts and suicide assistance with selfish motives on another. The psychiatrist was Dr Peter Baumann, who had resigned from EXIT in 2002 to establish his own organization, 'Suizidhilfe', after EXIT had adopted the moratorium that excluded mentally ill patients from its practice. Dr Baumann defended the absolute right to decide the time and manner of one's own death, including for non-terminally ill and mentally ill patients. He was released after three months in custody on the condition that he would not assist with any other suicide until the trial was over.[151]

In June 2007, the Basel Criminal Court found Dr Baumann guilty for negligent homicide (Article 117) in one case and assisting suicide with selfish motives (Article 115) in another, sentencing him to three years in prison, two of which on

[148] *Dr Y Case*, [3.2].

[149] *Haas* [2006] BGer 2A.48/2006 & 2A.66/2006, BGE 133 58; The analysis of the Federal Supreme Court's judgment can be found under Sect. 4.1.4 'The Haas Case'.

[150] *Dr Y Case*, [5].

[151] Lewy (2011), p. 109.

probation.[152] He had misjudged the decision-making capacity of a mentally ill patient. The patient had suffered from mental illness since 1986 and had attempted suicide before. He had visited Dr Baumann once on 4 April 2001, and after several phone calls, they had decided that assisted suicide would take place on 20 April 2001. Since Dr Baumann did not want to be accused of abusing his medical profession, the patient died by inhaling nitrous oxide (also known as the laughing gas) through a mask. Dr Baumann, who had called the police immediately after the patient's death, recorded the process as proof for the authorities. According to the expert opinion, Dr Baumann would have noticed the patient's incompetency if he had adequately examined the patient. In the other case, the process of assisted suicide was broadcasted on TV, which the Court interpreted as Dr Baumann's desire for publicity, which was a selfish motivation for assisting suicide. This was an essential argument because until then, the phrase 'selfish motives' had been interpreted to mean only financial interests.[153] However, the Criminal Court's broader interpretation was overturned by the Basel Court of Appeal, which acquitted Baumann of assisting suicide with selfish motives.[154] The Court of Appeal also disagreed with the Criminal Court on the classification of Dr Baumann's act in the first case and found him guilty of intentional homicide (Article 111), sentencing him to four years.

The decision was appealed both by the Prosecutor's Office and Dr Baumann before the Federal Supreme Court. The central questions were whether the patient in the first case had decision-making capacity and the nature of Dr Baumann's lack of effort for clarification. Based on previous psychiatric assessments, the patient's handwritten notes, and the fact that he had never sought treatment, the expert opinion had concluded that the patient was incompetent. Apart from an obsessive-compulsive disorder, the patient also had social phobia and suffered from severe depression. The Federal Supreme Court criticized Dr Baumann's conduct for replacing the normative requirement of capacity with his views on assisted suicide. Dr Baumann had mentioned before that he always wanted to help fulfil someone's wish to commit suicide as long as he could understand and empathize with it. Considering that Dr Baumann was a psychiatrist, the Court found his lack of effort to clarify the state of the patient's capacity and to objectify his assessment thereof intentional. It seemed to the Court that Dr Baumann was indifferent to the existence of capacity as long as he found the wish to die humanly empathetic and understandable. Therefore Dr Baumann was found guilty of intentional homicide.[155] In 2010, Dr Baumann was pardoned by the Basel cantonal parliament.[156]

---

[152] (2007) Doctor Sentenced over Assisted Suicides. In: SWI swissinfo.ch. https://www.swissinfo.ch/eng/doctor-sentenced-over-assisted-suicides/5988876.

[153] Bosshard (2008), p. 476.

[154] Lewy (2011), p. 110.

[155] *Baumann* [2009] BGer 6B_14/2009 & 6B_48/2009.

[156] Walther (2014) Leidenschaftlich Klar. In: Humanistischer Pressedienst. https://hpd.de/node/18453; Dr Baumann wrote a book about his experience with assisted suicide, see Baumann (2014).

3.1.4.6 Dignitas v Swissmedic

In an attempt to obtain, store and dispense NaP as an assisted suicide organization, Dignitas made an application to the Swiss Agency for Therapeutic Products (Swissmedic), which was rejected in November 2007. Upon appeal, the Federal Administrative Court decided that the rejection was proportionate on the grounds that it served the legitimate aim of preventing abuse. Dignitas brought the case before the Federal Supreme Court, arguing that it did not intend to surpass the prescription requirement but was rather interested in reflecting the recent developments in the regulation.[157]

According to Article 4(1)(a) of TPA, medicinal products are intended to have an effect 'in the diagnosis, prevention or treatment of diseases, injuries or handicaps'. The Federal Supreme Court held that this article did not exclude prescribing NaP in lethal doses for assisted suicide; however, the State's duty to strike a balance between the protection of life and the right to self-determination justified certain precautions, one of which was the prescription requirement. Although Article 14 (a) of NarcA provided a legal ground for granting a licence to international and national organizations to store narcotic drugs, this provision was aimed at humanitarian organizations and their work in emergency relief activities from a preservation of life perspective. Apart from having an entirely different goal, assisted suicide organizations did not have qualified expert staff that could guarantee an abuse-free use of the narcotic. A change contrary to the main aim of this provision should have been done by legislative means and not by circumvention through the judiciary system. Dismissing the appeal, the Court drew attention to the debates taking place at the parliamentary level.[158]

3.1.4.7 ERAS and Others

In 2015, 6 applicants, together with the *Echtes Recht auf Selbstbestimmung* (ERAS)[159] requested the Cantonal Medical Service of Zurich[160] to issue a declaratory order that would allow physicians to prescribe NaP to healthy, competent patients, to administer NaP if requested, and to prescribe NaP to an assisted suicide organization. One of the applicants, F, additionally asked to include a statement that

---

[157] *Dignitas v Swissmedic* [2008] BGer 2C_839/2008.

[158] *Dignitas v Swissmedic Case*, [2]-[3].

[159] ERAS, which stands in translation for the Real Right of Self-Determination, is an association established in May 2015 that aims to realize the right to self-determination in practice. According to ERAS, every competent individual should have access to medication when and if he or she chose to end his or her life. ERAS, Home. https://www.verein-eras.ch/de/home.

[160] The Cantonal Medical Service is a division within the Department of Health that is responsible for checking whether 'healthcare professionals and people who work in healthcare and medical institutions fulfil their professional duties and responsibilities properly'. Department of Health - Canton Zurich, About Us. https://www.zh.ch/en/gesundheitsdirektion.html.

prescribing NaP to healthy competent patients was permissible under the Health Act, TPA, and NarcA and was not in contradiction to the SAMS Guideline'04 or NCE's reports. After the Cantonal Medical Service decided not to respond to the applicants' request, they appealed to the Department of Health and the Administrative Court of Zurich, respectively, both of which dismissed the appeal. The case came before the Federal Supreme Court on 3 July 2017.[161]

The subject matter of the appeal was restricted to whether the Cantonal Medical Service was right not to respond to the applicants' request. The Court limited its examination to the procedural aspects of the case and did not elaborate on the substantive matter. A declaratory order could only be requested for a concrete personal legal interest. However, the applicants sought the recognition of physician-assisted suicide for healthy, competent individuals, arguing that they had a valid interest in clarifying the legal uncertainty surrounding assisted suicide. According to the applicants, although the right to choose the time and manner of one's own death was accepted, the lack of regulation caused a situation in which organizations without legislative powers were issuing restrictive guidelines or recommendations. The lengthy duration of the procedures made it very burdensome for someone to wait until he or she reached a point that life was no longer worth living and decided to end his or her life. As physicians and individuals, who defended the right to die with dignity, they had a justifiable interest in receiving a substantive assessment of their request.

The Court rejected the interest argument because the applicants did not face any concrete unreasonable disadvantages. If there was a specific case where the physician felt uncertain whether NaP could be prescribed, the physician could then ask for a declaratory order by providing the individual circumstances. Concerning the duration of the procedures, the Court agreed that certain circumstances would require more caution:

> An individual's right to self-determination over his or her own body and life is one of the basic manifestations of the development of personality within the meaning of Article 10(2) of the Constitution. Furthermore, an individual wishing to die is entitled to respect for his or her human dignity (Article 7 of the Constitution).[162]

According to the Court, the authorities should consider the time-sensitive nature of end-of-life decisions so that lengthy procedures did not cause erosion of this highly personal fundamental right. But in the instant case, neither of the applicants suffered any disadvantages, nor did their request possess any urgency. Therefore, the Court dismissed the appeal.

---

[161] *ERAS and others* [2018] BGer 2C_608/2017. The applicants informed the Court on 23 May 2018 that they lodged an application with the ECtHR complaining of the lengthy duration of the procedures. The ECtHR gave an inadmissibility decision based on the lack of victim status. ERAS (2019) Abschlägiger Bericht aus Strasbourg. https://www.verein-eras.ch/de/detail-reflexe?id=57.

[162] *Case of Eras and others*, [6.5.2] (author's translation).

3.1.4.8 The Preisig and Beck Cases

Erika Preisig, the president of the assisted suicide organization called Eternal Spirit, had assisted the suicide of a woman in 2016 without acquiring an expert psychiatric assessment. EXIT had rejected the 66-year-old woman's application since she had refused to be examined by a psychiatrist. Because there was no underlying psychical illness, her pain was believed to be psychological. After a post-mortem report stated that the woman lacked the decision-making capacity due to severe depression, the Public Prosecutor's Office asked for Dr Preisig's imprisonment for intentional or negligent homicide. The Basel Criminal Court ruled that the woman was able to assess her situation, and despite her psychological problems, she was capable of making an end-of-life decision. Although Dr Preisig was acquitted of murder, it is reported that the Court told Dr Preisig that this acquittal 'hanged by a thread' and her conduct was 'gravely negligent'.[163] She was found guilty of the mishandling of NaP. Dr Preisig was sentenced to a CHF 200.000 fine and 15-month imprisonment, suspended on probation for 4 years. During this time, Dr Preisig is not allowed to prescribe lethal drugs to individuals with mental illness.

The vice president of EXIT-ADMD, Pierre Beck, assisted the suicide of an 86-year-old woman who wanted to end her life together with her terminally ill husband although she, herself, was healthy. The couple died together in April 2017 with a lethal dose of NaP. The *Tribunal de Police* (Criminal Court) of Geneva fined Dr Beck CHF 2.400 with a probation period of 3 years for violating TPA. Dr Beck admitted that he had acted outside EXIT's boundaries; however, he argued that the wife had suffered from mental and existential anguish and was determined to end her life. The Court ruled that Dr Beck had acted out of personal convictions and overstepped the limits of assisted suicide in light of the SAMS Guidelines.[164]

Dr Beck appealed the decision, adding that the SAMS Guidelines referred to by the Court were outdated.[165] Dr Beck argued that in light of the wife's determination to end her life, he had to provide a way that was the 'lesser evil'. In April 2020, the Court of Appeal affirmed the Criminal Court's decision, finding a 'significant error'

---

[163] (2019) Sterbehelferin Erika Preisig wegen Medikament-Verstössen verurteilt. In: SWI swissinfo. ch. https://www.swissinfo.ch/ger/alle-news-in-kuerze/sterbehelferin-erika-preisig-wegen-medikament-verstoessen-verurteilt/45085538.

[164] Mansour (2019) A Genève, le médecin d'Exit coupable d'avoir repoussé les limites du suicide assisté. In: Le Temps. https://www.letemps.ch/suisse/geneve-medecin-dexit-coupable-davoir-repousse-limites-suicide-assiste.

[165] The guidelines applicable at the time of the incident were the Guideline'04. It is doubtful the outcome would have been any different under the Guideline'18. The wife's decision to end her life was motivated by fear of outliving her husband. Whether this situation would amount to an unbearable suffering within the meaning of the SAMS Guideline'18 is highly questionable. Even if so, Dr Beck had failed to get a detailed expert psychiatric assessment of the wife and did not ask for a third party confirmation whether the requirements of assisted suicide were met. Although the Criminal Court had not argued the wife's decision-making capacity, Dr Beck's conduct would still have been contrary to the SAMS Guideline'18 and TPA for not obtaining an expert psychiatric assessment.

in Dr Beck's conduct. According to the Court of Appeal, NaP could only be prescribed to patients close to the end of life and whose health was affected. Dr Beck announced that he would take the decision before the Federal Supreme Court.[166]

Although there seems to be a general reluctance towards making a comprehensive comment, the Federal Supreme Court could have another opportunity to clarify under which circumstances physicians can prescribe NaP for suicide assistance if Dr Beck goes through with his appeal. On several occasions, the Court has already underlined the importance of the patient's decision-making capacity and the physicians' duty of care, finally accepting assisted suicide as a voluntary medical activity. The case law sets clear that the right to decide the time and manner of one's own death does not constitute a right to access a prescription of NaP. While the Zurich Case limited the prescription of NaP in lethal doses to terminal cases, in the Haas Case, which will be examined later, the Federal Supreme Court showed more flexibility by establishing that the presence of a mental illness did not automatically exclude the option of assisted suicide. However, extra caution would be required when assessing the decision-making capacity, and only a physician, who possesses the necessary specialist knowledge, should do this assessment. In the Gross Case, which will also be examined later, the Federal Supreme Court expressly rejected the notion of unrestricted access to NaP, emphasizing the necessity of a medical indication for a prescription and its role in protecting public interest.[167] However, the term 'medical indication' does not provide sufficient clarity. The SAMS Guideline'18 finds it sufficient that the patient is suffering unbearably, and agrees that unbearableness is subjective. Considering that there have been many occasions where physicians have prescribed NaP to non-terminal patients while this was contrary to the guidelines of the time,[168] it is possible to envisage scenarios where the 'medical indication' requirement is interpreted loosely.

Although the Swiss Courts continuously refer to the SAMS Guidelines, the Guideline'18 caused serious debate and division amongst the medical profession. It is yet unknown how this will reflect in the case law. Perhaps it would help resolve the Swiss model's ambiguity if the Courts elaborated more in detail since several attempts for further regulation have failed in the parliament, which will be discussed next.

[166] Citroni (2020) Le vice-président d'Exit Suisse romande condamné en appel après un suicide assisté. In: RTS.ch. https://www.rts.ch/info/suisse/11288726-le-vice-president-d-exit-suisse-romande-condamne-en-appel-apres-un-suicide-assiste.html.

[167] See the Federal Supreme Court's decision under Sect. 4.1.5 'The Gross Case'.

[168] A study showed that between the years 1990–2000, 22% of assisted suicides with EXIT were non-terminal cases. However, the number of criminal prosecutions or professional proceedings does not correspond to this percentage. This does not reflect the approach in the Zurich Case or the SAMS Guidelines of the time period. Fischer et al. (2008), p. 813.

3.1.5 Administrative Aspect of the Swiss Model

The first attempt for a legislative change came in 1994 with the Ruffy Motion,[169] which asked for an addendum to Articles 114 and 115 of the Criminal Code that would legalize direct active euthanasia and explicitly regulate assisted suicide in cases of terminally ill patients. Considering the Report of the Working Group on 'Assisted Dying',[170] the Federal Council decided that there was a need for regulation on passive and indirect active euthanasia. There were, however, no grounds to legalize active euthanasia. The Federal Department of Justice and Police (FDJP) and FDHA were instructed to promote palliative care as part of the public health reforms.[171] An in-depth examination was necessary to establish proper principles for the regulation of passive and indirect active euthanasia, for which the Federal Council had suggested setting up a commission of experts.

In the meantime, two parliamentary initiatives were launched: the Cavalli Initiative[172] that asked for regulation following the Working Group's 'Assisted Dying' Report and the Vallender Initiative[173] that requested an amendment of Article 115, which would prohibit physician-assisted suicide and restrict the practice of assisted suicide organizations. The Legal Affairs Committee of the National Council, which favoured legalizing direct active euthanasia, decided to follow the Cavalli Initiative that would allow for an opportunity to solve the need for regulation while leaving the Vallender Initiative behind that was found restrictive and incompatible with the Cavalli Initiative.[174] Around the same time, a motion was brought by

---

[169]Motion 94.3370 Victor Ruffy (1994) Sterbehilfe. Ergänzung des Strafgesetzbuches (Swiss National Council).

[170]The Report had unanimously recommended passive and indirect active euthanasia to be regulated. The majority had recommended an addendum to Article 114 of the Criminal Code to legalize those exceptional situations for direct active euthanasia, while the minority opposed to any sort of relaxation. Although the Report refers to EXIT and its activities, it does not make any recommendation related to assisted suicide, except for stating that it is not a medical activity. Also the Report refers repeatedly to the SAMS Guidelines, which is another indication to the Guidelines' importance. Arbeitsgruppe Sterbehilfe (1999) Bericht der Arbeitsgruppe an Das Eidg. Justiz- und Polizeidepartement. https://www.bj.admin.ch/bj/de/home/gesellschaft/gesetzgebung/archiv/sterbehilfe.html.

[171]While discussing passive and indirect active euthanasia, the Federal Council had recognized the SAMS Guidelines, however stating that an area that 'affects life as the highest legal asset, should be regulated by the democratically legitimized legislator'. It is also noteworthy to mention that church positions were taken in to consideration in the report. Bundesrat (2000) Bericht des Bundesrates zum Postulat Ruffy, Sterbehilfe. Ergänzung des Strafgesetzbuches. https://www.bj.admin.ch/bj/de/home/gesellschaft/gesetzgebung/archiv/sterbehilfe.html, p. 14 (author's translation).

[172]Parlamentarische Initiative 00.441 Franco Cavalli (2000) Strafbarkeit der aktiven Sterbehilfe. Neuregelung (Swiss National Council).

[173]Parlamentarische Initiative 01.407 Dorle Vallender (2001) Verleitung und Beihilfe zur Selbsttötung. Neufassung von Artikel 115 StGB (Swiss National Council).

[174]Die Kommission für Rechtsfragen des Nationalrates (2001) Medienmitteilung: Sterbehilfe - Schmuggel und organisiertes Wirtschaftsverbrechen. In: Schweizer Parlament. https://www.parlament.ch/press-releases/Pages/2001/mm_2001-07-05_000_02.aspx.

Councillor Zäch that followed the course of the Cavalli Initiative and asked for regulation of indirect active and passive euthanasia in line with the SAMS Guidelines.[175]

At the end of 2001, the National Council refused to follow up on both initiatives and decided to go forward with the Zäch Motion instead.[176] After the Zäch Motion was found too narrow in scope, the Federal Council decided to launch another motion that would allow the necessary flexibility and instructed the National Council to submit proposals for the regulation of indirect active and passive euthanasia.[177] The FDJP set up a working group to analyse the issues of end-of-life and problems related to suicide tourism. The final report concluded that there was no need for regulation at the federal level on assisted suicide, suicide tourism, or indirect active and passive euthanasia.[178] Following this report, the Federal Council recommended that Parliament refrain from further regulation,[179] which was met with disappointment by the SAMS.[180] In a follow-up report, the FDJP stated that NaP regulations were sufficient to maintain its supervision.[181] However, discussions did not end there. Several motions, interpellations, parliament initiatives, and state initiatives were submitted in the following years, which were either rejected or not followed upon.[182] In a more in-depth analysis of organised assisted suicide, the FDJP

[175] Motion 01.3523 Guido Zäch (2001) Sterbehilfe. Gesetzeslücke schliessen statt Tötung erlauben (Swiss National Council).

[176] Swiss Parliament (2001) Amtliches Bulletin Nationalrat, Wintersession 11. Tagung der 46. Amtsdauer, pp. 1819–1835.

[177] Swiss Parliament (2003) Amtliches Bulletin Ständerat, Sommersession 19. Tagung der 46. Amtsdauer, pp. 616–618; Motion 03.3180 Komission für Rechtsfragen SR (2003) Sterbehilfe und Palliativmedizin (Swiss Council of State).

[178] FDJP (2006) Sterbehilfe und Palliativmedizin – Handlungsbedarf für den Bund? https://www.bj.admin.ch/bj/de/home/gesellschaft/gesetzgebung/archiv/sterbehilfe.html.

[179] FDJP (2006) Medienmitteilung: Sterbehilfe: Geltendes Recht durchsetzen. https://www.bj.admin.ch/ejpd/de/home/aktuell/news/2006/2006-05-311.html.

[180] SAMS (2006) Schreiben der SAMW an den Bundesrat zur Zulassung und Beaufsichtigung von Sterbehilfeorganisationen. https://www.samw.ch/de/Ethik/Themen-A-bis-Z/Sterben-und-Tod/Hintergrund-Sterben-Tod.html.

[181] FDJP (2007) Ergänzungsbericht zum Bericht "Sterbehilfe und Palliativmedizin – Handlungsbedarf für den Bund?" https://www.bj.admin.ch/bj/de/home/gesellschaft/gesetzgebung/archiv/sterbehilfe.html, para. [2.4].

[182] Some of these legislative attempts were: Motion 05.3352 FDP-Liberale Fraktion (2005) Expertenarbeiten zum Thema Sterbehilfe (Swiss National Council); Parlamentarische Initiative 06.453 Christine Egerszegi-Obrist (2006) Regelung der Sterbehilfe auf Gesetzesebene (Swiss National Council); Motion 07.3163 Hansruedi Stadler (2007) Gesetzliche Grundlage für die Aufsicht über die Sterbehilfeorganizationen (Swiss Council of States); Standesinitiative 08.317 Aargau (2008) Beihilfe zum Suizid. Änderung von Artikel 115 StGB; Standesinitiative 10.306 Basel-Landschaft (2010) Gesamtschweizerische Regelung der Suizidbeihilfe; Swiss Parliament (2012) Amtliches Bulletin Nationalrat, Herbstsession 5. Tagung der 49. Amtsdauer, pp. 1668–1674; Interpellation 14.3817 Francine John-Calame (2014) Sterbehilfe. Gesetzlicher Rahmen und Verhinderung von Auswüchsen (Swiss National Council); Standesinitiative 17.315 Neuenburg (2017) Bedingungen für die Suizidhilfe.

formulated options for regulation. However, it concluded that none of them would bring a substantial improvement to the current situation.[183] The Federal Council repeated its recommendation from 2006 on avoiding further regulation.[184]

The NCE, appointed by the Federal Council on 3 July 2001 as an independent panel of experts, researches on 'ethical issues of biotechnology in the medical area' to advise the government.[185] In July 2003, the NCE was asked to prepare a report covering the legal and ethical aspects of the end-of-life. Although the mandate was revoked later in 2004, NCE continued to work and published its report in 2005.

The extensive report examined many ethical questions, such as the compatibility of assisted suicide with the medical profession or the relationship between the right to self-determination and society. According to the NCE, 'the judgment of legitimacy of suicide or the decision to assist suicide remains with the individual'. However, assisted suicide carried a risk of abuse, which was why there should be binding criteria of due diligence under State supervision.[186] Due diligence was achieved if (1) the patient's decision-making capacity was intact (psychiatric evaluation was recommended in cases of mental illness), (2) the patient was suffering, (3) there was a diagnosis of a fatal or detrimental disease, (4) sufficient time had passed between the request and the act (waiting period) and (5) a second opinion was obtained. The NCE also drew attention to where suicide assistance could be provided. Health care institutions should previously decide if they would allow assisted suicide on their premises and make this decision transparent. Suicide companions should receive psychological support and necessary pharmacological training.[187]

The NCE divided cases with psychological elements into three groups; patients suffering only from a mental illness, patients with mental illness but a somatic illness causes the request for assisted suicide, and patients with advanced age. The difficulty of a reliable prognosis, various treatment options, the fact that assisted suicide would cause overall demotivation, and that the wish to die was usually an expression of mental illness excluded the first group from the option of assisted suicide. The NCE's general position for the second group was also negative; however, it recognized that there could be exceptional cases, and an evaluation of the subjective conditions would be necessary. The main concern for the third group was the autonomy of the suicide decision since capacity could be partial and subject to change. The risk of concealed pressure based on economic or family concerns could

[183]FDJP (2009) Organisierte Suizidhilfe: Vertiefte Abklärungen zu Handlungsoptionen und – Bedarf des Bundesgesetzgebers. https://www.bj.admin.ch/bj/de/home/gesellschaft/gesetzgebung/archiv/sterbehilfe.html.

[184]Bundesrat (2011) Bericht über Palliative Care, Suizidprävention und organisierte Suizidhilfe. https://www.bj.admin.ch/bj/de/home/gesellschaft/gesetzgebung/archiv/sterbehilfe.html.

[185]NCE (2018) Mission. https://www.nek-cne.admin.ch/en/about-us/mission/.

[186]NCE (2005) Beihilfe zum Suizid. Stellungnahme Nr. 9/2005, p. 47.

[187]NCE (2005) Beihilfe zum Suizid. Stellungnahme Nr. 9/2005, pp. 53–58.

not be ruled out. Although the same risk existed for patients with somatic illnesses, a realistic assessment was difficult for cases involving a mental illness.[188]

On the matter of organized assisted suicide, the NCE suggested that assisted suicide organizations should follow certain quality criteria and be under state supervision. Assuring the quality of these organizations would also solve the worries related to suicide tourism.[189] The NCE published a second report in 2006, elaborating on these quality criteria. In addition to the requirements listed in the first report, a few specific requirements were set out for assisted suicide organizations. The NCE recommended organizations not to assist patients who did not suffer from a severe illness. Despite the subjectivity of 'suffering', the duty of care and to protect life required the reasons behind a wish to end one's own life to be reasonably perceivable to a third party. Organizations must also make sure that the wish for assisted suicide was persistent instead of being a reaction to a temporary crisis. Since a decision to end one's own life must be free from any external pressure, the NCE excluded couple suicides. Repeated personal contact was necessary to examine the existence of these criteria, which would rule out suicide assistance upon a single meeting. Documentation was essential throughout the procedures and should include information on the illness, the state of suffering that the person experienced, the person's psychosocial environment, and life history to understand the situation better.[190]

The FDJP considered NCE's suggestions for its 2009 Report that focused on the matter of organized assisted suicide. One of the regulation options was the revision of Article 115 that would add due diligence criteria for assisted suicide organizations.[191] These criteria included two independent medical assessments of the decision-making capacity and the existence of an incurable disease with an immediate fatal prognosis. Although the NCE supported the effort for a regulation attempt, it did not find the FDJP's criteria appropriate. First of all, according to the SAMS Guideline'04, assisted suicide was not accepted as part of the medical profession. Therefore the involvement of not one but two physicians was contradictory to the SAMS' and NCE's views on assisted suicide. Second, limiting assisted suicide to people who were close to the end of life would cause arbitrariness. The NCE did not find it proportionate to exclude people with serious chronic illnesses, which could cause severe suffering even if death was not imminent.[192] However, the restriction of assisted suicide to terminal patients was in line with the Guideline'04. It seems contradictory that the NCE has used the SAMS Guidelines to support the first argument while going against it in the second one. In addition, assisted suicide

[188] NCE (2005) Beihilfe zum Suizid. Stellungnahme Nr. 9/2005, pp. 63–64.

[189] NCE (2005) Beihilfe zum Suizid. Stellungnahme Nr. 9/2005, pp. 63–64.

[190] NCE (2006) Sorgfaltskriterien im Umgang mit Suizidbeihilfe. Stellungnahme Nr. 13/2006.

[191] FDJP, 'Report 2009' (n 183) 25–27.

[192] NCE (2010) Vernehmlassungsantwort der NEK-CNE zu den bundesrätlichen Vorschlägen für eine Änderung von Art. 115 StGB/Art. 119 MStG. https://www.nek-cne.admin.ch/inhalte/Themen/Vernehmlassungsantworten/Vernehmlassungsantwort_NEK-CNE_Suizidbeihilfe_definitiv.pdf.

organizations only use NaP as their suicide method. With the prescription requirement, the involvement of the physician is already unavoidable.

Clarification attempts were not only made on the federal level. On the cantonal level, the Zurich Department of Public Prosecution and EXIT had made an agreement in June 2009, in which EXIT had agreed to financial transparency and an annual audit of its books. EXIT had also agreed to provide suicide assistance only to patients with severe suffering due to an illness, whose capacity to make an end-of-life decision was confirmed without a doubt, and only when the decision was well considered and constant. The examination of the decision-making capacity in cases of patients with mental illness was going to be stricter. Suicide assistance would only be provided after all alternatives were explained to the patient. Suicide companions were to be chosen carefully and trained well, limiting their assistance to a maximum of 12 patients a year. Their compensations for expenses while assisting were not to exceed CHF 500.[193]

The Federal Supreme Court declared this agreement void in June 2010 because many of the agreed-upon matters were within federal jurisdiction and could only be regulated by the Federal Government. The agreement was causing an extension of Article 115 of the Swiss Criminal Code by providing a list of requirements to be followed for non-prosecution, which was a guarantee a law enforcement agency could not give.[194]

Transparency of the assisted suicide organizations is vital to avoid any wrongdoings. However, this does not only entail financial transparency. Decision-making capacity is the most crucial aspect of any end-of-life decision. In the absence of such competence, the death of the patient cannot qualify as suicide. Therefore, the files on assisted suicide should be complete and informative, including detailed physician opinions. Due to data protection concerns, it is not expected that these files are made public. However, adapting a supervision system that respects the privacy of personal data is not impossible. It has been repeated that Article 115 of the Swiss Criminal Code provides sufficient supervision, as any unnatural death has to be reported to the authorities, and assisted suicide is classified as an unnatural death. Whether the sufficient supervision of the assisted suicide practice is achieved through the notification obligation is highly questionable. It is reported that even after the authorities have been notified, the investigation of whether there have been any wrongdoings is more of a formality than an actual in-depth examination.[195] According to the NRP 67 project carried out by the Swiss National Science Foundation, only half of all suicide cases have been forensically investigated, and it was concluded that '[t]here was, therefore, no satisfactory legal control, and the protection of autonomy and

[193] Die Oberstaatsanwaltschaft des Kantons Zürich and EXIT Deutsche Schweiz (2009) Vereinbarung über die organisierte Suizidhilfe. https://static.nzz.ch/files/4/7/6/EXIT-Vereinbarung2_1.2980476.pdf.

[194] *Case on the EXIT Agreement* [2010] BGer 1C_438/2009, BGE 136 II 415.

[195] Ackeret (2019) Die Sterbehilfe in der Schweiz ist längst ausser Kontrolle. In: SWI swissinfo.ch. https://www.swissinfo.ch/ger/standpunkt_die-sterbehilfe-in-der-schweiz-ist-laengst-ausser-kontrolle/44599878.

right to life were inadequately regulated'.[196] In such a highly delicate matter concerning human life and in light of the widely permissive practice, the lack of any regulation is difficult to comprehend. Exceeding the limits of what the drafters of Article 115 had initially envisaged, the assisted suicide practice has become a separate institution. Considering all the criticism towards assisted suicide organizations and the rising demand for assisted suicide both inland and outland, regulation would seem to be the natural expectation. To the surprise of many, the Swiss Government decided not to take any action. Questions on assisted suicide and its supervision usually received evasive answers. The last attempt was a postulate that came in front of the National Council in 2018, asking for the Federal Council to draw up a report on whether the current situation of the Swiss model continued to be compatible with the law. The postulate also included questions regarding the SAMS Guideline'18, control on the finances of assisted suicide organizations and suicide tourism. Referring to its report from 2011, the Federal Council commented that the legal situation had not changed since then and did not find it necessary to update its report.[197]

In an interpellation, the Government was asked whether assisted suicide was possible for healthy patients with advanced-age.[198] The Federal Council responded by referring to the NaP regulations and the SAMS Guidelines, which at the moment only covered terminal patients. However, the SAMS Guidelines have been updated the next year and it is unclear whether the Federal Council would still refer to the new Guideline'18 considering the conflict between SAMS and the FMH. The interpellation had also asked for statistical information on suicide tourism. Apparent from the Federal Council's answer, this information relied solely on the data provided by Dignitas.

3.1.6 Conclusion

The Swiss model of assisted suicide illustrates the necessity of adequately addressing both sides of the scale in the right to die debate. Focusing solely on personal autonomy risks overlooking other vital interests that can be impacted by the right to die practice.

[196] Swiss National Science Foundation & NRP 67 (2017) Synthesis Report NRP 67: End of Life, p. 33.

[197] Postulat 18.3554 Ida Glanzmann-Hunkeler (2018) Suizidhilfe in der Schweiz (Swiss National Council).

[198] Interpellation 17.3845 Sylvia Flückiger-Bäni (2017) Ausweitung der Sterbehilfe (Swiss National Council).

> There is a danger that these (assisted suicide) organizations will unilaterally focus on the principle of self-determination of people and thereby pay very little attention to the protection of life and duty of care in the sense of responsibility towards people at risk for suicide.[199]

Most founders of these organizations have already voiced their opinions on a more flexible practice of assisted suicide. Considering the minimum amount of scrutiny these assisted suicide organizations face, a unilateral focus on self-determination that argues for an unrestricted right to assisted suicide regardless of the existence of a medical indication is worrisome. Finding reasonable weight in the argument that regulation would legitimize these organizations by providing them governmental recognition is also quite difficult.[200] In the previously mentioned interpellation, the Federal Council was asked about the statistics regarding suicide tourism. It is peculiar that the only data relied on was retrieved from Dignitas' reports. Would the duty to protect vulnerable people from risk of abuse not require the authorities to atleast conduct their own research on the assisted suicide practice? Even if the Government continues to avoid regulating the practice, assisted suicide organizations are the reality of Switzerland. They have been subject to many debates in the Parliament and Court decisions. Since the Federal Supreme Court ruled that regulation of this matter was outside the competence of the Cantons, the responsibility lies with the Federal Government. The Federal Government's refusal to adopt a legislative framework leaves the Swiss model in an ambigious situation. Instead of burdening the physicians with the role of 'gatekeeper' and allowing assisted suicide organizations to dominate the practice, perhaps it is time to acknowledge the delicacy of the interests involved, such as protection of vulnerable people, right to self-determination and personal autonomy, and assure a proper balance among them, as it is the responsibility of modern democratic States.[201]

3.2 The Netherlands

In the Netherlands, the debate on euthanasia started in the early 1970s, leading up to the decriminalization of physician-assisted dying in 2002. Until then, there was 'a policy of pragmatic tolerance' apparent in the jurisprudence and guidelines of the medical association.[202]

The Dutch understanding of euthanasia is an act done with the sole intention of terminating the life of the patient upon his or her autonomous request. It does not

---

[199] NCE (2006) Sorgfaltskriterien im Umgang mit Suizidbeihilfe. Stellungnahme Nr. 13/2006, p. 3 (author's translation).

[200] This was one of the reasons that weighed against regulation in FDJP (2006) Sterbehilfe und Palliativmedizin – Handlungsbedarf für den Bund? p. 46; Bundesrat (2011) Bericht über Palliative Care, Suizidprävention und organisierte Suizidhilfe, p. 34.

[201] See Nisnevich (2012), p. 35.

[202] Broeckaert and Janssens (2005), p. 35.

refer to withdrawal or withholding of treatment, as they are refrainment from an action. It also does not refer to other medical procedures that hasten death as a side effect. Therefore, the differentiation between active and passive, direct and indirect, or voluntary and involuntary euthanasia is deemed unnecessary in the Dutch doctrine.[203] Although the distinction between euthanasia and physician-assisted suicide is acknowledged, this does not have specific relevance in the Dutch jurisprudence or literature. Physicians are bound by the same requirements and are equally responsible for both practices.[204]

Many factors have contributed to the Dutch approach towards euthanasia and allowed for a more liberal system compared to the other European States. One of these factors is the Dutch culture of physician-patient relationship. During the Nazi Occupation, an order was issued on the physicians' responsibilities, which concentrated on the rehabilitation of the patients, who were 'useful' to society. This order, which was issued by the Reich Commissar in the Occupied Netherlands Arthur Seyss-Inquart, would open the door to the infamous practices of involuntary euthanasia and sterilization. Able to foresee this order's implications, the Dutch physicians refused to comply and instead gave up their medical licences. Their refusal resulted in 100 physicians being sent to concentration camps.[205] The severe consequences did not diminish the Dutch physicians' determination to protect the best interests of their patients, which ultimately created a deeper trusting physician-patient relationship.[206]

Most people in the Netherlands have a long-lasting relationship with their general practitioner, namely their family physician, which allows for a strong bond. In principle, everyone is appointed a general practitioner, and the healthcare system works upon referral, which means the general practitioner refers the patient to a specialist or hospital if need be. The majority of the requests for physician-assisted dying are addressed to the general practitioners, who have known their patients for many years and are well aware of the individual factors contributing to such requests.[207] According to the Regional Euthanasia Review Committees (RTE), in 2019, 83.1% of all physician-assisted deaths were performed by general practitioners.[208]

The Dutch society has been very open in the euthanasia debate. In his famous work, the Medical Power and Medical Ethics, Dr van den Berg discussed how the changes in medicine have forced reconsidering the concepts of human dignity and

---

[203] Kimsma and Van Leeuwen (1993), p. 24.

[204] Cohen-Almagor (2004), p. 24. Since neither the Dutch jurisprudence nor the Dutch literature make any specific distinction between euthanasia and assisted suicide, the term euthanasia will refer to both physician-assisted dying practices under this section unless otherwise expressed.

[205] Alexander (1949), p. 45.

[206] Scherer and Simon (1999), p. 55.

[207] Cohen-Almagor (2004), p. 35.

[208] RTE (2020) Annual Report 2019, p. 17; All RTE annual reports can be found at https://english.euthanasiecommissie.nl/the-committees/documents/publications/annual-reports/2002/annual-reports/annual-reports.

unconditional respect for human life.[209] He focused on technological developments in medical care, specifically on the inhumane consequences a relentless medical approach could have. The goal to preserve life without observing its quality caused situations that were contrary to human dignity. Although Dr van den Berg's ideas were rather focused on involuntary euthanasia,[210] the book drew much attention to dignity at the end of life, building up to a favourable environment for an open debate on euthanasia.

3.2.1 Until 2002

The Dutch Criminal Code before 2002 prohibited killing at the victim's request and assisting with suicide.

> Section 293 – Any person who terminates the life of another person at that other person's express and earnest request, shall be liable to a term of imprisonment not exceeding twelve years or a fine of the fifth category.
>
> Section 294 – Any person who intentionally incites another person to commit suicide shall, if suicide follows, be liable to a term of imprisonment not exceeding three years or a fine of the fourth category.[211]

3.2.1.1 The Postma Case

The first famous case on euthanasia started nationwide discussions in 1973.[212] Dr Geertruda Postma had given her 78-year-old mother a lethal injection of morphine, intending to end her life. The mother was partially paralyzed due to a cerebral haemorrhage. She had repeatedly asked her daughter to end her life. After being brought on trial for mercy killing before the Leeuwarden Court, Dr Postma received considerable support from the public and other physicians, who came forward by confessing to similar decisions they had taken. During this time, the Dutch Association for Voluntary End of Life was founded as a response to the trial.[213]

The expert medical opinion presented to the Court stated that administrating pain relief medication that carried the risk of shortening the patient's life was widely accepted medical practice under certain conditions: if the patient is in a terminal

---

[209] van den Berg (1978), the original first edition was published in Dutch in 1969.

[210] Fenigsen (1990), p. 236.

[211] BWBR0001854 Criminal Code of 3 March 1881 (before the amendment of 1 April 2002) English translation available at https://www.legislationline.org/documents/section/criminal-codes/country/12/Netherlands/show.

[212] *Postma* [1973] Rechtbank Leeuwarden ECLI:NL:RBLEE:1973:AB5464.

[213] *Nederlandse Vereniging voor een Vrijwillig Levenseinde* (NVVE), founded in 1973, aims for the advancement of end-of-life decision as a human right. NVVE, About NVVE. https://www.nvve.nl/about-nvve.

phase of an incurable illness with unbearable physical or mental suffering and has requested from the physician to end his or her life. The Court adopted the expert opinion except for the condition that the patient must be in a terminal phase since, in some cases, patients could live on for several years with an incurable illness that nevertheless caused unbearable suffering. Dr Postma had met the conditions mentioned in the expert medical opinion. However, her primary intention was to end her mother's life rather than death being an unintended outcome.[214] The Court sentenced Dr Postma to suspended imprisonment of one week with a one-year probation. Dr Postma received a very light sentence considering the fact that mercy killing is punishable by up to 12 years imprisonment. The judgment was seen as a signal of leniency and sympathy, which ignited the discussions even further.[215]

After the Postma Case, the working group of the Royal Dutch Medical Association (KNMG) published a report stating that although euthanasia should remain illegal, certain conditions could give rise to a conflict of duties. This argument would later provide justifying grounds for euthanasia cases.[216] According to the report, euthanasia could only be considered under rare circumstances when the patient's suffering could not be relieved by other alternative means. For euthanasia to be considered acceptable, the request must be made by a competent patient in a hopeless situation. The physician should consult with a colleague on the request. Due to the difference of opinions among the medical profession, the working group advised the KNMG against taking an official stance on euthanasia.[217]

3.2.1.2 The Wertheim Case

Ms Wertheim, who was a voluntary euthanasia activist, was arrested for suicide assistance in 1981 after she had helped a 67-year-old woman end her life. The woman had repeatedly expressed her wish to die due to her physical and psychological sufferings and was referred to Ms Wertheim by her general practitioner.

According to the Rotterdam Criminal Court, assisted suicide could be justified if

(1) there was a persistent wish to die, which was well thought and autonomous,
(2) the person was suffering from unbearable pain,
(3) all other alternatives have been considered and exhausted,
(4) the person's death did not cause unnecessary suffering to others,
(5) a physician was involved in the decision-making and

[214] Griffiths et al. (1998), p. 52.
[215] Thomasma et al. (1998), p. 7.
[216] Otlowski (1997), p. 396.
[217] KNMG Working Group on Euthanasia (1975), p. 15.

(6) utmost care had been shown, including consultation with another physician and, if the person was not terminally ill, consultation with an expert such as a psychiatrist.[218]

Ms Wertheim was found guilty since these conditions were not met and sentenced to six months imprisonment with a one-year probation. After the Wertheim Case, the Board of Procurators-General[219] decided that cases concerning sections 293 and 294 of the Criminal Code would be referred to the Board to decide whether to prosecute. The conditions laid out in the Postma and Wertheim Cases would serve as guidelines to determine the necessity of a prosecution.[220]

3.2.1.3 The Schoonheim Case

The first euthanasia case before the Dutch Supreme Court was in 1984 and brought a new perspective to the debate.[221] Dr Schoonheim was the family physician of Mrs Barendregt, who was a 95-year-old severely ill, bedridden patient dependent on the nursing staff and who had continuously expressed her wish to die before she would lose her mental capacity. After her condition had severely deteriorated, Dr Schoonheim administered a lethal drug upon Mrs Barendregt's repeated requests. He had discussed the euthanasia request with another colleague, who had agreed that the patient would not regain her health, and Mrs Barendregt's son, who had also supported the decision.

Dr Schoonheim argued that the force majeure defence under section 40 of the Criminal Code justified his decision to perform euthanasia.[222]

> According to this defence, the duty of a doctor to abide by the law and to respect the life of the patient may be outweighed by the doctor's other duty to help a patient who is suffering unbearably and for whom, to end this suffering, there is no alternative but death.[223]

In the Dutch jurisprudence, a section 40 force majeure defence contains two grounds: 'necessity' and 'duress'. The necessity argument allows a lawful excuse to the physician, who has rationally weighed the interest of his patient against the interests protected under section 293. The duress or 'psychological compulsion' argument would generate an exemption from punishment because the physician has

---

[218] *Wertheim* [1981] Rechtbank Rotterdam ECLI:NL:RBROT:1981:AB7817; Griffiths et al. (1998), p. 59.

[219] The Board of Procurators-General is the governing body of the Netherland's Public Prosecution Service. It is tasked with developing the national investigation and prosecution policy of the Public Prosecution Service. Openbaar Ministerie, College van Procureurs-Generaal – Opdrachten. https://www.om-mp.be/nl/colpg/college-van-procureurs-generaal-opdrachten.

[220] Griffiths et al. (1998), p. 59.

[221] *Schoonheim* [1984] Hoge Raad ECLI:NL:HR:1984:AC8615.

[222] Dutch Criminal Code Art 40 'Any person who commits an offence under the compulsion of an irresistible force shall not be criminally liable.'

[223] Otlowski (1997), p. 398.

felt overpowered in the face of his patient's situation and felt as if there was no other way. The second argument has not been accepted as a justification for physicians who perform euthanasia, since physicians have to remain rational and calm from a professional standpoint. With the necessity argument, the physician seeks a balance between the patient's request for euthanasia and the obligation under section 293 and ultimately decides that the patient's interest is more important given the specific circumstances.[224]

The Alkmaar District Court accepted Dr Schoonheim's defence and decided for his acquittal. While it had been established that unbearable continuous suffering was necessary to justify euthanasia, in this case, the Court found continuous suffering caused by psychological pain to be sufficient. The Amsterdam Court of Appeal disagreed and found Dr Schoonheim guilty under section 293. However, it did not sanction him since he had acted with 'integrity and due caution'.[225] The case came before the Supreme Court.

Before the Supreme Court's judgment, a significant development took place. In 1982, the State Committee on Euthanasia was established by Royal Decree to advise the Government on euthanasia. Among many organizations, the State Committee had also asked the KNMG for an opinion, which finally issued its official statement on euthanasia. Although not taking a position for or against, the KNMG listed requirements of physician-assisted dying justifiable under the medical duty of care. These requirements were similar to those expressed in the Wertheim Case. The statement aimed to reflect the social changes and legal developments since the working group's report from 1973 and to provide some clarity into the legally uncertain area of euthanasia. The KNMG strongly recommended that only a physician would be able to perform euthanasia. This was not only because of the level of medical expertise necessary to comply with the conditions but also because a higher level of supervision was possible due to the accountability of physicians.[226] According to the guidelines laid down in the statement, the requirements of 'careful medical practice' that would justify euthanasia under the necessity defence were

(1) a persistent, autonomous, and well-informed decision by the patient,
(2) hopeless and unbearable suffering that need not be in a terminal phase,
(3) all alternatives acceptable to the patient have been exhausted and
(4) consultation with at least one other physician who is experienced in the field.

The KNMG had acknowledged the subjectivity of unbearable and hopeless suffering and how dependent it was as a concept to the individual norms and values of the person. The only objective aspect of hopeless unbearable suffering was whether medical knowledge and possible new medical developments expected in the short term could put the patient's situation in a new light. It was the physician's task to evaluate which medical and social possibilities existed to make the patient's life

[224] Elders and Wöretshofer (1992), p. 227.
[225] Cohen-Almagor (2004), p. 40.
[226] Otlowski (1997), pp. 410–411.

bearable. The KNMG did not find it appropriate to limit euthanasia only to terminal patients since non-terminal cases could also present unbearable suffering with no hope of relief.[227]

Because the KNMG had limited the assisted dying practice to the medical profession, it was interpreted as a willingness to take responsibility, which is thought to have made it more convenient for the Supreme Court to consider the necessity defence.[228] The Supreme Court ruled that the Amsterdam Court of Appeal should have considered the situation of necessity, which meant considering the unbearable suffering and loss of dignity experienced by the patient. Mrs Barendregt had requested euthanasia on several occasions due to her deteriorating health with no prospects of recovery. The amount of suffering the illness caused or was expected to cause, whether the patient would have the chance to die with dignity if the illness were to progress further, and whether there were other means to alleviate the pain caused by the illness were factors that should have been but were not considered by the Court of Appeal.[229] The Supreme Court stated that although euthanasia was prohibited under the Criminal Code, the professional duty of care might cause a physician to feel obliged to honour a patient's request to die. In such cases, the physician must act in line with medical ethics in order to argue the necessity defence. The case was sent to the Hague Court of Appeal, which followed the approach of the Supreme Court and acquitted Dr Schoonheim. Despite the lack of consensus on euthanasia among medical professionals, 'reasonable medical insight' could justify the act under certain circumstances.[230]

The Schoonheim Case was an important step regarding the necessity defence that effectively created an exception of section 293. The physician would have to make the initial assessment based on medical ethics whether the extent of the conflict justified such an exception.[231] Due to the vagueness of the term 'medical ethics' and the lack of consensus among physicians, the judgment was criticized for not clarifying which requirements should be met to uphold the necessity defence successfully.[232] Another criticized point was that the consulting physician was Dr Schoonheim's assistant, who worked in his practice.[233] The consultation process aims to get a neutral opinion that can adequately assess the diagnosis and whether euthanasia is the last option. The decision-making progress should have included a physician who was professionally and emotionally independent of the case.

[227] KNMG (1984), p. 995.

[228] Griffiths et al. (2008), p. 31.

[229] Leenen (1986), p. 350.

[230] *Schoonheim* [1986] Gerechtshof's-Gravenhage ECLI:NL:GHSGR:1986:AC8621.

[231] Otlowski (1997), p. 401.

[232] Leenen (1987), p. 201.

[233] Cohen-Almagor (2004), p. 41.

3.2.1.4 The Pols Case

Mrs M, 73-year-old, had been suffering from multiple sclerosis, and her health was deteriorating. In the face of her irremediable illness, Mrs M had asked her friend and psychiatrist, Dr Pols, to end her life. After Mrs M died, Dr Pols notified her general practitioner and the prosecutor.

Dr Pols's lawyer argued that she should not receive any punishment since her actions did not violate the law's purpose (absence of substantial violation) and additionally argued the force majeure defence. While the first argument was rejected, the Groningen District Court interpreted the force majeure defence as invoking the medical exception argument, which was theoretically acceptable. The District Court stated that under certain circumstances, a medical action might not be worthy of punishment if it was medically necessary and adequate. However, Dr Pols had not fulfilled the requirements of careful medical practice, as she had failed to consult with a colleague.[234]

The Leeuwarden Court of Appeal quickly eliminated the possibility of the medical exception argument as justifying grounds.[235] There were no indications that the drafters of the Criminal Code wanted to exclude euthanasia from the application of section 293. The drafters had discussed medical procedures, including abortion to save the mother's life, and decided not to include an explicit exception to the Criminal Code since standard medical procedures were naturally excluded. However, euthanasia was not a standard medical practice, and there was no consensus among physicians on the subject.[236] Dr Pols was found guilty and sentenced to two months imprisonment with two years probation. On appeal, the Supreme Court also rejected the defence of medical exception.[237]

3.2.1.5 The Remmelink Report

After the Schoonheim Case in 1984, the political party Democrats 66 (D66) submitted a proposal for a bill on euthanasia. However, the State Committee on Euthanasia had not published its report yet. The report was finally published in 1985, and the State Committee had proposed maintaining the prohibition on euthanasia while adding a second paragraph that would exempt euthanasia, which was carried out in line with careful medical practice, from punishment. D66's proposal was adapted to the State Committee's report and gained support in the Parliament, except from the Christian Democratic Appeal Party (CDA). Contrary to the State Committee's recommendation, the State Council issued a statement that it would prefer postponing a new legislative attempt until the case law developed further.

[234] *Pols* [1984] Rechtbank Groningen ECLI:NL:RBGRO:1984:AB7546.

[235] *Pols* [1984] Gerechtshof Leeuwarden ECLI:NL:GHLEE:1984:AC2140.

[236] Welie (1992), pp. 431–432.

[237] *Pols* [1986] Hoge Raad ECLI:NL:HR:1986:AC9531.

Because D66's proposal was awaiting and the matter of euthanasia legislation was already on its agenda, the Government presented a proposal of its own in 1987, according to which euthanasia would remain punishable under the Criminal Code, but requirements of careful medical practice would be incorporated into the Medical Practice Act. If the physicians comply with these conditions, there would be no prosecution against them. The Government's proposal was considered as an attempt to find a solution to the controversial topic through compromise between the supporters of legalization and the CDA.[238]

In 1988, there were two proposals on euthanasia, one from the D66 and the other from the Government. Neither of them gathered sufficient support from the Parliament. Since 1917, the Dutch Government consisted of a coalition, in which the CDA had been an essential part with the ability to block legislation. The CDA was rather more on the opposite side of the legalization of euthanasia.[239] In 1990, the Government appointed the Remmelink Commission (named after the chairman Attorney-General Professor Remmelink) to prepare a report on medical decisions at the end of life (MDEL) in the Netherlands. As part of the preparation for the Remmelink Report, a study was carried out in which many physicians were asked to participate.[240] Until then, deaths caused by euthanasia were usually declared as natural deaths, mostly out of fear from prosecution. This made it impossible to capture the real extent of the practice. The KNMG, in its statement from 1984, had already pointed out the complications of this situation and recommended that the prosecution policy should be clarified. Therefore, for the purposes of the Remmelink Report, the KNMG and the Ministry of Justice made an agreement stating that physicians, who would participate in the study, would be immune from criminal liability. They also agreed upon an ex post facto notification procedure for future cases of euthanasia:

(1) Cases of euthanasia will no longer be declared as natural deaths. Instead, the physician will notify the municipal pathologist that euthanasia has taken place and submit the following information: personal details of the patient and the course of the disease, details on the request for euthanasia, and how euthanasia was performed.
(2) The municipal pathologist will notify the prosecutor's office of the euthanasia case and submit the information provided to him or her alongside his or her autopsy findings.
(3) The prosecutor's office will decide based on the physician's compliance with the careful medical practice requirements whether to prosecute the case or not.

If the prosecutor decided to carry out an investigation, it was recommended that the police investigation be done discreetly with respect to the close ones of the patient. The officials should visit the physician not in uniforms but in civilian clothes and a

[238] Leenen (1989), pp. 523–524.
[239] Kimsma and Van Leeuwen (1993), pp. 22–23.
[240] van der Maas et al. (1991).

vehicle that was not recognizable as the police. The investigation should take place at the address of the physician and not the police station.[241]

The notification procedure provided some clarity and eased the fear from prosecution, allowing physicians to be more open about their practice, which was apparent from the increasing number of reported cases on euthanasia.[242] Since the immunity agreement encouraged physicians to be forthcoming, the study successfully gathered extensive information on the MDEL practice (including euthanasia, assisted suicide, termination of life without request, administration of an increasing dosage of pain medication, and non-treatment decisions), which constituted an estimated 38% of all deaths in 1990. Euthanasia accounted for 1.7% of all deaths in this time, while assisted suicide was at 0.2%. The study found that there were around 9.000 euthanasia and assisted suicide requests each year, and only about one-third were accepted.

A worrisome finding from the Remmelink Report was the 1.000 cases in which the physician had administered lethal medication to the patient with the intention to shorten life without being explicitly requested. In more than half of these 1.000 cases, euthanasia was either previously discussed with the patient or the patient had previously expressed a request for euthanasia if the situation should one day become unbearable. In the rest of the cases in which the patient was unable to communicate, the patient's family had been consulted. In most of these 1.000 cases, death was imminent by a few hours or days. The Commission did not see a cause for alarm since almost all these patients suffered unbearably, and their death was imminent. Although there was consensus on the explicit request requirement, some extreme suffering instances could cause the physician to take a medical decision in the patient's best interest without an explicit request.[243] The Commission also stated that most physicians were only open to the idea of euthanasia in cases where there was unbearable suffering with no other alternatives and if they had an emotional bond with the patient. Therefore, there was no need to worry about a 'slippery slope'.[244]

One might argue that when a patient is no longer able to communicate and suffers unbearably with death being imminent, an earlier request for euthanasia could justify ending the patient's life. Alternatively, sometimes, the patient has never been competent to express such a request, as is the case with neonates, and the physician would have to make a decision in the patient's best interest. However, can this decision be called euthanasia? The explicit, autonomous, and well-thought request of the patient is paramount even to begin considering the option of euthanasia, which is based on the right to self-determination. In the absence of a request, if the physician makes a decision for euthanasia considering the best interest of the patient, the focus shifts from self-determination to beneficence. The judgment of whether the

[241] KNMG (1990), pp. 1303–1301.

[242] Dillmann and Legemaate (1994), p. 84.

[243] van Delden et al. (1993), p. 26.

[244] van der Maas et al. (1991), p. 673.

suffering is unbearable would be on the physician. This shift has the consequence of disregarding patient autonomy.[245] When the patient has never had decision-making capacity, practices to relieve the patient from pain should not be classified as euthanasia in order to avoid confusion, even if that practice ends the patient's life. Perhaps this is a result of the difference in the Dutch approach. In the Netherlands, justification of euthanasia has been developed over the physician's duty of care, unlike the Swiss practice, which has focused on the right to self-determination.

The Government agreed with the Remmelink Report that withholding or withdrawing life-sustaining treatment that had become futile or had been refused by the patient and administration of pain medication that shortened life as a side effect were normal medical practices. However, ending a severely suffering patient's life without an explicit request could not be considered normal medical practice and was subject to prosecution. These cases should also be reported under the notification procedure. However, this extension of the notification procedure was criticized for causing an impression that cases of termination of life without request would be evaluated on the same basis as euthanasia.[246]

In light of the Remmelink Report, the Government withdrew its proposal from 1987 and drafted a new legislative proposal that would amend the Burial Act of 1991 instead.[247] The proposal, Bill 22572, was sent to the Parliament in April 1992. It aimed to give the notification procedure, which was agreed upon between the KNMG and the Ministry of Justice, legal status. The proposal was accepted by the Parliament in 1993 and came into force in 1994.[248] Although euthanasia remained a crime under the Criminal Code, the Government found a way to formally adopt an exception.[249] The amendment did not add the requirements of careful medical practice to the Burial Act. However, the questionnaire, which was aimed to determine whether the requirements of careful medical practice had been met, was added as an appendix to be filled in by the physicians for notification. Therefore, the general rule was that if a physician had complied with careful medical practice requirements in line with the case law and medical ethics while performing euthanasia, there would be no prosecution.

The study from 1990 was repeated in 1995 and 2001. The number of requests for a physician-assisted death rose from 8.900 in 1990 to 9700 both in 1995 and 2001. According to the death certificates, the percentage of deaths caused by euthanasia increased from 1.7 in 1990 to 2.4 in 1995 and 2.6 in 2001. Meanwhile, the percentage of physician-assisted suicide remained the same. Although it was not a high number to begin with (4% in 1990), the studies showed that the number of physicians, who are strongly opposed to euthanasia, had decreased (1% in 2001). In 1990, only 41% of the physicians had said they would never end a patient's life

[245] ten Have and Welie (1996), pp. 101–102.

[246] Dillmann and Legemaate (1994), p. 86; Gevers (1996), p. 332.

[247] BWBR0005009 Burial Act of 7 March 1991.

[248] Dillmann and Legemaate (1994), pp. 84–85.

[249] Thomasma et al. (1998), p. 11.

without an explicit request. This number rose to 45% in 1995 and 71% in 2001. While 64% of the physicians agreed to the right to decide the time and manner of one's own death in 1990 and 1995, this number dropped to 56% in 2001. The studies also showed that physicians became slightly more restrictive on the matter of euthanasia.[250]

The formalized notification procedure did not resolve the reporting problem in euthanasia cases entirely. While the reporting rate was 18% in 1990, it only increased to 41% in 1995.[251] The criminal nature of the notification procedure, where the physicians had to face prosecutors and be investigated, did not necessarily encourage transparency. To soften the process, the Government decided to create the RTE as a 'buffer' in 1998. Composed of a lawyer, a physician, an ethicist, these committees review reported cases and advise the prosecutors whether further legal action is necessary.[252]

Another institution was also established in 1998 to facilitate physicians' compliance with the consultation requirement. Support and Consultation on Euthanasia in the Netherlands (SCEN) is an initiative of the KNMG, founded by the Ministry of Health, Welfare and Support. What was first a regional project in Amsterdam became nationwide through an implementation period of three years starting, in 1999. More than 630 SCEN physicians, who have received special training, provide support, advice, and consultation on euthanasia. They work in shifts, and the on-call SCEN physician is reachable through a special telephone number. It is vital in a physician-assisted death procedure for the consultation to be independent, which the SCEN program can achieve. The KNMG provides training, registration, and supervision of SCEN physicians.[253] The SCEN program has contributed to a higher quality of the consultation process and successfully provided valuable support.[254]

3.2.1.6 The Kors and Duintjer Cases

The criteria of unbearable pain gained more depth with further cases that involved euthanasia requests motivated by psychological suffering. The first case was about a 25-year-old Maria, who was diagnosed with anorexia at the age of 8 by her paediatrician, Dr Kors. Upon her diagnosis, she was admitted to a special clinic from 1974 to 1977, underwent several treatments, and was hospitalised multiple times between 1979 and 1982. She also suffered from severe anxiety and obsessive behaviour. Her parents' divorce significantly impacted Maria and her younger brother, who had become seriously depressed and committed suicide in 1990. Her

---

[250] Onwuteaka-Philipsen et al. (2003), pp. 395–399.

[251] van der Wal et al. (1996), p. 1707.

[252] Griffiths et al. (2008), p. 32; The RTE will be explained further under Sect. 3.2.2 'The New Legal Framework of 2002: Euthanasia Act'.

[253] KNMG, Over SCEN. https://www.knmg.nl/advies-richtlijnen/scen/over-scen.htm.

[254] Jansen-van der Weide et al. (2004), pp. 372–373; Jansen-van der Weide et al. (2007), p. 106.

brother's suicide renewed Maria's wish to end her life, a request that she had expressed to Dr Kors on previous occasions. Maria was only 19 kilos, and in 16 years of treatment, she had never weighed more than 30 kilos. Determined to end her life, Maria refused tube feeding. Dr Kors consulted a psychiatrist, who reported that Maria was mentally competent, and there were no alternatives to relieve her from the mental suffering. Dr Kors concluded that Maria's situation was beyond hope and agreed to assist her with suicide. To help Dr Kors if he were to be prosecuted, Maria made a video recording explaining why she wanted to end her life. Dr Kors notified the authorities after Maria's assisted suicide took place.

While the prosecutor argued that there must be an underlying physical condition to justify euthanasia, Dr Kors's lawyer claimed that according to the principle of 'equality before the law', the policy on euthanasia could not be restricted to patients with somatic illnesses. The cause of suffering was not relevant as long as the patient was experiencing unbearable and irremediable pain. He also stated that the two pillars of the Dutch euthanasia policy, the right to self-determination and the principle of beneficence, provided sufficient grounds for patients whose suffering was not caused by a somatic illness to request an assisted death. The Court agreed that the patient's experience of suffering was the determining factor, and careful medical practice requirements had been fulfilled.[255]

The second case was about a psychiatrist, Dr Duintjer, who had assisted with the suicide of a patient by providing a lethal dose of cyclobarbital. The 50-year-old patient, Martha N, had suffered from depression and alcohol abuse for 25 years, accompanied by suicidal thoughts. She was admitted several times to psychiatric institutions and received various treatments with no success. She had attempted suicide three times during 1983–1984 and described her life as a 'big black hole'. Her general practitioner Dr W had arranged for her to meet with a pastor, who, after several meetings, agreed that her situation was 'hopeless'. When Martha requested suicide assistance for the first time in 1981, Dr W referred her to Dr Duintjer. Her last attempt of suicide with an overdose of sedatives, which she had acquired by falsified prescription, convinced Dr W and Dr Duintjer of her desperate desire to die. It should be noted that her previous suicide attempts were drinking chloride, setting herself on fire, and jumping out of a second-floor window. After signing a statement describing that her decision to end her life was taken in full consciousness, she committed suicide on 4 October 1985. Dr Duintjer reported the case to the prosecutor, who filed charges against him under section 294.

The Rotterdam District Court acquitted Dr Duintjer, ruling that requirements of careful medical practice had been met. Martha's decision to end her life was persistent, autonomous, and well-considered. Alternative measures did not relieve her unbearable suffering. The prosecutor appealed the decision, stating that psychiatric patients could not be regarded as mentally competent to make an end-of-life decision. The Hague Appeal Court rejected the prosecutor's argument and held that Martha was, in fact, mentally competent. Although criticizing Dr Duintjer for not

[255] Sneiderman and Verhoef (1996), pp. 393–396.

consulting an independent psychiatrist, the Appeal Court upheld the acquittal because there was enough evidence attesting to the unbearable and irremediable nature of Martha's suffering.[256]

The Cases of Kors and Duintjer dealt with euthanasia requests without an underlying somatic illness. Although the KNMG had not limited the concept of unbearable and hopeless suffering to only physical pain, most euthanasia cases concerned a patient in a dying phase wishing to avoid a painful end.[257] Perhaps this had caused a slightly wrong perception of which circumstances would qualify for physician-assisted death, as also indicated by the prosecutors' argument in the above cases ('must have an underlying somatic cause' and 'psychiatric patients are not mentally competent'). The Courts fixed this perception early on by clarifying that psychological suffering could cause unbearable and hopeless suffering.

3.2.1.7 The Chabot Case

The Supreme Court confirmed the scope of unbearable and hopeless suffering with the Chabot Case.[258] The 50-year-old Hilly Bosscher had lost her will to live after the loss of her two sons. The first committed suicide in 1986, and the second died from cancer in 1991, both at the age of 20. The day her second son had died, Mrs Bosscher attempted suicide. She did not see any meaning in life after losing her sons. She wanted assisted suicide to have a dignified death, and after being refused by her general practitioner, she contacted Dr Chabot via the NVVE. Despite her insistence on assisted suicide, Mrs Bosscher agreed to a trial therapy with Dr Chabot. After several meetings, Mrs Bosscher's determination to end her life did not waiver. She refused further treatment saying that 'motherhood was the core of her identity and her spirit had died with her sons'. After meetings that accumulated to 30 h over two months, Dr Chabot concluded that Mrs Bosscher had utterly given up on life and had no intention to improve her situation. She was neither clinically depressed nor did she suffer from any other psychiatric illness. She was mentally competent to make an end-of-life decision. Dr Chabot concluded that the only way to relieve his patient's suffering was to provide her with suicide assistance, and if he would not, she would eventually end her life on her own. He sent the transcripts of their meetings to four psychiatrists and one clinical psychologist, meanwhile consulting with a general practitioner and a theologian-ethicist. Except for one of the psychiatrists, who believed the case was not hopeless and treatment should continue, all consultants supported Dr Chabot's decision to comply with Mrs Bosscher's wish. However, none of them had met Mrs Bosscher in person. In 1991, four months after her second son's death, Mrs Bosscher ended her life with the assistance of Dr Chabot.[259]

---

[256] Sneiderman and Verhoef (1996), pp. 396–398.

[257] de Vries (2004), p. 379.

[258] *Chabot* [1994] Hoge Raad ECLI:NL:HR:1994:AD2122.

[259] Sneiderman and Verhoef (1996), pp. 398–402.

The Assen District Court acquitted Dr Chabot, and the Leeuwarden Court of Appeal upheld this decision. Dr Chabot's lawyer, who was also the lawyer of Dr Kors and Dr Duintjer, argued upon the two pillars of the Dutch euthanasia policy. In Mrs Bosscher's case, the right to self-determination and the principle of beneficence outweighed the duty to preserve life in the face of her unbearable and hopeless suffering. While the District Court agreed that there were no other alternatives to relieve Mrs Bosscher from her suffering, the Court of Appeal emphasized the importance of the physician's duty to show particular care in the absence of a somatic illness in assessing the authenticity of the wish to die. The case came before the Supreme Court.[260]

The prosecutor argued that the necessity defence did not justify euthanasia if the patient was not suffering from a terminal illness with physical pain. The Supreme Court found this argument too restrictive and ruled that the legality of euthanasia was a matter of balance between the duty to preserve life and the medical duty of care. It was upon the physician's professional assessment to determine whether a patient's suffering, which included subjective aspects, amounted to an extent that would outweigh the duty to preserve life. The patient did not need to be in a terminal phase. The Supreme Court also refused the prosecutor's argument that psychological suffering was not a sufficient justification for physician-assisted death. However, it emphasized the difficulty of evaluating the severity and hopelessness of non-somatic suffering and stated that particular care should be given to such cases. In addition to the lack of physical suffering, the prosecution argued that the patient, in this case, was mentally incapable of making an end-of-life decision. Psychological suffering would cast a shadow on the patient's capacity, interfering with the authenticity of the decision to end life. The Supreme Court rejected this argument as well. Unbearable and hopeless suffering could be either physical or psychological or carry both attributes. Even in cases of somatic terminal illnesses, one could not rule out the psychological elements caused by being close to death, which could very well play a role in the patient's decision. The mere presence of a mental illness did not automatically eliminate decision-making capacity. Therefore, the authenticity of the end-of-life decision should be subject to careful medical assessment.[261]

Although Dr Chabot had consulted several colleagues, none of the physicians examined the patient in person. To present the necessity defence in non-somatic cases, the Supreme Court required the consultant to meet the patient in person. Thus, Dr Chabot was found guilty of not performing proper due care. Despite the guilty verdict, no sentence was imposed on Dr Chabot.[262]

The consultation requirement had been breached in previous cases. However, the Court had still given acquittal decisions when the rest of the careful medical practice requirements had been fulfilled. In the Duintjer Case, when there was fairly enough evidence on the patient's suffering, failure to meet the consultation requirement was

[260] Sneiderman and Verhoef (1996), p. 403.

[261] Griffiths (1995a), pp. 236–239.

[262] Griffiths (1995a), pp. 236–239.

disregarded. Several experts had testified to the Court that Mrs Bosscher's situation was beyond remedy, and there were no other alternatives. Dr Chabot's consulting colleagues had stated that the transcripts of the meetings were so detailed that they did not need to meet Mrs Bosscher in person to understand her state of mind. Based on the previous case law, the Supreme Court could have acquitted Dr Chabot because it was unlikely that an in-person meeting with the consultant would have made any difference. By finding Dr Chabot guilty without imposing any sanctions, it seems like the Supreme Court wanted to stress the delicacy of end-of-life decisions in cases with psychological suffering and urge extra caution.[263]

After the Supreme Court's judgment, the Medical Disciplinary Tribunal reprimanded Dr Chabot, meanwhile stating that his actions had 'undermined confidence in the medical profession'.[264]

3.2.1.8 The Brongersma Case

In 1998, Mr Brongersma ended his life with the help of his general practitioner at the age of 86. Mr Brongersma, a former lawyer and senator, did not suffer from any physical or mental illness. Due to the deterioration of his physical condition from advanced age, he could not keep up the active lifestyle he once had and found this situation to be unbearable. He had attempted suicide once in 1996. After Mr Brongersma's requested physician-assisted suicide, his general practitioner invited two independent consultants, including a psychiatrist, to meet with Mr Brongersma. Both consultants agreed with the general practitioner that Mr Brongersma's wish to end his life was sincere and autonomous. When assisted suicide was reported to the authorities, the general practitioner explained the reasons for Mr Brongersma's wish to end his life as 'lonely, feeling of senselessness, physical deterioration, and a long-standing wish to die not associated with depression'. He also stated that life had become unbearable to Mr Brongersma. Authorities decided to prosecute.[265]

The expert witness opinions submitted to the Haarlem District Court stated that suffering did not necessarily depend on a medical indication, and one could find the quality of life unbearable due to other reasons. In such cases, the subjective circumstances related to the patient would come forward as a defining factor on the authenticity of the wish to die. The Court accepted existential suffering as justifiable grounds for physician-assisted suicide. Independent from the underlying cause and merely based on the presence of suffering, a physician could justify the decision to assist with a patient's death. Since there were no doubts about Mr Brongerma's decision-making capacity and considering that proper due care was performed

[263] Sneiderman and Verhoef (1996), pp. 403–405.
[264] Medical Disciplinary Tribunal (1995), p. 674 (Griffiths' translation at Griffiths (1995b), p. 895).
[265] Griffiths et al. (2008), p. 36.

during the process, including the consultations, together with the fact of the suffering experienced by Mr Brongersma, the general practitioner was found not guilty.[266]

The District Court's judgment departed from the case law that had established the necessity of a medical indication.[267] The KNMG also criticized it in a statement made by its Chairman who wrote, 'as the criterion of unbearable and hopeless suffering is extended, the request of the patient becomes central, and the medical professional judgment disappears to the background'.[268] This statement is once more a reminder that the Dutch practice of physician-assisted death does not stem purely from the right to self-determination but from the concept of medical duty of care towards the patient.

The Amsterdam Court of Appeal overruled the District Court's judgment. Two experts were asked whether the medical profession covered existential suffering, to which they both disagreed. According to the Court Appeal, it was doubtful whether the conflict of duties argument, namely the necessity defence, could be invoked despite the absence of a medical indication. Three questions were asked to the Supreme Court for a preliminary ruling: Could a physician agree to assist with dying in the absence of any somatic or mental illness? Was it part of a physician's duty to assist in cases of existential suffering? Was there a consensus among the medical profession about this matter?[269]

The Supreme Court took into account two expert witness opinions that both agreed there was no consensus on the matter of physician-assisted dying in cases of existential suffering. The experts stated that as far as existential suffering was not related to the realm of the medical profession, it would not provide grounds for the necessity defence that provided legitimacy to physician-assisted death. Repeating the necessity of a medical indication, the Court ruled that physicians must act within their professional competence.[270]

'Existential suffering', 'being tired of life', 'suffering from life' or 'completed life' are used as synonyms, and the Dijkhuis Committee appointed by the KNMG after the Brongersma Case defined existential suffering as

> suffering at the prospect of having to continue living in a manner in which there is no, or only a deficient, perceived quality of life, giving rise to a persisting desire to die, even though the absence or deficiency in quality of life cannot be explained in any or significant measure by an identifiable somatic or psychological condition.[271]

Physician-assisted death based on existential suffering has been debated during the parliamentary discussions for the 2002 Act. Despite the general sympathy towards

---

[266] *Brongersma-RB* [2000] Rechtbank Haarlem ECLI:NL:RBHAA:2000:AA7926.

[267] de Vries (2004), pp. 384–386.

[268] Hagenouw (2000) Nooit: u vraagt en arts draait. In: Trouw. https://www.trouw.nl/nieuws/nooit-u-vraagt-en-arts-draait~b9e7d35b/ (Griffiths's translation at Griffiths et al. (2008), p. 36.

[269] *Brongersma-GH* [2001] Gerechtshof Amsterdam ECLI:NL:GHAMS:2001:AD6753.

[270] *Brongersma-HR* [2002] Hoge Raad ECLI:NL:HR:2002:AE8772.

[271] KNMG (2011) Position Paper: The Role of the Physician in the Voluntary Termination of Life. https://www.knmg.nl/advies-richtlijnen/knmg-publicaties/publications-in-english.htm, p. 14.

the suffering one might have due to 'being tired of life', there was strong opposition against extending the competency of the medical profession to a non-medical situation.[272]

The Dutch case law so far portrays an approach that is different from that of Switzerland. The idea behind the Swiss model of assisted suicide is focused on the right to self-determination. Arguments for and against assisted suicide orbit around the right to decide the time and manner of one's own death. The Dutch approach stems from the medical duty of a physician to care for his or her patients, which means that

> euthanasia must remain based on medical considerations about causes and suffering. Euthanasia is an exception to a general rule – an option to an extreme situation – rather than the general rule itself. A justification for this exception is found in the medical context itself, with reference to the role of the doctor, serving the interests of the patient, and the nature of the doctor-patient relationship, in which a confidential discussion about life and death usually takes place.[273]

The right to self-determination realized itself in the conditions of euthanasia. Apart from the request condition, the patient's perspective on the 'hopeless and unbearable suffering' or what would qualify as a 'death with dignity' requires the expression of the right to self-determination. However, the main justifying grounds came from the concept of conflict of duties that a physician might face within the medical profession. While self-determination was the core of the end-of-life discussions in Switzerland, the Dutch debate centralized on the medical duty of care.[274]

3.2.2 *The New Legal Framework of 2002: Euthanasia Act*

After the election in 1994, the CDA was not part of the coalition government for the first time since 1917. The new Government, which continued for another term with the 1998 election, consisted of a coalition among the Labour Party (PvdA), the People's Party for Freedom and Democracy (VVD), and the D66. The D66 introduced another proposal for euthanasia legislation. The House of Representatives in November 2000 and the Senate in April 2001 approved the proposed bill, making the Netherlands the first Council of Europe State to legalize euthanasia. The Termination of Life on Request and Assistance with Suicide Act (Euthanasia Act) came into force on 1 April 2002.[275]

---

[272] Griffiths et al. (2008), p. 39.

[273] de Vries (2004), p. 388.

[274] Otlowski (1997), p. 402.

[275] BWBR0012410 Termination of Life on Request and Assistance with Suicide (Review Procedures) Act of 10 April 2001. English translation available at https://www.ieb-eib.org/ancien-site/pdf/loi-euthanasie-pays-bas-en-eng.pdf. The version provided under this link is from 2002, before the amendments of 2012, 2014, 2018 and 2020. However, these amendments did not bring major

The Euthanasia Act amended sections 293 and 294 of the Criminal Code by adding a second paragraph.

> Section 293(2): The offence referred to in subsection (1) shall not be punishable, if it is committed by a medical doctor who meets the requirements of due care referred to in section 2 of the Termination of Life on Request and Assisted Suicide (Review Procedures) Act and who informs the municipal forensic pathologist in accordance with section 7(2) of the Burial and Cremation Act.
>
> Section 294(2): Any person who intentionally assists in the suicide of person or provides him with the means thereto shall, if suicide follows, be liable to a term of imprisonment not exceeding three years or a fine of the fourth category. Section 293(2) shall apply mutatis mutandis.

According to section 2(1) of the Euthanasia Act, in order to meet the requirements of due care the physician must:

(a) be satisfied that the patient has made a voluntary and carefully considered request;
(b) be satisfied that the patient's suffering was unbearable, and that there was no prospect of improvement;
(c) have informed the patient about his situation and his prospects;
(d) have come to the conclusion, together with the patient, that there is no reasonable alternative in the light of the patient's situation;
(e) have consulted at least one other, independent physician, who must have seen the patient and given a written opinion on the due care criteria referred to in a. to d. above; and
(f) have terminated the patient's life or provided assistance with suicide with due medical care and attention.

Physician-assisted death will be justified if the physician follows the due care requirements, namely, careful medical practice requirements previously developed by the Courts and the KNMG. If a patient dies by euthanasia or assisted suicide, the physician will notify the municipal pathologist of the situation and file a report detailing the reasons for performing euthanasia.[276] The municipal pathologist will notify the RTE, which will evaluate the case and decide whether the requirements mentioned above are fulfilled.[277] Five regional review committees oversee five regions. The committees consist of a physician, a lawyer, an ethicist, and their alternates.[278] The members of the committees are appointed for four years by the Ministers of Justice and Health.[279] After receiving a notification, the secretary of the committee will make a preliminary assessment and decide whether the case is straightforward (prima facie compliance with the legal requirements) or non-straightforward (a case that raises questions on its compliance with the legal requirements). Straightforward cases will be reviewed at the committee's digital

changes that are relevant here. The only relevant change is that the members of the RTE are no longer appointed for a term of 6 years, but 4.

[276] Dutch Burial Act sec 7(2).

[277] Dutch Burial Act sec 10(2); The RTE is regulated under Chapter III sections 3–19 of the Dutch Euthanasia Act.

[278] RTE, The Committees. https://english.euthanasiecommissie.nl/the-committees/the-committees.

[279] Dutch Euthanasia Act sec 4(1).

meetings. Non-straightforward cases or straightforward cases that have raised additional questions during the digital meeting will be reviewed at the monthly committee meeting, and the involved parties can be invited to give further statements for clarification. The committee should notify the physician of the outcome of its assessment within six weeks. If it is concluded that the requirements have not been met, the committee will notify the Board of Procurators General and the Health and Youth Care Inspectorate. Otherwise, no further action is necessary.[280] The RTE is tasked to submit an annual report to the Ministers of Justice and Health on the statistics, including its remarks on the cases it has dealt with.[281] The RTE also published the Euthanasia Code 2018 – Review Procedures in Practice, which gives 'a practical overview of how the RTE interprets the due care criteria' and is regularly updated alongside relevant developments.[282]

If these requirements are met, the physician will be immune from criminal charges. In 2019, there were 6.361 reports of euthanasia cases, from which only four were found incompatible with the legal requirements.[283]

Under the Euthanasia Act, minors from the age of 12 can request euthanasia. Until 16 years old, parental consent is required. From 16 to 18, parental consent may be waived if the minor is considered to have a 'reasonable understanding of his interests', but the parents must nevertheless be involved in the decision-making process. The Euthanasia Act also regulates advance directives on euthanasia, by which patients over 16 years of age can request euthanasia for a future scenario of incompetency.[284]

3.2.3 Interpretations by the RTE

Physicians must act in accordance with the professional standards of medicine in all of their professional conduct, including euthanasia. However, the Euthanasia Act cannot cover every aspect and detail of the professional medical standards relating to euthanasia. The act lists only the general due care criteria. Therefore, there is a need for further clarification. The KNMG and the RTE are the most essential two institutions that play a significant role in the Dutch euthanasia practice. The KNMG publishes statements and guidelines on relevant questions. One of these guidelines, for example, describes the methods of performing euthanasia, such as the

[280] A step-by-step explanation of this process can be found at RTE, Review Procedure. https://english.euthanasiecommissie.nl/review-procedure.

[281] Dutch Euthanasia Act sec 17(1); All annual reports can be found at https://english.euthanasiecommissie.nl/the-committees/annual-reports.

[282] RTE (2019) Euthanasia Code 2018. https://english.euthanasiecommissie.nl/the-committees/code-of-practice.

[283] RTE (2020) Lichte stijging aantal euthanasiemeldingen. https://www.euthanasiecommissie.nl/actueel/nieuws/2020/4/17/jaarverslag-2019.

[284] Dutch Euthanasia Act sec 2(2), 2(3), 2(4).

choice of medication and details on preparation, which elaborates on section 2(1)(f) of the Euthanasia Act.[285] The Guidelines are regularly updated in line with medical developments. The RTE is the first instance of evaluating whether due care requirements have been met and the committees' decisions are published, which allows for better transparency. The annual reports summarise these decisions, statistics on the cases, and explanations on how the RTE interprets due care requirements. Since there are constant developments and debates on the Euthanasia Act's application, publications of the KNMG and the RTE provide clarification and guidance.

3.2.3.1 On 'Suffering'

One requirement of euthanasia is that there must be unbearable suffering with no prospects of recovery. The cause of suffering does not need to be based on somatic illnesses. It was clarified in the Chabot Case that the source of suffering, whether somatic or non-somatic, is irrelevant, and they can both be valid reasons for a euthanasia request. The unbearable state of suffering is subjective and thus contains individual elements, which the physician should take into account. Nevertheless, the suffering must be understandable to the physician.[286] In the view of the case law, the KNMG and the RTE believe that

> the suffering must have a medical dimension: it must fall within the physician's domain, that is to say within the scope of his responsibility and expertise. There must be a state that can be described as a disease or a medical condition. However, there need not be a single, dominant or life-threatening medical problem. For instance, the patient could be suffering from two (or more) diseases. The medical dimension to the suffering then lies in the combination of these medical conditions.[287]

Therefore, the suffering of a purely existential nature (the concept of 'completed life' as the RTE refers to) does not justify euthanasia.[288] As it was previously established in the Brongersma Case, there needs to be a medical indication that allows the physician to become involved. On the other hand, the deteriorating state of health due to advanced age, namely multiple geriatric syndromes, can be accepted as suffering in the meaning of the Euthanasia Act.

There are debates on whether psychiatric illnesses are somatic or non-somatic.[289] Developments in science, especially neuroscience, continue to change the outlook on psychology and psychiatric illnesses. Regardless of the debates, for the purposes

---

[285] KNMG (2012) Guidelines for the Practice of Euthanasia and Physician-Assisted Suicide. https://www.knmg.nl/advies-richtlijnen/knmg-publicaties/publications-in-english.htm.

[286] RTE (2019) Euthanasia Code 2018, p. 24.

[287] RTE (2019) Euthanasia Code 2018, p. 22.

[288] RTE (2019) Euthanasia Code 2018, pp. 52–53.

[289] Psychiatric illnesses might often have biological correlates. There are researches aiming to give neurophysiological explanations to psychiatric illnesses. See Rietschel (2014).

of euthanasia, psychiatric illnesses are considered non-somatic. As stated in the Chabot Case, when faced with a euthanasia request based on non-somatic reasons, physicians must show 'exceptional care' while determining the euthanasia request's authenticity since the decision-making capacity might be impaired. Although the law does not distinguish between euthanasia and assisted suicide, there seems to be a general understanding that when the suffering is not somatic, the only option will be assisted suicide.[290]

While the unbearable state of suffering is subjective, any recovery prospects are an objective medical assessment. Nevertheless, it is not without subjective elements. The assessment of possible alternatives to alleviate the patient's suffering depends on whether a given alternative treatment is acceptable to the patient. The RTE interprets lack of prospects of recovery as the following:

> The physician and the patient must together arrive at the conclusion that no reasonable alternatives are available to the patient. The perception and wishes of the patient are important. There is an alternative to euthanasia if there is a realistic way of alleviating or ending the suffering which may – from the patient's point of view – be considered reasonable. An invasive or lengthy intervention with a limited chance of a positive result will not generally be regarded as a 'reasonable alternative'. Generally, 'a reasonable alternative' intervention or treatment can end or considerably alleviate the patient's suffering over a longer period.[291]

The benefits expected from an alternative should outweigh the burden of the treatment on the patient, which will be assessed based on the patient's individual circumstances. According to the RTE, the patient has a 'large say' in what constitutes a reasonable alternative.[292] If a patient refuses a reasonable alternative treatment, the criteria of euthanasia will not have been met. This assessment requires extra caution when it concerns non-somatic suffering. The Dutch Association for Psychiatry (NVvP) has published guidelines on how to deal with euthanasia requests from patients with psychiatric illnesses.[293]

3.2.3.2 On 'Termination of Life Without an Explicit Request'

Terminating a person's life without that person's request lacks the crucial element of euthanasia, which is the request, and hence, cannot be classified as euthanasia. While the Remmelink Commission had considered the termination of life without a request under exceptional circumstances (administering lethal drugs to hasten the death of a terminal patient) to be normal medical practice and suggested that it would be

---

[290] Griffiths et al. (2008), p. 113.

[291] RTE (2019) Annual Report 2018, p. 38; Also addressed in RTE (2019) Euthanasia Code 2018, pp. 25–27.

[292] RTE (2019) Euthanasia Code 2018, p. 26.

[293] NVvP (2018) Levensbeëindiging op verzoek bij patiënten met een psychische stoornis. https://richtlijnendatabase.nl/richtlijn/levensbeeindiging_op_verzoek_psychiatrie/startpagina_-_levensbe_indiging_op_verzoek.html.

justified as a medical exception, this notion was rejected during parliamentary debates.[294] The Supreme Court dealt with this very matter in the van Oijen Case in 2004.[295]

In 1997, a general practitioner, Dr van Oijen, had administered medication that caused the death of his patient, who was an 85-year-old terminally ill woman staying in a nursing home. After she had fallen into a coma, Dr van Oijen prescribed palliative drugs to prevent her from suffering in case she would regain consciousness. The nursing home did not administer the prescribed drugs, fearing that they would cause the patient's death. According to Dr van Oijen, the nursing home had also neglected to wash and care for the patient since her death was expected shortly. When seeing this situation, Dr van Oijen consulted with the patient's daughter and administered an expired muscle relaxer, which he happened to have with him. The patient died, and Dr van Oijen reported the incident as a natural death. Suspicious of the circumstances, the director of the nursing home notified the authorities, and charges were brought against Dr van Oijen.

The Medical Disciplinary Tribunal found Dr van Oijen guilty of terminating life without a request, falsifying the death certificate, administering an expired drug, and keeping insufficient documentation. Since Dr van Oijen's motivation was to act in the best interest of his patient, he only received a warning from the Tribunal, which was the least severe sanction.[296]

The Amsterdam District Court and the Court of Appeal found Dr van Oijen guilty of murder and falsifying a death certificate. Both Courts rejected Dr van Oijen's necessity defence. Since the patient was in a coma, she was unconscious to feel any suffering. She had also stated that she did not want to die. While the District Court sentenced Dr van Oijen to a fine, the Court of Appeal sentenced him to one week imprisonment with two years probation.[297]

The Supreme Court dismissed Dr van Oijen's appeal, stating that terminating a patient's life without a request could be justified by the necessity defence only under extraordinary circumstances, under which the physician felt compelled to do what was in the best interest of the patient. This was not the case in Dr van Oijen's patient.[298] Dr van Oijen was convicted of murder. Nevertheless, the minimal sentence he received signals the Courts' leniency to his case. Although the necessity defence was not accepted in the van Oijen Case, the judgment did not eliminate the possibility of justification under extraordinary circumstances.

An example of extraordinary circumstances is severely ill newborns. 'Neonatal euthanasia' has been discussed since the 1990s. The Commission on the Acceptability of Medical Behaviour that Shortens Life, which was appointed by the KNMG, in 1990 and the Dutch Association for Paediatrics (NVK) in 1992 have

---

294 Griffiths et al. (2008), p. 40.

295 *van Oijen* [2004] Hoge Raad ECLI:NL:HR:2004:AP1493.

296 Griffiths et al. (2008), pp. 40–41.

297 *van Oijen* [2003] Gerechtshof Amsterdam ECLI:NL:GHAMS:2003:AF9392.

298 Griffiths et al. (2008), pp. 40–41.

issued reports on the subject, which generally considered the termination of life acceptable when the withdrawing treatment has left the newborn in a state of 'unacceptable suffering'.[299] In two cases from 1995, the Courts acquitted two physicians who had terminated the lives of two newborn babies. The newborns were both severely ill with no chance of survival. After withdrawing all life-sustaining treatment, the newborns were believed to be in a state of severe suffering. The physicians' actions were found justified.[300] The Groningen Protocol, which was written in 2004 by Professor Eduard Verhagen, head of the Paediatrics Department at the University of Groningen, outlines criteria that provide physicians with guidelines on neonatal termination of life.[301] In 2005 the NVK adopted the Groningen Protocol as the national guideline.[302] There is a Review Committee on Late-Term Abortions and Neonatal Termination of Life that oversees compliance with due care requirements.[303]

3.2.3.3 On 'Terminal Sedation'

Palliative sedation means intermittent or continuous sedation that could range from a low-level consciousness to a complete state of unconsciousness. It is a method chosen to ease the patient's pain and provide comfort. As a subdivision of palliative sedation, terminal sedation refers to continuous deep sedation until death takes its course. It is often combined with withdrawing or withholding of life-sustaining treatment, such as artificial nutrition and hydration because treatment is usually deemed medically futile at this stage.[304] While many consider terminal sedation normal medical practice, the blurry line between terminal sedation and termination of life has caused discussions. Some consider there to be no difference between the administration of lethal medication to a patient upon request (euthanasia) and the continuous administration of pain medication that sedates the patient until death occurs (terminal sedation), classifying the latter as 'euthanasia in disguise' or 'slow euthanasia'.[305] Practically there might not be much of a difference: the patient's life comes to an end. Morally, however, it is the intention of the act that distinguishes these practices. The primary goal of euthanasia is to end life, while terminal sedation is aimed to alleviate pain. Death is not intended but occurs as a secondary outcome,

---

[299] Griffiths et al. (2008), pp. 217–226.

[300] Griffiths et al. (2008), pp. 227–228.

[301] See Verhagen (2006).

[302] NVK (2014) Richtlijn: Levensbeëindiging bij pasgeborenen, actieve. https://www.nvk.nl/themas/kwaliteit/richtlijnen/richtlijn?componentid=6881303&tagtitles=Neonatologie.

[303] Beoordelingscommissie Late Zwangerschapsafbreking en Levensbeëndiging bij Pasgeborenen, Over ons. https://www.lzalp.nl/over-ons.

[304] Rietjens et al. (2008), p. 813.

[305] See Tännsjö (ed) (2004); In this book, 'Terminal Sedation: Euthanasia in Disguise?', several authors discuss whether terminal sedation is used as a substitute for euthanasia. One of the authors, Helga Kuhse, calls terminal sedation 'slow euthanasia'.

which is referred to as the doctrine of double effect.[306] However, many researchers have stated that properly administered pain medication in adequate and careful dosages does not hasten death.[307]

A television program caused controversy when it revealed that some physicians choose terminal sedation to avoid the notification procedure of euthanasia.[308]While terminal sedation accounted for approximately 5.7% of all deaths in 2001, this number increased to 7.1% in 2005. In the meantime, the percentage of euthanasia cases decreased from 2.6 in 2001 to 1.7 in 2005.[309] These numbers seem to coincide with the claim that physicians opt for terminal sedation rather than euthanasia in order to avoid the procedural hassles of the notification procedure. However, increasing awareness and knowledge of palliative care could also explain these numbers. The head of the Board of Procurators General, Mr de Wijkerslooth, had argued that the consequences of a physician's act should be determinative rather than the subjective intention and that terminal sedation should be included in the Euthanasia Act. Mr de Wijkerslooth's call was perceived as interference in normal medical practice, and while receiving a negative reaction from physicians and the KNMG, it was rejected both by the Ministers of Health and Justice.[310]

Another comparative study of terminal sedation and euthanasia from 2002 disclosed that the decision was discussed with the patient in 61% and the family in 93% of terminal sedation cases. In 4% of the terminal sedation cases the physician had decided without consulting the patient or the family, but the patient had previously requested euthanasia.[311] In 17% of terminal sedation cases, hastening death was the explicit intention. 96% of deaths occurred within a week.[312] Loss of dignity and the feeling of dependence were cited more often as reasons for requesting euthanasia than for terminal sedation. Terminal sedation decisions were mostly based on physical elements, like pain or difficulty breathing.[313] This is probably the most crucial outcome of the study. Concepts related to personal autonomy and dignity play a more significant role in euthanasia requests than physical suffering does. Sufficient palliative care and pain management would not be able to replace the demand for euthanasia entirely.

Although the Government rejected to include it in the Euthanasia Act, the medical profession was asked to draw up a national guideline on palliative sedation. The

[306] McIntyre (2019) Doctrine of Double Effect. In: Zalta EN (ed) The Stanford Encyclopedia of Philosophy. https://plato.stanford.edu/archives/spr2019/entries/double-effect/.

[307] McIntyre (2019) Doctrine of Double Effect; Fohr (1998), p. 319; Badarau et al. (2019), p. 57.

[308] van Kolfschooten (2003), pp. 1352–1353.

[309] van der Heide et al. (2007), p. 1960.

[310] Sheldon (2003), p. 465.

[311] Rietjens et al. (2006), p. 750.

[312] Rietjens et al. (2006), pp. 751–752.

[313] Rietjens et al. (2006), p. 751.

KNMG adopted the National Guideline for Palliative Sedation in 2005 and revised it in 2009.[314] Palliative sedation is considered normal medical practice.[315] The Guideline divides palliative sedation into two groups: continuous sedation until death, which refers to terminal sedation, and intermittent sedation.[316] Continuous sedation until the time of death is medically acceptable when there is unbearable suffering, which is caused by refractory symptoms that could not be treated by other means.[317] Existential suffering is not excluded, as it is acknowledged that existential suffering might cause unbearable pain to the patient that cannot be alleviated with regular means. These patients are usually very close to death, and numerous physical problems accompany their suffering. In these cases, terminal sedation can be considered after consulting with experts of psychology or spiritual counsellors. However, existential suffering without any refractory symptoms is not accepted as a sufficient reason for palliative sedation.[318] Death must be imminent by one or two weeks. Artificial nutrition and hydration can be withheld only because death is foreseeable within a maximum of two weeks.[319] The decision-making process should include the patient, the patient's family, and the healthcare team. The physician will act in the best interest of the patient, and if there is a disagreement between the physician and the patient's family, the physician will have the final say.[320] Since continuous sedation is considered normal medical practice, there is no obligation of consultation like there is in euthanasia. However, if the treating physician does not have sufficient knowledge of palliative care, it is good medical practice to consult an expert.[321] According to the Guideline, continuous sedation is not an alternative to euthanasia, and the two practices must be clearly distinguished. The aim is to lower the consciousness to a level that the patient does not experience unbearable pain; therefore, adequate usage of sedatives is crucial.[322] The Guideline explains the proper medication and dosages for palliative sedation and emphasizes the importance of documentation. It also acknowledges the value of good communication by informing the patient's family and friends as well as the importance of supporting the healthcare team.[323]

---

[314] KNMG (2009) Guideline for Palliative Sedation. https://www.knmg.nl/advies-richtlijnen/knmg-publicaties/publications-in-english.htm.

[315] KNMG (2009) Guideline for Palliative Sedation, p. 55.

[316] KNMG (2009) Guideline for Palliative Sedation, p. 20.

[317] The Guideline refers to a refractory symptom when 'none of the conventional modes of treatment is effective or fast-acting enough, and/or if these modes of treatment are accompanied by unacceptable side-effects.' KNMG (2009) Guideline for Palliative Sedation, p. 22.

[318] KNMG (2009) Guideline for Palliative Sedation, pp. 24–25.

[319] KNMG (2009) Guideline for Palliative Sedation, pp. 25–27.

[320] KNMG (2009) Guideline for Palliative Sedation, pp. 31–33.

[321] KNMG (2009) Guideline for Palliative Sedation, p. 30.

[322] KNMG (2009) Guideline for Palliative Sedation, pp. 66–69.

[323] KNMG (2009) Guideline for Palliative Sedation, p. 51.

The physician's intention is another factor that separates euthanasia from terminal sedation. In one case, a physician had administered sedatives to a terminal patient after consulting with the patient's family. The patient died 15 min later, and charges of murder were brought against the physician. The physician was acquitted since there was no clear indication of an intention to terminate life.[324] Prognosis, medical history, choice of medication, and dosage are all identifying tools to determine the physician's intention. Although terminal sedation is classified as normal medical practice, it should be treated carefully.[325] There should be sufficient grounds to justify putting a patient in a continuous unconscious state until death because 'one does not take a person's consciousness away for less than grave reasons.'[326]

The practice of terminal sedation has been mostly in line with the KNMG guidelines.[327] However, there seems to be an increase in the practice, especially by general practitioners with patients over 80 years old and cancer patients. A problematic finding was that a palliative care expert was consulted only in 1 out of 5 cases.[328] Whether the increase means terminal sedation is used as a substitute for euthanasia by general practitioners is unknown. It could also be a result of raising awareness of palliative care. Over time, the definition of 'suffering' extended from physical pain to non-physical pain, such as existential distress. Whether it is a general change in the perception of dignity or an increase of respect towards the personal understanding of dignity, subjective considerations are not as easily excluded. Studies have shown that non-physical elements are quoted more frequently than before as reasons for terminal sedation.[329]

3.2.3.4 On 'Non-residents'

There has been the impression that physician-assisted death is only available to Dutch nationals or residents of the Netherlands despite the lack of such a requirement under the Euthanasia Act. Perhaps this impression was created intentionally in fear of the Netherlands becoming the next hotspot for death tourism.[330] The Gov-

[324]Griffiths et al. (2008), pp. 42–43.

[325]The KNMG refers to continuous sedation as a 'radical medical procedure'. KNMG (2009) Guideline for Palliative Sedation, p. 7.

[326]Janssens et al. (2012), p. 667.

[327]Swart et al. (2012), p. 262.

[328]Rietjens et al. (2019), pp. 1367–1372.

[329]Heijltjes (2020), pp. 841–843.

[330]Enthoven (2017) Deur staat open voor euthanasietoerisme. NJB 38:2035. https://www.njb.nl/blogs/deur-staat-open-voor-euthanasietoerisme/.

ernment finally clarified the situation in 2017[331] by updating the website on euthanasia that now states:

> A physician who performs euthanasia should be convinced that the due care criteria of the Termination of Life on Request and Assisted Suicide (Review Procedures) Act are met.
>
> This means that the physician has to have sufficient knowledge concerning the patient's medical history to be able to assess whether the patient's suffering is unbearable and without prospect of improvement. In addition, the physician has to be convinced that the patient's request is voluntary and well-considered.
>
> This concerns a complex and multi-faceted assessment, and it is up to the physician to decide whether this is possible in case of a request done by a person who does not reside in the Netherlands and has only recently arrived here.[332]

As long as the physician feels confident that due care requirements have been met, there is no obstacle for a non-resident to receive physician assistance in dying in the Netherlands. It can be argued that if the Government had serious concerns about death tourism, a provision could have been included in the Euthanasia Act limiting the practice to residents only. However, it does not seem likely that this issue could have simply been forgotten during the parliamentary discussions. It is more in line with the general Dutch approach that it would be left to the physician's discretion.

3.2.3.5 On 'Demedicalized Assisted Suicide'

The end-of-life debate in the Netherlands has rather evolved around the morality of serving the patient's best interest. It has been a medical discussion, and the case law is focused on the physician's duty of care. Though self-determination has played an identifying role in justifying physician-assisted death, the core of its legitimacy stemmed from the physician's duty. The physician's duty of care for the patient outweighs the prohibition to kill under severe circumstances in which the patient is suffering gravely. The amount of suffering endured by the patient renders the interest protected by sections 293 and 294 of the Criminal Code meaningless, and under those exceptional circumstances, the physician cannot be held guilty to have set them aside. Based on this idea, the conditions that would indicate such a situation, namely the requirements of careful medical practice, include elements of the right to self-determination. There should be an autonomous well-thought request for an assisted death, a discussion on other possible alternatives with the patient, consultation with another expert who might see an alternative that was not considered;

---

[331] Enthoven states that, before the change, the Government's website stated 'The Act is only applicable to people who have a medical relationship with a physician who is subject to Dutch law. This means that people who do not reside in the Netherlands cannot apply for euthanasia or physician-assisted suicide under the Act.' Enthoven (2017) Deur staat open voor euthanasietoerisme.

[332] Government of the Netherlands, Is euthanasia allowed? https://www.government.nl/topics/euthanasia/is-euthanasia-allowed.

otherwise, the physician would not be serving the best interest of the patient. The requirements of euthanasia are indicators that illustrate the physician had indeed been thinking of the patient's best interest, which is why he or she does not need to receive punishment.

The Swiss debate on end-of-life evolved on another path. The centre of the discussion was self-determination, which needed to be weighed against the State's duty to protect the vulnerable. The criteria set out for assisted suicide are an outcome of a compromise. The right to self-determination is limited in the face of the State's interests, and the criteria show when it is permitted to uphold the individual interest. Contrary to the Dutch practice, the evolvement of the Swiss model of assisted suicide has been kept away as much as possible from the medical sphere.

Patients who do not meet the physician-assisted death requirements or who have been rejected by their physician look for other solutions. Some patients want to avoid the procedures of physician-assisted dying or assume that their circumstances do not meet the requirements but wish to keep their options open nonetheless. The feeling of reassurance in case of future suffering is a motivating factor in the search for other options.[333]

Several Dutch organizations, such as the NVVE, give information on effective ways to end one's own life, namely demedicalized assisted suicide (DAS). The often-used methods for an effective ending of life are refraining from food and fluids, or self-collecting lethal medication.[334] While distributing information on ways to commit suicide has not been an issue in the Netherlands, assisted suicide organizations, which would provide similar assistance to those of the Swiss organizations, have faced some problems. Since the Dutch model of assisted death is based on the medical profession, the involvement of a non-physician falls outside the regularly accepted practice.

The organization *de Einder*, founded in 1995, offers open discussions and information on suicide to people who would like to have control over the time and manner of their death. When faced with a suicide wish, the reaction is often prejudiced and focused on curing such a wish rather than hearing it out. Open discussions on end-of-life options often reassure people who wish to maintain their independence and autonomy on the time and manner of their death. The basic idea of having an available course of action can give peace of mind and ease many worries, enhancing the quality of life.[335] *De Einder* pursues a non-judgmental supportive approach 'to promote and, if desired, provide professional counselling to people who want assisted suicide with respect to their personal autonomy.'[336] The organization's support has included, on occasion, being present for the suicide and offering guidance if necessary. A counsellor was found guilty and sentenced to

[333] Hagens et al. (2014), p. 462.

[334] Hagens et al. (2017), p. 543.

[335] Hagens et al. (2021), p. 45.

[336] de Einder, Historie van Stichting de Einder. https://www.deeinder.nl/de-einder/organisatie/historie/.

twelve months imprisonment, eight of which conditional, on violation of section 294 of the Criminal Code. The Court found that the counsellor had overstepped his limits by actively assisting with suicide. In another case, the founder of *de Einder* had provided medication to a woman who wanted to end her life. He was found guilty, but due to his remorse, received a probationary sentence.[337]

According to a study, only 21% of the Dutch public supports the legalization of DAS. However, when faced with a concrete scenario, the percentage increased to 62. The public places its trust in physicians at the end of life. However, if the physician refuses to assist, a patient with physical suffering receives empathy, and DAS is accepted as an alternative. The accepted form of assistance is providing information to the person wishing to end his or her life. Obtaining drugs for the person wishing to commit suicide is less approved.[338]

The *Expertisecentrum Euthanasie* (formerly known as End-of-life Clinic) was established in 2012 by the NVVE to provide a 'safety net' for euthanasia requests. Physicians can refuse to grant their patients' euthanasia requests due to moral reasons, hesitation, concerns of compliance with the law, lack of experience, etc. Based on their specialization in euthanasia, the *Expertisecentrum Euthanasie* aims to provide guidance and support to physicians in the euthanasia process and offer an alternative to those patients whose euthanasia requests have been rejected by their own physicians.[339] The *Expertisecentrum Euthanasie* operates under the requirements of due care set forth by the Euthanasia Act.

3.2.3.6 On 'Dementia'

The Dutch practice has not limited the interpretation of suffering to the present physical or psychological pain. It is accepted that suffering also includes the anticipation of an undignified situation, which can be a legitimate reason for requesting euthanasia.[340] Oftentimes, people fear the future possibility of losing their mental capacity and becoming dependent on the support of others. Fear of an undignified end can have different meanings to each person. Some consider the end stages of dementia undignified and, therefore, request euthanasia with an advance directive.

In 2018, two cases were reported to the RTE that involved patients in an advanced stage of dementia who were no longer mentally competent. Euthanasia was based on an advance directive in each case. 144 cases concerned patients in an early stage of dementia who were still competent and able to communicate their request at the time

[337] Griffiths et al. (2008), p. 47.

[338] Schoonman et al. (2014), pp. 844–845.

[339] Expertisecentrum Euthanasie, Over ons. https://expertisecentrumeuthanasie.nl/over-ons/.

[340] Griffiths et al. (2008), p. 73.

of euthanasia.[341] The RTE's annual reports do not reveal a rapidly increasing number in euthanasia of patients with dementia.

A case concerning a euthanasia request via an advance directive by a patient with dementia came before the District Court of The Hague in 2019.[342] In 2016, a physician performed euthanasia on a 74-year-old woman with advanced dementia. The incident raised some eyebrows due to the circumstances of the euthanasia procedure.[343] The patient had signed an advance directive in 2012, in which she had made a euthanasia request, including a dementia clause, with the wish to avoid being admitted to a nursing home. Her mother had passed away under similar circumstances, and she had hoped to avoid the same ending. She wanted to end her life 'when I am still to some degree decisionally competent but no longer able to live at home with my husband'. When the patient revised her advance directive in 2015, she said 'when I myself think the time is ripe' that euthanasia would be the course of action, further stating 'trusting that, by the time the quality of my life has become so poor that [. . .] euthanasia will be performed at my request'. The patient had discussed her advance directive with her family and with both her general practitioner and geriatrician, who concluded the patient was competent to make such a request at the time. She repeated her wish to die to her family but said 'not now'. Before her admission to the nursing home, when euthanasia was discussed with the general practitioner, the patient believed that euthanasia would be 'going too far'. When she was admitted to the nursing home, the patient was no longer in a state of competence to grasp the idea of euthanasia or her health condition. Although she expressed her wish to die, she would conclude that her situation was 'not that bad yet'. The physician consulted with two independent SCEN physicians, both of whom agreed the due care criteria had been met, and the advance directive would replace the oral request at that point of time since the patient was no longer competent and did suffer unbearably and hopelessly. Because she was refusing to take any medication, the physician first added a sedative to the patient's coffee. Despite the sedative, the patient woke up and resisted the injection of the euthanasia medication. The procedure was continued nevertheless, and the RTE was notified.[344]

The physician justified continuing the euthanasia procedure based on the patient's history, her wish not to be admitted to a nursing home, and the advance directive drawn up when the patient was competent. The committee pointed out the wording of the advance directive. Although the interpretation of the advance directive was possible and sometimes necessary, the specific wording chosen by the patient, such as 'when I myself think', 'at my request' and 'when I am still to some degree

[341] RTE (2019) Annual Report 2018, p. 13.

[342] *Case on Dementia* [2019] Rechtbank Den Haag ECLI:NL:RBDHA:2019:9506.

[343] Cheng (2018) Dutch probe "appalling" euthanasia of dementia patient. In: Associated Press. https://apnews.com/article/8278f8a6224a47e88b46ea434eda26b4.

[344] RTE (2016) 2016-85, Elderly-Care Specialist, Dementia, Not Acted in Accordance with the Due Care Criteria. https://english.euthanasiecommissie.nl/judgments/dementia/documents/publications/judgments/2016/2016-85/2016-85.

decisionally competent', indicated that the patient thought she would be able to make her euthanasia request herself when the time came. According to the RTE, considering her postponements and resistance, the advance directive should not have been interpreted to replace an oral request. In addition, the physician had 'overstepped a boundary' in the method of performing euthanasia. Even if the patient were no longer competent to request euthanasia and an advance directive were to replace the oral request, this would not rule out the patient's competence to reject an injection. In euthanasia cases, the committee emphasized that coercion or any act similar to that end should be avoided. Instead of opting for an extreme scenario, the physician should have taken the time to reconsider the current situation.[345]

After the RTE found that the physician had not complied with the due care criteria, the Medical Disciplinary Tribunal gave the physician a warning, finding that she had failed to meet the requirements.[346] The District Court of Hague dismissed the criminal case brought against the physician by ruling that a current request for euthanasia was not required since the patient had advanced dementia and prior request had already been established through an advance directive. The premedication was also done in consultation with the family and was not a careless decision.[347] The Supreme Court was asked to clarify in the public interest whether the physician had the duty to verify a current request at the time of euthanasia in case of an incompetent patient with advanced dementia. Upholding the District Court's decision, the Supreme Court stated that physicians should consider the specific circumstances of each patient to 'deduce' whether the prior request covers the current situation and whether the patient's condition amounts to unbearable suffering.[348] In these exceptional cases, two independent physicians must be consulted.[349] The circumstances of the euthanasia procedure and the patient's resistance were not fully discussed in the decision.

Section 2(2) of the Euthanasia Act states:

> If a patient aged sixteen or over who is no longer capable of expressing his will, but before reaching this state was deemed capable of making a reasonable appraisal of his own interests, has made a written declaration requesting that his life be terminated, the attending physician may comply with this request.

The Euthanasia Code 2018 further clarifies advance directives for patients with dementia. In order for an advance directive to replace an oral request when the patient is no longer competent, the advance directive must be sufficiently clear. The validity of an advance directive does not depend on how recent it is. However, since an advance directive reflects the patient's wishes, a directive that is more recent or

[345] RTE (2016) 2016-85, Elderly-Care Specialist, Dementia, Not Acted in Accordance with the Due Care Criteria.

[346] Mahase (2019).

[347] *Case on Dementia-RB*, [5.3].

[348] *Case on Dementia* [2020] Hoge Raad ECLI:NL:HR:2020:712, [5.3.2]; Sheldon (2020).

[349] *Case on Dementia-HR*, [4.9].

has been regularly updated or discussed will carry greater significance than an older one. A physician must consider:

(a) To what degree or in what way did the patient reaffirm his written directive (either orally or otherwise) when he was still decisionally competent?
(b) If the patient is no longer capable of (effective) communication, has there been anything in his behaviour or utterances that contradicts his wishes as set out in the advance directive?
(c) Immediately prior to termination of life, is the patient's state one that he described in his advance directive as being a situation in which he would wish for his life to be terminated?[350]

The Euthanasia Code 2018 also states that if there is an indication of an objection, euthanasia cannot be performed. In cases of patients with advanced dementia, the directive must be 'evidently applicable to the current situation'. The physician must be satisfied that there is no 'contraindication' to the termination of life and the patient is under unbearable suffering.[351] If it is likely that the patient will experience unnecessary pain or confusion due to the state of mind, the RTE considers that administering premedication to calm the patient could be part of due medical care depending on the specific circumstances.[352]

3.2.4 Conclusion

The Netherlands has a culture of open debate on end-of-life matters that started as early as the seventies. Compared to the other European States, the Dutch practice is quite liberal. Professor Theo Boer, who had been a strong supporter of the legalization of euthanasia and a member of the RTE for nine years, believes there is a real risk of a slippery slope. According to Boer, apart from the rising number of euthanasia cases, the scope of euthanasia practice has extended since the Euthanasia Act has entered into force. Euthanasia for mentally ill patients or patients with dementia is reported more often than before. What is once perceived to be a 'last resort' had become the 'normality'.[353] Another member of the RTE resigned her post, criticizing the euthanasia practice for patients with dementia.[354]

The statistics reflect a rise in euthanasia cases. However, this increase does not necessarily mean that there is an abuse of the legislative boundaries. The awareness

[350] RTE (2019) Euthanasia Code 2018, pp. 38–39.
[351] RTE (2019) Euthanasia Code 2018, p. 45.
[352] RTE (2019) Euthanasia Code 2018, p. 40.
[353] Doughty (2014) Don't make our mistake: As assisted suicide bill goes to Lords, Dutch watchdog who once backed euthanasia warns UK of 'slippery slope' to mass deaths. In: Daily Mail. https://www.dailymail.co.uk/news/article-2686711/Dont-make-mistake-As-assisted-suicide-bill-goes-Lords-Dutch-regulator-backed-euthanasia-warns-Britain-leads-mass-killing.html.
[354] Cook (2018) Dissent in Dutch Euthanasia Bureaucracy. In: BioEdge. https://www.bioedge.org/bioethics/dissent-in-dutch-euthanasia-bureaucracy/12569.

of end-of-life options has increased; meanwhile, the notification procedure has settled in. Not only are the patients informed of their choices, but also the physicians are more aware of the terminological differences between euthanasia and other MDEL. The control mechanism set out by the Euthanasia Act and performed by the RTE is transparent enough to evaluate the euthanasia practice objectively. The medical profession has been involved in the euthanasia debate early on and continues to take part in supporting the legal framework with explanatory guidelines and statements. With its freedom and boundaries, the Dutch practice of euthanasia is the outcome of intense collaboration over several decades.

3.3 Belgium

In Belgium, the legal framework for euthanasia was adopted shortly after the Netherlands. The Belgian Act on Euthanasia came into force on 23 September 2002 and has been amended three times since then.[355] Alongside the Euthanasia Act, two other acts were adopted concerning patient rights and palliative care to complement the legislation on end-of-life matters.[356] Unlike in the Netherlands, euthanasia and assisted suicide are not regulated as separate criminal offences under the Belgian Criminal Code.[357] Prior to its legalization, the act of euthanasia would be prosecuted under other crimes listed in the Criminal Code, such as murder.

3.3.1 Until 2002

The movement in favour of legislation on euthanasia started in the 1980s with the establishment of two organizations: the *Association pour le droit de mourir dans la dignité – Belgique* (ADMD) in 1981 and the *Recht op Waardig Sterven* (RWS) in 1983. However, it was not until 1995 that the parliamentary debates gained motion.[358] Although there had been several legislative proposals before the Parliament, they did not have any substantial impact.[359] Similar to the situation in the Netherlands, the opposition of the Christian-democratic parties affected the pro-

[355] 2002009590 Belgian Act on Euthanasia of 28 May 2002 (23 March 2020) (amended 10 November 2005, 24 February 2014 and 15 March 2020); English translation without the amendment of 15 March 2020 can be found in Jones et al. (2017), pp. 305–315.

[356] 2002022737 Belgian Act on Patients' Rights of 22 August 2002 (31 December 2018); 2002022868 Belgian Act on Palliative Care of 14 June 2002 (21 March 2018).

[357] 1867060850 Belgian Criminal Code of 8 June 1867 (4 May 2020).

[358] Cohen-Almagor (2009), p. 188.

[359] Broeckaert (2001), p. 95.

cess.[360] In 1996, both the House of Representatives and the Senate requested the Belgian Advisory Committee on Bioethics (ACB)[361] to draw up a recommendation on the regulation of euthanasia, palliative care, advance directives, and other issues related to the end-of-life.[362]ACB limited its recommendation to the question of whether there was a need for euthanasia legislation, which was defined as an 'act performed by a third party who intentionally puts an end to a person's life at the request of the said person'.[363] ACB further limited the scope of its recommendation to 'hopeless' cases concerning competent patients. Other MDEL had been excluded. Opinion No 1 reflected a divided position on the ethical acceptability of euthanasia while providing four proposals on how to deal with the question of legislation.

The first proposal was a legislative amendment to decriminalize euthanasia.[364] The second was establishing an 'ex post facto procedural regulation' that set certain requirements. Euthanasia would remain illegal; however, the physician would be protected from criminal liability if the requirements were fulfilled. This proposal was influenced by the pre-legislation solution developed by the Dutch courts.[365] Requirements were listed as unbearable suffering experienced by the patient, a well-considered and constant request for euthanasia, consultation with another physician, and informing the relatives and the nursing staff of the euthanasia decision.[366] The third and most discussed proposal was an 'a priori procedural regulation', which meant that all end-of-life decisions would be made through a collegial deliberation. This proposal took the view that not just euthanasia but all end-of-life decisions should be subject to an ethical assessment beforehand since a set of legal rules could not answer the specificity of each case. The physician and the patient would make a joint decision after consultations with the nursing team. In case of a euthanasia request, the ethical assessment would include a non-physician appointed by the local ethics committee and social supervision. The a priori procedure would provide the physician with legal security since the consultation process would confirm a situation of necessity.[367] The fourth and last proposal was to maintain the legal prohibition on euthanasia.[368] Despite the lack of consensus in Opinion No 1, ACB

[360] Broeckaert (2001), p. 95.

[361] ACB was established in 1993 as an independent committee to provide opinions on questions raised in the fields of healthcare, biology and medicine upon request from authorities or on its own initiative. In 1996, the ACB had divided its organization into six commissions, one of which dealt with euthanasia, and received its first assignment on the matter of end-of-life decisions. FPS Public Health, About Us. https://www.health.belgium.be/en/about-us-1.

[362] ACB (1997) Opinion No 1 of 12 May 1997 Concerning the Advisability of a Legal Regulation on Euthanasia. https://www.health.belgium.be/en/opinion-no-1-legal-regulation-euthanasia, p. 1.

[363] ACB (1997) Opinion No 1, p. 1.

[364] ACB (1997) Opinion No 1, p. 2.

[365] See Sect. 3.2.1 'Until 2002' for the Dutch Jurisprudence.

[366] ACB (1997) Opinion No 1, p. 2.

[367] ACB (1997) Opinion No 1, p. 3.

[368] ACB (1997) Opinion No 1, p. 3.

unanimously urged the Government to carry out a broad democratic debate on the matter.[369]

ACB delivered its second opinion on euthanasia in 1999, which was focused on 'active termination of the lives of persons incapable of expressing their wishes'.[370] Incapability to express one's wish refers to the lack of one's capacity to make an autonomous decision (a prerequisite of euthanasia), and it could be based on legal or factual reasons, such as being a minor or loss of consciousness due to an accident.[371] The ACB divided its approach into three groups: Group A (patients incapable of expressing their wishes at the moment but previously having expressed their wishes via an advance directive or having designated a person of trust), Group B (patients incapable of expressing their wishes and not having drawn up an advance directive or designated a person of trust when they had the opportunity) and Group C (patients who have never been capable of expressing their wishes, such as newborns, minors and patients with severe mental disorders).[372] The first proposal in Opinion No 9 was to legally recognize the possibility of active termination of life for patients from Group A, who were in a 'hopeless situation'.[373] If the patient had made an advance directive or had designated a person of trust, the physician should base his or her decision on the patient's previously expressed wishes as much as possible. Although under extreme circumstances, the hopeless situation of a patient from Group B could provide grounds for the necessity defence and justify active termination of life, ACB recommended that it should not be given legal recognition due to the risk of abuse. The legal guardians of patients from Group C could request termination of life. However, the physician should only proceed if there was consensus among the family members and if such an act is advisable under the specific circumstances.[374] The second proposal was, while not giving euthanasia legal recognition, to allow active termination of life only under exceptional circumstances for Group A patients in a terminal stage.[375] An a priori consultation procedure, similar to the one

[369] ACB (1997) Opinion No 1, p. 4.

[370] ACB (1999) Opinion No 9 of 22 February 1999 Concerning Active Termination of the Lives of Persons Incapable of Expressing Their Wishes. https://www.health.belgium.be/en/opinion-no-9-active-termination-lives-persons-incapable-expressing-their-wishes.

[371] ACB (1999) Opinion No 9, p. 6.

[372] ACB (1999) Opinion No 9, pp. 10–12.

[373] 'Hopeless situation' refers to when a patient in a terminal stage has 'no prospect of any recovery' with only a few hours or days to live. However, a situation can still be hopeless even if the patient is not in an immediate terminal stage but nevertheless has no hopes of recovery. ACB gives the example of a newborn suffering from an incurable illness with only few years to live, patients in a persistent vegetative state or patients with dementia. While it can take years for death to take its course in these cases, there is an irremediable illness that will ultimately cause death. ACB (1999) Opinion No 9, p. 3.

[374] ACB (1999) Opinion No 9, pp. 13–14.

[375] It is assumed that the patient had previously requested the termination of his or her life under such circumstances.

described in Opinion No 1, should take place.[376] The third proposal was to maintain the legal prohibition of active termination of lives of patients incapable of expressing their wishes. Supporters of this proposal believed that the complete ban was the only way to protect vulnerable members of the society.[377]

Opinion No 9 presented a more divided committee than Opinion No 1. However, members of the committee shared the common opinion that palliative care needed further development and that the regulation on death certificates was not adequate to ensure the reliability of cause of death statements. They also agreed on the patients' right to refuse life-prolonging treatment and the need for more transparency in end-of-life decision-making procedures.[378]

A majority of ACB members were in favor of an 'a priori procedural regulation' in the Opinion No 1 as a compromise solution, and this understanding grew more potent within the Parliament, including the Christian-democratic party.[379] After the 1999 elections, the new Government was formed without the Christian-democratic party, *Christen-Democratisch en Vlaams* (CD&V). Perhaps their absence led to the departure from proceeding with the priori procedure proposal, since the majority's proposal in the Parliament was closer to the ex post facto procedure proposal in ACB's Opinion No 1 and broader in its content.[380]

The Flemish Palliative Care Federation (FPZV) suggested including a 'palliative filter' for euthanasia. According to the FPZV, there was an underestimation of palliative care options and a false assumption that every physician had sufficient palliative care knowledge. By requiring the attending physician to consult with a palliative care specialist, both the physician and the patient would have a better understanding of the available options.[381] Although the National Council of Ordomedic and the Commission for Public Health of the House of Representatives supported this amendment to the draft bill, the efforts to include consultation with a palliative care specialist within the requirements of euthanasia failed.[382] Jans believes the reason behind the unwillingness to amend the draft bill was:

> If the government were to fall in the time needed for the Senate to discuss a changed bill, the risk of the Christian Democrats coming to power again was deemed too great. As enough members of the majority thought – and some said: 'Better to have an imperfect law on euthanasia now, than to risk having no law at all.[383]

Even if the palliative filter is not explicitly included among the requirements of euthanasia, the physician always carries the duty to act with due care. Suppose the physician, who receives a euthanasia request, does not have sufficient knowledge on

---

[376] ACB (1999) Opinion No 9, pp. 14–15.

[377] ACB (1999) Opinion No 9, pp. 15–16.

[378] ACB (1999) Opinion No 9, p. 17.

[379] Jans (2005), p. 170.

[380] Broeckaert (2001), pp. 99–101; Jans (2005), p. 170.

[381] Broeckaert and Janssens (2005), pp. 38–42.

[382] Lewy (2011), pp. 73–74; Jans (2005), p. 172.

[383] Jans (2005), p. 172.

palliative care. In that case, it is common sense and in accordance with due medical care that the physician should consult a palliative care specialist to present his or her patient with all available options and come to a decision in good conscience. While it is explicitly stated under the Dutch Euthanasia Act that physicians must act with due medical care, adding such a requirement to the Belgian Euthanasia Act was found redundant since physicians are always under the obligation to comply with due medical care.[384]

Contrary to the Netherlands, where the KNMG had been actively involved from the very beginning in the process that led to the legislation, the Belgian medical associations were neither as active as their Dutch counterparts nor have they supported the legislation.[385] A year after ACB's Opinion No 9, the National Council of the Order of Physicians (Ordomedic)[386] made a statement that did not express particular support for legislation on euthanasia. The National Council recognized that certain exceptional circumstances could give rise to a conflict of duties—not to cause death deliberately and allow the patient to die with dignity—and stated that physicians must be able to justify their decision in light of necessity. Although the necessity defence did not provide a sense of security, the National Council pointed out that any medical decision taken by physicians could be subject to scrutiny. Furthermore, the National Council drew attention to the fact that there had been no prosecution or disciplinary action against physicians who have openly admitted they were performing euthanasia.[387]

Euthanasia was being practiced before the legislation was adopted in 2002. A study made in Flanders revealed that the portion of deaths caused by end-of-life decisions with the explicit intention to shorten life was estimated at around 10% in 1998.[388] The number of euthanasia and physician-assisted suicide cases was estimated at 705, and the number of termination of life without the patient's explicit request cases (by administering lethal medication) was significantly higher with an estimation of 1.796. The highest portion belonged to withholding or withdrawing potentially life-prolonging treatment with the explicit intention to shorten life with an estimated case number of 3.261, and in 73% of these cases the decision was neither discussed with the patient nor had the patient express a prior wish to that end.[389] Comparing this situation to the Netherlands, the authors of the study concluded that 'perhaps less attention is given to requirements of careful end-of-

---

[384] Nys (2017), p. 12.

[385] Cohen-Almagor (2009), p. 196.

[386] Physicians have to be registered with the Ordomedic to practice medicine in Belgium. The National Council is the body of the Ordomedic responsible with the establishment of principles, which form the code of medical ethics. It is also responsible to give the Government advice on medical matters. Ordomedic, Wie zijn we? https://www.ordomedic.be/nl/orde/wie-zijn-we/.

[387] Ordomedic (2000) Implication médicale dans le cadre de la vie finissante – Euthanasie, a087001. https://ordomedic.be/fr/avis/ethique/euthanasie/implication-medicale-dans-le-cadre-de-la-vie-finissante-euthanasie.

[388] Deliens et al. (2000), p. 1810.

[389] Deliens et al. (2000), pp. 1809–1810.

life practice in a society with a restrictive approach than in one with an open approach that tolerates and regulates euthanasia and PAS [physician-assisted suicide]'.[390] While in most cases the patient was not competent at the time of the decision to make a request, 16% of the patients were competent at the time of the decision to withhold or withdraw possibly life-sustaining treatment, and 12% in termination of life without the patient's explicit request cases.[391] Whether it is fear of prosecution or a prevailing paternalistic approach of medicine, the reason behind taking such a decision without discussing it first with the patient, who was competent at the time, is hard to understand.[392] What is clear from the study is that illegal end-of-life practices were not uncommon before the legal framework was set in place.[393]

Despite the illegality of the practice, there were hardly any prosecutions against physicians.[394] Unlike the rich Dutch jurisprudence, there is no similar background in Belgium.[395] This might indicate that there was already a level of tolerance existent towards the practice of euthanasia before its decriminalization.[396] Indeed, studies have shown that public acceptance of euthanasia had increased drastically from the 1980s to the end of the 1990s.[397] On the other hand, however, Belgian physicians did not show explicit support to the legislative process as the medical profession in the Netherlands had.[398] Lewy writes that many physicians have considered the legislation as 'the intrusion of politics into the practice of medicine'.[399] Nevertheless, the Euthanasia Act was adopted on 28 May 2002 and gave legitimacy to an already existent practice.

3.3.2 The Legal Framework

3.3.2.1 Exclusion of Assisted Suicide

Section 2 of the Euthanasia Act defines euthanasia as 'intentionally terminating life by someone other than the person concerned, at the latter's request', a definition that was taken from the Dutch neighbour.[400] Although including assisted suicide was

[390] Deliens et al. (2000), p. 1811.
[391] Deliens et al. (2000), p. 1809.
[392] Another report based on the same study from 1998 focused on the general practitioners role in end-of-life decisions: Bilsen (2004), p. 286.
[393] Lewy (2011), p. 70.
[394] Cohen-Almagor (2009), p. 189.
[395] Adams and Nys (2003), pp. 353–354.
[396] MacKeller (2017), p. 222.
[397] Cohen et al. (2006), p. 667.
[398] Adams and Nys (2003), p. 373.
[399] Lewy (2011), p. 82.
[400] Saad (2017), p. 184.

proposed during parliamentary debates, it seems to be deliberately excluded from the act.[401] The reason for this might be because, contrary to the Netherlands, aiding suicide is not defined as a punishable offence in the Belgian Criminal Code. However, this does not mean that helping someone to commit suicide will not constitute a crime under other sections of the Criminal Code. Another reason that might explain the exclusion of assisted suicide could be the political scene in the Belgian Parliament in which the Euthanasia Act has been passed. It is said that 'the term "aiding suicide", for a great many members of the parliament, came to mean literally simply killing someone at his/her request, with no additional conditions.'[402] Due to this misconception, including assisted suicide to the debate would attract more opposition, and the majority did not want to delay passing the Euthanasia Act.[403] The situation in the Belgian Parliament proves how important it is to define the terminology correctly in the right to die debate.

The Federal Commission for Control and Evaluation of Euthanasia (CFCEE), a commission established under the Euthanasia Act for the supervision of euthanasia practice, stated in 2004 that it would hold physician-assisted suicide cases to the same requirements of euthanasia as was established under the law.[404] In physician-assisted suicide cases, the physician does preparatory procedures, leaving the final act to the patient. As long as the dying process would happen under the physician's supervision, the CFCEE did not see a difference in the physician's responsibility.[405] Although this approach is understandable, it is noteworthy that a commission without legislative powers has provided an interpretation that effectively extends the application of the law when there is a clear definition that excludes assisted suicide and the legislator's explicit refusal to include it in the Euthanasia Act.[406]

3.3.2.2 Adults and Emancipated Minors

According to section 3(1) of the Euthanasia Act, legally competent adults and legally competent emancipated minors[407] can request euthanasia. The request must be

[401] Nys (2017), pp. 9–10.

[402] Nys (2005), p. 40.

[403] Nys (2005), p. 40.

[404] Ordomedic (2003) Avis relatif aux soins palliatifs, à l'euthanasie et à d'autres décisions médicales concernant la fin de vie, a100006. https://ordomedic.be/fr/avis/deontologie/consentement-eclaire/avis-relatif-aux-soins-palliatifs-a-l-euthanasie-et-a-d-autres-decisions-medicales-concernant-la-fin-de-vie.

[405] CFCEE (2004) Rapport Euthanasie 2004, p. 24; All reports of the CFCEE can be found at https://organesdeconcertation.sante.belgique.be/fr/organe-d'avis-et-de-concertation/commission-federale-de-controle-et-devaluation-de-leuthanasie.

[406] Nys (2017), p. 1011; Montero (2017), pp. 36–37.

[407] 'Emancipated minors are those minors who, in accordance with Belgian law, are legally competent to autonomously make decisions that touch upon their person, as a result of marriage that, subject to the provision of weighty reasons by the minor, is approved by the juvenile court or,

autonomous and well-considered. The patient must be ‘in a medically hopeless condition experiencing constant and unbearable physical or mental suffering that cannot be alleviated, resulting from a serious and incurable disorder caused by an illness or accident’.

When the patient meets these requirements, section 3(2) outlines the conditions that the physician should meet.

> Without prejudice to any supplementary conditions the physician may want to provide to his/her intervention, he/she must, beforehand, and in each case:
> 1) Inform the patient about his/her state of health and life expectancy, discuss with the patient his/her request for euthanasia and mention the therapeutic possibilities which may still be envisaged as well as the possibilities offered by palliative care and their consequences. He/She must come to the conviction, together with the patient, that there is no reasonable alternatives in his/her condition and that the patient’s request is completely voluntary;
> 2) Ascertain the continued physical or mental suffering of the patient and of the recurring nature of his/her request. To this end, the physician has several conversations with the patient over a reasonable period of time, taking into account the evolution of the patient’s condition;
> 3) Consult another physician about the serious and incurable nature of the disorder specifying the reasons for this consultation. The physician consulted takes note of the medical records, examines the patient and ascertains the constant, unbearable nature of the physical or mental suffering that cannot be alleviated. The physician consulted drafts a report about the results of this consultation. The physician consulted must be independent of the patient as well as the attending physician and must be competent to give an opinion about the disorder in question. The attending physician informs the patient about the results of this consultation;
> 4) If a nursing team exists that has regular contact with the patient, discuss the request of the patient with the nursing team or its members;
> 5) If the patient so desires, discuss his/her request with those close to the patient whom he/she appoints;
> 6) Verifies that the patient has had the opportunity to discuss his/her request with the persons that he/she wanted to meet.

Section 3(3) sets out additional requirements for cases where death is not imminent in the near future. In addition to the requirements above, if the patient is not in a terminal phase, a second consultation is required from an independent physician, who is either a psychiatrist or a specialist in the specific illness concerning the patient, to report on the situation of the patient and attest to the autonomy of the euthanasia request. There should also be a one-month waiting period between the written euthanasia request and the act of euthanasia.

Section 3(4) regulates the formal requirements of the euthanasia request. The euthanasia request must be in writing, dated, and signed by the patient. If the patient is unable to write or sign the request, a person appointed by the patient and who does not have any material interest in the patient’s death will draw up the document in the

---

when they have reached the age of 15, on the basis of an order by the juvenile court.’ Van Assche et al. (2019), p. 243.

presence of the patient and the physician. The reasons why the patient cannot draw up the document himself or herself should also be explained. The amendment of 28 February 2014 added a paragraph to section 3(4) that provides the possibility of psychological assistance for persons involved in the process.

Legally competent adults and legally competent emancipated minors can draw up advance directives requesting euthanasia. According to section 4, the physician can perform euthanasia based on an advance directive if the patient has a severe and incurable disorder caused by an illness or an accident and if the condition is irreversible. The advance directive must be in writing, dated, and signed in front of two witnesses. The patient shall appoint one or more persons of trust, who will inform the physician of the advance directive's existence when the time arrives. Advance directives had a 5-year validity until the last amendment to the Euthanasia Act on 15 March 2020. Advance directives are now indefinitely valid according to the amended section 4(1) subparagraph 6. Before performing euthanasia, the physician must consult another independent physician to confirm the irreversible nature of the patient's situation and discuss the advance directive with the nursing team of the patient and the trusted person or persons. Advance directives are registered with the offices of the National Registry.

Section 14 sets forth a conscience clause, meaning no one can be forced to participate in euthanasia procedures, and no physician can be compelled to perform euthanasia. A physician, who refuses to perform euthanasia, will inform the patient about this decision and the reasons behind it 'in a timely fashion'. If the refusal is based on medical grounds, the physician should add this to the patient's medical records. The 2020 amendment brought three crucial changes to section 14.[408] First, a new subparagraph was added that states 'no written or unwritten clause can prevent a physician from practising euthanasia under the legal requirements' (new subparagraph 4), which means that healthcare institutions can no longer prevent their physicians from practicing euthanasia. This concerned particularly the Catholic healthcare institutions. Second, the old subparagraph 4 has been changed and divided into two subparagraphs that regulate refusal to practice euthanasia based on reasons of conscience (new subparagraph 5) and medical reasons (new subparagraph 6). According to the new subparagraph 5, a physician, who refuses to practice euthanasia based on reasons of conscience, will have to inform the patient of this refusal within seven days after the euthanasia request has been made. If a physician refuses the euthanasia request based on medical reasons, the physician should notify the patient in good time and make note of his or her reasons in the patient's file. The third change is that, according to the new subparagraph 7, physicians are now obliged to provide the patient with the contact information of a euthanasia centre or association if they are not willing to carry out the patient's request. The physician also has to send the patient's medical records to the physician, who is designated by the patient, within four days of the request.

[408] 2020040680 Act amending the Belgian legislation on euthanasia of 15 March 2020, sec 3 (author's translation).

It is reported that some healthcare institutions were forcing their patients to go through palliative care before carrying out their euthanasia request.[409] While it is a prerequisite to inform the patient of all available options, the patient can nevertheless refuse palliative treatment. However, some institutions' insistence on palliative care as a way of preventing euthanasia is said to be the motivation behind the new subparagraph 4 that prohibits healthcare institutions from forbidding euthanasia on their premises.[410] Additionaly, it has been argued that publicly funded healthcare institutions should not be able to prohibit euthanasia or abortion, which are patients' rights within the legal framework.[411] In fact, the amendment is in line with a judgment from 2016. A 74-year-old woman with terminal lung cancer was a resident at a Catholic nursing home. After her physician was not allowed into the facility to carry out her euthanasia request, the family had to move her home, where the physician could administer the necessary drugs for euthanasia. The children later sued the nursing home for causing unnecessary suffering to their mother, and the court fined the nursing home, stating that it did not have the right to intervene in the relationship between a patient and his or her physician.[412]

It might be questioned whether section 14(4) of the Euthanasia Act interferes with the freedom of religion of healthcare institutions. Thc Legislation Section of the Belgian Council of State[413] finds the aim of section 14(4), which is to allow the exercise of personal autonomy on both the patient's and the physician's side, proportionate to the restriction it imposes on healthcare institutions. Section 14 (4) restricts healthcare institutions only from introducing a clause into the work agreement with their physicians that prohibits physicians from practicing euthanasia and not from adopting their own policies on the matter. Therefore, according to the Legislation Section, the interference on the freedom of religion is justifiable.[414] However, even if a healthcare institution adopts a non-euthanasia policy due to its

---

[409] Hope (2020) Catholic hospitals forcing palliative care on patients who request euthanasia. In: The Brussels Time. https://www.brusselstimes.com/belgium/94850/catholic-hospitals-forcing-palliative-care-on-patients-who-request-euthanasia-legal-right-filter-bishops-morgen-tijd/.

[410] Hope (2020) Parliament Approves Change to Euthanasia Law. In: The Brussels Time. https://www.brusselstimes.com/news/belgium-all-news/98832/parliament-approves-change-to-euthanasia-law-advance-directive-living-will/. Acc

[411] Temmerman (2015) Als je als ziekenhuis abortus en euthanasie weigert, moet je het ook durven zeggen. In: De Morgen. https://www.demorgen.be/es-bdff7b1b.

[412] Heneghan (2016) Catholic nursing home fined thousands in euthanasia case. In: The Tablet. https://www.thetablet.co.uk/news/5792/catholic-nursing-home-fined-thousands-in-euthanasia-case.

[413] The Council of State is Belgium's Administrative Supreme Court and is divided into two sections: Legislation, which is an advisory body providing advice to the Parliament on legislative proposals, and Administrative Litigation, which is the judicial body. Council of State, Proceedings. http://www.raadvst-consetat.be/?page=procedure&lang=en.

[414] Belgian House of Representatives (2020) Proposition de loi modifi ant la loi du 28 mai 2002 relative à l'euthanasie, en ce qui concerne la suppression de la durée de validité de la déclaration anticipée - Avis du Conseil d'État No 66.816/AG – 66.817/AG du 29 Janvier 2020, Doc 55 0523/011. https://www.lachambre.be/FLWB/PDF/55/0523/55K0523011.pdf, pp. 15–17.

philosophy or religious views, such a policy is nothing more than a mere statement since the law effectively prohibits its implementation.

3.3.2.3 Euthanasia for Minors

3.3.2.3.1 Amendment of 2014

An amendment to the Euthanasia Act on 24 February 2014 added the phrase 'a minor with the ability of discernment' into section 3(1) subparagraph 1, extending the euthanasia practice to minors (persons under the age of 18). This is different from emancipated minors who are considered adults from a legal point of view.

According to section 3(1) subparagraph 4, if a minor with the capacity of discernment is in 'a medically hopeless condition of constant and unbearable physical suffering resulting from a serious and incurable disorder caused by illness or accident, that cannot be alleviated and that will result in death in the near future', he or she could request euthanasia. In addition to the requirements listed above for legally competent adults and emancipated minors, section 3(2) subparagraph 7 sets forth that a child psychiatrist or psychologist be consulted to confirm the minor's capacity. According to section 3(4), the minor's legal representatives (parent/s or guardian) should give their written consent to euthanasia. The amendment does not state any age limitation. As long as the decision-making capacity can be proved, the minor will be able to request euthanasia.

Some of the arguments raised in favour of the amendment for minors were eliminating discrimination based on age and providing a legal framework to an already existent practice. Some members argued in a joint meeting of the Committees for Justice and Social Affairs[415] that minors, who have the right to refuse life-sustaining treatment under the Patients' Rights Act,[416] should also have the right to request euthanasia. If age, by itself, was the determining factor of suitability for euthanasia, emancipated minors should not have been allowed to take a life-ending decision either.[417] When the amendment was proposed in the Senate, it was stated that euthanasia was an act of humanity at the end of life, and this option should not

[415] Committees of the Senate or the Chamber of Representatives examine legislative proposals and can organize hearings to this end. Temporary committees can be set up to discuss specific legislative proposals. Belgian Senate, Introduction in Belgian Parliamentary History. https://www.senate.be/english/federal_parliament_en.html, para. 5.3.

[416] Sec 12(2) 'The patient is involved in the exercise of his/her rights with due regard for his/her age and maturity. The rights summarised in this Law can be independently exercised by the patient who is a minor if (s)he can be considered as being able to reasonably assess his/her best interests.' English translation by the Federal Commission on Patients Rights (2007) Patients' rights – an invitation to dialogue available at https://www.health.belgium.be/en/health/taking-care-yourself/patient-related-themes/patients-rights, p. 15.

[417] Verenigde Commissies voor de Justitieen voor de Sociale Aangelegenheden (2013) Hoorzittingen Euthanasie, Zitting 2012–2013. https://www.senate.be/actueel/homepage/docs/euthanasie.pdf, pp. 117, 121, 160.

have been taken away from minors. Furthermore, physicians were already administering a lethal medication that hastened or caused the death of a minor in severe pain, and amending the legislation would reflect the reality.[418]

Although minors have the right to refuse treatment, this does not by itself justify a need to amend the Euthanasia Act. Presenting the right to refuse treatment as a justification for euthanasia would fail to observe the legal, medical, psychological, and ethical differences between withholding or withdrawing treatment and actively terminating the life of another person upon request.

Regarding minors, the National Council of Ordomedic had already stated in 2003 that 'from a medical ethics viewpoint, the mental age of a patient is more important than his chronological age'.[419] Sometimes a minor, who has a terminal illness that causes unbearable suffering, could possess the mental capacity to evaluate his or her situation and make a well-considered autonomous end-of-life decision. Under such circumstances, prohibiting euthanasia for minors with the capacity of discernment might render discriminatory results. However, considering the especially vulnerable nature of minors and the general interest to protect the vulnerable, the decision to extend the euthanasia practice to minors should have perhaps been subject to further extensive debate and not taken hastily, which seems to be the case with the 2014 amendment.[420]

Over 170 paediatricians had signed an open letter, asking the Parliament to postpone the amendment.[421] Several paediatricians and paediatric palliative care specialists have criticized the 2014 amendment for being rushed into adoption without discussing it with the experts in the field of healthcare for minors.[422] The political rush for legislation without proper debate caused an impression that there was a pressing social demand for euthanasia in minors, which was actually not the case. This became apparent in the following years after the amendment. In 2016–2017, there were only three euthanasia cases concerning minors that were reported to the CFCEE.[423] While there were no cases reported in 2018, only one minor's euthanasia case was reported in 2019.[424]

---

418 Belgian Senate (2013) Proposition de loi modifiant la loi du 28 mai 2002 relative à l'euthanasie en vue de l'étendre aux mineurs, Session de 2012–2013, Doc 5-2170/1. https://www.senate.be/www/webdriver?MItabObj=pdf&MIcolObj=pdf&MInamObj=pdfid&MItypeObj=application/pdf&MIvalObj=83890023, pp. 2–3.

419 Ordomedic (2003) Avis relatif aux soins palliatifs, à l'euthanasie et à d'autres décisions médicales concernant la fin de vie (author's translation).

420 Montero (2017), p. 41; van Gool and de Lepeleire (2017), p. 185; van de Walle (2017), p. 6.

421 Watson (2014), p. g1633.

422 (2020) Fin de vie des enfants : une loi inutile et précipitée. In: La Libre Belgique. https://www.lalibre.be/debats/opinions/fin-de-vie-des-enfants-une-loi-inutile-et-precipitee-52e93c5b3570e5b8eeea1a00.

423 CFCEE (2018) Rapport Euthanasie 2018, p. 12.

424 CFCEE (2019) Euthanasie - Chiffres de l'année 2018. https://organesdeconcertation.sante.belgique.be/fr/documents/euthanasie-chiffres-de-lannee-2018. CFCEE (2020) Euthanasie -

Although the argument was made that amending the Euthanasia Act would reflect an already existing end-of-life practice for minors, a closer examination of the study cited in favour of this argument reveals that the existing practice was not euthanasia.[425] The study had concentrated on medical end-of-life decisions in minors. The most frequent decisions were the administration of drugs to alleviate pain and symptoms with a possible life-shortening effect and non-treatment. The third and least frequent decision was the use of drugs with the explicit intention to hasten death, and in none of these cases, the patient had made a request to end his or her life.[426] The patient was either unconscious or too young to discuss such a decision.[427] Although the study might corroborate a general need to discuss medical end-of-life decisions in minors, it certainly does not illustrate a pressing need to amend the Euthanasia Act to include minors since none of the cases in the study can be classified as euthanasia.

3.3.2.3.2 Constitutional Court Decision Upholding the 2014 Amendment

Three associations challenged the 2014 amendment before the Belgian Constitutional Court, asking for its annulment.[428] They argued that the 2014 amendment was incompatible with the right to life and the State's duty to protect life. Furthermore, they criticized the State for not fulfilling its obligation to protect minors and for treating them equally with adults while they needed special protection due to their vulnerable state. Applicants also stated that the 2014 amendment failed to set out criteria to clarify the consultation procedure where a psychiatrist or psychologist must assess the minor's capacity of discernment. It was further argued that the requirement of parental consent constituted 'a direct and irreversible violation of the minor's moral and physical integrity, as well as a violation of his right to life'.[429]

The Constitutional Court evaluated the case in light of Articles 22 (right to respect for private and family life), 22b, and 23 (right to human dignity) of the Constitution,[430] Articles 2, 3, and 8 of the ECHR, and Article 6 of the Convention on the

Chiffres de l'année 2019. https://organesdeconcertation.sante.belgique.be/fr/documents/euthanasie-chiffres-de-lannee-2019, p. 1.

425 Pousset et al. (2010) cited in Verenigde Commissies voor de Justitieen voor de Sociale Aangelegenheden (2013) Hoorzittingen Euthanasie, p. 4.

426 Pousset et al. (2010), p. 549.

427 Pousset et al. (2010), p. 551.

428 *Case on the 2014 Amendment* [2015] Cour constitutionnelle Judgment No 153/2015, English translation of the case as provided under the Court's official website has been used and can be found at http://www.const-court.be/public/e/2015/2015-153e.pdf.

429 *Case on the 2014 Amendment*, [7]-[8].

430 1994021048 Belgian Constitution of 17 February 1994 (17 March 2021) relevant articles have not changed since the date of this case, English translation available at https://www.dekamer.be/kvvcr/pdf_sections/publications/constitution/GrondwetUK.pdf. Art 22*bis* regulates children's rights: 'Each child is entitled to have his or her moral, physical, mental and sexual integrity

Rights of the Child that protects children's right to life.[431] Considering the already established right to decide the time and manner of one's own death within the ECtHR's case law, the margin of appreciation attributed to member States in this regard and the State's positive obligation to protect minor's life, the Court examined

> whether or not the contested Act [2014 amendment] establishes a fair balance between, on the one hand, the right ensuing from the right to respect for private life to make life-ending decisions in order to avoid an undignified and distressing end to life and, on the other hand, the right ensuing from the right to life and to physical integrity of vulnerable persons to increased protective measures put in place by the legislature.[432]

What needed to be examined was whether the legislator had put sufficient safeguards in place to ensure the protection of minors.

First, the Court evaluated the legislator's intention behind the 2014 amendment. The amendment did not intend to simply extend the exact euthanasia practice applicable to adults and emancipated minors to non-emancipated minors. It was intended to provide the option of euthanasia to minors with the capacity of discernment, who were in a state of constant and unbearable physical suffering caused by a medically futile condition and whose death was foreseeable in the near future. Purely mental suffering was exempted from the euthanasia practice for minors. Additionally, their condition had to be terminal with death expected in the near future. These additional requirements differentiated them from euthanasia in adults and emancipated minors.[433] Second, the physician had to make sure that the minor's constant and unbearable physical suffering could not be alleviated, and according to the consultation obligation set under section 3(2)(3) of the Euthanasia Act, an independent physician had to confirm the minor's medical condition in order to guarantee 'an objective and correct diagnosis'.[434] Third, the attending physician was obliged to determine the nature of the euthanasia request, whether it was voluntary, well-considered, constant, and free from external pressure per section 3(1)(2). Under section 7(6), the physician also had to describe the elements that gave reassurance to the nature of the euthanasia request in the registration form submitted to the CFCEE.[435] Fourth, section 3(2)(7) regulated how the minor's capacity of discernment should be ascertained. It was discussed during the parliamentary proceedings that it was better to evaluate the capacity of discernment on a case-by-case basis taking into account each patient's specific circumstances, including the medical

respected. Each child has the right to express his or her views in all matters affecting him or her, the views of the child being given due weight in accordance with his or her age and maturity. Each child has the right to benefit from measures and facilities which promote his or her development. In all decisions concerning children, the interest of the child is a primary consideration. [...]'

[431] United Nations, General Assembly, Convention on the Rights of the Child, 20 November 1989, United Nations, Treaty Series, vol 1577, 3.

[432] *Case on the 2014 Amendment*, [20].

[433] *Case on the 2014 Amendment*, [21].

[434] *Case on the 2014 Amendment*, [22].

[435] *Case on the 2014 Amendment*, [23].

condition and level of maturity. The assessment of the capacity of discernment was more of a medical assessment than a legal one. Therefore, it was reasonable for the legislature not to provide more detailed criteria within the Euthanasia Act.[436] The attending physician had to consult a child psychiatrist or psychologist to examine the minor and confirm the capacity of discernment. The Court emphasized that the opinion of the psychiatrist or psychologist was binding. If the child psychiatrist or psychologist did not agree that the minor had the capacity of discernment, euthanasia could not be performed. The applicants had claimed that the amendment did not provide the child psychiatrist or psychologist to be independent. The Court rejected this claim referring to the Code of Medical Ethics and the Royal Decree of 2 April 2014, which provided that psychiatrists and psychologists do not accept assignments for which they cannot be objective and independent.[437] Lastly, the legal representatives of the minor had to give their consent, and this requirement provided an additional safeguard.[438]

Considering the safeguards set forth by the Euthanasia Act for the practice of euthanasia in minors, the Court did not agree with the applicants that the 2014 amendment had failed to take into account the different situation of minors.[439] The Court ruled that the Euthanasia Act was

> based on a fair balance between, on the one hand, the right of every person to make life-ending decisions in order to avoid an undignified and distressing end to life, a right that follows from the right to respect for private life, and, on the other hand, the minor's right to measures aimed at preventing abuses in the performance of euthanasia, a right that follows from the right to life and physical integrity.[440]

3.3.2.4 Patients with Psychiatric Illnesses

The National Council of Ordomedic published an advice in 2019 on euthanasia for patients with psychiatric illnesses, laying out additional ethical requirements due to the sensitive and challenging nature of these cases.[441] According to this ethical guideline, the treating physician and the two consulting physicians should meet together in person to evaluate the situation, allowing for interdisciplinary collaboration. The three physicians should then write a report of their assessment, including any diverging opinions. The National Council also recommends that healthcare providers in regular contact with the patient, alongside the psychologist and/or

[436] *Case on the 2014 Amendment*, [24.5].

[437] *Case on the 2014 Amendment*, [24.7].

[438] *Case on the 2014 Amendment*, [25].

[439] *Case on the 2014 Amendment*, [28].

[440] *Case on the 2014 Amendment*, [26].

[441] Ordomedic (2019) Directives déontologiques pour la pratique de l'euthanasie des patients en souffrance psychique à la suite d'une pathologie psychiatrique, a165002. https://ordomedic.be/fr/avis/ethique/euthanasie/directives-deontologiques-pour-la-pratique-de-l-euthanasie-des-patients-en-souffrance-psychique-a-la-suite-d-une-pathologie-psychiatrique.

psychiatrists involved in the patient's treatment, participate in the consultation process.[442]

The Euthanasia Act requires a hopeless medical situation with constant unbearable suffering that cannot be alleviated. The determination of whether a psychiatric illness is irremediable poses a difficult question. The National Council states that the physician must ensure that all evidence-based treatments have been tried. If the patient refuses a reasonable, evidence-based treatment, the euthanasia request should not be accepted. The National Council also warns against therapeutic relentlessness. From an objective medical-psychiatric perspective, the physician must determine whether sufficient effort has been made for treatment.[443]

While the Euthanasia Act requires a one-month waiting period between the request and the act of euthanasia, the National Council urges for a longer timespan for psychiatric patients. It is found unacceptable to carry out a euthanasia request without giving sufficient time for possible treatment options. It is not described how long an acceptable time period should be. However, the headline of the section is *une maladie de plusieurs années*, meaning a disorder of several years.[444]

The Euthanasia Act provides that the euthanasia request is discussed with the family or third persons designated by the patient if the patient gives consent. The National Council acknowledges the harm that can be caused to third parties by the lack of communication and encourages the involvement of family and loved ones in the process unless there is a good reason against it. It further states that 'the support of third parties and the protection of society are inextricably linked to the issue of the euthanasia practice for psychiatric patients'.[445]

Recognizing the difficulty of determining the effective capacity[446] of a patient with psychiatric illness, the National Council refers to the Advisory Opinion of the Flemish Association for Psychiatry on 'how to deal with a euthanasia request in psychiatry in the current legal framework?' of 2017.[447]

---

[442] Ordomedic (2019) Directives déontologiques pour la pratique de l'euthanasie des patients en souffrance psychique à la suite d'une pathologie psychiatrique, para. 1.

[443] Ordomedic (2019) Directives déontologiques pour la pratique de l'euthanasie des patients en souffrance psychique à la suite d'une pathologie psychiatrique, para. 2.

[444] Ordomedic (2019) Directives déontologiques pour la pratique de l'euthanasie des patients en souffrance psychique à la suite d'une pathologie psychiatrique, para. 3.

[445] Ordomedic (2019) Directives déontologiques pour la pratique de l'euthanasie des patients en souffrance psychique à la suite d'une pathologie psychiatrique, para. 4.

[446] A patient with a psychiatric illness might possess the legal capacity of discernment, but oftentimes, the patient's judgment can be influenced by his or her mental state. The National Council uses the term 'effective capacity' to refer to this distinction.

[447] Ordomedic (2019) Directives déontologiques pour la pratique de l'euthanasie des patients en souffrance psychique à la suite d'une pathologie psychiatrique, para. 5. The Flemish Association for Psychiatry (VVP) has mostly followed the guidelines of its Dutch counterpart, NVvP. Due to the delicate nature of psychiatric cases, the guidelines provide specific guidance on how to determine capacity in psychiatric patients in accordance with medical ethics. Details will not be mentioned here. VVP (2017) Hoe omgaan met een euthanasieverzoek in psychiatrie binnen het huidig wettelijk kader? https://vvponline.be/bibliotheek.php?item=451&s=Presentatie_en_lezing.

Even before the 2020 amendment to the Euthanasia Act that added section 14(7) regarding the referral obligation, the National Council had already stated that the physician who refuses to practice euthanasia based on conscientious reasons must refer the patient to another physician.[448]

A survey published in 2020 showed that almost 75% of psychiatrists think euthanasia should remain a legal option for psychiatric patients.[449] A significant number of psychiatrists (94.6%) agreed that psychiatric illnesses could cause unbearable suffering. While 88% of the psychiatrists were of the opinion that a psychiatric patient could make an autonomous, well-thought euthanasia request, 83.7% believed that a psychiatric illness could lead to a medically hopeless situation. However, when asked if the evaluation of a euthanasia request was compatible with a psychotherapeutic relationship, only 52.7% of the psychiatrists responded affirmatively.[450] The survey also revealed worries about the insufficient practice of due care during the evaluation of the euthanasia request.[451] When it came to the psychiatrist's role in the euthanasia procedure, the willingness of active participation was not as high. Most psychiatrists (68%) stated that they would refer their patients to a colleague, but only 8.4% were willing to perform euthanasia on their own patients.[452] It should be noted that the survey had only a 40% response rate.[453] While the results should be considered with caution, the survey reflects a certain hesitance towards playing an active role in the euthanasia of psychiatric patients.

The Brothers of Charity in Belgium, a religious organization based on the Catholic faith, owns 12 psychiatric hospitals.[454] After the Catholic nursing home was fined for not allowing euthanasia on its premises,[455] the Brothers of Charity in Belgium made a statement regarding their view on euthanasia. After emphasizing the respect for patient autonomy, it was stated that euthanasia would be possible in these hospitals if due care criteria were met.[456] This change was done before the amendment to the Euthanasia Act in 2020 that prohibits healthcare institutions from

[448] Ordomedic (2019) Directives déontologiques pour la pratique de l'euthanasie des patients en souffrance psychique à la suite d'une pathologie psychiatrique, para. 6.

[449] Verhofstadt et al. (2020), p. 378.

[450] Verhofstadt et al. (2020), p. 379.

[451] Verhofstadt et al. (2020), p. 378.

[452] Verhofstadt et al. (2020), p. 381.

[453] Verhofstadt et al. (2020), pp. 380–381.

[454] Brothers of Charity was first founded in 1807 in Belgium and is now active in 30 countries. Its general administration is in Rome. Brothers of Charity, Founder. https://brothersofcharity.org/who-are-the-brothers/founder/?lang=en; For the Belgian branch's information see Broeders van Liefde, Wie zijn we? https://broedersvanliefde.be/wie-zijn-we.

[455] See text to footnote no. 412.

[456] Thijs (2017) Euthanasie mag nu ook van Broeders van Liefde. In: De Morgen. https://www.demorgen.be/nieuws/euthanasie-mag-nu-ook-van-broeders-van-liefde~b4e72386/. The 2017 statement is no longer on the official website. However, an English translation of the statement can be found at Protection of Conscience Project (2017) Brothers of Charity: Vision of Euthanasia Adjusted. https://www.consciencelaws.org/religion/religion053-001.aspx.

adopting a no-euthanasia policy. The General Administration of the Brothers of Charity voiced their disapproval of the statement, and together with the Vatican, urged the Belgian branch to amend their approach.[457] After an almost three-year dialogue, the Vatican finally announced in 2020 that the psychiatric hospitals of the Brothers of Charity in Belgium could no longer enjoy the 'Catholic' title.[458]

3.3.2.5 Notification Procedure

The physician, who has performed euthanasia, should notify the CFCEE within 4 working days. The CFCEE is composed of 16 members appointed for a four-year term by a royal decree after deliberations by the Council of Ministers. According to section 6 of the Euthanasia Act, the members of the commission should consist of 8 physicians (of whom at least 4 are professors at a Belgian University), 4 professors of law (at a Belgian University) or lawyers, and 4 from groups, which focus on patients with an incurable illness. Members of the legislative organs, the Federal Government, the regional or community governments cannot be on the commission. The commission's constitution should respect the linguistic plurality of Belgium, meaning each linguistic group should be represented by at least three candidates of each gender. The commission has two presidents, Dutch-speaking and French-speaking, elected by the respective linguistic group.

The physician will report each euthanasia case by filing a registration form with the required information foreseen under section 7 of the Euthanasia Act (information on the patient, persons involved, advance directive if there is one, circumstances of the patient's case, etc.). The first part of the registration form includes the personal information of the persons involved, such as names and addresses. The second part consists of the factual circumstances of the case. The commission will review the second part of the registration form and, if necessary, decide with a simple majority vote to reveal the first part. The physician can be asked to provide additional information from the medical records. According to section 8 of the Euthanasia Act, the commission will decide within two months whether euthanasia was in accordance with the legal criteria. If the commission decides by a two-third-majority vote that the criteria have not been fulfilled, it will forward the report to the prosecutorial authorities.

---

[457] Brothers of Charity (2017) The Vatican's Response to the Issue of Euthanasia with the Organization of the Brothers of Charity in Belgium. https://brothersofcharity.org/the-vaticans-response-to-the-issue-of-euthanasia-with-the-organization-of-the-brothers-of-charity-in-belgium/?lang=en; Brothers of Charity (2017) Press Release from the Brothers of Charity Generalate, Rome. https://brothersofcharity.org/press-release-from-the-brothers-of-charity-generalate_02_10_2017/?lang=en.

[458] Ladaria (2020) Letter to the Superior General of the Congregation of the "Brothers of Charity", Regarding the Accompaniment of Patients in Psychiatric Hospitals of the Congregation's Belgian Branch. http://www.vatican.va/roman_curia/congregations/cfaith/documents/rc_con_cfaith_doc_20200330_lettera-fratellidellacarita-belgio_en.html.

There are some differences between the Dutch RTE and the CFCEE. They were both intended to function as a buffer system in addition to their supervisory functions. While the workload is divided among five committees in the Netherlands, only one commission oversees all the cases in Belgium. This might perhaps cause the CFCEE not to be able to properly evaluate each case in detail. The RTE can invite physicians reporting euthanasia cases for additional inquires, allowing more back and forth feedback between the committee and the physician. Meanwhile, the CFCEE is restricted to the extent of the medical records. In addition to an annual report, the RTE publishes its decisions for better transparency. The CFCEE only gives an overview in its reports.

Like the SCEN in the Netherlands, *LevensEinde InformatieForum* (LEIF) was founded in 2003 to provide support and information to healthcare professionals in end-of-life decision-making and to train physicians on euthanasia and possibilities of palliative care. LEIF-physicians can provide the mandatory consultation required by law for euthanasia decisions.[459] While LEIF operates in the Flanders region, the ADMD helped found a similar forum for the Walloon region called *Le Forum EOL* (End Of Life Forum).[460]

3.3.3 Conclusion

Within the 15 months after the Euthanasia Act entered into force, there were 259 reported euthanasia cases.[461] This number has increased steadily in the following years (2004: 349, 2005: 393, 2006: 429, 2007:495, 2008: 704, 2009: 822, 2010: 953, 2011: 1.133, 2012: 1432, 2013: 1.807, 2014:1.928, 2015: 2.002, 2016: 2.028, 2017: 2.309, 2018: 2.359, 2019: 2.656).[462] According to the CFCEE's report in 2014, the increasing numbers can be explained by raising awareness of the legal framework on euthanasia and available end-of-life options.[463] As the practice settles in and physicians become more aware of the legal requirements, the fear of prosecution would naturally decrease.[464] Although this might explain the initial increase within the first few years after the Euthanasia Act has come into force, euthanasia cases have multiplied by seven since 2004. As years go by, it is questionable whether the same argument could be presented as the singular reason for the increase.

---

[459] LEIF, LEIFartsen en het LEIFartsenforum. https://leif.be/vragen-antwoorden/leifartsen/.

[460] Le Forum EOL, Origine et Objectifs. http://www.eol.admd.be/.

[461] CFCEE (2004) Rapport Euthanasie 2004, p. 7.

[462] CFCEE (2006) Rapport Euthanasie 2006, p. 15; CFCEE (2008) Rapport Euthanasie 2008, p. 15; CFCEE, (2010) Rapport Euthanasie 2010, p. 15; CFCEE (2012) Rapport Euthanasie 2012, p. 7; CFCEE (2014) Rapport Euthanasie 2014, p. 7; CFCEE (2016) Rapport Euthanasie 2016, p. 14; CFCEE (2018) Rapport Euthanasie 2018, p. 2; CFCEE (2020) Rapport Euthanasie 2020, p. 2.

[463] CFCEE (2014) Rapport Euthanasie 2014, p. 27.

[464] In a comparative study, fear of legal consequences as a reason to reject a patient's euthanasia request had decreased from 23.4% in 2007 to 2% in 2013. Dierickx et al. (2015), p. 1705.

What might indeed indicate a slippery slope is the percentage of euthanasia cases in non-terminal patients, which has doubled since 2002 (2002–03: 22 at 8.5%, 2004: 24 at 7%, 2005: 27 at 7%, 2006: 26 at 6%, 2007: 28 at 6%, 2008: 49 at 7%, 2009: 67 at 8%, 2010: 80 at 8.4%, 2011: 114 at 10%, 2012: 167 at 11.6%, 2013: 266 at 14.7%, 2014: 295 at 15.3%, 2015: 299 at 14.8%, 2016: 279 at 13.8%, 2017: 375 at 16.2%, 2018: 345 at 14.6%, 2019: 449 at 16.9%).[465] The number of euthanasia cases in patients with neuropsychiatric diagnosis (Alzheimer's, dementia, depression) has increased since its decriminalization. While only 9 cases were reported for 2004–2005,[466] there were 105 cases in 2018–2019.[467] However, the percentage of euthanasia in patients with psychiatric conditions has remained between 1 and 4, with a slight spike between 2012 and 2015. The CFCEE was satisfied that requirements under the Euthanasia Act were being met and proper due care was shown.[468] Again, the increase in numbers might be the result of rising awareness and practice without fear of prosecution. But reasons of subjective attributes, such as being tired of life, fear of future suffering, fear of becoming dependent on others, and loss of dignity as the disease progresses, mostly belong to cases where death is not imminent. A raise in non-terminal euthanasia numbers can also mean that the scope of euthanasia practice has extended its initially intended limits. Indeed, the National Council of Ordomedic has not supported euthanasia for non-terminal patients. In 2001, the National Council stated that a thorough evaluation of euthanasia requests from non-terminal patients would reveal a request due to misinformation or lack of proper treatment, or a request motivated by relational, social, or financial reasons.[469]

According to the CFCEE's reports, only one case in 2015 was referred to the prosecutorial authorities since the legislation on euthanasia entered into force.[470] It has been 18 years since the decriminalization of euthanasia. It is difficult to say with complete certainty if the fact that there had been only one referral means complete compliance with the legal requirements. It could also be evidence that the legal framework is not being followed adequately, indicating a slippery slope.[471] These statistics raise the question of whether the CFCEE is effectively provides adequate supervision to the Belgian practice of euthanasia.

---

[465] CFCEE (2004) Rapport Euthanasie 2004, p. 8; CFCEE (2006) Rapport Euthanasie 2006, p. 15; CFCEE (2008) Rapport Euthanasie 2008, p. 15; CFCEE (2010) Rapport Euthanasie 2010, p. 15; CFCEE (2012) Rapport Euthanasie 2012, p. 8; CFCEE (2014) Rapport Euthanasie 2014, p. 8; CFCEE (2016) Rapport Euthanasie 2016, p. 6; CFCEE (2018) Rapport Euthanasie 2018, p. 3; CFCEE (2020) Rapport Euthanasie 2020, p. 3.

[466] CFCEE (2006) Rapport Euthanasie 2006, p. 22.

[467] CFCEE (2020) Rapport Euthanasie 2020, p. 40.

[468] CFCEE (2016) Rapport Euthanasie 2016, pp. 53–57.

[469] Ordomedic (2001) Euthanasie, a094007. https://ordomedic.be/fr/avis/ethique/euthanasie/euthanasie-1.

[470] CFCEE (2016) Rapport Euthanasie 2016, p. 10.

[471] Saad (2017), p. 204.

3.4 The United Kingdom

The Suicide Act 1961 (or 1961 Act) decriminalized suicide in the UK. While it is not a crime to commit suicide, assisting someone with suicide is punishable by up to 14 years of imprisonment under section 2(1). According to section 2(4), prosecutions in assisted suicide cases are subject to the Director of Public Prosecutions' (DPP) consent.

> 2(1) A person who aids, abets, counsels or procures the suicide of another, or an attempt by another to commit suicide, shall be liable on conviction on indictment to imprisonment for a term not exceeding fourteen years.
>
> 2(4) No proceedings shall be instituted for an offence under this section except by or with the consent of the Director of Public Prosecutions.

Assisted dying has been debated in the UK Parliament several times. After the famous Airedale NHS Trust v Bland Case,[472] the House of Lords Committee on Medical Ethics recommended not to make any changes to the law that would allow assisted suicide or euthanasia, to which the House of Lords agreed.[473]

In 2004, Lord Joffe introduced the Assisted Dying for the Terminally Ill Bill to the House of Lords that aimed 'to enable an adult who has capacity and who is suffering unbearably as a result of a terminal illness to receive medical assistance to die at his own considered and persistent request'.[474] Upon Lord Joffe's proposal, a Select Committee was established to examine and report on the Bill.[475] The Select Committee published a detailed report that included a wide range of evidence gathered from assisted suicide organizations, medical associations and authorities from the Netherlands, Belgium, Switzerland and Oregon, US.[476] Based on its assessment, the Select Committee gave recommendations on what to consider if such a bill were adopted. However, Lord Joffe's Bill did not go any further than a proposal. During the debates on the adoption of the Coroners and Justice Act in 2009, Lord Falconer proposed an amendment that would allow assisted suicide for the terminally ill, which was rejected by 194 votes to 141.[477] In addition, the Coroners and Justice Act, which amended section 2 of the 1961 Act, re-enacted

[472]The Bland Case was about the withdrawal of life-sustaining treatment from a patient who was in a persistent vegetative state with no hopes of recovery. After a distinction was made between euthanasia and withdrawal of treatment, the House of Lords accepted that there was no duty to continue treatment if there was no prospect of improvement. Although the omission would cause death, withdrawing life-sustaining treatment was lawful since treatment was no longer in the best interest of the patient. *Airedale NHS Trust v Bland* [1993] UKHL 17, [1993] AC 789.

[473]HL Deb 9 May 1994 Vol 554 Col 1349, col 1354.

[474]United Kingdom, Assisted Dying for the Terminally Ill HL Bill 17, Session 2003-04.

[475]HL Deb 10 March 2004 Vol 658 Cols 1316–1324.

[476]Select Committee of the Assisted Dying for the Terminally Ill Bill, *Assisted Dying for the Terminally Ill Bill* (HL 2004-05, 86-I, II, III).

[477]HL Deb 7 July 2009 Vol 712 Cols 596–636.

the prohibition of assisted suicide.[478] The current version of section 2 of the 1961 Act reads:

> (1) A person ("D") commits an offence if—
>
> (a) D does an act capable of encouraging or assisting the suicide or attempted suicide of another person, and
> (b) D's act was intended to encourage or assist suicide or an attempt at suicide.
> (1A) The person referred to in subsection (1)(a) need not be a specific person (or class of persons) known to, or identified by, D.
> (1B) D may commit an offence under this section whether or not a suicide, or an attempt at suicide, occurs.
> (1C) An offence under this section is triable on indictment and a person convicted of such an offence is liable to imprisonment for a term not exceeding 14 years.

Although attempts in the Parliament at decriminalizing assisted suicide were not successful, the following case law portrays the British approach towards assisted suicide and what can perhaps be called a cautious and indirect step towards flexibility under the blanket ban on assisted suicide.

3.4.1 The Z Case

An significant development in 2009 was the House of Lords judgment in the Z Case.[479] Mrs Z, who was suffering from an incurable and terminal illness that caused deterioration of her motor functions, wanted to travel to Switzerland to end her life with the help of Dignitas. Since she had become increasingly disabled due to her illness, her husband made the travel arrangements to honour her wish and informed the local authority of their plan. The local authority obtained an injunction from a Black J of the High Court to stop Mrs Z from leaving the country. Mrs Z appealed the injunction before the High Court.

A psychiatric assessment was asked to examine Mrs Z, and it was concluded that Mrs Z had possessed legal capacity and that her decision to end her life was autonomous. Hedley J stated:

> Human freedom, if it is to have real meaning, must involve the right to take what others may see as unwise or even bad decisions in respect of themselves; were that not so, freedom would be largely illusory. It follows that the court has no basis in law for exercising the jurisdiction so as to prohibit Mrs Z from taking her own life. The right and responsibility for such a decision belongs to Mrs Z alone. [...]

[478] United Kingdom, Coroners and Justice Act 2009 (1 February 2010) sec 59. The reason behind this re-enactment was, with technological developments and cybersuicide in mind, to 'simplify and modernise the language of sec 2 of the 1961 Act to increase public understanding and to reassure people that the provision applies as much to actions on the internet as to actions offline', rather than a reaction against assisted suicide in the context of the right to die. HC Deb 26 January 2009 Vol 487 Col 35, col 68.

[479] *Local Authority v Z* [2004] EWHC 2817 (Fam).

> In the circumstances here, Mrs Z's best interests are no business of mine.[480]

However, the situation of Mr Z in the role of the assistor was not as clear. To realize her wish, Mrs Z required assistance, which would constitute a criminal act. After shortly reminding of the discretionary power given to the DPP by the 1961 Act section 2(4) and referring to Airedale NHS Trust v Bland,[481] Hedley J ruled that it was beyond the local authority's duties to seek the continuation of the injunction. After lifting the injunction, Hedley J concluded the judgment by stating:

> This case affords no basis for trying to ascertain the court's views about the rights or wrongs of suicide, assisted or otherwise. This case simply illustrates that a competent person is entitled to take their own decisions on these matters and that that person alone bears responsibility for any decision so taken. That is the essence of what some will regard as God-given free will and what others will describe as the innate right of self-autonomy. It illustrates too that the civil court, and in this context, especially the family court, will be slow to restrain behaviour consistent with the rights of others simply because it is unlawful where adequate powers are vested in the criminal justice agencies.[482]

Although the judgment did not go into a detailed evaluation, it signalled a balancing act among the sanctity of life, the right to self-determination, and the respect for human dignity, concluding that the sanctity of life did not always prevail. The judgment accepted that Articles 2, 3 and 8 of the Convention were engaged in the matter. The relationship between these articles and how they would balance against each other would have to be determined in light of the specific circumstances of a given case.[483] Hedley J's subtle reminder of the 1961 Act section 2(4) and that it was not always in the public interest to prosecute assisted suicide cases indicated that the Court would not recommend prosecution against Mr Z.[484]

The DPP's discretionary power regarding prosecutions in assisted suicide cases and the vagueness of its policy has been subject to criticism.[485] The House of Lords dealt with this matter in more detail in the following case.

---

[480] *Local Authority v Z Case*, [12]-[13].

[481] Hedley J quotes Hoffman LJ stating 'A conflict between the principles of the sanctity of life and the individual's right of self-determination may therefore require a painful compromise to be made. In the case of the person who refuses an operation without which he will certainly die, one or other principle must be sacrificed. We may adopt a paternalist view, deny that his autonomy can be allowed to prevail in so extreme a case, and uphold the sanctity of life. Sometimes this looks an attractive solution, but it can have disturbing implications. Do we insist upon patients accepting life-saving treatment which is contrary to their strongly held religious beliefs? Should one force-feed prisoners on hunger strike? English law is, as one would expect, paternalist towards minors. But it upholds the autonomy of adults. A person of full age may refuse treatment for any reason or no reason at all, even if it appears certain that the result will be his death.' *Bland Case*, 827.

[482] *Local Authority v Z Case*, [21].

[483] *Local Authority v Z Case*, [18].

[484] de Cruz (2005), p. 262.

[485] Williams (2010), p. 182.

3.4.2 *The Purdy Case*

Ms Debbie Purdy was a 45-year-old woman who was diagnosed with multiple sclerosis in 1995. In 2007, her health started to deteriorate severely. She was planning to use either Dignitas's services or travel to Belgium, where euthanasia is legal. She did not want to end her life prematurely and would rather wait until the point that her life became unbearable. However, once she arrived this stage, it would no longer be possible for her to end her life without assistance, as she would not be able to travel alone. Although her husband was willing to assist her with her travel, Ms Purdy did not want to risk her husband going to prison.

In December 2007, Ms Purdy had asked the DPP to publish his policy on prosecutions in assisted suicide cases and, if there was no such policy, to set up one that outlined which criteria the DPP took into consideration when using his discretionary power under the 1961 Act section 2(4). The DPP responded that there was no such policy and, referring to the Pretty Case, providing one would be unlawful.[486] Ms Purdy started judicial proceedings, arguing that the DPP's refusal to clarify his policy violated her rights under Article 8 of the Convention.

In the Pretty Case, the House of Lords had ruled that Article 8 of the Convention was not engaged in a way to confer a right to decide the time and manner of one's death.[487] Following the House's jurisprudence, both the High Court and the Court of Appeal dismissed Ms Purdy's claims.[488] The case came before the House.[489]

Lord Hope, who delivered the judgment, evaluated the matter in three tiers. Did Article 2(1) of the 1961 Act apply to Ms Purdy's case? Was there interference with her rights under Article 8 of the Convention? If there was, was this interference in accordance with the law under paragraph 2 of Article 8?

Assisting suicide is not an ancillary crime that depends on the suicide taking place. Therefore, even if the suicide does not occur within the jurisdiction of England and Wales, meaning if someone travels to Switzerland, assisting with the travel will nevertheless constitute a crime under section 2(1) of the 1961 Act.[490]

The Code for Crown Prosecutors, issued by the DPP as head of the Crown Prosecutors Service, lays down the general principles to be followed when deciding whether to prosecute a crime.[491] According to the Code, the decision to prosecute

---

[486] R (Purdy) v the Director of Public Prosecutions [2009] EWCA Civ 92, para. 12.

[487] Contrary to the House of Lords, the ECtHR had found interference with Mrs Pretty's rights under Article 8, which was nevertheless justifiable under paragraph 2. See Sect. 4.1.3.3.3 'On Article 8 of the Convention'.

[488] *Purdy Case-CA*, [54].

[489] *Purdy Case-HL*. Purdy was the last judgment given by the House of Lords before the Supreme Court was established.

[490] *Purdy Case-HL*, [23].

[491] DPP (2018) The Code for Crown Prosecutors. https://www.cps.gov.uk/publication/code-crown-prosecutors. The fifth edition (2004) referred to in the Purdy Case can be found at https://1library.net/document/qo50p4my-the-code-for-crown-prosecutors.html.

shall be based on the Full Code Test that contains two stages: the evidential stage, which means there should be a realistic prospect of conviction, and the public interest stage, which means that prosecution should be in the public interest. Factors of public interest will be dependent on the individual case, but the Code provides an exemplary non-exhaustive list of factors to take into consideration, such as the degree of harm caused by the crime, whether the victim was in a vulnerable state, whether it was an act of misjudgement or misunderstanding or the proportionality of prosecution in light of the likely penalty that will be given to the crime.[492]

Until the hearing, there had been 115 people who travelled to another country for assisted suicide with the help of their family or friends. Among those 115 cases, only 8 had been referred to the DPP to decide on whether to prosecute and, apart from 2, none of them were prosecuted due to lack of evidence. In December 2008, the DPP had decided not to prosecute the case against Daniel James' parents and one friend, who had helped Daniel travel to Switzerland, where he ended his life. The decision was based on the lack of public interest in prosecution and was announced by the DPP, which was an unusual situation since none of the previous decisions were made public.[493] In light of the Daniel James decision, it was unlikely that Mr Purdy would be prosecuted if he had helped his wife travel to Switzerland. However, the factors weighing in on the DPP's Daniel James decision were not clearly set out. Ms Purdy argued that the DPP's refusal to provide information in order to clarify this situation constituted a violation of her rights under Article 8 of the Convention.

Lord Hope agreed that Article 8 was indeed engaged, departing from the House's previous Pretty judgment.[494] Lord Hope then evaluated whether the interference with Ms Purdy's right was in accordance with the law. Three questions were to be answered: Was there a legal basis for the restriction in the domestic law? Was this restriction sufficiently accessible and foreseeable for the individual to understand its scope? Finally, was the restriction arbitrary?

While section 2(1) of the 1961 Act satisfied these requirements, the main question at hand was whether section 2(4), which conferred a discretionary power upon the DPP, provided sufficient clarity. A discretionary power provided by law was accessible and foreseeable if the scope and manner of its exercise were sufficiently clear.[495] The purpose of section 2(4) was to provide consistency of practice and

---

[492] DPP (2004) The Code for Crown Prosecutors, para. 4.14.

[493] The DPP's decision on prosecution in Daniel James's case is no longer available on the Crown Prosecution Service's (CPS) website. The details of the decision can be found at: Mullock (2009).

[494] *Purdy Case-HL*, [34]-[39]. In the House's Pretty judgment, Lord Hope had given a dissenting opinion finding an engagement of Article 8 of the Convention, with which the ECtHR had agreed. *Pretty v Director of Public Prosecutions and Secretary of State for the Home Department* [2001] UKHL 61, [2002] 1 AC 800, [100]; *Pretty Case*, [64].

[495] *Purdy Case-HL*, [41]. Lord Hope also cites Hasan and Chaush v Bulgaria, in which the ECtHR had stated, 'In matters affecting fundamental rights it would be contrary to the rule of law, one of the basic principles of a democratic society enshrined in the Convention, for a legal discretion granted to the executive to be expressed in terms of an unfettered power. Consequently, the law must indicate with sufficient clarity the scope of any such discretion conferred on the competent

central control in sensitive or controversial areas of criminal law.[496] To avoid arbitrary proceedings, the police, who brought cases to the prosecutors' attention, and the Crown Prosecutors, who decided whether or not to proceed, must have guidance. This guidance was accomplished with the Code for Crown Prosecutors, which is classified as 'law' within the meaning of Article 8(2) of the Convention. Therefore, Lord Hope asked whether the Code satisfied the requirements of accessibility and foreseeability.

In his decision concerning Daniel James, the DPP had stated that many of the factors listed in the Code did not apply to the case of assisted suicide because of the latter's specific nature. He had considered additional factors, such as the fact that the parents and friend had not influenced Daniel in his decision and had nothing to gain from his death. Although it was claimed that the DPP's evaluation in Daniel James' case could provide an example for Ms Purdy, Lord Hope disagreed and stated that there was nothing in the Code that offered guidance to 'a highly unusual and extremely sensitive case of this kind'.[497] Even though the nature of these cases, such as Ms Purdy's, made the decision of prosecution highly dependent on the individual circumstances, there was an apparent gap between what section 2(1) of the 1961 Act stated and how section 2(4) was being applied in practice. Therefore, Lord Hope concluded that the DPP could not be excused 'from the obligation to clarify what his position is to the factors that he regards as relevant for and against prosecution in this very special and carefully defined class of case'.[498] Baroness Hale added that in the Pretty Case, the ECtHR had found section 2(1) in accordance with the Convention because of the flexibility provided by section 2(4). Hence, the application of this discretionary power should have been made clear.[499]

With the House's departure from its former Pretty jurisprudence, the Purdy Case was an important development for assisted suicide. Mrs Pretty had asked for a promise of non-prosecution from the DPP, unlike Ms Purdy, who wanted a clarification of policy on how discretion was applied in the decision-making on prosecutions. While the DPP does not have the power to guarantee non-prosecution, he is authorized to make a prosecution policy. However, this is not the only reason behind Ms Purdy's success. The House could have decided that although Article 8 of the Convention was engaged, not issuing a specific policy on assisted suicide was in accordance with the law based on balancing individual interests with the public interest in light of the margin of appreciation. However, the House went further by demanding more explicit guidelines from the DPP, which signals a change towards a more accepting approach to assisted suicide. While welcomed by the supporters of the right to die, many have criticized the House's decision for being 'unsound if not

---

authorities and the manner of its exercise.' *Hasan and Chaush v Bulgaria* [GC] App no 30985/96 ECHR 2000-XI, [84].

496 *Purdy Case-HL*, [46].

497 *Purdy Case-HL*, [53].

498 *Purdy Case-HL*, [55].

499 *Purdy Case-HL*, [63].

unconstitutional'[500] or 'improper'.[501] It ought to be left to the Parliament to resolve this highly controversial area rather than the DPP since such a policy would 'effectively decriminalize assisted suicide'.[502] Although assisted suicide remains a crime, the fact that the Court had based its judgment on personal autonomy could invite more challenges.[503]

Shortly after the House's Purdy judgment, the DPP published its policy on assisted suicide.[504] The policy provides a non-exhaustive list of public interest factors to be taken into account while deciding whether to prosecute a case on assisting suicide, in conjunction with the Code's guidance. The factors that weigh against prosecution are listed as the following:

(1) the victim had reached a voluntary, clear, settled and informed decision to commit suicide;
(2) the suspect was wholly motivated by compassion;
(3) the actions of the suspect, although sufficient to come within the definition of the offence, were of only minor encouragement or assistance;
(4) the suspect had sought to dissuade the victim from taking the course of action which resulted in his or her suicide;
(5) the actions of the suspect may be characterised as reluctant encouragement or assistance in the face of a determined wish on the part of the victim to commit suicide;
(6) the suspect reported the victim's suicide to the police and fully assisted them in their enquiries into the circumstances of the suicide or the attempt and his or her part in providing encouragement or assistance.[505]

It is also important that the suspect did not stand to gain anything from the victim's death and that the victim was not physically capable of doing the act of assistance herself. The policy states some factors in favour of prosecution that clearly discourage any establishment of an assisted suicide organization and the involvement of a healthcare professional. Some of these factors are as the following:

(11) the suspect was unknown to the victim and encouraged or assisted the victim to commit or attempt to commit suicide by providing specific information via, for example, a website or publication;

(12) the suspect gave encouragement or assistance to more than one victim who were not known to each other;

(13) the suspect was paid by the victim or those close to the victim for his or her encouragement or assistance;

---

500 Keown (2013), p. 46.

501 Cartwright (2009), p. 474.

502 Williams (2010), p. 192.

503 Cleary (2010), p. 304.

504 DPP (2010, updated 2014) Suicide: Policy for Prosecutors in Respect of Cases of Encouraging or Assisting Suicide. https://www.cps.gov.uk/legal-guidance/suicide-policy-prosecutors-respect-cases-encouraging-or-assisting-suicide#a01.

505 DPP (2010, updated 2014) Suicide: Policy for Prosecutors in Respect of Cases of Encouraging or Assisting Suicide, para. 45.

(14) the suspect was acting in his or her capacity as a medical doctor, nurse, other healthcare professional, a professional carer [whether for payment or not], or as a person in authority, such as a prison officer, **and the victim was in his or her care;**

[. . .]

(16) the suspect was acting in his or her capacity as a person involved in the management or as an employee (whether for payment or not) of an organization or group, a purpose of which is to provide a physical environment (whether for payment or not) in which to allow another to commit suicide.[506]

The decision in favour of or against prosecution will be based on a balance of these factors, which should be considered in light of each case's specific circumstances. Although the starting point for the Purdy Case that led to the policy was assisting someone to travel to another country where assisted suicide is legally allowed, the policy is not restricted to this scenario. Therefore, the policy is also applicable to assisted suicides that take place within England and Wales.[507] The policy does not include factors regarding the state of illness suffered by the person wishing to end his or her life. The only listed factor related to the health status is whether the affected person was physically able to perform the act that constituted the assistance.[508]

3.4.3 The Martin Case

The Nicklinson Case, which will be evaluated under Chapter C, dealt with the question of whether section 2(1) of the 1961 Act was incompatible with the Convention. Alongside Mr Nicklinson and Mr Lamb's appeals, the Supreme Court (successor to the House of Lords in its judicial function) dealt with a third appeal from an applicant referred to as Martin.[509] Martin had suffered a brainstem stroke in 2008 at the age of 43. He was unable to move and could only communicate with slow hand movements and with the help of an eye-blink computer. Regarding his situation intolerable and undignified, Martin wanted to end his life through the help of Dignitas, for which he needed assistance. As his wife did not want to take part in his death and Martin did not want to involve anyone else from his family, he needed assistance from either one of his carers or an organization. He sought an order for the DPP to clarify and modify his policy 'to enable responsible people, including, but

[506] DPP (2010, updated 2014) Suicide: Policy for Prosecutors in Respect of Cases of Encouraging or Assisting Suicide, para. 43.

[507] DPP (2010, updated 2014) Suicide: Policy for Prosecutors in Respect of Cases of Encouraging or Assisting Suicide, para. 8.

[508] DPP (2010, updated 2014) Suicide: Policy for Prosecutors in Respect of Cases of Encouraging or Assisting Suicide, para. 43.10.

[509] R (Nicklinson and another) v Ministry of Justice, R (AM) v Director of Public Prosecutions [2014] UKSC 38, [2015] AC 657.

not limited to, carers who are willing to do so, to know that they could assist Martin in committing suicide through Dignitas without the risk of being prosecuted'.[510]

After the High Court had dismissed his application, the case came before the Court of Appeal. Martin claimed that the DPP's policy on assisted suicide was not clear enough to be in accordance with the law under Article 8(2) of the Convention and therefore constituted an interference with his rights. After evaluating the ECtHR's case law on foreseeability and the House's judgment in the Purdy Case, the Court decided that there was considerable uncertainty on how the factors listed in the policy, especially factors 6 (lack of compassion), 13 (receiving payment), and 14 (healthcare professional or carer) under paragraph 43, would be taken into account in cases such as Martin's, if a healthcare professional or a third party who is neither family nor close friend were to be willing to assist with suicide. Therefore, the Court ruled that the DPP should provide more clarity into this aspect.[511]

While this was the conclusion of Lord Dyson and Elias LJ, Lord Judge CJ disagreed on the grounds that the DPP's policy did, in fact, provide Martin or anyone who wanted to assist him with the necessary information to make an informed decision. He stated:

> Paragraph 14 addresses the risks which can arise when someone in a position of authority or trust, and on whom the victim would therefore depend to a greater or lesser extent, assisting in the suicide in circumstances in which, just because of the position of authority and trust, the person in authority might be able to exercise undue influence over the victim. As I read this paragraph it does not extend to an individual who happens to be a member of a profession, or indeed a professional carer, brought in from outside, without previous influence or authority over the victim, or his family, for the simple purposes of assisting the suicide after the victim has reached his or her own settled decision to end life, when, although emotionally supportive of him, his wife cannot provide the necessary physical assistance. [...]
>
> Naturally, it would come as no surprise at all for the DPP to decide that a prosecution would be inappropriate in a situation where a loving spouse or partner, as a final act of devotion and compassion assisted the suicide of an individual who had made a clear, final and settled termination to end his or her own life. The Policy does not limit, and we know from the responses to the consultation process, deliberately does not restrict the decision to withhold consent to family members or close friends acting out of love and devotion. The Policy certainly does not lead to what would otherwise be an extraordinary anomaly, that those who are brought in to help from outside the family circle, but without the natural love and devotion which obtains within the family circle, are more likely to be prosecuted than a family member when they do no more than replace a loving member of the family, acting out of compassion, who supports the "victim" to achieve his desired suicide. The stranger brought into this situation, who is not profiteering, but rather assisting to provide services which, if provided by the wife, would not attract a prosecution, seems to me most unlikely to be prosecuted. In my respectful judgment this Policy is sufficiently clear to enable Martin, or

[510] *Nicklinson Case-SC*, [9]-[11].

[511] R (Nicklinson and another) v Ministry of Justice, R (AM) v Director of Public Prosecutions [2013] EWCA Civ 961 [124]-[148].

> anyone who assists him, to make an informed decision about the likelihood of prosecution.[512]

Upon appeal, the Supreme Court reiterated that the prosecutorial discretion aimed to serve the public interest, which had to be based on several factors that would be weighed according to the specific circumstances of each given case.[513] The Court did not agree with Lord Judge CJ that paragraph 43.14 of the DPP's policy on assisted suicide was sufficiently clear. In the Purdy Case, the House had stated the necessity of a policy but refrained from dictating its contents.[514] Following the same approach, the Court ruled that it would be appropriate to leave it to the DPP to resolve any discrepancy between her views and the wording of the policy if there were one. The Court also expressed its expectation from the DPP to resolve the confusion concerning paragraph 43.14 since the DPP had stated that Lord Judge CJ's approach did, in fact, reflect her view.[515]

Shortly after the Supreme Court's Judgment, the DPP modified the policy by underlining the phrase in paragraph 43.14 'and the victim was in his or her care' and adding an explanatory footnote that stated:

> For the avoidance of doubt the words "and the victim was in his or her care" qualify all of the preceding parts of this paragraph [43.14]. This factor does not apply merely because someone was acting in a capacity described within it: it applies only where there was, in addition, a relationship of care between the suspect and the victims such that it will be necessary to consider whether the suspect may have exerted some influence on the victim.

It is more likely that the physician would have more influence on a patient with whom they have had a long-lasting relationship. In the Netherlands, one of the justifying grounds for the physician's involvement with a patient's request for an assisted death was the very nature of the trusting relationship that would be built after a long period of time. Instead of an influencing factor, being under the physician's care is seen as means to understand and confirm the reasons behind the patient's request to die. What is perceived as a positive element in evaluating the authenticity of an assisted death request in the Netherlands and Belgium is listed as a factor that might contribute to a decision in favour of prosecution in the UK. Of course, one could also argue that as long as it is proven that the patient had made an autonomous

---

[512] *Nicklinson Case-CA*, [185]-[186].

[513] *Nicklinson Case-SC*, [249].

[514] *Nicklinson Case-SC*, [141].

[515] *Nicklinson Case-SC* [143], [193], [251], [323]. The Court did not hesitate to express their expectation from the DPP to resolve the confusion concerning paragraph 43.14, though she was not bound to follow Lord Judge CJ's interpretation. 'Given that, in an important respect, the 2010 Policy does not appear to reflect what the DPP intends, it seems to me inevitable that she will take appropriate steps to deal with the problem, particularly in the light of the impressive way in which her predecessor reacted to the decision in Purdy. However, if the confusion is not sorted out, then, at least in my view, the court's powers could be properly invoked to require appropriate action, but, as I have said, it seems very unlikely that this will be necessary.' [146].

decision independent from anyone's influence, this factor would not weigh in favour of prosecution. Nevertheless, this is another example of different approaches in the matter of assisted dying and of the different results such approaches can create.

3.4.4 The Martin v GMC Case

Another case brought by Martin was about the General Medical Council's (GMC) guidance.[516] Martin wanted to travel to Switzerland, where he would receive the assistance of Dignitas to end his life. In order to assist him, Dignitas required Martin's medical records, which could only be provided by a physician. He also wanted advice on methods to end his life at home. However, according to the GMC's guidance, any physician who would assist Martin in either way would risk facing disciplinary action, causing the physicians to be reluctant to help. Martin argued before the High Court that the GMC's guidance violated his rights under Articles 8 and 10 of the Convention.[517]

In addition to the Good Medical Practice guidance, the GMC has published two other documents that are relevant for assisted suicide: 'Guidance for the Investigation Committee and case examiners when considering allegations about a doctor's involvement in encouraging or assisting suicide'[518] and 'When a patient seeks advice or information about assistance to die'.[519] Although they are not strictly binding, failing to comply with the GMC's guidance could lead to the physician being found unfit to practice and to the loss of the medical registration. According to the Guidance for Investigation Committee:

> Where patients raise the issue of assisting suicide, or ask for information that might encourage or assist them in ending their lives, doctors should be prepared to listen and to discuss the reasons for the patient's request but they must not actively encourage or assist the patient as this would be a contravention of the law. Any advice or information they give in response should be limited to an explanation that it is a criminal offence for them to encourage or assist a person to commit or attempt suicide. For the avoidance of doubt, this

[516]The GMC is responsible for the medical practice and qualification of physicians in the UK and, according to the Medical Act 1983, sets the medical standards to be followed in the practice of the medical profession. GMC, Our role and the Medical Act 1983. https://www.gmc-uk.org/about/what-we-do-and-why/our-mandate.

[517]*R (AM) v General Medical Council* (Martin v GMC) [2015] EWHC 2096 (Admin).

[518]GMC (2013) Guidance for the Investigation Committee and case examiners when considering allegations about a doctor's involvement in encouraging or assisting suicide. https://www.gmc-uk.org/-/media/documents/dc4317-guidance-for-ftp-decision-makers-on-assisting-suicide-51026940.pdf.

[519]GMC (2013, last updated 2015) When a patient seeks advice or information about assistance to die. https://www.gmc-uk.org/ethical-guidance/ethical-guidance-for-doctors/when-a-patient-seeks-advice-or-information-about-assistance-to-die; See also GMC (2014) Revised guidance for doctors on giving advice to patients on assisted suicide. https://www.gmc-uk.org/-/media/documents/12%2D%2D-revised-guidance-for-doctors-on-assisted-suicide_pdf-80652843.pdf.

> does not preclude doctors from providing objective advice about the lawful clinical options (such as sedation and other palliative care) which would be available if a patient were to reach a settled decision to kill himself, or agreeing in advance to palliate the pain and discomfort involved should the need for it arise. Doctors should continue to care for their patients and must be respectful and compassionate. We recognise that doctors will face challenges in ensuring that patients do not feel abandoned while ensuring that the advice or information that they provide does not encourage or assist suicide. Doctors are not required to provide treatments that they consider will not be of overall benefit to the patient, or which will harm the patient. Respect for a patient's autonomy cannot justify illegal action.[520]

A question of impaired fitness to practice might arise when a physician provides the patient with reports knowingly that they would be used for assisted suicide (submitting medical records to Dignitas) or provides the patient with information regarding methods of committing suicide.[521] If the patient brings up the subject of assisted suicide, the physician must

> limit any advice or information in response, to:
> i. an explanation that it is a criminal offence for anyone to encourage or assist a person to commit or attempt suicide, and
> ii. objective advice about the lawful clinical options (such as sedation and other palliative care) which would be available if a patient were to reach a settled decision to kill them self. For avoidance of doubt, this does not prevent a doctor from agreeing in advance to palliate the pain and discomfort involved for such a patient should the need arise for such symptom management.[522]

While the Court agreed that the GMC guidance could discourage physicians from providing the kind of assistance asked by Martin and that Article 8 was engaged in the matter, it rejected the notion that the guidance should be modified. The reasons that justified the blanket ban on assisted suicide, namely the protection of the vulnerable, equally justified the GMC guidance.[523] The Court also stated:

> If the position were that section 2 [of the 1961 Act] would in exceptional cases infringe article 8 save for the fact that the discretion conferred upon the DPP is capable of being so exercised as to render it compatible, there would be room for the argument now being advanced. It could be said that the GMC guidance undermines the mechanism which secures compliance with article 8. It was indeed argued by Martin in the earlier case that this was the proper reading of the decision of *Pretty* in the Strasbourg Court, that Martin was an exceptional case, and that accordingly the DPP had to indicate in his policy that it was unlikely that a doctor would be prosecuted for assisting him in the ways he sought. Both the Court of Appeal and the Supreme Court rejected this submission, finding that section 2 is compatible with article 8 even as a blanket ban. Its conformity with article 8 was dependent neither on the existence of the prosecutorial discretion nor the way that it is exercised.[524]

---

[520] GMC (2013) Guidance for the Investigation Committee and case examiners when considering allegations about a doctor's involvement in encouraging or assisting suicide, para. 10.

[521] GMC (2013) Guidance for the Investigation Committee and case examiners when considering allegations about a doctor's involvement in encouraging or assisting suicide, para. 19.

[522] GMC (2013, last updated 2015) When a patient seeks advice or information about assistance to die, para. 6.b.

[523] *Martin v GMC Case*, [42].

[524] *Martin v GMC Case,* [41].

However, disregarding the prosecutorial discretion might not reflect the full extent of the ECtHR's consideration in the Pretty Case. While referring to the statistics of prosecution decisions on assisted suicide cases, the ECtHR had held:

> The Court does not consider therefore that the blanket nature of the ban on assisted suicide is disproportionate. The Government have stated that flexibility is provided for in individual cases by the fact that consent is needed from the DPP to bring a prosecution and by the fact that a maximum sentence is provided, allowing lesser penalties to be imposed as appropriate... It does not appear to be arbitrary to the Court for the law to reflect the importance of the right to life, by prohibiting assisted suicide while providing for a system of enforcement and adjudication which allows due regard to be given in each particular case to the public interest in bringing a prosecution, as well as to the fair and proper requirements of retribution and deterrence.[525]

In her concurring opinion in the Purdy Case, Baroness Hale had emphasized the prosecutorial discretion and the contribution this flexibility had made to the ECtHR's judgment. Referring to the paragraph cited above, Baroness Hale wrote:

> Both sides have understandably gained comfort from that passage. For the DPP, it justifies a blanket ban coupled with flexible enforcement. For Ms Purdy, it contemplates that there will be individual cases in which the deterrent effect of a prosecution would be a disproportionate interference with the autonomy of the person who wishes to end her life. Moreover, in an argument which was not raised in *Pretty*, if the justification for a blanket ban depends upon the flexibility of its operation, it cannot be "in accordance with the law" unless there is greater clarity about the factors which the DPP and his subordinates will take into account in making their decisions.[526]

3.4.5 Recent Developments

In the Nicklinson Case, five judges had expressed a degree of discontent with the current state of law.[527] Although the Supreme Court had not given an incompatibility decision and instead referred to the Parliament, the judgment was considered to contain a strong message that the Parliament should address the matter of assisted suicide.[528] Considering the statements made by the majority of the Supreme Court, MP Rob Morris introduced a similar bill to Lord Falconer's Assisted Dying Bill to the House of Commons in September 2015.[529] The Assisted Dying (No 2) Bill addressed competent adult patients who were terminally ill with a life expectancy of fewer 6 months. Assisted suicide would be subject to a judge's approval with a cooling period of 14 days. Concerns about assisted suicide becoming a substitute

---

[525] *Pretty Case*, [76].

[526] *Purdy Case-HL*, [63].

[527] *Nicklinson Case-SC*, [111] (Lord Neuberger), [186] (Lord Mance), [205] (Lord Wilson), [301] (Lady Hale), [335] (Lord Kerr).

[528] Downie (2016), p. 95.

[529] United Kingdom, Assisted Dying (No 2) HC Bill 7, Session 2015-16.

alternative for palliative care, the unintended extension of assisted suicide over time, the risk of abuse for the elderly population, and the possibility of the right to die to become a duty to die were raised during the debates in the House of Commons. The rising statistics in the Netherlands for euthanasia cases were given as a counterargument as a worrisome example.[530]

The former DPP, Keir Starmer, also made a statement in which he cautiously addressed the inequality of the situation caused by the DPP's policy on assisted suicide. While 'compassionate and amateur assistance from the nearest and dearest' was accepted, professional assistance from a physician could not be obtained unless the person had the means to travel to Switzerland to receive such assistance from Dignitas.[531]

Members of the House of Commons have expressed both support and objection through studies as well as examples of personal experiences. After a heated debate, a second reading for the Assisted Dying (No 2) Bill was rejected by 330 votes to 118.

In a case that came before the High Court, Noel Conway sought a judicial review of section 2(1) of the 1961 Act on the basis that it was incompatible with Articles 8 and 14 of the Convention. The Court refused Conway's application stating:

> The core reason for doing so is that Parliament has reconsidered the issue of assisted dying following the decision of the Supreme Court in Nicklinson, as that court encouraged it to do. Both the House of Commons and the House of Lords have debated the matter in the context of bills proposing a relaxation of the strict application of section 2(1). The result is that Parliament has decided, at least for the moment, not to provide for legislative exceptions to section 2(1) of the 1961 Act. The policy of the DPP has also been subject to parliamentary scrutiny and debate. That controls the practical application of the statutory provision. The Strasbourg court has ruled that the question whether there should be exceptions to a blanket ban on assisting suicide falls within the margin of appreciation of the State parties to the ECHR. Whilst the Nicklinson case recognised a jurisdiction in the courts to issue a declaration of incompatibility in these circumstances, even where Parliament had struck the balance for itself, the Supreme Court also recognised that Parliament was better placed to resolve these sensitive issues. [. . .] I do not consider that it is arguable that a declaration of incompatibility should be made, in the light of the post Nicklinson parliamentary consideration of this very difficult moral issue.[532]

Subsequent applications to the Court of Appeal and the Supreme Court have also been rejected on the same grounds.[533] Recently, Phil Newby, who is suffering from a motor neurone disease, asked for a judicial review of the ban on assisted suicide under Articles 2 and 8 of the Convention. The High Court refused Mr Newby's application.

> In the context of repeated and recent parliamentary debate, where there is an absence of significant change in societal attitude expressed through Parliament, and where the courts

530 HC Deb 11 September 2015 Vol 599 Col 653, Cols 656–724.

531 HC Deb 11 September 2015 Vol 599 Col 653, Col 674.

532 R (Conway) v Secretary of State for Justice [2017] EWHC 640 (Admin) [5].

533 R (Conway) v Secretary of State for Justice [2018] EWCA Civ 1431; R (Conway) v Secretary of State for Justice [2018] UKSC B1.

> lack legitimacy and expertise on moral (as opposed to legal) questions, in our judgment the courts are not the venue for arguments which have failed to convince Parliament. [. . .]
>
> How is a court positioned to conclude whether such an estimated level of abuse to the vulnerable is, or is not, proportionate, as a balance to the enfranchisement of assisted suicide benefitting those facing such a tragic quandary as that before the Claimant? In our judgment, there are some questions which, plainly and simply, cannot be 'resolved' by a court as no objective, single, correct answer can be said to exist. On issues such as the sanctity of life there is no consensus to be gleaned from evidence. The private views of judges on such moral and political questions are irrelevant, and spring from no identifiable legal principle. We struggle to see why any public conclusion judges might reach on matters beyond the resolution of evidence should carry more weight than those of any other adult citizen.[534]

The Court of Appeal has also refused Mr Newby's application.[535] Paul Lamb from the Nicklinson Case renewed his application in 2019, arguing that the current law was discriminatory for people with severe disabilities who could not end their own lives without help from another. He claimed that the public opinion on assisted dying had changed overtime and therefore, the Court should assess his claims in this new light. However, his application was rejected on the same grounds that it was upon the Parliament to decide whether to make a change.[536]

It seems unlikely that the Courts in the UK will take a different approach and find incompatibility of section 2(1) of the 1961 Act with the Convention in the near future. Although the matter has been repeatedly brought to the Parliament's attention over the years, none of the proposals gathered sufficient support. Lord Falconer introduced the latest proposal to the House of Lords in January 2020.[537] Around the same time, the House of Commons discussed the current situation and whether there was a need for a change. Despite the tone of sympathy surrounding the debate, worries of adequate safeguards and the possibility of a slippery slope were emphasized while expressing a need for more research and evidence. MPs Christine Jardine and Karin Smyth pointed out the discriminatory nature of the current situation, in which only people with more than £10.000 were able to receive suicide assistance by travelling to Switzerland. MP Kevin Hollinrake drew attention to the latest surveys, which revealed that most British people favoured changing the legislation, and currently, there was concern that the Parliament was 'out of step with the public'.[538]

According to a recent survey, 84% of the British people supported changing the law to enable the option of assisted suicide for terminally ill patients.[539] The medical

---

[534] R (Newby) v Secretary of State for Justice [2019] EWHC 3118 (Admin) [40], [42].

[535] (2020) Assisted dying: Terminally ill man's judicial review rejected. In: BBC. https://www.bbc.com/news/uk-england-leicestershire-51311089.

[536] (2019) Paralysed Leeds man Paul Lamb loses "right to die" case. In: BBC. https://www.bbc.com/news/uk-england-leeds-50852790.

[537] United Kingdom, Assisted Dying HL Bill 69, Session 2019-21.

[538] HC Deb 23 January 2020 Vol 670 Col 186WH, Col 200WH.

[539] Dignity in Dying (2019) Dignity in Dying Poll. In: Yonder. https://yonderconsulting.com/poll/dignity-in-dying/. The question asked was: 'Currently it is illegal for a doctor to help someone with

profession reserves, however, more caution. The British Medical Association (BMA) carried out a research project on end-of-life care and physician-assisted dying in 2015, which revealed that many people were uninformed on the details of the practical aspects of assisted dying, and not many had given serious thought to end-of-life matters.[540] While some physicians believed that enabling physician-assisted dying would improve the physician-patient relationship by respecting patients' choices and relieving pain and suffering, many were worried about the negative impacts. Physicians were mostly worried that physician-assisted death would cause changes to their fundamental role as healers and increase suspicion and distrust towards their profession.[541]

In March 2019, the Royal College of Physicians (RCP) adopted a neutral position on assisted dying after surveying its members.[542] Until 2021, the BMA maintained a position of opposition to assisted dying and insisted that neither physician-assisted suicide nor euthanasia be legalized.[543] According to a survey held by the BMA in 2020, 40% of its members who have participated thought that the BMA's position on physician-assisted suicide should be supportive. While 33% opposed, 21% were in favour of a neutral position.[544] The top two cited reasons in support of changing the law to allow physician-assisted suicide were 'the importance of patient choice' and the physician's role to 'relieve suffering'.[545] Members in favour of a legislative change also mentioned the need for clear guidelines and the possibility of conscientious objection.[546] The top reasons cited against physician-assisted suicide were

---

a terminal illness to end their life, even if the person considers their suffering unbearable and they are of sound mind. A proposed new law would allow terminally ill adults the option of assisted dying. This would mean being provided with life-ending medication, to take themselves, if two doctors were satisfied they met all of the safeguards. They would need to be of sound mind, be terminally ill and have 6 months or less to live, and a High Court judge would have to be satisfied that they had made a voluntary, clear and settled decision to end their life, with time to consider all other options. Whether or not you would want the choice for yourself, do you support or oppose this proposal for assisted dying becoming law?'

540 BMA (2016) End-of-Life Care and Physician-Assisted Dying: 3 - Reflections and Recommendations. https://www.bma.org.uk/advice-and-support/ethics/end-of-life/end-of-life-care-and-physician-assisted-dying-project, p. 65ff.

541 BMA (2016) End-of-Life Care and Physician-Assisted Dying: 3 - Reflections and Recommendations, pp. 71–73.

542 While 43.4% thought the position should remain opposed, 31.6% thought the RCP should be supportive and 25% were neutral. The RCP defines assisted dying as physician-assisted suicide for terminally ill patients. RCP (2020) The RCP Clarifies Its Position on Assisted Dying. https://www.rcplondon.ac.uk/news/rcp-clarifies-its-position-assisted-dying.

543 BMA (2021) How have the law and BMA policy developed over the past twenty years? https://www.bma.org.uk/media/4401/bma-pad-policy-law-and-timeline-aug-2021.pdf.

544 For the purposes of the survey, capable adult patients who 'have either a terminal illness or serious physical illness causing intolerable suffering that cannot be relieved' are considered eligible for physician-assisted suicide. BMA (2020) Physician-Assisted Dying Survey. https://www.bma.org.uk/advice-and-support/ethics/end-of-life/physician-assisted-dying-survey, p. 10.

545 BMA (2020) Physician-Assisted Dying Survey, p. 21.

546 BMA (2020) Physician-Assisted Dying Survey, p. 22.

contradiction with medical ethics and the physicians' role, the risk to vulnerable patients, the need for better palliative care, and the legal liability of physicians. While some members were worried about the possibility of a slippery slope, some had objections based on personal ethical or religious beliefs.[547] Only 30% favoured the BMA adopting a supportive position on euthanasia (23% neutral, 40% opposed).[548] In September 2021, the BMA changed its position of opposition to neutral.[549]

3.5 Germany

3.5.1 Section 217 of the Criminal Code

Suicide and assisted suicide are not prohibited by law in Germany. Although a practice similar to that of Switzerland never developed, there have been concerns about the establishment of assisted suicide organizations. Many Germans wishing for assisted suicide travel to the Swiss neighbour.[550] There have been attempts to establish similar assisted suicide organizations in Germany as well. However, these attempts have faced several complications.[551] To remedy the legal gap,[552] the Parliament passed an amendment to the Criminal Code in 2015. Section 217 of the Criminal Code stated:

(1) Whoever, with the intention of assisting another person to commit suicide, provides, procures or arranges the opportunity for that person to do so and whose actions are intended as a recurring pursuit incurs a penalty of imprisonment for a term not exceeding three years or a fine.
(2) A participant whose actions are not intended as a recurring pursuit and who is either a relative of or is close to the person referred to in subsection (1) is exempt from punishment.[553]

---

[547] BMA (2020) Physician-Assisted Dying Survey, pp. 22–23.

[548] BMA (2020) Physician-Assisted Dying Survey, p. 37.

[549] BMA (2021) Physician-Assisted Dying. https://www.bma.org.uk/advice-and-support/ethics/end-of-life/the-bmas-position-on-physician-assisted-dying.

[550] Almost 47% of the members, who have ended their lives through the assistance of Dignitas, are from Germany. Dignitas, Accompanied Suicide of Members of Dignitas, by Year and by Country of Residency 1998–2020.

[551] Kamann (2014) Befördert Sterbehelfer Kusch sich selbst ins Aus? In: Welt. https://www.welt.de/politik/deutschland/article127971004/Befoerdert-Sterbehelfer-Kusch-sich-selbst-ins-Aus.html; Schmidt and Ulrich (2009) Court Expected to Rule on Assisted Suicide Case. In: Spiegel. https://www.spiegel.de/international/germany/deadly-business-court-expected-to-rule-on-assisted-suicide-case-a-602390.html.

[552] The states of Saarland, Thüringen and Hessen had submitted a proposal in 2006. BR-Dr 230/06. Later, the Federal Government submitted a draft proposal in 2012. BT-Dr 17/11126.

[553] German Criminal Code of 13 November 1998 (19 June 2019), English translation by (Micheal Bohlander, revised and updated by Ute Reusch) the German Federal Ministry of Justice and

Section 217 prohibited providing suicide assistance in a 'business-like' manner.[554] It was acknowledged that the constitutional guarantees of physical integrity under Article 2(2) and the protection of the right to free development of personality under Article 2(1) in conjunction with human dignity under Article 1(1) of the Basic Law founded a right to self-determination, which included the right to decide one's own death.[555] Although a complete ban would fall contrary to the fundamental rights, it was found necessary to prevent the 'social normalization' of assisted suicide that could become a factor of pressure on some members of the society. Therefore, the State had to reconcile an area of conflict between the right to self-determination and the protection of human life.[556]

Even if assisted suicide organizations would operate as non-profit organizations, frequency and effectiveness were essential elements to their services. Therefore, the business-like model of assisted suicide did not just refer to material gain but also included the specialized professional manner of providing suicide assistance. According to the drafters, 'business-like' should be understood as 'granting, procuring or mediating the opportunity to commit suicide as a permanent or recurring activity [. . .] irrespective of the intention to make profit and irrespective of a connection with an economic or professional activity'.[557] The business-like occupation of assisted suicide had the danger of causing pressure on some members of the society, who would otherwise not have considered suicide.[558] The promotion of assisted suicide carried the risk of tampering with the autonomous nature of the individual's decision.[559] Therefore, the first subsection was aimed to prevent the

Consumer Protection and the German Federal Office of Justice available at https://www.gesetze-im-internet.de/englisch_stgb/index.html.

554 In the original German text, the adjective used for 'recurring pursuit' is *geschäftsmäßig*, to which the literal translation is 'business-like'. The translator's choice to use the term 'recurring pursuit' is perhaps to capture the intention behind the section. Using the word 'business' might give the false impression that only commercial suicide assistance would be criminalized. However, the legislator's intention was to prohibit acts that were not necessarily commercial 'but designed to be repeated'. BT-Dr 18/5373, p. 2 (author's translation). Nevertheless, the author will use the direct translation of *geschäftsmäßig*: business-like.

555 Art 1(1) 'Human dignity shall be inviolable. To respect and protect it shall be the duty of all state authority.'

Art 2(1) 'Every person shall have the right to free development of his personality insofar as he does not violate the rights of others or offend against the constitutional order or the moral law.'

Art 2(2) 'Every person shall have the right to life and physical integrity. Freedom of the person shall be inviolable. These rights may be interfered with only pursuant to a law.' Basic Law of the Federal Republic of Germany of 23 May 1949 (1 January 2021) English translation by (Christian Tomuschat, David P Currie, Donald P Kommers and Raymond Kerr, in cooperation with the Language Service of the German Bundestag) the German Federal Ministry of Justice and Consumer Protection and the German Federal Office of Justice available at https://www.gesetze-im-internet.de/englisch_gg/index.html.

556 BT-Dr 18/5373, pp. 2–3, 10.

557 BT-Dr 18/5373, p. 17 (author's translation).

558 BT-Dr 18/5373, pp. 11–12.

559 BT-Dr 18/5373, p. 17.

establishment of assisted suicide organizations, such as those in Switzerland. Subsection 2, on the other hand, excluded non-business-like suicide assistance from criminal liability, namely suicide assistance carried out for reasons of compassion.[560]

Section 217 had been criticized for disproportionately restricting the right to self-determination and ultimately causing a duty to continue living upon those who wanted to end their lives as an expression of personal autonomy. The prohibition was also criticized for being unfounded. There was no evidence attesting to a possible social normalization of suicide and unwarranted pressure on the vulnerable to choose death. The exception provided by subsection 2 for compassionate suicide assistance mainly carried out by family or close friends was not understandable. While the legislator aimed to prevent unwarranted pressure on vulnerable members of the society, it had neglected the pressure one might feel due to becoming a 'burden' to one's family.[561] In fact, it is more likely that one's family or close friends would have more influence on one's self rather than an organization, to which one has no emotional connection.

Mostly agreeing with these criticisms, the German Federal Constitutional Court struck down section 217 as unconstitutional in 2020. The Constitutional Court's decision will be analysed after an overview of the Federal Administrative Court's approach to NaP for assisted suicide purposes.

3.5.2 Aftermath of the ECtHR's Koch Judgment

NaP is listed under Annex III of the Narcotic Drugs Act.[562] Drugs under Annex III can either be obtained through a prescription in accordance with section 4(1)(3)(a) or through a licence granted by the German Federal Institute for Drugs and Medical Devices (Federal Institute) in accordance with section 3(1)(1) of the Narcotic Drugs Act. According to section 5(1)(6),

> The issue of a licence pursuant to section 3 shall be refused if [. . .]
>
> 6. the kind and purpose of the trade for which application has been made do not comply with the purpose of this Act to ensure the required medical care of the population, but at the same time to preclude, as far as possible, the abuse of narcotic drugs [. . .]

The Koch Case concerned a request for a licence to obtain NaP for the purpose of assisted suicide. Pursuant to section 5(1)(6), the Federal Institute had refused to grant the licence, and the German Courts had dismissed the applicant's appeal as

560 BT-Dr 18/5373, p. 19.

561 Stiller (2020), pp. 252–257.

562 German Act on the Trade of Narcotic Drugs of 28 July 1981 (9 June 2021) (Narcotic Drugs Act) English translation available at https://www.bundesgesundheitsministerium.de/fileadmin/Dateien/3_Downloads/Gesetze_und_Verordnungen/GuV/N/Narcotic_Drugs_18_12_2009.pdf.

inadmissible.[563] The ECtHR had found a violation of the applicant's right under Article 8 of the Convention on the grounds that the German Courts had failed to examine the merits of the case. Following the ECtHR's judgment, the applicant re-initiated legal proceedings before the German Courts asking to determine the illegality of the refusal to grant the licence to obtain to NaP for assisted suicide.

The Federal Administrative Court issued a landmark decision, in which it was reaffirmed that the right to decide the time and manner of one's own death in cases of severely and incurably ill persons was part of the right to self-determination derived from the fundamental rights to free development of personality and human dignity under the Basic Law. The protection of this right was not limited to situations where the dying process had already begun. Severely and incurably ill people could decide to end their lives before the final dying phase started, and this decision should also be respected.[564] Although not directly intended, the restriction caused by section 5(1)(6) of the Narcotic Drugs Act affected seriously and incurably ill persons who had decided to end their lives by using a narcotic drug that would ensure them a painless and safe death.[565] While interpreting section 5(1)(6) of the Narcotics Drug Act, constitutional guarantees had to be taken into consideration.

Apart from respecting the right to self-determination, the State had an obligation to protect life under Article 2(2) of the Basic Law. Alongside the goal to protect life, section 5(1)(6) also aimed to protect the vulnerable and prevent the abuse of narcotic drugs, which were legitimate purposes.[566] Although the individual could not demand the State to provide them with the means to commit suicide, the right to self-determination gained more weight when the individual was in an extreme state of emergency due to a severe and incurable illness. In such circumstances, the State's duty to protect life took second place. The Court further stated that the State could not simply abandon the person in such a helpless situation when the person was even more dependent on the respect and protection of his or her autonomy. Therefore, Section 5(1)(6) had to be interpreted in a way that would allow an exception.[567] According to the Court, an exception would be the case under these requirements:

> if - firstly - the severe and incurable disease is connected with grave physical suffering, in particular severe pain, which results in unbearable psychological strain for the affected person and cannot be reduced sufficiently (. . .), if - secondly - the affected person is able to take decisions and has made the free and earnest choice to end his or her life, and if he or she - thirdly - does not have any other reasonable option to carry out the wish to die.[568]

The refusal to grant a licence for NaP in such cases forced an obligation upon the affected person to continue living under circumstances unbearable to that person. In

---

[563] See Sect. 4.1.5 'The Koch Case'.

[564] *Koch (2)* [2017] BVerwG 3 C 19.15, [24].

[565] *Koch (2) Case*, [26].

[566] *Koch (2) Case*, [29]-[30].

[567] *Koch (2) Case*, [27]-[28].

[568] *Koch (2) Case*, [31] English translation available at the Federal Administrative Court's website https://www.bverwg.de/en/020317U3C19.15.0.

light of human dignity and the state of distress and helplessness of the affected person, the State's duty to protect life gave way to a duty to allow access to NaP for assisted suicide.[569]

Elaborating on the third requirement, the Court stated that while a reasonable alternative to assisted suicide would be the withdrawal of life-sustaining treatment, this could only be a viable alternative if death could be expected in the foreseeable future after the treatment had been withdrawn. If withdrawing the treatment would only cause further deterioration of the person's health for an indefinite period of time, it would not be a reasonable alternative. Seeking a prescription for NaP was not an alternative either since the physicians' involvement carried legal risks regarding criminal liability and the law governing the medical profession. Neither could assisted suicide services provided abroad be considered as a reasonable alternative as the Basic Law required the State to guarantee the protection of the fundamental rights within its own jurisdiction.[570]

According to the Court, access to NaP could actually constitute necessary medical care within the meaning of section 5(1)(6). In an extreme state of emergency, assisted suicide could be considered a therapeutic act when there were no other alternatives. This interpretation of section 5(1)(6) did not fall contrary to section 217 of the Criminal Code either, as it did not constitute a business-like service of assisted suicide.[571]

Although the Federal Institute had argued that it did not have a list of requirements to make a reliable assessment of whether there was a situation of extreme emergency, the Court ruled that the absence of procedural rules did not save the Federal Institute from acting in accordance with the fundamental rights. The difficulty of such an assessment was neither more nor less than the assessment of capacity in cases of refusal of life-sustaining treatment or the determination of the presumed will of an unconscious patient. Therefore, the Court found the Federal Institute's refusal to grant a licence for NaP without examining whether there was a situation of extreme emergency unlawful.[572]

Despite the Federal Administrative Court's judgment, the Ministry of Health instructed the Federal Institute not to accept any licence applications to obtain NaP.[573] In an expert opinion written by the former Federal Constitutional Court judge Prof Dr Udo di Fabio on behalf of the Federal Institute, the Federal Administrative Court's judgment was strongly criticized for being constitutionally unsustainable, for replacing the legislature's will with its own legal policy, and for

---

[569] *Koch (2) Case*, [32].

[570] *Koch (2) Case*, [34]-[36].

[571] *Koch (2) Case*, [37]-[38].

[572] *Koch (2) Case*, [42].

[573] Müller-Neuhof (2018) Wie die Regierung beschloss, das höchstrichterliche Urteil zu ignorieren. In: *D*er Tagesspiegel. https://www.tagesspiegel.de/politik/sterbehilfe-wie-die-regierung-beschloss-das-hoechstrichterliche-urteil-zu-ignorieren/22928052.html.

violating the separation of powers principle.[574] Upon reports of the high number of unprocessed applications made to the Federal Institute, the Free Democratic Party (FDP) asked the Government to clarify the criteria of processing the applications.[575] The Government responded that in light of the State's duty to protect life, it could not be the task of the State to actively support the killing of a person. The aim of drafting Section 217 of the Criminal Code was to prevent assisted suicide from becoming a normal treatment option. To that same end, new regulations on palliative and hospice care had been passed in 2015. To the questions regarding the Government's views on the Federal Administrative Court's judgment, the Government responded that the deliberations were not yet finalized and awaited the finalization of the aforementioned opinion by Prof Dr di Fabio.[576] In a second inquiry, the FDP asked among other things for the Government's response to the Ministry of Health's instruction to the Federal Institute to reject all applications, to which the Government did not give a clear answer.[577] The Government's responses, especially the Ministry of Health's reaction, clearly indicate dissatisfaction with the Federal Administrative Court's judgment. Responses also show that none of the applications for a licence to obtain NaP have been approved.[578]

The Federal Administrative Court emphasized the limits to its approach in a following case. The applicants were a married couple, who did not suffer from any severe and incurable illness but rather wished to end their lives together on their own terms. The applicants had requested from the Federal Institute to grant a licence for NaP, which was rejected in November 2014. The Administrative Court and the Higher Administrative Court had dismissed the applicants' appeal on the basis that section 5(1)(6) of the Narcotic Drugs Act did not allow obtaining a licence for narcotic drugs for the purpose of assisted suicide and that there was no right to access lethal drugs inherent in the right to a self-determined death.[579]

The applicants claimed that the restrictive interpretation of section 5(1)(6) violated their rights under Articles 4(1), (2) and 6(1) of the Basic Law, alongside Article 8 of the Convention.[580] The Federal Institute opposed by stating that the previous judgment of the Federal Administrative Court from 2 March 2017 foresaw an exception only in a situation of emergency caused by a severe illness and that the

---

[574] di Fabio (2017) Erwerbserlaubnis letal wirkender Mittel zur Selbsttötung in Existenziellen Notlagen - Rechtsgutachten zum Urteil des Bundesverwaltungsgerichts vom 2. März 2017-3 C 19/15. https://www.bfarm.de/SharedDocs/Downloads/DE/Service/Presse/Rechtsgutachten.pdf?__blob=publicationFile&v=2, pp. 99ff.

[575] BT-Dr 19/1860.

[576] BT-Dr 19/2090.

[577] BT-Dr 19/9847.

[578] Since the Federal Administrative Court's judgment on 2 March 2017 until 10 May 2020, there had been 174 applications, none of which were approved. BT-Dr 19/19411.

[579] Case against the Federal Institute [2019] BVerwG 3 C 6.17, [5].

[580] Basic Law Art 4(1) 'Freedom of faith and of conscience and freedom to profess a religious or philosophical creed shall be inviolable.' Art 4(2) 'The undisturbed practice of religion shall be guaranteed.' Art 6(1) 'Marriage and the family shall enjoy the special protection of the state.'

applicants did not meet this requirement. The Federal Administrative Court repeated its conclusion from its earlier judgment and ruled that section 5(1)(6) of the Narcotic Drugs Act should be interpreted in light of the fundamental rights, which entailed an exception for severe and incurably ill persons in cases of extreme distress. In situations other than that described, however, the restriction caused by section 5(1)(6) was in balance to its legitimate aim, which was the State's duty to protect life. Therefore, any interference would also be justified under Article 8(2) of the Convention.[581]

In November 2019, the Federal Administrative Court made a reference to the Constitutional Court pursuant to Article 100(1) of the Basic Law to resolve the question of whether the prohibition to obtain NaP due to section 5(1)(6) of the Narcotic Drugs Actwas compatible with Articles 2(1) and 1(1) of the Basic Law. Six applicants had brought a case against the Federal Institute's refusal to grant a licence to obtain NaP, claiming that they did meet the requirements established in the previous case by the Federal Administrative Court.

The Constitutional Court dismissed the submission. In the meantime, the Constitutional Court had found section 217 of the Criminal Code unconstitutional and declared it void. Under the Constitutional Court's procedural rules, constitutionality questions should only be submitted after a complete consideration of all relevant facts. The Federal Administrative Court's question of constitutionality regarding section 5(1)(6) of the Narcotic Drugs Act was based on the fact that persons wishing to end their lives did not have access to assistance due to the criminal liability under section 217 of the Criminal Code. In light of the landmark decision, which will be analysed next, the Constitutional Court did not find it necessary to rule on the matter and dismissed the submission.[582]

3.5.3 Unconstitutionality of Section 217

In February 2020, the Constitutional Court declared section 217 of the Criminal Code void because it violated the general right of personality enshrined in Article 2(1) taken in conjunction with Article 1(1) of the Basic Law.[583] The Court stated:

> The specific guarantees deriving from the general right of personality give effect to the notion of autonomous self-determination that is rooted in human dignity. This right ensures the basic conditions for the individual to find, develop and protect their identity and individuality in self-determination. Notably, the self-determined protection of one's personality requires that the individual can control their life on their own terms and is not forced into ways of living that are fundamentally irreconcilable with their idea of self and their personal identity. [...]

---

[581] *Case against the Federal Institute*, [17]-[26].

[582] [2020] BVerfG 1 BvL 2/20.

[583] *Case on Sec 217* [2020] BVerfG 2 BvR 2347/15.

> In terms of human personality the decision to end one's own life is of the most vital significance to one's existence. It reflects one's personal identity and is a central expression of the person capable of self-determination and personal responsibility. For the individual, the purpose of life, and whether and for what reasons they might consider ending their own life, is a matter of highly personal beliefs and convictions. The decision to commit suicide concerns fundamental questions of human existence and has a bearing on one's identity and individuality like no other decision. Therefore, the general right of personality in its manifestation as right to a self-determined death is not limited to the right to refuse, of one's own free will, life-sustaining treatments and thus let a terminal illness run its course. The right to a self-determined death also extends to cases where the individual decides to take their own life. The right to take one's own life guarantees that the individual can determine their fata autonomously in accordance with their ideas of self and can thus protect their personality ([...]).[584]

Most importantly, the Court did not condition the right to a self-determined death to the existence of 'situations defined by external causes', namely the presence of a severe or incurable illness.

> Restricting the scope of protection to specific causes or motives would essentially amount to an appraisal of the motives of the person seeking to end their own life, and thereby a substantive predetermination, which is alien to the Basic Law's notion of freedom. Such a restriction would lead to considerable difficulties in drawing distinctions; furthermore, it would come into conflict with the concept of human dignity and the free development of one's personality in self-determination and personal responsibility, which is fundamental to the Basic Law. The right to a self-determined death is rooted in the guarantee of human dignity enshrined in Art. 1(1) GG; this implies that the decision to end one's own life, taken on the basis of personal responsibility, does not require any explanation or justification. Art. 1(1) GG protects human dignity, the way humans understand themselves as individuals and become aware of themselves. What is decisive is the will of the holder of fundamental rights, which eludes any appraisal on the basis of general values, religious precepts, societal norms for dealing with life and death, or considerations of objective rationality... Where an individual decides to end their own life, having reached this decision based on how they personally define quality of life and a meaningful existence, their decision must, in principle, be respected by state and society as an act of autonomous self-determination.[585]

According to the Court, the right to a self-determined death also included the right to seek and if offered, receive assistance to that end. If realizing the decision to end one's own life was only possible through a third party's assistance, including expert help by a physician, the protection of this right meant a prohibition of restrictions against such means.[586] Section 217 of the Criminal Code interfered with the right to a self-determined death by criminalizing business-like suicide assistance. Therefore, it must be evaluated whether this interference was in accordance with the law.

Although section 217 served a legitimate aim of protecting life and preventing assisted suicide from becoming normality that resulted in social pressure endangering self-determination, and although this measure was suitable to achieve its

---

[584] *Case on Sec 217*, [207], [209], English translation available at the Federal Constitution Court's website https://www.bundesverfassungsgericht.de/e/rs20200226_2bvr234715en.html.

[585] *Case on Sec 217*, [210].

[586] *Case on Sec 217*, [212]-[213].

legitimate aim, the Court did not find the interference proportionate. Despite the importance of section 217's legitimate aim, the State exceeded the limits by rendering the decision of a self-determined death impossible and failing to leave sufficient space for personal autonomy, leaving the individual with no reasonable option in cases in which committing suicide without assistance is not possible.[587] When balancing personal autonomy and the right to self-determination with the State's duty to protect life and the vulnerable, the Court took the following formulation:

> Where the protection of life undermines the protection of autonomy, it contradicts the central understanding of a community which places human dignity at the core of its order of values and thus commits itself to respecting and protecting the free human personality as the highest value of its Constitution. Given the vital significance for self-determination and respect for one's personality that can be attached to the freedom to commit suicide, it must always be ensure that realistic possibilities of committing suicide are available.[588]

Section 217 does not criminalize suicide assistance provided as a non-recurring act carried out by a family member or close friend out of compassion. However, this exemption did not provide a realistic alternative in the Court's opinion. The person wishing to end his or her life in a comfortable and safe manner required a physician's participation, at least by prescribing the lethal medication. Due to the regulations governing the medical profession, physicians were not willing to provide assistance.[589] The fact that suicide assistance could be received abroad did not present a realistic alternative, as the State had to guarantee the protection of the fundamental rights within its own jurisdiction.[590] The Court also stated that the protection of the vulnerable did not justify the complete restriction of personal autonomy in the decision of a self-determined death.[591]

In addition to the rights of the person who made an autonomous decision to end his or her life, section 217 also interfered with the rights of the person who wished to provide suicide assistance by criminalizing their actions. The constitutional protection of a self-determined death extended its protection to persons willing to assist as well. The threat of penalty infringed the occupational freedom under Article 12(1) of the Basic Law for physicians and lawyers who wanted to provide suicide assistance.[592] The Court ruled that the fundamental right to occupational freedom could only be restricted when the occupation caused harm to the public by its nature and

---

[587] *Case on Sec 217*, [228]-[277].

[588] *Case on Sec 217*, [277].

[589] *Case on Sec 217*, [278]-[297]. The Court also referred to the sample Professional Code of Conduct for German Physicians published by the German Medical Association. In its last version from 2018, Article 16 clearly prohibits assisted dying. Bundesärztekammer (2018) (Muster-) Berufsordnung für die in Deutschland tätigen Ärztinnen und Ärzte. https://www.bundesaerztekammer.de/recht/berufsrecht/muster-berufsordnung-aerzte/muster-berufsordnung/.

[590] *Case on Sec 217*, [300].

[591] *Case on Sec 217*, [301].

[592] Basic Law Art 12(1) 'All Germans shall have the right freely to choose their occupation or profession, their place of work and their place of training. The practice of an occupation or profession may be regulated pursuant to a law.'

that this did not apply to suicide assistance, even if it were provided in a business-like manner.[593] The Court did not accept the same argument for assisted suicide organizations because they did not exercise a professional activity within the meaning of Article 12(1).[594]

While ruling that section 217 of the Criminal Code was void, the Court stated that the legislator could regulate organized assisted suicide by placing safeguards to ensure the authenticity of the decision for a self-determined death. However, any such regulation could not set substantive prerequisites for suicide assistance, such as the existence of a severe or incurable illness. Additionally, changes to the legal framework applicable to the medical profession and controlled substances were necessary to maintain coherence in the legal framework.[595]

The Constitutional Court's judgment has great importance for the supporters of the right to die. In its reasoning, the Court focused on the right to self-determination and built up to a conclusion that prevents the legislator from setting criteria based on the diagnosis of the individual wishing to end his or her life. If the person possesses the decision-making capacity and has arrived autonomously at the decision of a self-determined death, he or she should be eligible for an assisted suicide. Granting assistance cannot be dependent on whether the person has an incurable illness or is in unbearable pain. The Court has made a liberal assessment compared to the Netherlands or Belgium or even Switzerland. Although generously interpreted and superficially implemented, the Swiss assisted suicide organizations require a medical indication. Despite the step-by-step relaxation of its meaning due to the subjectivity of 'unbearable suffering', the Dutch and Belgian practices maintain the condition of a medical indication. In Germany, the Court skipped the process of gradually relaxing the criteria and ruled straight forward that the right to self-determination prohibited the search for a medical indication. Therefore, the legislator would have to make the necessary adjustments to the legal framework and allow physicians to prescribe NaP even if the situation of the person asking for an assisted suicide does not fall within the medical profession. Currently, the German Medical Association is discussing a change to Article 16 of the sample Code of Professional Conduct that prohibits physician-assisted suicide.[596] The Federal Administrative Court's judgment in 2015 had a much more restrictive approach and would have allowed for more control over the distribution of NaP. Considering that the earlier judgment was not embraced in the slightest, it is yet to be seen if the Constitutional Court's judgment will face any resistance.

---

593 *Case on Sec 217*, [312].

594 *Case on Sec 217*, [313].

595 *Case on Sec 217*, [337]-[342].

596 (2020) Sterbehilfe auf Agenda des Deutschen Ärztetages. In: aerzteblatt.de. https://www.aerzteblatt.de/nachrichten/sw/Sterbehilfe?s=sterbehilfe&p=1&n=1&nid=116866.

3.6 Recent Developments in Other Council of Europe Member States

The right to die has been gaining considerable attention in other Council of Europe member States. The Italian Constitutional Court decided in September 2019 that under certain circumstances, the prohibition on assisted suicide violated the right to self-determination.[597] The strictly limited area in which the Court had identified an interference with the right to self-determination related only to persons, who were affected by an incurable illness that caused intolerable physical or psychological suffering, who depended on medical life-supporting treatment, and who were mentally competent to make an informed decision.[598] Grounding its reasoning on the right to refuse treatment, the Court stated:

> If, indeed, the primary importance of the value of life does not rule out the duty to respect the patient's decision to end his or her life by means of suspending healthcare treatments – even when this requires action by third parties [. . .] – there is no reason for the same value to become an absolute obstacle, supported by criminal liability, to accepting the patient's request for assistance in preventing the slower decline which results from the suspension of life support devices. As for the need to protect the most vulnerable individuals, it is clear that persons with incurable illnesses who experience high levels of pain may generally be ascribed to this category. But it is also opportune to observe that if those who are kept alive by artificial means of support are legally considered to be able, under certain conditions, to take the decision to end their existence by suspending such treatment, there is no reason why the same persons, under certain conditions, cannot also decide to end their existence with the help of others.[599]

The Italian legislature has not yet adopted a regulation following the Constitutional Court's decision. However, in November 2021, the ethical board of the health authority of Marche has given the green light to a 43-year-old patient's request for assisted suicide. The patient, who is referred to as Mario, was left quadriplegic after a car accident 11 years ago.[600]

In December 2020, the Austrian Constitutional Court also found the blanket ban on assisted suicide unconstitutional, stating

> On the one hand, free self-determination encompasses the individual's decision how to conduct his/her life. On the other hand, free self-determination also includes the decision if and for what reasons an individual wants to end his/her life in dignity. All of that depends on the individual's convictions and attitudes and is a matter of autonomous decision-making.

---

[597] *DJ Fabo* [2019] Italian Constitutional Court Judgment No 242/2019. Fabiano Antoniani, also known as DJ Fabo, was left with tetraplegia after a car accident in 2014. Marco Cappato drove him to Switzerland, where DJ Fabo would receive suicide assistance from Dignitas. After he informed the authorities, Mr Cappato was prosecuted in Italy for assisting DJ Fabo.

[598] *DJ Fabo Case*, [2.3.1], English translation of the case as provided on the Court's official website has been used and can be found at https://www.cortecostituzionale.it/documenti/download/doc/recent_judgments/Sentenza_n_242_del_2019_Modugno_en.pdf.

[599] *DJ Fabo Case*, [2.3.8].

[600] Martuscelli (2021) Italian authorities clear way for country's first assisted suicide. In: Politico. https://www.politico.eu/article/italy-authorities-first-assisted-suicide/.

> The right to free self-determination, as derived from the Constitution, covers not only the decision by and the action of the person willing to commit suicide, but also that person's right to avail himself/herself of the assistance of a third party (willing to provide such assistance). The person willing to commit suicide may, in various ways, be dependent on another person's assistance in order to actually implement his/her self-determined decision to end his/her life by the means chosen. Hence, the person willing to commit suicide has the right to selfdetermined dying in dignity; to this end, he/she must have the possibility of using the assistance of a willing third party.[601]

Due to the importance of the right to self-determination, the Court refused the Government's argument that it enjoyed a wide margin of appreciation in the matter of assisted dying.[602] Similar to the German Constitutional Court's approach, the Austrian Constitutional Court also did not make assisted suicide dependent on the existence of an irremediable condition or unbearable suffering. An interesting difference in the Austrian approach was that the Court did not see the matter as an attempt to strike a balance between Articles 2 and 8 of the Convention. Alongside the right to self-determination, Article 2 also obliged the State to permit assisted dying since it was '*a priori* wrong to infer a duty to live from the right to protection of life enshrined in Article 2 and thus [made] the subject of this fundamental right an addressee of the State's duty of protection'.[603]

The Austrian Parliament passed a law regulating assisted suicide under strict requirements, effective after 1st of January 2022.[604] According to section 6 of the new law, a competent adult, who has a persistent autonomous request to end his or her life, is eligible for assisted suicide if he or she is unbearably suffering from (1) a terminal illness or (2) a serious incurable illness with symptoms that permanently impair the person. The request must be supplemented with two physician assessments, one of who should be a palliative care specialist, in line with section 7. Section 8 sets a 12-week waiting period, which can be reduced to two weeks in cases where the patient is suffering unbearably and has entered the terminal phase.

The majority of the public supports the legalization of physician-assisted dying in Spain.[605] The Parliament recently passed a law legalizing assisted dying, which came into force three months after its publication in the Official Gazette on 25 March 2021.[606] Assisted dying has been on the Portuguese Parliament's agenda as well.[607] In Ireland, a bill on assisted dying has passed the second stage and is waiting to be

---

[601] *Austrian Case on Assisted Suicide* [2020] VfGH G 139/2019-71 31, English translation of the case as provided under the Court's official website has been used and can be found at https://www.vfgh.gv.at/downloads/G_139-2019_EN_shortened_Version_Website.pdf.

[602] *Austrian Case on Assisted Suicide*, p. 33.

[603] *Austrian Case on Assisted Suicide*, p. 33.

[604] Austria, Federal Act on the Establishment of Dying Wills (*Bundesgesetz über die Errichtung von Sterbeverfügungen – Sterbeverfügungsgesetz, StVfG*) BGBI. I Nr. 242/2021, 31 December 2021.

[605] Bernal-Carcelén (2020), p. 113.

[606] Spain, The Organic Law for the Regulation of Euthanasia (*Ley Orgánica 3/2021, de 24 de marzo, de regulación de la eutanasia*) BOE no 72, 25 March 2021, 34037–34049.

[607] Demony (2020) Pro-Euthanasia Bills Get Green Light in Portugal, Negotiations Ahead. In: Reuters. https://www.reuters.com/article/idUSKBN20E2F4.

reviewed by a select committee.[608] Although we are still far away from a European consensus, the right to die continues to be a subject of heated debate.

3.7 Canada

Canada is one of the exemplary jurisdictions in the development of the right to die. Despite the primary focus on the ECtHR and its member States, it is beneficial to analyse the two cornerstone cases from the Canadian jurisprudence for a better perspective. Developments in one legal system tend to influence others, especially in the field of human rights where the values originate from the mere existence of humans as individuals. This is seen in the case law of the ECtHR and some of its member States where referral has been made to the Canadian Supreme Court's judgments. Two specific cases will be examined here: first, the Rodriguez Case from 1993, which had upheld the prohibition on physician-assisted suicide and second, the Carter Case from 2015, which has struck down the same provision, ultimately decriminalizing physician-assisted suicide.

3.7.1 The Rodriguez Case

Before moving on to the circumstances of the case, the relevant provisions will be laid out for a better understanding of the decisions.

> Canadian Criminal Code
>
> Section 241: Counselling or Aiding Suicide: Every one who (a) counsels a person to commit suicide, or (b) aids or abets a person to commit suicide, whether suicide ensues or not, is guilty of an indictable offence and liable to imprisonment for a term not exceeding fourteen years.[609]
>
> Canadian Charter of Rights and Freedoms
>
> Section 1: Rights and freedoms in Canada: The Canadian Charter of Rights and Freedoms guarantees the rights and freedoms set out in it subject only to such reasonable limits prescribed by law as can be demonstrably justified in a free and democratic society.
>
> Section 7: Life, liberty and security of person: Everyone has the right to life, liberty and security of the person and the right not to be deprived thereof except in accordance with the principles of fundamental justice.
>
> Section 12: Treatment or punishment: Everyone has the right not to be subjected to any cruel and unusual treatment or punishment.

---

608 Ireland, Dying with Dignity Bill 24 of 2020; Hurley (2020) Dáil Passes Dying with Dignity Bill Aimed at Legalising Assisted Dying. In: RTÉ. https://www.rte.ie/news/politics/2020/1007/1170121-dying-with-dignity/.

609 Canadian Criminal Code, RSC 1985, c C-46 (before the amendment of 16 June 2016).

> Section 15(1): Equality before and under law and equal protection and benefit of law: Every individual is equal before and under the law and has the right to the equal protection and equal benefit of the law without discrimination and, in particular, without discrimination based on race, national or ethnic origin, colour, religion, sex, age or mental or physical disability.[610]

Mrs Rodriguez was a 42-year-old woman, suffering from amyotrophic lateral sclerosis with a life expectancy of 2 to 14 months at the time of the judgment.[611] She wished to receive assistance from a medical professional to end her own life when the time came she no longer believed it would be possible to continue living in a dignified manner. Mrs Rodriguez applied to the Supreme Court of British Columbia, arguing that the criminalization of assisted suicide by section 241(b) of the Criminal Code violated her right to liberty and security under section 7 of the Charter, amounted to a cruel treatment under section 12 and was discriminatory by ignoring her specific circumstances under section 15. Mrs Rodriguez asked the Court to strike down section 241(b), or strike down section 241(b) but suspend the application of the judgment until the Parliament considered the matter meanwhile giving her permission to seek physician-assisted suicide or exclude the group of terminally ill patients from the application of section 241(b).[612]

3.7.1.1 Judgment of the Supreme Court of British Columbia

J Melvin, sitting for the Supreme Court of British Columbia, did not agree with Mrs Rodriguez that the law restricted her from deciding on the time and manner of her death. Rather, it was the physician who was being restricted by the prohibition under section 241(b) of the Criminal Code from providing Mrs Rodriguez with suicide assistance. However, allowing a physician to assist with the suicide of a patient was contrary to the sanctity of life that was inherent in the Canadian Charter and the ethical duties of physicians. J Melvin further stated that the rights under sections 7 and 12 of the Charter were protected against State interference within the context of the criminal justice system. This was not the case for Mrs Rodriguez since she would not face criminal proceedings based on section 241(b) of the Criminal Code. It was Mrs Rodriguez's illness that might have deprived her of her wish, but not State interference. Therefore, J Melvin ruled that there was no violation of sections 7 and

[610] Canadian Charter of Rights and Freedoms, Part I of the Constitution Act, 1982, Schedule B to the Canada Act 1982 (UK), 1982, c 11.

[611] Amyotrophic lateral sclerosis (ALS), which is also called motor neuron disease or Lou Gehrig disease, causes progressive destruction of the nerve cells leading to the loss of muscle functions over time and eventual paralyses. Although there is no harm to the mental capacities of the patient, the disease has no treatment, and death is inevitable, which is usually by suffocation as the breathing muscles lose their function. Death is usually expected within 3 to 5 years after the onset of the disease. Editors of Encyclopedia Britannica (2020) Amyotrophic Lateral Sclerosis. In: Encyclopædia Britannica. https://www.britannica.com/science/amyotrophic-lateral-sclerosis.

[612] Rodriguez v British Columbia (Attorney General) [1992] 18 WCB (2d) 279, [1993] BCWLD 347.

12. J Melvin also referred to a previous case concerning suicide, where a court had ruled that section 7 did not include a right to die.[613] As to Mrs Rodriguez's claim under section 15, J Melvin ruled that section 241(b) of the Criminal Code provided equal protection to all individuals and there was no discrimination against individuals with a physical disability. Section 241(b) aimed to protect the vulnerable, and even if there were a violation of sections 7, 12, and 15 of the Charter, it would be justifiable under section 1. J Melvin dismissed Mrs Rodriguez's application and the case came before the British Columbia Court of Appeal.[614]

3.7.1.2 Judgment of the British Columbia Court of Appeal

The Court of Appeal upheld the decision of the Supreme Court of British Columbia. While Chief Justice McEachern gave a dissenting opinion, Justices Hollinrake and Proudfoot voted for the dismissal of the appeal for different reasons.

CJ McEachern referred to the Morgentaler Case, a case on abortion that had emphasized the importance of human dignity inherent in the Charter, as a starting point to establish his argument in favour of Mrs Rodriguez.[615] CJ McEachern stated

[613] *Burke v Prince Edwards Island* (1991) 93 Nfld PEIR 356 (Supreme Court-Trial Division of Prince Edward Island). The applicant, who was a prisoner at the time, had attempted suicide, and after being rescued, he had started fasting with the intention to end his life. The officials wanted to force-feed him, and the applicant claimed force-feeding was in violation of his Charter rights, claiming s 7 had guaranteed a right to die. Although the judgment was given expeditiously without elaborative assessment, the Court agreed with the applicant that force-feeding or treatment against his will was a violation of s 7. However, the Court rejected the argument that a right to die was inherent within s 7.

[614] *Rodriguez Case-BCSC*, 6–23.

[615] *R v Morgentaler* (1988) 1 SCR 30 (SCC). The Morgentaler Case concerned three doctors who performed illegal abortions under s 251 of the Criminal Code (in force at the time of the decision) that required abortions to be performed only at accredited hospitals and with a certification acquired by the Therapeutic Abortion Committee. Approval for an abortion was given only when the pregnancy endangered the health of the woman. This led women who wished to end their pregnancy in the absence of health issues to search for other means that sometimes meant abortions performed by non-professionals. Dr Morgentaler and two of his colleagues believed that the Criminal Code was restricted women's rights and challenged the law based on the Canadian Charter. By a majority of five to two, the Supreme Court found a violation of s 7 of the Charter. From the majority, CJ Dickson and J Lamer stated: 'State interference with bodily integrity and serious state-imposed psychological stress, at least in the criminal law context, constitutes a breach of security of the person [. . .] Forcing a woman, by threat of criminal sanction, to carry a foetus to term unless she meets certain criteria unrelated to her own priorities and aspirations, is a profound interference with a woman's body and thus an infringement of security of the person.' (32–33) J Wilson further stated: 'To be able to decide what to do and how to do it, to carry out one's own decisions and accept their consequences, seems to me essential to one's self-respect as a human being, and essential to the possibility of that contentment. Such self-respect and contentment are in my judgment fundamental goods for human beings, the worth of life itself being on condition of having or striving for them. If a person were deliberately denied the opportunity of self-respect and that contentment, he would suffer deprivation of his essential humanity.' (164–165) The two other judges in the majority

that the Charter covered the quality and dignity of an individual's life.[616] Contrary to the Supreme Court of British Columbia, CJ McEachern found that section 241(b) of the Criminal Code engaged Mrs Rodriguez's rights under section 7 of the Charter by way of having 'the effect of imposing continued physical and psychological suffering upon her'.[617] He continued to evaluate whether the infringement caused by section 241(b) of the Criminal Code was in accordance with the principles of fundamental justice, but reached the conclusion that 'any provision which imposes an indeterminate period of senseless physical and psychological suffering upon someone who is shortly to die anyway cannot conform with any principle of fundamental justice'.[618] CJ McEachern ruled that the limitation caused by section 241(b) of the Criminal Code did not satisfy the condition of minimal impairment and therefore, could not be justified under section 1 of the Charter.[619] As a result, Mrs Rodriguez and the physician, who were to assist her with suicide, should be exempt from the application of section 241(b) of the Criminal Code if the criteria listed by CJ McEachern were followed. This exemption was provided only for Mrs Rodriguez and anyone else who found herself or himself in a similar situation had to apply to the courts for an exemption.[620]

Although agreeing with a prima facia violation of section 7, J Hollinrake ruled that this violation was justified under the principles of fundamental justice, and there was no need for an evaluation under section 1. J Hollinrake stated that the Morgentaler Case was a reflection of changing public opinion, which was made clear through legislation prior to the Court's judgment. However, physician-assisted suicide had not yet been voiced as a public concern through the Parliament, and there was no indication to that end. The Court would be overstepping its boundaries if it were to dictate a right to die despite the absence of signs of supportive public

---

only found the procedural requirements inconvenient as they caused delays in receiving necessary medical treatment, ultimately violating s 7. They kept their argument limited to cases where the pregnancy endangered the health of the woman, unlike the other three judges.

[616] Rodriguez v British Columbia (Attorney General) (1993) CanLII 1191 (BCCA) [50].

[617] *Rodriguez Case-BCCA*, [60].

[618] *Rodriguez Case-BCCA*, [75].

[619] If there is a violation of a Charter right that is not in accordance with the principles of fundamental justice, such a violation might nevertheless be justified under sec 1. Whether or not a violation is justified by sec 1 is determined through 'the Oakes test'. According to the Oakes test, any restriction to a Charter right (1) must pursue a pressing and substantial objective, and (2) must be proportionate to its objective. A restriction is proportionate if there is a rational connection between the objective and the means to achieve it, if there is minimal impairment to the relevant Charter right and if the effects of the restriction are proportional. *R v Oakes* (1986) 1 RCS 103 (SCC) 105–106; *Rodriguez Case-BCCA*, [82].

[620] CJ McEachern listed a detailed procedural order that included, among other things, the confirmation of Mrs Rodriguez's autonomous and well-considered decision to end her life, the terminal and hopeless nature of her illness, and the unbearable physical or severe psychological suffering experienced by her. The authenticity of her decision had to be confirmed by an independent psychiatrist. The final act that ended Mrs Rodriguez's life was to be carried out by herself. *Rodriguez Case-BCCA*, [100]-[110].

opinion, especially in a matter that involved highly philosophical and moral discussions.[621]

J Proudfoot agreed with J Hollinrake except for the approach to the Morgentaler Case. In her opinion, Morgentaler was about the preservation of health, contrary to this case that concerned the ending of life. Moreover, Morgentaler was a criminal case, and the criminal action had already occurred prior to the Court's judgment. However, there was no criminal action on which a judgment could be given in the present case. According to J Proudfoot, Mrs Rodriguez sought a declaration to protect an unknown person from future criminal liability, which could not be granted by any legal authority.[622] J Proudfoot furthermore agreed that physician-assisted suicide was a controversial topic in many aspects and should be left to the Parliament to resolve.[623]

Mrs Rodriguez's appeal was dismissed by two votes to one by the British Columbia Court of Appeal, and the case came before the Supreme Court of Canada (SCC).

3.7.1.3 Judgment of the Supreme Court of Canada

The following questions were to be answered by the Court:

> Does s. 241(b) of the Criminal Code of Canada infringe or deny, in whole or in part, the rights and freedoms guaranteed by ss. 7, 12 and 15(1) of the Canadian Charter of Rights and Freedoms?
>
> If so, is it justified by s. 1 of the Canadian Charter of Rights and Freedoms and therefore not inconsistent with the Constitution Act, 1982?[624]

The appeal was dismissed by a majority of 5 (Justices Sopinka, La Forest, Gonthier, Iacobucci, and Major) to 4 (Justices L'Hereux-Dubé, McLachlin, Cory, and CJ Lamer).

3.7.1.3.1 Justice Sopinka on Behalf of the Majority

J Sopinka did not agree with the argument that section 7 could not be engaged because Mrs Rodriguez's situation was not caused by State interference. He also rejected the argument that section 7 was not applicable since Mrs Rodriguez was not within the criminal justice system.[625] Based on the Morgentaler Case, J Sopinka stated:

---

[621] *Rodriguez Case-BCCA*, [142]-[144].

[622] *Rodriguez Case-BCCA*, [168].

[623] *Rodriguez Case-BCCA*, [172].

[624] Rodriguez v British Columbia (Attorney General) (1993) 3 SCR 519 (SCC) 543.

[625] *Rodriguez Case-SCC*, 584–585.

> There is no question [...] that personal autonomy, at least with respect to the right to make choices concerning one's own body, control over one's physical and psychological integrity, and basic human dignity are encompassed within the security of the person, at least to the extent of freedom from criminal prohibitions which interfere with these.[626]

Section 241(b) of the Criminal Code had the effect of preventing Mrs Rodriguez from seeking assistance to end her life, when she was no longer physically capable of doing so herself, and forcing her to face an end she feared and found undignified. Since section 241(b) impinged on Mrs Rodriguez's personal autonomy, her right to security ('considered in the context of the life and liberty interest') under section 7 of the Charter was engaged. Therefore, it should be examined whether this engagement was in accordance with the principles of fundamental justice.[627]

The life, liberty, or security interest of the person that is being subject to restriction must be balanced against principles of fundamental justice, 'upon which there is some consensus that they are vital or fundamental to our societal notion of justice' and which can be 'identified with some precision and applied to situations in a manner which yields an understandable result'.[628] When deciding which fundamental principles were at play, one should look at the historical background and the rationality behind the provisions together while considering the changes or developments within the society. The prohibition on assisted suicide served the State's purpose to protect life and the vulnerable, which was part of the notion of the sanctity of life. Suicide and attempted suicide were decriminalized in Canada in 1972. However, decriminalization of suicide was not an indication that personal autonomy had overruled the State's interest in protecting life, but an acknowledgement that a criminal approach towards a person who had attempted suicide was not the appropriate response.[629] J Sopinka then considered the difference between refusing life-sustaining treatment and active termination of life by euthanasia or physician-assisted suicide. The Law Reform Commission had emphasized the risk of abuse inherent in decriminalizing assisted suicide for the terminally ill and the difficulty in determining with certainty the intention of the person assisting with suicide.[630] Although it remained against decriminalizing assisted suicide, the Law Reform Commission suggested an amendment to section 241(b) of the Criminal Code by which prosecution of suicide assistance would be dependent on a written authorization from the Attorney General. By doing so, the special circumstances of people suffering unbearably from a terminal illness could be taken into consideration. However, the Reform Commission retracted its suggestion later in a report due to

---

[626] *Rodriguez Case-SCC*, 588.

[627] *Rodriguez Case-SCC*, 588–589.

[628] *Rodriguez Case-SCC*, 590–591.

[629] *Rodriguez Case-SCC*, 597–598.

[630] Law Reform Commission of Canada (1982) Euthanasia, Aiding Suicide and Cessation of Treatment, Working Paper 28. http://www.lareau-law.ca/LRCWP28.pdf, pp. 52–55.

the negative reaction.[631] J Sopinka considered this to be a clear sign that public opinion did not support a change in the legislation.[632] Other jurisdictions had similar approaches to assisted suicide and a blanket ban seemed to be the norm. J Sopinka also referred to the R v UK Case,[633] in which section 2 of the UK's 1961 Suicide Act was evaluated under Article 8 of the ECHR, and no incompatibility was found. Evidence suggesting the existence of an involuntary active euthanasia practice in the Netherlands was considered a side effect of relaxing the complete ban on assisted dying.[634]

Although the sanctity of life was not an absolute notion and could be limited with considerations of personal autonomy and human dignity, there was a recognized distinction between passive and active forms of medical end-of-life decisions. Legally allowing physician-assisted suicide could undermine the respect for human life. Considering the risk of abuse and the difficulty of providing adequate safeguards, the blanket ban on physician-assisted suicide was in accordance with the fundamental principles of justice and there was no violation of section 7 of the Charter.[635]

Moving on to the assessment of whether there was a violation of section 12 of the Charter, J Sopinka held that a mere prohibition within the Criminal Code, which applied to every member of the society, could not, on its own, constitute cruel and unusual treatment. There needed to be 'more active state process in operation, involving an exercise of state control over the individual, in order for the state action in question, whether it be positive action, inaction or prohibition' in order to talk about treatment within the meaning of section 12. This was, however, not the case in Mrs Rodriguez's situation. Therefore, section 241(b) of the Criminal Code did not violate section 12 of the Charter.[636]

J Sopinka did not find it necessary to elaborate on whether the prohibition on assisted suicide caused a discriminatory situation for terminally ill patients, who were not physically able to end their own lives, within the meaning of section 15 of the Charter. According to J Sopinka, any violation of section 15 would nevertheless be saved by section 1. As mentioned before, section 241(b) of the Criminal Code served the legitimate purpose of protecting people's lives against the intervention of others. A blanket ban was the best means to achieve that purpose because an exception to the prohibition on assisted suicide carried the risk of becoming a slippery slope due to the difficulty of establishing adequate safeguards.[637]

---

[631] Law Reform Commission of Canada (1983) Euthanasia, Aiding Suicide and Cessation of Treatment, Report 20. http://www.lareau-law.ca/LRCReport20.pdf; For a critical analysis of Working Paper 28 and Report 20 see Samek (1984).

[632] *Rodriguez Case-SCC*, 600–601.

[633] See Sect. 4.1.1 'The R v UK Case'.

[634] *Rodriguez Case-SCC*, 601–605.

[635] *Rodriguez Case-SCC*, 605–608.

[636] *Rodriguez Case-SCC*, 612.

[637] *Rodriguez Case-SCC*, 613–615.

J Sopinka dismissed the case while concluding that section 241(b) of the Criminal Code did not violate sections 7 and 12 of the Charter, and the assumed violation of section 15 was justified under section 1.

3.7.1.3.2 Dissenting Opinion of Chief Justice Lamer

CJ Lamer was of the opinion that section 241(b) of the Criminal Code infringed the right to equality under section 15 of the Charter insofar as the blanket ban on assisted suicide deprived people, who were physically not able to end their own life without the assistance of another, of their option to choose suicide.[638] Referring to the Andrews Case,[639] CJ Lamer described discrimination as the following:

> [A] distinction, whether intentional or not but based on grounds relating to personal characteristics of the individual or group, which has the effect of imposing burdens, obligations, or disadvantages on such individual or group not imposed upon others, or which withholds or limits access to opportunities, benefits, and advantages available to other members of society.[640]

CJ Lamer emphasized that while an intent to discriminate was not required, it was sufficient that the provision in question had an adverse effect on a certain group of people due to their specific characteristics. Although section 241(b) of the Criminal Code applied to all individuals and had no intention of discriminating, it did nevertheless cause inequality by preventing people physically unable to end their own lives without assistance from choosing suicide, which was an option legally available to others.[641] Since this inequality amounted to a discriminatory situation within the meaning of section 15 of the Charter, CJ Lamer evaluated whether the infringement could be saved under section 1.[642] Although section 241(b) of the Criminal Code aimed to protect the vulnerable, the context of this protection had changed once attempted suicide had been decriminalized. It was evident not only from the decriminalization of suicide but also from the developments within the medical field in patients' rights, for example the right to refuse life-sustaining treatment, that self-determination had gained considerable importance. CJ Lamer further stated:

> An individual's right to control his or her own body does not cease to obtain merely because that individual has become dependant on others for the physical maintenance of that body; indeed, in such circumstances, this type of autonomy is often most critical to an individual's feeling of self-worth and dignity.[643]

---

[638] *Rodriguez Case-SCC*, 544.

[639] Andrews v Law Society of British Columbia (1989) 1 SCR 143 (SCC).

[640] *Rodriguez Case-SCC*, 545–546.

[641] *Rodriguez Case-SCC*, 549–551.

[642] *Rodriguez Case-SCC*, 552.

[643] *Rodriguez Case-SCC*, 559–560.

Despite its legitimate aim, it had to be evaluated whether section 241(b) of the Criminal Code was proportionate or, in other words, whether it struck 'a reasonable balance'.[644] The necessity of a blanket ban on assisted suicide was based on the argument that it could not be positively determined if suicide assistance was motivated only by reasons of compassion. However, according to CJ Lamer, this argument falsely assumed that every person who needed the assistance of another to commit suicide would be vulnerable. Despite the valid concerns over the risk of abuse, the blanket ban on assisted suicide was overreaching as it affected people who were neither vulnerable nor in need of protection and who were capable of making an autonomous decision. Especially the dire circumstances under which Mrs Rodriguez found herself could not be ignored. CJ Lamer concluded that the blanket ban did not comply with the minimal impairment condition and that the violation of section 15 was not saved under section 1.[645] Therefore, section 241(b) should be declared invalid, subject to a one-year suspension during which the Parliament could decide how to address the matter and until then, a constitutional exemption should be made available to Mrs Rodriguez following the conditions laid out by CJ Lamer, which were similar to those in J McEachern's dissenting opinion in the Court of Appeal's judgment. Until the Parliament would address the matter, others could apply to the Court to receive a constitutional exemption as well. While the conditions for Mrs Rodriguez would serve as a guideline, each case would need to be examined on its own merits. CJ Lamer also stated that the person did not need to be terminally ill to receive suicide assistance since that condition did not comply with his evaluation under section 15.[646]

3.7.1.3.3 Dissenting Opinion of Justices L'Hereux-Dubé and McLachlin

J McLachlin wrote for the dissenting opinion that the matter at hand with the present case was not one of discrimination under section 15, but rather one related to section 7 of the Charter.[647] J McLachlin did not agree that the lack of broad acceptance of physician-assisted suicide or the fact that the Parliament had not addressed the matter should be determinative in considering Mrs Rodriguez's claim. The prohibition on assisted suicide had the effect 'to deny to some people the choice of ending their lives solely because they [were] physically unable to do so'.[648] In light of the Morgentaler Case, J McLachlin stated that 'security of the person [had] an element of personal autonomy, protecting individuals' dignity and privacy with respect to decisions concerning their own body'.[649] Therefore, the question to be answered was

[644] *Rodriguez Case-SCC*, 561.

[645] *Rodriguez Case-SCC*, 567–569.

[646] *Rodriguez Case-SCC*, 578–580.

[647] *Rodriguez Case-SCC*, 616.

[648] *Rodriguez Case-SCC*, 617.

[649] *Rodriguez Case-SCC*, 618.

whether the limitation caused by section 241(b) of the Criminal Code on Mrs Rodriguez's freedom to make a decision concerning her own body was in accordance with the principles of fundamental justice. According to J McLachlin, considerations of the risk of abuse and respect for life belonged under section 1 of the Charter; and these considerations had no place under the principles of fundamental justice. J McLachlin disagreed with J Sopinka's statement that active participation in another's death was 'intrinsically morally and legally wrong'.[650] The criminal justice system took into considerations the circumstances under which death had occurred and accepted the possibility of justifying an act that caused the death of another, for example self-defense. Therefore, it could not be said that the State had an absolute interest in punishing all types of involvement in someone else's death. J McLachlin did not accept the argument that allowing assisted suicide would diminish the value of life either. The value of life was a subjective concept that depended on the individual's view on and expectation from his or her life. Mrs Rodriguez was arbitrarily denied the choice to end her life that was legally available to other people due to her physical status, resulting in the violation of section 7.[651] Once it was established that section 241(b) of the Criminal Code caused arbitrariness, the burden of proof to demonstrate that this arbitrariness could be saved in light of societal interests under section 1 of the Charter was on the State.

According to J McLachlin, the justification of section 241(b) of the Criminal Code was based on two concerns: first, fear that assisted suicide would be used as a 'cloak' for murder and second, the consent of the person, who wishes to end their life, would not be voluntary.[652] Although these fears were real, they were not sufficient to override Mrs Rodriguez's right under section 7 of the Charter. While other provisions of the Criminal Code would continue to punish criminal acts carried out under the pretext of assisted suicide, an additional safeguard of requiring a court order could ensure that only those who had made an autonomous decision would receive suicide assistance. In light of the possibility of a less restrictive measure, the violation of section 7 could not be justified under section 1.[653]

J McLachlin disagreed that the matter should be left to the Parliament. The Parliament had already acted on the subject of suicide and assisted suicide. The question before the Court concerned the manner in which the Parliament had acted, namely whether the way it had chosen to act was 'fundamentally fair to all'.[654]

[650] *Rodriguez Case-SCC*, 601, cited by J McLachlin at 623.

[651] *Rodriguez Case-SCC*, 624.

[652] *Rodriguez Case-SCC*, 625–626.

[653] *Rodriguez Case-SCC*, 626–628.

[654] *Rodriguez Case-SCC*, 629.

3.7.1.3.4 Dissenting Opinion of Justice Cory

Essentially agreeing with the other dissenting opinions, J Cory found applicability of both sections 7 and 15 of the Charter. As an integral part of life, death was also subject to constitutional protection and '[s]tate prohibitions that would force a dreadful, painful death on a rational but incapacitated terminally ill patient [were] an affront to human dignity'.[655] Since patients were already allowed to choose a dignified death by refusing life-sustaining treatment, J Cory found no reason to prohibit exercising one's choice of a dignified death with the help of a third party in cases of terminally ill patients. J Cory agreed with the remedy proposed by CJ Lamer.[656]

3.7.2 *The Carter Case*

22 years after the Rodriguez Case, the SCC overturned its judgment that upheld the blanket ban on assisted suicide and unanimously struck down section 241(b) of the Criminal Code with the Carter Case.[657]

Although the relevant law was the same as in the Rodriguez Case, the Court took into consideration the developments in the area of end-of-life decisions and changes in the social perception of the matter while interpreting the sections of the Charter relevant to the case.

Gloria Taylor was diagnosed with ALS in 2009, the same disease suffered by Mrs Rodriguez. Ms Taylor did not want to 'live in a bedridden state, stripped of dignity and independence' and, therefore, wanted to obtain a physician's assistance in dying. As she did not have the financial means to travel to Switzerland for suicide assistance, section 241(b) of the Criminal Code forced her into a dilemma between ending her life prematurely while she was still physically able to do so on her own or living out a painful end that she considered miserable and degrading.[658]

Kay Carter has suffered from spinal stenosis since 2008.[659] Her physical condition was deteriorating rapidly, and she suffered chronic pain. Kay Carter asked her daughter, Lee Carter, and her son-in-law, Hollis Johnson, to help her arrange a trip to Switzerland, where she could end her life with the assistance of Dignitas. After Lee Carter and Hollis Johnson had helped her with the arrangements, Kay Carter ended

[655] *Rodriguez Case-SCC*, 630.

[656] *Rodriguez Case-SCC*, 631.

[657] *Carter v Canada (Attorney General)* 2015 SCC 5, [2015] 1 SCR 331.

[658] *Carter Case-SCC*, [12]-[13].

[659] Spinal stenosis occurs when the narrowing of the spaces within the spine causes pressure to the nerves. Symptoms can vary depending on the severity and location. Mayo Clinic (2020) Spinal Stenosis. https://www.mayoclinic.org/diseases-conditions/spinal-stenosis/symptoms-causes/syc-20352961.

her life in the Dignitas clinic in 2010. Although Lee Carter and Hollis Johnson did not face prosecution, they believed that Kay Carter should have been able to choose physician-assisted death in Canada rather than having to travel somewhere else.[660]

Based on sections 7 and 15 of the Charter, the applicants challenged section 241 (b) and other related sections of the Criminal Code that prohibit physician-assisted dying before the Supreme Court of British Columbia.[661]

3.7.2.1 Judgment of the Supreme Court of British Columbia

After evaluating the current status of medical end-of-life practices in Canada, J Smith for the Supreme Court of British Columbia examined a large number of evidence consisting of expert witness testimonies on the ethical acceptability of physician-assisted dying, the position of medical associations, public opinion, and committee reports on physician-assisted dying and prosecution policies on assisted suicide cases.[662] Based on the evidence, J Smith concluded that there was a consensus on the 'extremely high value' of human life and that current medical end-of-life decisions (palliative sedation and withdrawal or withholding treatment) were ethically acceptable.[663] Although there was no consensus on the acceptability of physician-assisted dying, there was, nevertheless, a strong consensus that if it were to be accepted as ethical, it would only be so when it was 'consistent with the patient's wishes and best interests, and in order to relieve suffering'.[664] Afterward, J Smith continued to examine to a great extent the situation in jurisdictions that are permissive of physician-assisted dying,[665] including the Netherlands, Belgium, and Switzerland. J Smith stated that 'although none of these systems [had] achieved perfection', the view was that 'they work well in protecting patients from abuse while allowing competent patients to choose the timing of their deaths'.[666] Furthermore, evidence suggested that legitimizing physician-assisted dying would not necessarily have a negative impact on palliative care or physician-patient relationship.[667]

---

[660] *Carter Case-SCC*, [17]-[18].

[661] Apart from s 241(b), the applicants had challenged ss 14, 21, 22 and 222 of the Criminal Code as well. The applicants were accompanied by the British Columbia Civil Liberties Association (BCCLA), a non-governmental organization that raises funds and takes an active part in litigation on matters of civil liberties and human rights. The Notice of Civil Claim submitted by the applicants to the Supreme Court of British Columbia can be found at BCCLA (2012) Carter v Canada Case Documents. https://bccla.org/2012/12/carter-et-al-v-attorney-general-of-canada/.

[662] *Carter v Canada (Attorney General)* [2012] BCSC 886 (BCSC) [232]-[307].

[663] *Carter Case-BCSC*, [357].

[664] *Carter Case-BCSC*, [358].

[665] *Carter Case-BCSC*, [359]-[645].

[666] *Carter Case-BCSC*, [685].

[667] *Carter Case-BCSC*, [739], [746].

Regarding the evidence on the Dutch and Belgian practices, J Smith acknowledged that the legal frameworks in these States were aimed to regulate an already existing practice in the medical culture and that considerable progress had been achieved towards that end.[668] The history in the Netherlands and Belgium that had led to the respective legal frameworks was not comparable to Canada since there was no existing practice and Canadian physicians had been compliant with the ban on physician-assisted suicide. Thus, it was difficult to deduce whether there would be a compliance problem with the safeguards if the ban were to be lifted.[669]

Considering whether it was possible to place adequate safeguards, J Smith concluded that 'the risk inherent in permitting physician-assisted death [could] be identified and very substantially minimized through a carefully-designed system imposing stringent limits that [were] scrupulously monitored and enforced'.[670] Upon examining a large amount of evidence and finding that the SCC's judgment in the Rodriguez Case did not prevent her from ruling on the case in hand, J Smith found a violation of sections 7 and 15 of the Charter that could not be saved under section 1.[671]

3.7.2.2 Judgment of the British Columbia Court of Appeal

By a two-to-one vote, the Court of Appeal set aside J Smith's decision. The majority, Justices Newbury and Saunders, ruled that both the Court of Appeal and the Supreme Court of British Columbia were bound by the SCC's judgment in the Rodriguez Case. It had already been decided that section 241(b) of the Criminal Code did not engage section 7 of the Charter, and any alleged violation of section 15 would be justified under section 1. The SCC's assessment in the Rodriguez Case applied to the present case as well, and the developments since then did not affect the outcome.[672] In agreement with J Smith, CJ Finch stated that section 241(b) of the Criminal Code deprived the applicants of their rights under section 7 of the Charter, that this deprivation did not comply with the minimal impairment condition and therefore could not be justified under section 1.[673]

3.7.2.3 Judgment of the Supreme Court of Canada

After the Court of Appeal's dismissal, the case came before the SCC. Before moving on to the evaluation of section 241() of the Criminal Code's compatibility with

668 *Carter Case-BCSC*, [660].

669 *Carter Case-BCSC*, [680], [683].

670 *Carter Case-BCSC*, [883].

671 *Carter Case-BCSC*, [1009]-[1383].

672 *Carter v Canada (Attorney General)* [2013] BCCA 435 (BCCA) [322]-[324].

673 *Carter Case-BCCA*, [171], [177].

sections 7 and 15 of the Charter, the Court assessed whether J Smith was bound by the Court's judgment in the Rodriguez Case. The Court stated that lower courts could reconsider matters that had already been settled by higher courts when the case brought into question a new legal issue or when there have been changes to the circumstances or evidence that have a considerable impact on the court's assessment.[674] Both of these conditions were met. Since the Rodriguez Case, the legal framework relating to the analysis under section 7 of the Charter and the evidence on the risk of abuse had developed in a way that could lead to a different conclusion. Therefore, J Smith was not mistaken in her decision to reconsider the case.[675] The Court moved on to its evaluation under section 7.

The Court agreed with J Smith that the prohibition on physician-assisted dying interfered with the right to life under section 7 only as far as it put some individuals like Ms Taylor into a dilemma of having to choose a premature death while they were still physically able to end their own lives without assistance.[676] Considerations of human dignity and personal autonomy belonged under the rights to liberty and security.[677] The Court stated

> An individual's response to a grievous and irremediable medical condition is a matter critical to their dignity and autonomy. The law allows people in this situation to request palliative sedation, refuse artificial nutrition and hydration, or request the removal of life-sustaining medical equipment, but denies them the right to request a physician's assistance in dying. This interferes with their ability to make decisions concerning their bodily integrity and medical care and thus trenches on liberty. And, by leaving people like Ms. Taylor to endure intolerable suffering, it impinges on their security of person.[678]

Referring to the AC v Manitoba Case, the Court emphasized the importance of patient autonomy in medicine, namely the freedom of competent individuals 'to make decisions about their bodily integrity', and the protection of this autonomy, which was guaranteed by section 7 of the Charter.[679] Whether the patient's decision to refuse treatment carried the risk of death did not negate his or her right to self-determination.[680] The Court accepted that in cases of patients who suffered unbearably from a severe and irremediable condition, the decision to choose physician-assisted suicide could be a 'deeply personal response' stemming from the individual's 'sense of dignity and personal integrity' and should be protected under the rights to liberty and security.[681]

---

[674] *Carter Case-SCC*, [44].

[675] *Carter Case-SCC*, [45]-[48].

[676] *Carter Case-SCC*, [58]; *Carter Case-BCSC*, [1322].

[677] *Carter Case-SCC*, [62].

[678] *Carter Case-SCC*, [66].

[679] *Carter Case-SCC*, [67]; citing *AC v Manitoba (Director of Child and Family Services)* 2009 SCC 30, [2009] 2 SCR 181, [39].

[680] *Carter Case-SCC*, [67]; The majority in the AC Case used the phrase 'the right to decide one's own fate' *AC v Manitoba Case*, [40].

[681] *Carter Case-SCC*, [69]; citing J Smith *Carter Case-BCSC*, [1326].

The Court moved on to evaluate whether the deprivation caused by section 241 (b) of the Criminal Code was in accordance with the principles of fundamental justice. Based on its case law on section 7, the Court named three central principles: 'laws that impinge on life, liberty and security of the person must not be arbitrary, overbroad, or have consequences that are grossly disproportionate to their object'.[682]

The Court rejected the Attorney General's claim that the objective of section 241 (b) of the Criminal Code was 'the preservation of life'. Agreeing with J Smith, the Court specified a narrower objective, which was the protection of the vulnerable.[683] This is an important point that signals a shift in the Court's approach towards physician-assisted dying. In Rodriguez, J Sopinka had also defined the objective as the protection of the vulnerable. However, the preservation of life had played a determining role in his arguments and led to a different balance under the principles of fundamental justice.[684] The Court made it clear that claims of morality and public interests were to be addressed under the analysis of section 1 of the Charter.[685]

Since the blanket ban achieved the objective of protecting the vulnerable, the Court did not find section 241(b) of the Criminal Code arbitrary.[686] After establishing a rational connection, the Court examined whether the prohibition on physician-assisted suicide reached outside of the scope of its objective, namely whether it was overbroad. The Court agreed with J Smith that section 241 (b) exceeded its objective by affecting those who were not vulnerable.[687] The argument that a blanket ban was the most practical way of ensuring the protection of the vulnerable because it was difficult to distinguish who was actually in need of protection was not accepted. Whether the State had chosen the least restrictive way of ensuring its objective was a matter to consider under the section 1 analysis.[688] Since the Court had already established that the prohibition on physician-assisted suicide was overbroad, it did not find it necessary to evaluate whether the prohibition was also grossly disproportionate to its objective.[689]

The Court did not examine whether there was a violation of section 15 since it was already established that section 7 had been violated.

---

[682] *Carter Case-SCC*, [72]; referring to *Canada (Attorney General) v Bedford* 2013 SCC 72, [2013] SCR 1101, [96]-[123].

[683] *Carter Case-SCC*, [74]-[78]; referring to *Carter Case-BCSC*, [1190].

[684] *Rodriguez Case-SCC*, 595.

[685] *Carter Case-SCC*, [79]-[80]. This was another important difference between Rodriguez and Carter. In Rodriguez, only J McLachlin had made this distinction. Under the analysis of principles of fundamental justice, the burden of proof is on the individual who claims there has been an interference with his or her Charter rights. The State carries the burden of proof under sec 1 when demonstrating that such interference is necessary in light of the societal interests. *Bedford Case*, [123]-[129].

[686] *Carter Case-SCC*, [84].

[687] *Carter Case-SCC*, [86]; referring to *Carter Case-BCSC*, [1136].

[688] *Carter Case-SCC*, [88].

[689] The Court nevertheless agreed with J Smith that the deprivation caused by the prohibition on physician-assisted suicide was severe. *Carter Case-SCC*, [90].

According to the Court's case law, justifiably balancing a violation of section 7 with competing societal interests under section 1 of the Charter was difficult. Although it was accepted that section 241(b) of the Criminal Code served 'a pressing and substantial objective', it had to be examined whether it was proportionate.[690] At this point, the Court reminded of the 'high degree of deference' accorded to the legislature when dealing with complex social issues. However, the blanket nature of the legislature's response somewhat reduced the degree of deference.[691]

The proportionality of the blanket ban on assisted suicide depended on whether this measure had a rational connection to its objective, whether it was minimally impairing the rights of the individuals it affected and whether the benefits of the prohibition outweighed its negative effects. The Court accepted the rational connection between the prohibition on assisted suicide and its objective to protect the vulnerable.[692] To identify if the prohibition satisfied the condition of minimal impairment, the Court asked whether the blanket ban was the 'least drastic means of achieving the legislative objective'.[693] In light of the vast amount of evidence examined, J Smith had concluded that a blanket ban was not the least drastic measure to achieve the objective of protecting the vulnerable. It was possible to establish safeguards to prevent abuse. The Attorney General argued before the Court that evidence had also shown problems with compliance with the law in permissive jurisdictions. According to the Attorney General, it was an error to attribute these compliance problems to cultural differences and to suppose they would not occur in Canada.[694]

New evidence was presented to the Court by Professor Etienne Montero regarding the euthanasia practice in Belgium, suggesting that the safeguards were not effective in preventing the practice from extending. To demonstrate the existence of a slippery slope, Professor Montero gave examples of euthanasia cases in minors and patients with psychiatric illnesses. The Court responded by pointing out the discretion exercised by the supervisory body, CFCEE, in interpreting the legal framework and the fact that the Belgian Parliament had not taken any measures to restrict that discretion. The Court agreed that the particular historical background of the Belgian practice limited the insight it could offer on how a possible practice in Canada would operate.[695]

The Attorney General further argued that many components affected a patient's decision-making capacity, and a blanket ban on assisted suicide was necessary due to the difficulty of identifying vulnerability. The Court found no viable reason to assume that a patient, who had the capacity to refuse life-sustaining treatment, would be more vulnerable when deciding to request suicide assistance. The risks relating to

[690] *Carter Case-SCC*, [95]-[96]; see *R v Oakes Case*.

[691] *Carter Case-SCC*, [97]-[98].

[692] *Carter Case-SCC*, [100].

[693] *Carter Case-SCC*, [103].

[694] *Carter Case-SCC*, [108].

[695] *Carter Case-SCC*, [110]-[113].

capacity already existed in other medical end-of-life decisions.[696] Towards the Attorney General's argument of an inevitable slippery slope in the absence of a blanket ban, the Court responded: 'Anecdotal examples of controversial cases abroad were cited in support of this argument, only to be countered by anecdotal examples of systems that work well. The resolution of the issue before us falls to be resolved not by competing anecdotes, but by the evidence.'[697] The Court found no error in J Smith's assessment of the evidence and agreed that the blanket ban on assisted suicide did not comply with the minimal impairment condition.[698] Since it was established that section 241(b) of the Criminal Code was not minimally impairing, the Court did not find it necessary to assess whether the benefits of the prohibition outweighed its negative impacts.

Section 241(b) of the Criminal Code violated Ms Taylor's right to life, liberty, and security under section 7 of the Charter, and this violation was not saved by section 1. The Court declared sections 14[699] and 241(b) of the Criminal Code void to the extent they prohibited physician-assisted dying for a competent adult who gave clear consent and who suffered intolerably due to a 'grievous and irremediable medical condition'. The invalidity declaration was suspended for 12 months in order to provide the Parliament with enough time to address the matter. Since Ms Taylor had passed away before the judgment, the Court did not provide an exemption for these 12 months.[700]

3.7.3 Aftermath of the Carter Case

In response to the Carter Case, the Senate and the House of Commons appointed a Special Joint Committee to make recommendations for a legal framework on physician-assisted dying.[701] Upon the Special Joint Committee's report, the Parliament passed Bill C-14, legislation on medical assistance in dying (MAID) in 2016,

---

[696] *Carter Case-SCC*, [114]-[115].

[697] *Carter Case-SCC*, [120].

[698] *Carter Case-SCC*, [121].

[699] 'No person is entitled to consent to have death inflicted on him, and such consent does not affect the criminal responsibility of any person by whom death may be inflicted on the person by whom consent is given.'

[700] Referring to an 'irremediable' condition, the Court noted that the patient could not be forced to receive a treatment that was unacceptable to them. *Carter Case-SCC*, [127]-[129].

[701] Canada, Parliament (11 Dec 2015) Journals of the Senate, 42nd Parl, 1st Sess, No 6, p. 55; Canada, Parliament (11 Dec 2015) Journals of House of Commons, 42nd Parl, 1st Sess, No 7, p. 50.

amending the relevant sections of the Criminal Code.[702] According to the new section 241.1 of the Criminal Code, MAID is described as:

> the administering by a medical practitioner or nurse practitioner of a substance to a person, at their request, that causes their death; or
>
> the prescribing or providing by a medical practitioner or nurse practitioner of a substance to a person, at their request, so that they may self-administer the substance and in doing so cause their own death.

Section 241.2(1) lays out the eligibility requirements for MAID.

> A person may receive medical assistance in dying only if they meet all of the following criteria:
> (a) they are eligible — or, but for any applicable minimum period of residence or waiting period, would be eligible — for health services funded by a government in Canada;
> (b) they are at least 18 years of age and capable of making decisions with respect to their health;
> (c) they have a grievous and irremediable medical condition;
> (d) they have made a voluntary request for medical assistance in dying that, in particular, was not made as a result of external pressure; and
> (e) they give informed consent to receive medical assistance in dying after having been informed of the means that are available to relieve their suffering, including palliative care.

According to section 241.2(2), a person has a grievous and irremediable medical condition if all of the following criteria have been met:

> (a) they have a serious and incurable illness, disease or disability;
> (b) they are in an advanced state of irreversible decline in capability;
> (c) that illness, disease or disability or that state of decline causes them enduring physical or psychological suffering that is intolerable to them and that cannot be relieved under conditions that they consider acceptable; and
> (d) their natural death has become reasonably foreseeable, taking into account all of their medical circumstances, without a prognosis necessarily having been made as to the specific length of time that they have remaining.

The 'reasonably foreseeable natural death' requirement has received intense criticism for being vague and in contradiction with the Carter judgment.[703] Immediately after the MAID Act was adopted, the 28-year-old Julia Lamb, who was suffering from a degenerative neuromuscular disorder, challenged the reasonable foreseeability requirement before the Supreme Court of British Columbia.[704] After the Attorney General had submitted evidence that Ms Lamb was, in fact, eligible for a MAID, the case was adjourned. The evidence presented to the Court was an expert witness statement that said Ms Lamb would be eligible for a MAID if she expressed an

---

[702] Canada, Parliament, Special Joint Committee on Physician-Assisted Dying (Feb 2016) Medical Assistance in Dying: A Patient-Centred Approach, 42nd Parl, 1st Sess; An Act to amend the Criminal Code and to make related amendments to other Acts (medical assistance in dying) 2016.

[703] Downie and Scallion (2018), pp. 24–25; McMorrow (2018), pp. 86–87.

[704] BCCLA (2016) Lamb v. Canada Case Documents. https://bccla.org/our_work/lamb-v-canada-case-documents/.

intention to refuse treatment. The fact that her health condition would deteriorate in the absence of treatment was sufficient.[705] This evidence has been perceived as a clarification to the end that reasonable foreseeability was 'within the control of patients'.[706] More challenges were brought before the Ontario and Quebec Superior Courts of Justice. The Ontario Court stated that reasonable foreseeability of one's natural death was a 'person-specific question', which did not require the presence of a terminal illness or condition.[707] The Quebec Court ruled that the reasonably foreseeable natural death requirement under section 241.2(2)(d) of the Criminal Code violated sections 7 and 15 of the Charter and was not saved under section 1. Therefore, it was void.[708]

Considering the developments in the Lamb Case and the judgment of the Quebec Court, the Government responded with a proposal for an amendment, which was approved and came into force on 17 March 2021.[709] The amendment of 2021 repealed the reasonably foreseeable natural death requirement and set forth additional safeguards for those whose death is not reasonably foreseeable under new section 241.2(3.1). These safeguards include a consultation requirement and a waiting period. Furthermore, patients who are only suffering from a mental illness are excluded from the MAID practice with the recent amendment. This exclusion will be in effect until 17 March 2023, giving the Government time to evaluate adequate safeguard measures for the safe practice of MAID for patients whose only medical condition is a mental illness.[710]

Following section 241.31(3) of the Criminal Code, the Minister of Health adopted a federal regulation for monitoring MAID practice in July 2018.[711] Health Canada published its second annual report on MAID in June 2021 using the data from the federal monitoring system. According to the report, 2.5% of all deaths in 2020 were caused by MAID, with a total number of 7.595 cases (2016: 1.018, 2017: 2.838, 2018: 4.478, 2019: 5.660).[712] It should be kept in mind that before the

---

[705] BCCLA (2019) RELEASE: BC Supreme Court adjourns BC Civil Liberties Association's assisted dying case. https://bccla.org/news/2019/09/release-b-c-supreme-court-adjourns-b-c-civil-liberties-associations-assisted-dying-case/.

[706] Downie (2019) A Watershed Month for Medical Assistance in Dying. In: Policy Options-Institute for Research on Public Policy. https://policyoptions.irpp.org/magazines/september-2019/a-watershed-month-for-medical-assistance-in-dying/.

[707] *AB v Canada (Attorney General)* 2017 ONSC 3759, 139 OR (3d) 139, [79]-[83].

[708] *Truchon c Procureur général du Canada* 2019 QCCS 3792 [764]-[767] (this judgment is only enforceable in the province of Quebec).

[709] An Act to amend the Criminal Code (medical assistance in dying) 2021.

[710] Canadian Criminal Code (after the amendment of 17 March 2021) sec 241.2(2.1); Government of Canada (2021) Medical assistance in dying. https://www.canada.ca/en/health-canada/services/medical-assistance-dying.html.

[711] Canadian Regulations for the Monitoring of Medical Assistance in Dying, SOR/2018-166 (1 November 2019).

[712] Health Canada (2021) Second Annual Report on Medical Assistance in Dying in Canada, 2020. https://www.canada.ca/en/health-canada/services/medical-assistance-dying/annual-report-2020.html, p. 14.

regulation came into force in November 2018, reporting was on a voluntary basis. The increase in numbers is most likely due to the adoption of the monitoring system on a federal level and raising awareness of the possibility of MAID.

References

(2004) Exit lockert Moratorium für Sterbebegleitung. In: SWI swissinfo.ch. https://www.swissinfo.ch/ger/exit-lockert-moratorium-fuer-sterbebegleitung/4194608

(2007) Death Tourism Tops Swiss Word List. In: SWI swissinfo.ch. https://www.swissinfo.ch/eng/death-tourism-tops-swiss-word-list/6299814

(2007) Doctor Sentenced over Assisted Suicides. In: SWI swissinfo.ch. https://www.swissinfo.ch/eng/doctor-sentenced-over-assisted-suicides/5988876

(2007) Es gibt ein Leben vor dem Tod. In: Neue Zürcher Zeitung. https://www.nzz.ch/es_gibt_ein_leben_vor_dem_tod-1.587887

(2008) Mit Luftballon-Gas in den Tod. In: Neue Zürcher Zeitung. https://www.nzz.ch/mit_luftballon-gas_in_den_tod-1.691954

(2009) Sterbehilfe für kerngesunde Frau. In: Der Bund. https://www.derbund.ch/zeitungen/schweiz/sterbehilfe%2D%2Dfuer-kerngesunde-frau/story/24525418

(2010) Dignitas schickte Schizophrenen in den Tod. In: Tages Anzeiger. https://m.tagesanzeiger.ch/articles/20026089

(2010) Dozens of Urns with Human Ashes Found in Lake Zurich. In: HeraldNet. https://www.heraldnet.com/news/dozens-of-urns-with-human-ashes-found-in-lake-zurich/

(2018) Dignitas-Gründer Minelli vor Bezirksgericht Uster. In: Top Online. https://www.toponline.ch/news/zuerich/detail/news/dignitas-gruender-minelli-vor-bezirksgericht-uster-0088378/

(2018) Freispruch für Minelli - aber kein Freipass. In: Zürcher Oberländer. https://zueriost.ch/bezirk-pfaffikon/pfaffikon/freispruch-fuer-minelli-aber-kein-freipass/1063802

(2019) Paralysed Leeds man Paul Lamb loses "right to die" case. In: BBC. https://www.bbc.com/news/uk-england-leeds-50852790

(2019) Sterbehelferin Erika Preisig wegen Medikament-Verstössen verurteilt. In: SWI swissinfo.ch. https://www.swissinfo.ch/ger/alle-news-in-kuerze/sterbehelferin-erika-preisig-wegen-medikament-verstoessen-verurteilt/45085538

(2020) Assisted dying: Terminally ill man's judicial review rejected. In: BBC. https://www.bbc.com/news/uk-england-leicestershire-51311089

(2020) Fin de vie des enfants : une loi inutile et précipitée. In: La Libre Belgique. https://www.lalibre.be/debats/opinions/fin-de-vie-des-enfants-une-loi-inutile-et-precipitee-52e93c5b3570e5b8eeea1a00

(2020) Official Referendum Results Released. In: Electoral Commission. https://elections.nz/media-and-news/2020/official-referendum-results-released/

(2020) Sterbehilfe auf Agenda des Deutschen Ärztetages' In: aerzteblatt.de. https://www.aerzteblatt.de/nachrichten/sw/Sterbehilfe?s=sterbehilfe&p=1&n=1&nid=116866

ACB (1997) Opinion No 1 of 12 May 1997 Concerning the Advisability of a Legal Regulation on Euthanasia. https://www.health.belgium.be/en/opinion-no-1-legal-regulation-euthanasia

ACB (1999) Opinion No 9 of 22 February 1999 Concerning Active Termination of the Lives of Persons Incapable of Expressing Their Wishes. https://www.health.belgium.be/en/opinion-no-9-active-termination-lives-persons-incapable-expressing-their-wishes

Achermann F (2018) Gedanken zur Ablehnung der SAMW Richtlinie "Umgang mit Sterben und Tod" durch die FMH. Schweiz Ärzteztg 99(46):1614. https://doi.org/10.4414/saez.2018.17341

Ackeret M (2019) Die Sterbehilfe in der Schweiz ist längst ausser Kontrolle. In: SWI swissinfo.ch. https://www.swissinfo.ch/ger/standpunkt_die-sterbehilfe-in-der-schweiz-ist-laengst-ausser-kontrolle/44599878

Adams M, Nys H (2003) Comparative reflections on the Belgian Euthanasia Act 2002. Med L Rev 11(3):353–376. https://doi.org/10.1093/medlaw/11.3.353
Aeschlimann J (2018) Sistierung der Zusammenarbeit mit der SAMW. Schweiz Ärzteztg 99(42): 1452. https://doi.org/10.4414/saez.2018.17260
AGEAS (2018) Stellungnahme der AGEAS zu den SAMW-Richtlinien "Umgang mit Sterben und Tod". Schweiz Ärzteztg 99(42):1451. https://doi.org/10.4414/saez.2018.17261
Alexander L (1949) Medical science under dictatorship. N Eng J Med 241(2):39–47. https://doi.org/10.1056/NEJM194907142410201
Andorno R (2013) Nonphysician-assisted suicide in Switzerland. Camb Q Healthc Ethics 22:246–253. https://doi.org/10.1017/s0963180113000054
Arbeitsgruppe Sterbehilfe (1999) Bericht der Arbeitsgruppe an das Eidg. Justiz- und Polizeidepartement. https://www.bj.admin.ch/bj/de/home/gesellschaft/gesetzgebung/archiv/sterbehilfe.html
Badarau DO, de Clercq E, Helger BS (2019) Continuous deep sedation and euthanasia in pediatrics: does one really exclude the other for terminally ill patients? J Med Philos 44(1):50–70. https://doi.org/10.1093/jmp/jhy033
Bär W, Zollinger U, Sigrist T, Walz F (2019) Unverständlicher Entscheid. Schweiz Ärzteztg 100(7):202. https://doi.org/10.4414/saez.2019.17590
Barnikol M (2018) Die Regelung der Suizidbeihilfe in den neuen SMW-Richtlinien. Schweiz Ärzteztg 99(41):1392–1396. https://doi.org/10.4414/saez.2018.17179
Baumann P (2014) Die Freiheit zum Sterben: Menschliche Autonomie am Ende. Weiss J (ed) Chronos, Zurich
BCCLA (2012) Carter v Canada Case Documents. https://bccla.org/2012/12/carter-et-al-v-attorney-general-of-canada/
BCCLA (2016) Lamb v. Canada Case Documents. https://bccla.org/our_work/lamb-v-canada-case-documents/
BCCLA (2019) RELEASE: BC Supreme Court adjourns BC Civil Liberties Association's assisted dying case. https://bccla.org/news/2019/09/release-b-c-supreme-court-adjourns-b-c-civil-liberties-associations-assisted-dying-case/
Belgian House of Representatives (2020) Proposition de loi modifi ant la loi du 28 mai 2002 relative à l'euthanasie, en ce qui concerne la suppression de la durée de validité de la déclaration anticipée - Avis du Conseil d'État No 66.816/AG – 66.817/AG du 29 Janvier 2020, Doc 55 0523/011. https://www.lachambre.be/FLWB/PDF/55/0523/55K0523011.pdf
Belgian Senate (2013) Proposition de loi modifiant la loi du 28 mai 2002 relative à l'euthanasie en vue de l'étendre aux mineurs, Session de 2012-2013, Doc 5-2170/1. https://www.senate.be/www/webdriver?MItabObj=pdf&MIcolObj=pdf&MInamObj=pdfid&MItypeObj=application/pdf&MIvalObj=83890023
Belgian Senate, Introduction in Belgian Parliamentary History. https://www.senate.be/english/federal_parliament_en.html
Beoordelingscommissie Late Zwangerschapsafbreking en Levensbeëndiging bij Pasgeborenen, Over ons. https://www.lzalp.nl/over-ons
Bernal-Carcelén I (2020) Euthanasia: trends and opinions in Spain. Rev Esp Sanid Penit 22(3): 112–115. https://doi.org/10.18176/resp.00020
Betty D (2009) Call Dignitas to account. In: The Guardian. https://www.theguardian.com/commentisfree/2009/apr/03/assisted-suicide-mental-health
Bilsen J, Stichele RV, Mortier F, Bernheim J, Deliens L (2004) The incidence and characteristics of end-of-life decisions by GPs in Belgium. Fam Prac 21(3):282–289. https://doi.org/10.1093/fampra/cmh312
BMA (2016) End-of-life care and physician-assisted dying: 3 - reflections and recommendations. https://www.bma.org.uk/advice-and-support/ethics/end-of-life/end-of-life-care-and-physician-assisted-dying-project
BMA (2020) Physician-assisted dying survey. https://www.bma.org.uk/advice-and-support/ethics/end-of-life/physician-assisted-dying-survey

BMA (2021) How have the law and BMA policy developed over the past twenty years? https://www.bma.org.uk/media/4401/bma-pad-policy-law-and-timeline-aug-2021.pdf

BMA (2021) Physician-assisted dying. https://www.bma.org.uk/advice-and-support/ethics/end-of-life/the-bmas-position-on-physician-assisted-dying

Bondolfi A (2004) Switzerland - defending assisted death. In: Council of Europe Publishing (ed) Euthanasia: volume II - National and European perspectives. Council of Europe, Strasbourg

Bondolfi S (2020) Why assisted suicide is "normal" in Switzerland. In: SWI swissinfo.ch. https://www.swissinfo.ch/eng/why-assisted-suicide-is%2D%2Dnormal%2D%2Din-switzerland-/45924614

Borasio GD (2015) Sorgfaltskriterien nicht erfüllt. Schweiz Ärzteztg 96(47):1736. https://doi.org/10.4414/saez.2015.04169

Bosshard G (2008) Switzerland. In: Griffiths J, Weyers H, Adams M (eds) Euthanasia and law in Europe, 2nd edn. Hart Publishing, Oxford, pp 463–482

BR-Dr 230/06

Brauer S, Bolliger C, Strub J-D (2015) Swiss physicians' attitudes to assisted suicide: a qualitative and quantitative empirical study. Swiss Med Wkly 145:w14142. https://doi.org/10.4414/smw.2015.14142

Broeckaert B (2001) Belgium: towards a legal recognition of euthanasia. Eur J Health L 8:95–107

Broeckaert B, Janssens R (2005) Palliative care and euthanasia. Belgian and Dutch perspectives. In: Schotsmans P, Meulenbergs T (eds) Euthanasia and palliative care in the low countries. Peeters, Leuven, pp 35–70

Broeders van Liefde, Wie zijn we? https://broedersvanliefde.be/wie-zijn-we

Brothers of Charity (2017) Press Release from the Brothers of Charity Generalate, Rome. https://brothersofcharity.org/press-release-from-the-brothers-of-charity-generalate_02_10_2017/?lang=en

Brothers of Charity (2017) The Vatican's Response to the Issue of Euthanasia with the Organization of the Brothers of Charity in Belgium. https://brothersofcharity.org/the-vaticans-response-to-the-issue-of-euthanasia-with-the-organization-of-the-brothers-of-charity-in-belgium/?lang=en

Brothers of Charity, Founder. https://brothersofcharity.org/who-are-the-brothers/founder/?lang=en

BT-Dr 17/11126

BT-Dr 18/5373

BT-Dr 19/1860

BT-Dr 19/2090

BT-Dr 19/9847

BT-Dr 19/19411

Bundesärztekammer (2018) (Muster-)Berufsordnung für die in Deutschland tätigen Ärztinnen und Ärzte. https://www.bundesaerztekammer.de/recht/berufsrecht/muster-berufsordnung-aerzte/muster-berufsordnung/

Bundesblatt (1918) Botschaft des Bundesrates an die Bundesversammlung zu einem Gesetzesentwurf enthaltend das schweizerische Strafgesetzbuch (BBI 1918 IV 1)

Bundesblatt (1918) Schweizerisches Strafgesetzbuch, Entwurf des Bundesrates an die Bundesversammlung (BBI 1918 IV 103)

Bundesrat (2000) Bericht des Bundesrates zum Postulat Ruffy, Sterbehilfe. Ergänzung des Strafgesetzbuches. https://www.bj.admin.ch/bj/de/home/gesellschaft/gesetzgebung/archiv/sterbehilfe.html

Bundesrat (2011) Bericht über Palliative Care, Suizidprävention und organisierte Suizidhilfe. https://www.bj.admin.ch/bj/de/home/gesellschaft/gesetzgebung/archiv/sterbehilfe.html

Burkhardt SE (2011) L'assistance au décès à l'aube du XXIème siècle. Privatdozent Thesis, University of Geneva. https://doi.org/10.13097/archive-ouverte/unige:14584

Bütikofer C (2010) Dignitas-Mitglied: Mehrere 100000 Franken für Freitod bezahlt. In: Aargauer Zeitung. https://www.aargauerzeitung.ch/panorama/vermischtes/dignitas-mitglied-mehrere-100000-franken-fuer-freitod-bezahlt-8663015

Canada, Parliament (11 Dec 2015) Journals of House of Commons, 42nd Parl, 1st Sess, No 7

Canada, Parliament (11 Dec 2015) Journals of the Senate, 42nd Parl, 1st Sess, No 6
Canada, Parliament Special Joint Committee on Physician-Assisted Dying (Feb 2016) Medical Assistance in Dying: A Patient-Centred Approach, 42nd Parl, 1st Sess
Cartwright N (2009) Commentary. 48 years on: is the suicide act fit for purpose? Med L Rev 17(3): 467–476. https://doi.org/10.1093/medlaw/fwp022
CEC (2007) Suizidbeihilfe in Akutspitälern: die Haltung der Zentralen Ethikkommission der SAMW. https://www.samw.ch/de/Ethik/Themen-A-bis-Z/Sterben-und-Tod/Hintergrund-Sterben-Tod.html
Centre Hospitalier Universitaire Vaudois (CHUV) (2007) Directive institutionelle concernant l'assistance au suicide. Bioethica Forum 54:14–19
CFCEE (2004) Rapport Euthanasie 2004. All CFCEE reports can be found at https://organesdeconcertation.sante.belgique.be/fr/organe-d'avis-et-de-concertation/commission-federale-de-controle-et-devaluation-de-leuthanasie
CFCEE (2006) Rapport Euthanasie 2006
CFCEE (2008) Rapport Euthanasie 2008
CFCEE (2010) Rapport Euthanasie 2010
CFCEE (2012) Rapport Euthanasie 2012' (22 May 2012)
CFCEE (2014) Rapport Euthanasie 2014' (24 June 2014)
CFCEE (2016) Rapport Euthanasie 2016' (9 August 2016)
CFCEE (2018) Rapport Euthanasie 2018
CFCEE (2019) Euthanasie - Chiffres de l'année 2018. https://organesdeconcertation.sante.belgique.be/fr/documents/euthanasie-chiffres-de-lannee-2018
CFCEE (2020) Euthanasie - Chiffres de l'année 2019. https://organesdeconcertation.sante.belgique.be/fr/documents/euthanasie-chiffres-de-lannee-2019
CFCEE (2020) Rapport Euthanasie 2020
Cheng M (2018) Dutch probe "appalling" euthanasia of dementia patient. In: Associated Press. https://apnews.com/article/8278f8a6224a47e88b46ea434eda26b4
Citroni F (2020) Le vice-président d'Exit Suisse romande condamné en appel après un suicide assisté. In: RTS.ch. https://www.rts.ch/info/suisse/11288726-le-vice-president-d-exit-suisse-romande-condamne-en-appel-apres-un-suicide-assiste.html
Cleary CC (2010) From "personal autonomy" to "death-on-demand": will Purdy v. DPP legalize assisted suicide in the United Kingdom. B C Int'l & Comp L Rev 33(2):289–304
Cohen J, Marcoux I, Bilsen J, Deboosere P, van der Wal G, Deliens L (2006) Trends in acceptance of euthanasia among the general public in 12 European countries (1981-1999). Eur J Public Health 16(6):663–669. https://doi.org/10.1093/eurpub/ckl042
Cohen-Almagor R (2004) Euthanasia in the Netherlands: the policy and practice of mercy killing. Springer, Dordrecht
Cohen-Almagor R (2009) Euthanasia policy and practice in Belgium: critical observations and suggestions for improvement. Issues L & Med 24(3):187–218
Cook M (2011) Swiss back off restrictions on assisted suicide. In: BioEdge. https://www.bioedge.org/bioethics/bioethics_article/swiss_back_off_restrictions_on_assisted_suicide
Cook M (2018) Dissent in Dutch euthanasia bureaucracy. In: BioEdge. https://www.bioedge.org/bioethics/dissent-in-dutch-euthanasia-bureaucracy/12569
Council of State, Proceedings. http://www.raadvst-consetat.be/?page=procedure&lang=en
Cox S (2009) The report - Dignitas: assisted suicide in Switzerland. In: BBC. https://www.bbc.co.uk/sounds/play/b00jdnsl
de Cruz P (2005) Commentary. The terminally ill adult seeking assisted suicide abroad: the extent of the duty owed by a local authority. Med L Rev 23(2):257–267. https://doi.org/10.1093/medlaw/fwi015
de Einder, Historie van Stichting de Einder. https://www.deeinder.nl/de-einder/organisatie/historie/
de Vries U (2004) A Dutch perspective: the limits of lawful euthanasia. Annals Health L 13(2): 365–392

Deliens L, Mortier F, Bilsen J, Cosyns M, Stichele RV, Vanoverloop J, Ingels K (2000) End-of-life decisions in medical practice in Flanders, Belgium: a nationwide survey. Lancet 356(9244): 1806–1811. https://doi.org/10.1016/s0140-6736(00)03233-5

Demony C (2020) Pro-euthanasia bills get green light in Portugal, negotiations ahead. In: Reuters. https://www.reuters.com/article/idUSKBN20E2F4

Department of Health - Canton Zurich, About Us. https://www.zh.ch/en/gesundheitsdirektion.html

di Fabio U (2017) Erwerbserlaubnis letal wirkender Mittel zur Selbsttötung in Existenziellen Notlagen - Rechtsgutachten zum Urteil des Bundesverwaltungsgerichts vom 2. März 2017-3 C 19/15. https://www.bfarm.de/SharedDocs/Downloads/DE/Service/Presse/Rechtsgutachten.pdf?__blob=publicationFile&v=2

Die Kommission für Rechtsfragen des Nationalrates (2001) Medienmitteilung: Sterbehilfe - Schmuggel und organisiertes Wirtschaftsverbrechen. In: Schweizer Parlament. https://www.parlament.ch/press-releases/Pages/2001/mm_2001-07-05_000_02.aspx

Die Oberstaatsanwaltschaft des Kantons Zürich and EXIT Deutsche Schweiz (2009) Vereinbarung über die organisierte Suizidhilfe. https://static.nzz.ch/files/4/7/6/EXIT-Vereinbarung2_1.2980476.pdf

Dierickx S, Deliens L, Cohen J, Chambaere K (2015) Comparison of the expression and granting of requests for euthanasia in Belgium in 2007 vs 2013. JAMA Intern Med 175(10):1703–1706. https://doi.org/10.1001/jamainternmed.2015.3982

Dignitas (2014) How Dignitas works. http://www.dignitas.ch/images/stories/pdf/so-funktioniert-dignitas-e.pdf

Dignitas (2020) Members of DIGNITAS by country of residency. http://www.dignitas.ch/images/stories/pdf/statistik-mitglieder-wohnsitzstaat-31122020.pdf

Dignitas (2021) Rückblick 2020 und Ausblick 2021. http://www.dignitas.ch/images/stories/pdf/medienmitteilung-29012020.pdf

Dignitas, Accompanied Suicide of Members of Dignitas, by Year and by Country of Residency 1998-2020. http://www.dignitas.ch/index.php?option=com_content&view=article&id=32&Itemid=72&lang=en

Dignitas, Information-Brochure. http://www.dignitas.ch/images/stories/pdf/informations-broschuere-dignitas-e.pdf

Dignity in Dying (2019) Dignity in Dying Poll. In: Yonder. https://yonderconsulting.com/poll/dignity-in-dying/

Dillmann RJM, Legemaate J (1994) Euthanasia in the Netherlands: the state of the legal debate. Eur J Health L 1:81–87

Doughty (2014) Don't make our mistake: as assisted suicide bill goes to Lords, Dutch watchdog who once backed euthanasia warns UK of 'slippery slope' to mass deaths. In: Daily Mail. https://www.dailymail.co.uk/news/article-2686711/Dont-make-mistake-As-assisted-suicide-bill-goes-Lords-Dutch-regulator-backed-euthanasia-warns-Britain-leads-mass-killing.html

Downie J (2016) Permitting voluntary euthanasia and assisted suicide: law reform pathways for common law jurisdictions. QUT L Rev 16(1):84–112. https://doi.org/10.5204/qutlr.v16il.613

Downie J (2019) A watershed month for medical assistance in dying. In: Policy Options- Institute for Research on Public Policy. https://policyoptions.irpp.org/magazines/september-2019/a-watershed-month-for-medical-assistance-in-dying/

Downie J, Scallion K (2018) Foreseeably unclear: the meaning of the reasonably foreseeable criterion for access to medical assistance in dying in Canada. Dalhousie L J 41(1):23–57

DPP (2004) The Code for Crown Prosecutors. https://1library.net/document/qo50p4my-the-code-for-crown-prosecutors.html

DPP (2010, updated 2014) Suicide: Policy for Prosecutors in Respect of Cases of Encouraging or Assisting Suicide. https://www.cps.gov.uk/legal-guidance/suicide-policy-prosecutors-respect-cases-encouraging-or-assisting-suicide#a01

DPP (2018) The Code for Crown Prosecutors. https://www.cps.gov.uk/publication/code-crown-prosecutors

Editors of Encyclopedia Britannica (2020) Amyotrophic Lateral Sclerosis. In: Encyclopædia Britannica. https://www.britannica.com/science/amyotrophic-lateral-sclerosis
Elders JLM, Wöretshofer J (1992) Euthanasia in the Netherlands: current court decisions and legislation. In: Alexander GJ (ed) International perspectives on aging. Martinus Nijhoff Publishers, Dordrecht, pp 209–240
Enthoven L (2017) Deur staat open voor euthanasietoerisme. NJB 38:2035. https://www.njb.nl/blogs/deur-staat-open-voor-euthanasietoerisme/
ERAS (2019) Abschlägiger Bericht aus Strasbourg. https://www.verein-eras.ch/de/detail-reflexe?id=57
ERAS, Home. https://www.verein-eras.ch/de/home
Ernst C (2001) Assistierter Suizid in der Stadtzürcher Alters- und Krankenheimen. Schweiz Ärzteztg 82(6):293–295. https://doi.org/10.4414/saez.2001.07970
EXIT - Deutsche Schweiz (2021) EXIT Haupt-Infobroschüre “Selbstbestimmt bis ans Lebensende”, 3rd edn. Exit (Deutsche Schweiz), Zurich. https://exit.ch/downloads/
EXIT - Deutsche Schweiz, Statuten. https://exit.ch/verein/der-verein/statuten/
EXIT - Deutsche Schweiz, Werden Sie Mitglied. https://pv.exit.ch/register
EXIT - Suisse Romande (2020) Bulletin EXIT No 72. https://www.exit-romandie.ch/nos-bulletins-fr1263.html
EXIT - Suisse Romande (2021) Bulletin EXIT No 74. https://www.exit-romandie.ch/nos-bulletins-fr1263.html
Expertisecentrum Euthanasie, Over ons. https://expertisecentrumeuthanasie.nl/over-ons/
Falconer B (2010) Death becomes him. In: The Atlantic. https://www.theatlantic.com/magazine/archive/2010/03/death-becomes-him/307916/
FDJP (2006) Medienmitteilung: Sterbehilfe: Geltendes Recht durchsetzen. https://www.bj.admin.ch/ejpd/de/home/aktuell/news/2006/2006-05-311.html
FDJP (2006) Sterbehilfe und Palliativmedizin – Handlungsbedarf für den Bund? https://www.bj.admin.ch/bj/de/home/gesellschaft/gesetzgebung/archiv/sterbehilfe.html
FDJP (2007) Ergänzungsbericht zum Bericht “Sterbehilfe und Palliativmedizin – Handlungsbedarf für den Bund?” https://www.bj.admin.ch/bj/de/home/gesellschaft/gesetzgebung/archiv/sterbehilfe.html
FDJP (2009) Organisierte Suizidhilfe: Vertiefte Abklärungen zu Handlungsoptionen und –Bedarf des Bundesgesetzgebers. https://www.bj.admin.ch/bj/de/home/gesellschaft/gesetzgebung/archiv/sterbehilfe.html
Federal Commission on Patients Rights (2007) Patients' rights – an invitation to dialogue. https://www.health.belgium.be/en/health/taking-care-yourself/patient-related-themes/patients-rights
Fenigsen R (1990) Euthanasia in the Netherlands. Issues L & Med 6(3):229–245
Fischer S, Huber CA, Imhof L, Imhof RM, Furter M, Ziegler SJ, Bosshard G (2008) Suicide assisted by two Swiss right-to-die organisations. J Med Ethics 34(11):810–814. https://doi.org/10.1136/jme.2007.023887
FMH (2018) Medienmitteilung: Ärztekammer befürwortet eine partnerschaftliche Tarifrevision. https://www.fmh.ch/files/pdf21/medienmitteilung_aerztekammer_befuerwortet_eine_partnerschaftliche_tarifrevision.pdf
FMH (1997, last updated 2020) Standesordnung der FMH. https://www.fmh.ch/ueber-die-fmh/statuten-reglemente.cfm#i112408
FMH (2018) Stellungnahme: Richtlinien “Umgang mit Sterben und Tod”. https://www.fmh.ch/files/pdf20/Stellungnahme_der_FMH_Richtlinien_Umgang_mit_Sterben_und_Tod.pdf
Fohr SA (1998) The double effect of pain medication: separating myth from reality. Palliat Med 1(4):315–328. https://doi.org/10.1089/jpm.1998.1.315
FPS Public Health, About Us. https://www.health.belgium.be/en/about-us-1
Frith M (2004) Couple who died after suicide clinic visit “not terminally ill”. In: The Independent. https://www.independent.co.uk/news/world/europe/couple-who-died-after-suicide-clinic-visit-not-terminally-ill-733208.html

Gevers S (1996) Euthanasia: law and practice in the Netherlands. Br Med Bull 52(2):326–333. https://doi.org/10.1093/oxfordjournals.bmb.a011547

GMC (2013) Guidance for the Investigation Committee and case examiners when considering allegations about a doctor's involvement in encouraging or assisting suicide. https://www.gmc-uk.org/-/media/documents/dc4317-guidance-for-ftp-decision-makers-on-assisting-suicide-51026940.pdf

GMC (2013, last updated 2015) When a patient seeks advice or information about assistance to die. https://www.gmc-uk.org/ethical-guidance/ethical-guidance-for-doctors/when-a-patient-seeks-advice-or-information-about-assistance-to-die

GMC (2014) Revised guidance for doctors on giving advice to patients on assisted suicide. https://www.gmc-uk.org/-/media/documents/12%2D%2D-revised-guidance-for-doctors-on-assisted-suicide_pdf-80652843.pdf

GMC, Our role and the Medical Act 1983. https://www.gmc-uk.org/about/what-we-do-and-why/our-mandate

Government of Canada (2021) Medical assistance in dying. https://www.canada.ca/en/health-canada/services/medical-assistance-dying.html

Government of the Netherlands, Is euthanasia allowed? https://www.government.nl/topics/euthanasia/is-euthanasia-allowed

Griffiths J (1995a) Assisted suicide in the Netherlands: the Chabot Case. Mod L Rev 58(2):232–248. https://doi.org/10.1111/j.1468-2230.1995.tb02006.x

Griffiths J (1995b) Assisted suicide in the Netherlands: the postscript to Chabot. Mod L Rev 58(6):895–897. https://doi.org/10.1111/j.1468-2230.1995.tb02060.x

Griffiths J, Bood A, Weyers H (1998) Euthanasia and law in the Netherlands. Amsterdam University Press, Amsterdam

Griffiths J, Weyers H, Adams M (2008) Euthanasia and law in Europe, 2nd edn. Hart Publishing, Oxford

Guillod O, Schmidt A (2005) Assisted suicide under Swiss law. Eur J Health L 12(1):25–38. https://doi.org/10.1163/1571809054663140

Hafter E (1912) Zum Tatbestand: Anstiftung und Beihilfe zum Selbstmord. MschKrim 8:397–430

Hagenouw R (2000) Nooit: u vraagt en arts draait. In: Trouw. https://www.trouw.nl/nieuws/nooit-u-vraagt-en-arts-draait~b9e7d35b/

Hagens M, Pasman HRW, Onwuteaka-Philipsen BD (2014) Cross-sectional research into counselling for non-physician assisted suicide: who asks for it and what happens? BMC Health Serv Res 14:455–464. https://doi.org/10.1186/1472-6963-14-455

Hagens M, Snijdewind MC, Evenblij K, Onwuteaka-Philipsen BD, Pasman HRW (2021) Experiences with counselling to people who wish to be able to self-determine the timing and manner of one's own end of life: a qualitative in-depth interview study. J Med Ethics 47(1):39–46. https://doi.org/10.1136/medethics-2019-105564

Hagens M, Onwuteaka-Philipsen BD, Pasman HRW (2017) Trajectories to seeking demedicalised assistance in suicide: a qualitative in-depth interview study. J Med Ethics 43(8):543–548. https://doi.org/10.1136/medethics-2016-103660

Hasler T (2018) Er hat sich nicht bereichert: Dignitas-Gründer freigesprochen. In: Tages Anzeiger. https://www.tagesanzeiger.ch/zuerich/region/er-hat-sich-nicht-bereichert-dignitasgruender-freigesprochen/story/23093108

Hauri R, Aufgaben der Kantonsärzte. In: VKS/AMCS. https://www.vks-amcs.ch/de/home/merkblaetter/aufgaben-der-kantonsaerzte

HC Deb 11 September 2015 Vol 599 Col 653

HC Deb 23 January 2020 Vol 670 Col 186WH

HC Deb 26 January 2009 Vol 487 Col 35

Health Canada (2021) Second Annual Report on Medical Assistance in Dying in Canada, 2020. https://www.canada.ca/en/health-canada/services/medical-assistance-dying/annual-report-2020.html

Heijltjes MT, van Thiel GJMW, Rietjens JAC, van der Heide A, de Graeff A, van Delden JJM (2020) Changing practices in the use of continuous sedation at the end of life: a systematic review of literature. J Pain Symptom Manage 60(4):828–846.e3. https://doi.org/10.1016/j.jpainsymman.2020.06.019

Heneghan T (2016) Catholic nursing home fined thousands in euthanasia case. In: The Tablet. https://www.thetablet.co.uk/news/5792/catholic-nursing-home-fined-thousands-in-euthanasia-case

Hirsch A (2009) Debbie Purdy wins "significant legal victory" on assisted suicide. In: The Guardian. https://www.theguardian.com/society/2009/jul/30/debbie-purdy-assisted-suicide-legal-victory

HL Deb 7 July 2009 Vol 712 Cols 596-636

HL Deb 9 May 1994 Vol 554 Col 1349

HL Deb 10 March 2004 Vol 658 Cols 1316-1324

Hope A (2020) Catholic hospitals forcing palliative care on patients who request euthanasia. In: The Brussels Time. https://www.brusselstimes.com/belgium/94850/catholic-hospitals-forcing-palliative-care-on-patients-who-request-euthanasia-legal-right-filter-bishops-morgen-tijd/

Hope A (2020) Parliament approves change to euthanasia law. In: The Brussels Time. https://www.brusselstimes.com/news/belgium-all-news/98832/parliament-approves-change-to-euthanasia-law-advance-directive-living-will/

Hôpitaux Universitaires de Genève (HUG) (2007) Recommandations du Conseil d'Ethique Clinique des HUG concernant l'assistance au suicide. Bioethica Forum 54:21–23

Hurley S (2020) Dáil passes dying with dignity bill aimed at legalising assisted dying. In: RTÉ. https://www.rte.ie/news/politics/2020/1007/1170121-dying-with-dignity/

Hurst SA, Mauron A (2017) Assisted suicide in Switzerland: clarifying liberties and claims. Bioethics 31(3):199–208. https://doi.org/10.1111/bioe.12304

Interpellation 14.3817 Francine John-Calame (2014) Sterbehilfe. Gesetzlicher Rahmen und Verhinderung von Auswüchsen (Swiss National Council)

Interpellation 17.3845 Sylvia Flückiger-Bäni (2017) Ausweitung der Sterbehilfe (Swiss National Council)

Ireland, Dying with Dignity Bill 24 of 2020

Jans J (2005) The Belgian "Act on Euthanasia": clarifying context, legislation, and practice from an ethical point of view. Soc Christ Ethics 25(2):163–177

Jansen-van der Weide MC, Onwuteaka-Philipsen BD, van der Wal G (2004) Implementation of the project "Support and Consultation on Euthanasia in The Netherlands" (SCEN). Health Policy 69(3):365–373. https://doi.org/10.1016/j.healthpol.2004.04.010

Jansen-van der Weide MC, Onwuteaka-Philipsen BD, van der Wal G (2007) Quality of consultation and the project "Support and Consultation on Euthanasia in the Netherlands" (SCEN). Health Policy 80(1):97–106. https://doi.org/10.1016/j.healthpol.2006.03.005

Janssens R, van Delden JM, Widdershoven GAM (2012) Palliative sedation: not just normal medical practice. Ethical reflections on the Royal Medical Association's Guideline on palliative sedation. J Med Ethics 38(11):664–668. https://doi.org/10.1136/medethics-2011-100353

Jones DA, Gastmans C, MacKeller C (eds) (2017) Euthanasia and assisted suicide: lessons from Belgium. Cambridge University Press, Cambridge

Kaiser V (2018) Zur Debatte der umstrittenen SAMW Richtlinien. Schweiz Ärzteztg 99(40):1363. https://doi.org/10.4414/saez.2018.17164

Kamann M (2014) Befördert Sterbehelfer Kusch sich selbst ins Aus? In: Welt. https://www.welt.de/politik/deutschland/article127971004/Befoerdert-Sterbehelfer-Kusch-sich-selbst-ins-Aus.html

Keown J (2013) Five flawed arguments for decriminalising Euthanasia. In: Alghrani A, Bennett R, Ost S (eds) The criminal law and bioethical conflict: walking the tightrope. bioethics, medicine and and the criminal law, vol 2. Cambridge University Press, New York, pp 30–48

Kimsma GK, Van Leeuwen E (1993) Dutch euthanasia: background, practice and present justifications. Camb Q Healthc Ethics 2(1):19–35. https://doi.org/10.1017/S096318010000058X

KNMG (1984) KNMG-standpunt inzake euthanasie. Medisch Contact 31:990–997

KNMG (1990) Richtlijnen en meldingsprocedure euthanasie en hulp bij zelfdoding. Medisch Contact 44:1303–1301

KNMG (2009) Guideline for palliative sedation. https://www.knmg.nl/advies-richtlijnen/knmg-publicaties/publications-in-english.htm

KNMG (2011) Position paper: the role of the physician in the voluntary termination of life. https://www.knmg.nl/advies-richtlijnen/knmg-publicaties/publications-in-english.htm

KNMG (2012) Guidelines for the practice of euthanasia and physician-assisted suicide. https://www.knmg.nl/advies-richtlijnen/knmg-publicaties/publications-in-english.htm

KNMG, Over SCEN. https://www.knmg.nl/advies-richtlijnen/scen/over-scen.htm

KNMG Working Group on Euthanasia (1975) Discussienota van de Werkgroep Euthanasie. Medisch Contact 30(1):7–16

Kuhse H (2004) Why terminal sedation is no solution to the euthanasia debate. In: Tännsjö T (ed) Terminal sedation: euthanasia in disguise? Springer, Dordrecht, pp 57–70

Kuhn H (2019) Seniorenbewilligung – pragmatische Lösungsansätze. Schweiz Ärzteztg 100(19): 663–665. https://doi.org/10.4414/saez.2019.17817

Ladaria CLF (2020) Letter to the Superior General of the Congregation of the "Brothers of Charity", Regarding the Accompaniment of Patients in Psychiatric Hospitals of the Congregation's Belgian Branch. http://www.vatican.va/roman_curia/congregations/cfaith/documents/rc_con_cfaith_doc_20200330_lettera-fratellidellacarita-belgio_en.html

Law Reform Commission of Canada (1982) Euthanasia, Aiding Suicide and Cessation of Treatment, Working Paper 28. http://www.lareau-law.ca/LRCWP28.pdf

Law Reform Commission of Canada (1983) Euthanasia, Aiding Suicide and Cessation of Treatment, Report 20. http://www.lareau-law.ca/LRCReport20.pdf

Le Forum EOL, Origine et Objectifs. http://www.eol.admd.be/

Leenen HJJ (1986) Supreme Court's decision on euthanasia in the Netherlands. Med Law 5:349–351

Leenen HJJ (1987) Euthanasia, assisted suicide and the law: developments in the Netherlands. Health Policy 8(2):197–206. https://doi.org/10.1016/0168-8510(87)90062-5

Leenen HJJ (1989) Dying with dignity: developments in the field of euthanasia in the Netherlands. Med Law 8(5):517–526

Leidig M (2005) Dignitas is investigated for helping healthy woman to die. BMJ 331:1160. https://doi.org/10.1136/bmj.331.7526.1160-a

LEIF, LEIFartsen en het LEIFartsenforum. https://leif.be/vragen-antwoorden/leifartsen/

Lewy G (2011) Assisted death in Europe and America: four regimes and their lessons. Oxford University Press, Oxford

Luchsinger P (2018) SAMW-Richtlinie zu "Umgang mit Sterben und Tod". Schweiz Ärzteztg 99(41):1399–1400. https://doi.org/10.4414/saez.2018.17182

MacKeller C (2017) Some possible consequences arising from the normalisation of euthanasia in Belgium. In: Jones DA, Gastmans C, MacKeller C (eds) Euthanasia and assisted suicide: lessons from Belgium. Cambridge University Press, Cambridge, pp 219–234

Mahase E (2019) Euthanasia: Dutch doctor is acquitted in landmark test case. BMJ 366:l5555. https://doi.org/10.1136/bmj.I5555

Mansour F (2019) A Genève, le médecin d'Exit coupable d'avoir repoussé les limites du suicide assisté. In: Le Temps. https://www.letemps.ch/suisse/geneve-medecin-dexit-coupable-davoir-repousse-limites-suicide-assiste

Martuscelli C (2021) Italian authorities clear way for country's first assisted suicide. In: Politico. https://www.politico.eu/article/italy-authorities-first-assisted-suicide/

Mathwig F (2010) Zwischen Leben und Tod: Die Suizidhilfediskussion in der Schweiz aus theologisch-ethischer Sicht. Theologischer Verlag, Zürich

Mayo Clinic (2020) Spinal Stenosis. https://www.mayoclinic.org/diseases-conditions/spinal-stenosis/symptoms-causes/syc-20352961

McIntyre A (2019) Doctrine of double effect. In: Zalta EN (ed) The Stanford encyclopedia of philosophy. https://plato.stanford.edu/archives/spr2019/entries/double-effect/

McMorrow T (2018) MAID in Canada: debating the constitutionality of Canada's new medical assistance in dying law. Queen's L J 44(1):69–119

Medical Disciplinary Tribunal (1995) Psychiater berispt voor hulp bij zelfdoding, Uitspraak Medisch Tuchtcollege Amsterdam d. d. 6 februari 1995. Medisch Contact 21:668–674

Minelli LA (2008) The European Convention on Human Rights protects the right of suicide. In: Birnbacher D, Dahl E (eds) Giving death a helping hand: physician-assisted suicide and public policy. An international perspective. International library of ethics, law, and the new medicine, vol 38. Springer, Dordrecht, pp 149–157

Montero E (2017) The Belgian experience of euthanasia since its legal implementation in 2002. In: Jones DA, Gastmans C, MacKeller C (eds) Euthanasia and assisted suicide: lessons from Belgium. Cambridge University Press, Cambridge, pp 26–48

Motion 01.3523 Guido Zäch (2001) Sterbehilfe. Gesetzeslücke schliessen statt Tötung erlauben (Swiss National Council)

Motion 03.3180 Komission für Rechtsfragen SR (2003) Sterbehilfe und Palliativmedizin (Swiss Council of States)

Motion 05.3352 FDP-Liberale Fraktion (2005) Expertenarbeiten zum Thema Sterbehilfe (Swiss National Council)

Motion 07.3163 Hansruedi Stadler (2007) Gesetzliche Grundlage für die Aufsicht über die Sterbehilfeorganizationen (Swiss Council of States)

Motion 94.3370 Victor Ruffy (1994) Sterbehilfe. Ergänzung des Strafgesetzbuches (Swiss National Council)

Müller-Neuhof J (2018) Wie die Regierung beschloss, das höchstrichterliche Urteil zu ignorieren. In: Der Tagesspiegel. https://www.tagesspiegel.de/politik/sterbehilfe-wie-die-regierung-beschloss-das-hoechstrichterliche-urteil-zu-ignorieren/22928052.html

Mullock A (2009) Commentary. Prosecutors making (bad) law? Med L Rev 17(2):290–299. https://doi.org/10.1093/medlaw/fwp009

NCE (2005) Beihilfe zum Suizid. Stellungnahme Nr. 9/2005

NCE (2006) Sorgfaltskriterien im Umgang mit Suizidbeihilfe. Stellungnahme Nr. 13/2006

NCE (2010) Vernehmlassungsantwort der NEK-CNE zu den bundesrätlichen Vorschlägen für eine Änderung von Art. 115 StGB/Art. 119 MStG. https://www.nek-cne.admin.ch/inhalte/Themen/Vernehmlassungsantworten/Vernehmlassungsantwort_NEK-CNE_Suizidbeihilfe_definitiv.pdf

NCE (2018) Mission. https://www.nek-cne.admin.ch/en/about-us/mission/

Nisnevich YA (2012) Political and legal concept of modern democratic state. Am J Sociol 2(3): 32–37. https://doi.org/10.5923/j.sociology.20120203.01

NVK (2014) Richtlijn: Levensbeëindiging bij pasgeborenen, actieve. https://www.nvk.nl/themas/kwaliteit/richtlijnen/richtlijn?componentid=6881303&tagtitles=Neonatologie

NVVE, About NVVE. https://www.nvve.nl/about-nvve

NVvP (2018) Levensbeëindiging op verzoek bij patiënten met een psychische stoornis. https://richtlijnendatabase.nl/richtlijn/levensbeeindiging_op_verzoek_psychiatrie/startpagina_-_levensbe_indiging_op_verzoek.html

Nys H (2005) Physician assisted suicide in Belgian law. Eur J Health Law 12(1):39–41. https://doi.org/10.1163/1571809054663131

Nys H (2017) A discussion of the legal rules on euthanasia in Belgium briefly compared with the rules in Luxembourg and the Netherlands. In: Jones DA, Gastmans C, MacKeller C (eds) Euthanasia and assisted suicide: lessons from Belgium. Cambridge University Press, Cambridge, pp 7–25

Ogden RD, Hamilton WK, Whitcher C (2010) Assisted suicide by oxygen deprivation with helium at a swiss right-to-die organization. J Med Ethics 36(3):174–179. https://doi.org/10.1136/jme.2009.032490

Oltermann P (2018) David Goodall, Australia's oldest scientist, ends his own life aged 104. In: The Guardian. https://www.theguardian.com/society/2018/may/10/david-goodall-australias-oldest-scientist-ends-his-own-life-at-104

Onwuteaka-Philipsen BD, van der Heide A, Koper D, Keij-Deerenberg I, Rietjens JAC, Rurup ML, Vrakking AM, Georges JJ, Muller MT, van der Wal G, van der Maas P (2003) Euthanasia and other end-of-life decisions in the Netherlands in 1990, 1995, and 2001. Lancet 362(9381): 395–399. https://doi.org/10.1016/S0140-6736(03)14029-9

Openbaar Ministerie, College van Procureurs-Generaal – Opdrachten. https://www.om-mp.be/nl/colpg/college-van-procureurs-generaal-opdrachten

Ordomedic (2000) Implication médicale dans le cadre de la vie finissante – Euthanasie, a087001. https://ordomedic.be/fr/avis/ethique/euthanasie/implication-medicale-dans-le-cadre-de-la-vie-finissante-euthanasie

Ordomedic (2001) Euthanasie, a094007. https://ordomedic.be/fr/avis/ethique/euthanasie/euthanasie-1

Ordomedic (2003) Avis relatif aux soins palliatifs, à l'euthanasie et à d'autres décisions médicales concernant la fin de vie, a100006. https://ordomedic.be/fr/avis/deontologie/consentement-eclaire/avis-relatif-aux-soins-palliatifs-a-l-euthanasie-et-a-d-autres-decisions-medicales-concernant-la-fin-de-vie

Ordomedic (2019) Directives déontologiques pour la pratique de l'euthanasie des patients en souffrance psychique à la suite d'une pathologie psychiatrique, a165002. https://ordomedic.be/fr/avis/ethique/euthanasie/directives-deontologiques-pour-la-pratique-de-l-euthanasie-des-patients-en-souffrance-psychique-a-la-suite-d-une-pathologie-psychiatrique

Ordomedic, Wie zijn we? https://www.ordomedic.be/nl/orde/wie-zijn-we/

Otlowski M (1997) Voluntary euthanasia and the common law. Oxford University Press, New York

Palomino E (2017) How to die in Colombia: a constitutional dilemma. Asia Pacific J Health L & Ethics 10(2):51–68

Parlamentarische Initiative 00.441 Franco Cavalli (2000) Strafbarkeit der aktiven Sterbehilfe. Neuregelung (Swiss National Council)

Parlamentarische Initiative 01.407 Dorle Vallender (2001) Verleitung und Beihilfe zur Selbsttötung. Neufassung von Artikel 115 StGB (Swiss National Council)

Parlamentarische Initiative 06.453 Christine Egerszegi-Obrist (2006) Regelung der Sterbehilfe auf Gesetzesebene (Swiss National Council)

Petermann FT (2008) Die geltende Regelung für Natrium-Pentobarbital: Ein legistischer Rubik's Cube? AJP/PJA 11:1413–1431

Postulat 18.3554 Ida Glanzmann-Hunkeler (2018) Suizidhilfe in der Schweiz (Swiss National Council)ve

Pousset G, Bilsen J, Joachim C, Chambaere K, Deliens L, Mortier F (2010) Medical end-of-life decisions in children in Flanders, Belgium: a population-based postmortem survey. Arch Pediatr Adolesc Med 164(6):547–553. https://doi.org/10.1001/archpediatrics.2010.59

Protection of Conscience Project (2017) Brothers of Charity: vision of euthanasia adjusted. https://www.consciencelaws.org/religion/religion053-001.aspx

RCP (2020) The RCP clarifies its position on assisted dying. https://www.rcplondon.ac.uk/news/rcp-clarifies-its-position-assisted-dying

Rietjens JAC, van Delden JJM, van der Heide A, Vrakking AM, Onwuteaka-Philipsen BD, van der Maas PJ, van der Wal G (2006) Terminal sedation and euthanasia. Arch Intern Med 166(7): 749–753. https://doi.org/10.1001/archinte.166.7.749

Rietjens JAC, van Delden JJM, Onwuteaka-Philipsen BD, Buiting H, van der Maas P, van der Heide A (2008) Continuous deep sedation for patients nearing death in the Netherlands: descriptive study. BMJ 336(7648):810–813. https://doi.org/10.1136/bmj.39504.531505.25

Rietjens JAC, Heijltjes MT, van Delden JJM, Onwuteaka-Philipsen BD, van der Heide A (2019) The rising frequency of continuous deep sedation in the Netherlands, a repeated cross-sectional survey in 2005, 2010 and 2015. J Am Med Dir Assoc 20(11):1367–1372. https://doi.org/10.1016/j.jamda.2019.06.012

Rietschel M (2014) Mental disorders are somatic disorders, a comment on M. Stier and T. Schramme. Front Psychol 5(53):1–3. https://doi.org/10.3389/fpsyg.2014.00053

RTE (2016) 2016-85, Elderly-Care Specialist, Dementia, Not Acted in Accordance with the Due Care Criteria. https://english.euthanasiecommissie.nl/judgments/dementia/documents/publications/judgments/2016/2016-85/2016-85
RTE (2019) Annual Report 2018. https://english.euthanasiecommissie.nl/the-committees/annual-reports
RTE (2019) Euthanasia Code 2018. https://english.euthanasiecommissie.nl/the-committees/code-of-practice
RTE (2020) Annual Report 2019. https://english.euthanasiecommissie.nl/the-committees/annual-reports
RTE (2020) Lichte stijging aantal euthanasiemeldingen. https://www.euthanasiecommissie.nl/actueel/nieuws/2020/4/17/jaarverslag-2019
RTE, Review Procedure. https://english.euthanasiecommissie.nl/review-procedure
RTE, The Committees. https://english.euthanasiecommissie.nl/the-committees/the-committees
Ruth HEH (2011) Suizidbeihilfe – eine ärztliche Tätigkeit? Die Diskussion in der schweizerischen Akademie der medizinischen Wissenschaften 1995-2004. Dissertation, University of Bern
Saad TC (2017) Euthanasia in Belgium: legal, historical and political review. Issues L & Med 32(2): 183–204
Samek R (1984) Euthanasia and law reform. Ottawa L R 17(1):86–115
SAMS (1976) Medizinisch-ethische Richtlinien für die Sterbehilfe
SAMS (1981) Medizinisch-ethische Richtlinien für die Sterbehilfe
SAMS (1995) Medizinisch-ethische Richtlinien für die ärztliche Betreuung sterbender und zerebral schwerst geschädigter Patienten
SAMS (2004, updated 2013) Medizinisch-ethische Richtlinien - Betreuung von Patientinnen und Patienten am Lebensende
SAMS (2006) Schreiben der SAMW an den Bundesrat zur Zulassung und Beaufsichtigung von Sterbehilfeorganisationen. https://www.samw.ch/de/Ethik/Themen-A-bis-Z/Sterben-und-Tod/Hintergrund-Sterben-Tod.html
SAMS (2006) Zur Praxis der Suizidbeihilfe in Akutspitälern: die Position der SAMW. https://www.samw.ch/de/Ethik/Themen-A-bis-Z/Sterben-und-Tod/Hintergrund-Sterben-Tod.html
SAMS (2018) Medizin-ethische Richtlinien - Umgang mit Sterben und Tod
SAMS (2019) Medizin-ethische Richtlinien - Urteilsfähigkeit in der medizinischen Praxis
SAMS, Portrait. https://www.samw.ch/en/Portrait.html
Säuberli H (2019) Fehlendes Vertrauen der Ärztekammer der FMH in ihre Mitglieder. Schweiz Ärzteztg 100(7):202. https://doi.org/10.4414/saez.2019.17586
Scheidegger D (2018) Diskussion um die SAMW-Richtlinien "Umgang mit Sterben und Tod". Schweiz Ärzteztg 99(46):1613. https://doi.org/10.4414/saez.2018.17337
Scherer JM, Simon RJ (1999) Euthanasia and the right to die: a comparative view. Rowman & Littlefield Publishers, Lanham
Schmidt C, Ulrich A (2009) Court expected to rule on assisted suicide case. In: Spiegel. https://www.spiegel.de/international/germany/deadly-business-court-expected-to-rule-on-assisted-suicide-case-a-602390.html
Schoonman MK, van Thiel GJMW, van Delden JJM (2014) Non-physician-assisted suicide in the Netherlands: a cross-sectional survey among the general public. J Med Ethics 40(12):842–848. https://doi.org/10.1136/medethics-2013-101736
Schwarzenegger C (2007) Das Mittel zur Suizidbeihilfe und das Recht auf den eigenen Tod (lange Version). Schweiz Ärzteztg 88(19):1–9. https://doi.org/10.4414/saez.2007.1217
Select Committee of the Assisted Dying for the Terminally Ill Bill, *Assisted Dying for the Terminally Ill Bill* (HL 2004-05, 86-I, II, III)
Sheldon T (2003) "Terminal sedation" different from Euthanasia, Dutch ministers agree. BMJ 327(7413):465. https://doi.org/10.1136/bmj.327.7413.465-a
Sheldon T (2020) Doctors can fulfil euthanasia request if patient develops dementia, rules Dutch Supreme Court. BMJ 369:m1652. https://doi.org/10.1136/bmj.m1652

Sillgitt A (2007) Letzte Ausfahrt Parkplatz. In: Der Spiegel. https://www.spiegel.de/panorama/sterbehilfe-letzte-ausfahrt-parkplatz-a-516121.html
Sneiderman B, Verhoef M (1996) Patient autonomy and the defence of medical necessity: five dutch euthanasia cases. Alta L Rev 34(2):374–415. https://doi.org/10.29173/alr1086
Sperling D (2019) Suicide tourism: understanding the legal, philosophical, and socio-political dimensions. Oxford University Press, Oxford
Srinivas R (2009) Exploring the potential for American death tourism. Mich St U J Med & L 13:91–122
Stalder H (2019) Ist Leiden nicht Sache der Medizin? Schweiz Ärzteztg 100(3):66. https://doi.org/10.4414/saez.2019.17421
Standesinitiative 08.317 Aargau (2008) Beihilfe zum Suizid. Änderung von Artikel 115 StGB
Standesinitiative 10.306 Basel-Landschaft (2010) Gesamtschweizerische Regelung der Suizidbeihilfe
Standesinitiative 17.315 Neuenburg (2017) Bedingungen für die Suizidhilfe
Stiller L (2020) Sterbehilfe und assistierter Suizid - Zur Bedeutung des Patientenwillens für die Rechtfertigung von Sterbehilfe und Suizidassistenz. Dike, Nomos, Baden-Baden
Stooss C (1893) Die Grundzüge des schweizerischen Strafrechts, im Auftrage des Bundesrathes vergleichend dargestellt, vol 2. H. Georg, Basel
Stooss C (1894) Schweizerisches Strafgesetzbuch: Vorentwurf im Auftrage des schweizerischen Bundesrates. Georg & Co, Basel
Strebel D (2007) Eine Insiderin klagt an. In: Beobachter. https://www.beobachter.ch/gesellschaft/sterbehilfe-eine-insiderin-klagt
Suter D (2012) EXIT (Deutsche Schweiz) 1982-2012: Ein Überblick: 30 Jahre Einsatz für Selbstbestimmung. Sutter B (ed) EXIT Deutsche Schweiz, Zurich. https://exit.ch/fileadmin/user_upload/download/broschueren/exit_30-Jahre-Broschuere_DE.pdf
Swart SJ, van der Heide A, Brinkkemper T, van Zuylen L, Perez R, Rietjens J (2012) Continous palliative sedation until death: practice after introduction of the Dutch national guide. BMJ Support Palliat Care 2(3):256–263. https://doi.org/10.1136/bmjspcare-2011-000063
Swiss National Science Foundation & NRP 67 (2017) Synthesis Report NRP 67: End of Life. http://www.nfp67.ch/en/News/Pages/11121-news-nfp67-synthesis-report.aspx
Swiss Parliament (2001) Amtliches Bulletin Nationalrat, Wintersession 11. Tagung der 46. Amtsdauer
Swiss Parliament (2003) Amtliches Bulletin Ständerat, Sommersession 19. Tagung der 46. Amtsdauer
Swiss Parliament (2012) Amtliches Bulletin Nationalrat, Herbstsession 5. Tagung 49. Amtsdauer
Temmerman M (2015) Als je als ziekenhuis abortus en euthanasie weigert, moet je het ook durven zeggen. In: De Morgen. https://www.demorgen.be/es-bdff7b1b
ten Have HAMJ, Welie JVM (1996) Euthanasia in the Netherlands. Crit Care Clin 12(1):97–108. https://doi.org/10.1016/S0749-0704(05)70217-7
Thijs T (2017) Euthanasie mag nu ook van Broeders van Liefde. In: De Morgen. https://www.demorgen.be/nieuws/euthanasie-mag-nu-ook-van-broeders-van-liefde~b4e72386/
Thomasma DC, Kimbrough-Kushne T, Kimsma GK, Ciesielski-Carlucci C (eds) (1998) Asking to die: inside the Dutch debate about euthanasia. Springer, Dordrecht
Thommen M (2018) Criminal law. In: Thommen M (ed) Introduction to Swiss law. Carl Grossman Verlag, Berlin, Bern
Todd D (2015) The Story at the Heart of Friday's Supreme Court Ruling on Assisted Suicide. In: Vancouver Sun. https://vancouversun.com/news/staff-blogs/b-c-woman-chooses-a-dignified-death-in-switzerland
Tännsjö T (ed) (2004) Terminal sedation: euthanasia in disguise? Springer, Dordrecht
Triviño MA (2018) Colombia has regulated euthanasia for children and adolescents. In: LatinAmerican Post. https://latinamericanpost.com/20090-colombia-has-regulated-euthanasia-for-children-and-adolescents
United Kingdom, Assisted Dying for the Terminally Ill HL Bill 17, Session 2003-04

United Kingdom, Assisted Dying HL Bill 69, Session 2019-21
United Kingdom, Assisted Dying (No 2) HC Bill 7, Session 2015-16
Universitätsspital Zürich (2007) Suizidbeihilfe und Spital: Umgang mit Patienten des USZ, die sich mit Hilfe ei- ner Sterbehilfeorganisation das Leben nehmen wollen. Bioethica Forum 54:28–29
Van Assche K, Raus K, Vanderhaegen B, Sterckx S (2019) "Capacity of discernment" and euthanasia on minors in Belgium. Med Law Rev 27(2):242–266. https://doi.org/10.1093/medlaw/fwy027
van de Walle J-P (2017) Euthanasia of minors in Belgium. In: European Institute of Bioehtics. https://www.ieb-eib.org/docs/pdf/2017-01/doc-1554801216-19.pdf
van Delden JJM, Pijnenborg L, van der Maas P (1993) The Remmelink Study: two years later. Hastings Cent Rep 23(6):24–27
van den Berg JH (1978) Medical power and medical ethics. Norton, New York
van der Heide A, Onwuteaka-Philipsen BD, Rurup ML, Buiting HM, van Delden JJM, Hanssen-de Wolf JE, Janssen AGJM, Pasman HRW, Rietjens JAC, Prins CJM, Deerenberg IM, Gevers JKM, van der Maas PJ, van der Wal G (2007) End-of-life practices in the Netherlands under the Euthanasia Act. N Eng J Med 356(19):1957–1965. https://doi.org/10.1056/NEJMsa071143
van der Maas P, van Delden JJM, Pijnenborg L, Looman CWN (1991) Euthanasia and other medical decisions concerning the end of life. Lancet 338(8768):669–674. https://doi.org/10.1016/0140-6736(91)91241-L
van der Wal G, van der Maas PJ, Bosma JM, Onwuteaka-Philipsen BD, Willems DL, Haverkate I, Kostense PF (1996) Evaluation of the notification procedure for physician-assisted death in the Netherlands. N Eng J Med 335(22):1706–1711. https://doi.org/10.1056/NEJM199611283352228
van Gool S, de Lepeleire J (2017) Euthanasia in children: keep asking the right questions. In: Jones DA, Gastmans C, MacKeller C (eds) Euthanasia and assisted suicide: lessons from Belgium. Cambridge University Press, Cambridge, pp 173–187
van Kolfschooten F (2003) Dutch television report stirs up euthanasia controversy. Lancet 361(9366):1352–1353. https://doi.org/10.1016/S0140-6736(03)13090-5
Verenigde Commissies voor de Justitieen voor de Sociale Aangelegenheden (2013) Hoorzittingen Euthanasie, Zitting 2012-2013. https://www.senate.be/actueel/homepage/docs/euthanasie.pdf
Verhagen E (2006) End of life decisions in newborns in the Netherlands: medical and legal aspects of the Groningen Protocol. Med Law 25(2):399–407
Verhofstadt M, Audenaert K, Van den Broeck K, Deliens L, Mortier F, Titeca K, Pardon K, Chambaere K (2020) Belgian psychiatrists' attitudes towards, and readiness to engage in, euthanasia assessment procedures with adults with psychiatric conditions: a survey. BMC Psychiatry 20:374–383. https://doi.org/10.1186/s12888-020-02775-x
Vuilleumier-Koch S (2019) Der Arzt und der assistierte Suizid. Schweiz Ärzteztg 100(12):419. https://doi.org/10.4414/saez.2019.17695
VVP (2017) Hoe omgaan met een euthanasieverzoek in psychiatrie binnen het huidig wettelijk kader? https://vvponline.be/bibliotheek.php?item=451&s=Presentatie_en_lezing
Walther C (2014) Leidenschaftlich Klar. In: Humanistischer Pressedienst. https://hpd.de/node/18453
Watson R (2014) Belgium extends euthanasia law to children. BMJ 348:g1633. https://doi.org/10.1136/bmj.g1633
Welie JVM (1992) The medical exception: physicians, euthanasia and the Dutch criminal law. J Med Philos 17(4):419–437. https://doi.org/10.1093/jmp/17.4.419
Williams G (2010) Assisting suicide, the code for crown prosecutors and the DPP's discretion. Comm L World Rev 39(2):181–203. https://doi.org/10.1350/clwr.2010.39.2.0203
Yu C-E, Wen J, Meng F (2020) Defining physician-assisted suicide tourism and travel. J Hosp Tour Res 44(4):694–703. https://doi.org/10.1177/1096348019899437

Chapter 4
The Right to Die Under the European Convention on Human Rights

Examining the case law of the ECtHR in detail is vital for understanding the trend in the jurisprudence and determining whether an argument can be made in favour of the right to die strong enough to force its applicability on the member states. As the interpreter of the Convention,[1] the Court's approach on the matter will be indicative of the direction in which the right to die is headed.

4.1 Case Law of the European Court of Human Rights

4.1.1 The R v UK Case

Until 1998, the European Commission of Human Rights (the Commission) received individual applications, and only those which were well-founded were sent to the Court.[2] The first-ever application about assisted suicide, which came before the Commission, was the R v UK Case.[3]

The applicant, who was a member of EXIT, was sentenced to 18 months in prison by the British courts for aiding and abetting suicide and conspiring to aid and abet suicide. He had counselled people by putting them in contact with another EXIT member to help them carry out their wishes for an assisted suicide. The applicant had

[1]European Convention on Human Rights and Fundamental Freedoms (European Convention on Human Rights, as amended).

[2]Before the amendment to the Convention by Protocol No. 11 on 01/11/1998, Section III of the original text regulated a Commission/Court system. Individual applications, regulated under Articles 25–32 of Section III, were to be made solely to the Commission. If the application was well founded and a friendly settlement could not be reached by the Commission, the case would be referred to the Court within three months period. Zwart (1994), pp. 23–29.

[3]*R v the United Kingdom* (1983) 33 DR 270 (European Commission of Human Rights).

D. N. Kayacan, *The Right to Die with Dignity*, European Union and its Neighbours in a Globalized World 6, https://doi.org/10.1007/978-3-031-04516-5_4

claimed that his motive was compassion, and his imprisonment based on the Suicide Act of 1961 had violated his rights under Articles 8 and 10 of the Convention.

While the Commission recognized that the wish to end one's life 'might be thought to touch directly on the private lives of those who sought to commit suicide', the sphere of Article 8 did not, however, cover the applicant's privacy interests in helping those who wished to commit suicide, by 'virtue of their trespass on the public interest of protecting life'.[4]

The Commission accepted the interference claim with regard to Article 10, the freedom of expression of the applicant. However, it ruled that this interference was justified when considering the legitimate interest pursued by the State in criminalizing assistance in suicide. 'It recognizes the right of the State under the Convention to guard against the inevitable criminal abuses that would occur, in the absence of legislation, against the aiding and abetting of suicide.'[5] Even if the applicant's intentions were only to help those who were suffering and autonomously had a wish to die, that fact did not eliminate the State's justification to protect its citizens. The application was found manifestly ill-founded and declared inadmissible.

4.1.2 The Sanles Sanles Case

After the Commission's R v UK decision, the Court received the first application on the matter of assisted suicide in 2000 and declared it inadmissible.[6] In 1968, Ramón Sampedro Cameán had an accident that had left him with tetraplegia at the age of 25.[7] In April 1993, Mr Sampedro started searching for a legal remedy in order to receive assistance from his physician to end his life. The Barcelona Court of First Instance dismissed his request because it was incompatible with the Criminal Code, and the Corunna Provincial Court upheld this decision. Mr Sampedro brought an appeal to the Constitutional Court in December 1996, claiming that the refusal to grant a legal remedy to end his life through the assistance of his physician was an infringement of his 'rights to human dignity and the free development of the personality, to life and to physical and psychological integrity, and to a fair trial'.[8] However, Mr Sampedro died in January 1998 before the Constitutional Court could

[4] *R v UK Case*, [13].

[5] *R v UK Case*, [17].

[6] *Sanles Sanles v Spain (dec)* App no 48335/99 ECHR 2000-XI.

[7] Tetraplegia, also known as quadriplegia, is a physical condition that is caused by spinal cord injury and results in the loss of function in four limbs and the torso. The spinal cord injury can be *complete* (loss of sensory and motor functions) or *incomplete* (if there is some sensory or motor function remaining). The severity of the symptoms is based on many factors. It could cause difficulty in breathing and severe pain. However, death is not imminent, and with proper care, life expectancy is usually long. Mayo Clinic (2019) Spinal Cord Injury. https://www.mayoclinic.org/diseases-conditions/spinal-cord-injury/symptoms-causes/syc-20377890.

[8] *Sanles Sanles Case*, 2.

render a judgment, through the help of a person or persons unknown. Before he died, Mr Sampedro had appointed Mrs Sanles, his sister-in-law, as his legal heir to continue the proceedings he had started. Mrs Sanles informed the Constitutional Court about the situation. In November 1998, the Constitutional Court dismissed the appeal on the grounds that Mrs Sanles did not have locus standi in the proceedings, as the rights Mr Sampedro's had claimed were highly personal in nature and could not be transferred to a third party.[9]

Mrs Sanles lodged an application to the ECtHR, claiming that denying Mr Sampedro's 'right to a dignified life, or to non-interference with his wish to put an end to his undignified life' violated Articles 2, 3, 5, and 9 of the Convention.[10] Since Mr Sampedro was unable to commit suicide by himself, refusing him to receive assistance also accumulated to discrimination under Article 14. Complaining about the lengthy proceedings that did not consider the urgency of Mr Sampedro's situation, the applicant also claimed a violation of Article 6.

The ECtHR stated that the right to die with dignity, whether or not it existed as a right to receive assistance for committing suicide, would be very personal and could not be transferred.[11] Therefore, Mrs Sanles could not claim violation of the Convention rights on behalf of Mr Sampedro. Even if Mrs Sanles could bring an application as a victim herself, the Court did not agree that the domestic courts' proceedings were lengthy enough to count as a violation of Article 6 of the Convention. The application was dismissed.

4.1.3 The Pretty Case

4.1.3.1 Circumstances of the Case

The first case concerning assisted suicide that was brought to the Court to be examined on the merits was the Pretty Case.[12] Mrs Pretty was a 43-year-old woman suffering from motor neuron disease, which causes 'progressive destruction' of the nerve cells leading to the loss of functions of muscles overtime and eventually paralyses. Although there is no harm to the patient's mental capacities, the disease has no treatment, and death is inevitable, which is usually caused by suffocation as the breathing muscles lose their function.[13] When the case came before the Court, Mrs Pretty was already in a state where she was paralyzed from the neck down, had lost her speech for the better part, and was being fed with a tube. Having her mental capacities intact, she feared the end that was coming and did not wish to endure the

---

[9] *Sanles Sanles Case*, 3.

[10] *Sanles Sanles Case*, 5.

[11] *Sanles Sanles Case*, 8.

[12] *Pretty v the United Kingdom* App no 2346/02 ECHR 2002-III.

[13] See footnote 611 under 3.7.1 'The Rodriguez Case'.

pain, which she found to be humiliating and undignified. Since it was no longer possible for her to end her life alone, she wanted her husband to assist her in suicide but worried that he might face criminal charges for his assistance after she passed away.

According to section 2(1) of the 1961 Act, Mr Pretty faced the risk of prosecution if he were to assist his wife in suicide. Therefore, Mrs Pretty had requested from the DPP to guarantee that her husband would not be prosecuted for his assistance. Her request had been refused on the ground that immunity for a future crime could not be granted ahead of time. Mrs Pretty had challenged the DPP's refusal before the British Courts and claimed that the 1961 Act, which criminalized her husband's assistance, was incompatible with Articles 2,3,8,9, and 14 of the Convention, however, without any success.

4.1.3.2 Judgment of the House of Lords

After the DPP had refused to grant immunity to her husband, Mrs Pretty appealed the decision before the Divisional Court in August 2001. Her appeal was rejected within two months in October 2001, as the Divisional Court did not find any incompatibility between the 1961 Act and the Convention. The Divisional Court's decision was appealed before the House of Lords (the House), only to be dismissed in November 2001. In its decision, the House evaluated Mrs Pretty's claims and all possible violations of the Convention rights.[14]

Considering the claim of violation of Article 2 of the Convention, which covers the right to life, the House stated that such an article protecting the sanctity of life could not be interpreted as including a negative aspect in terms of a right to die. To support its position, the House referred to a previous judgment by the Court, which identified a 'positive obligation on the authorities to take preventive operational measures to protect an individual whose life is at risk from the criminal acts of another individual'.[15] In the face of the State's duty to protect life, it could not be concluded that the State also carried a duty to enable end-of-life decisions.

The House referred to two previous British cases that had established a general principle on end-of-life decisions. The Bland Case was about the withdrawal of treatment from a patient who was in a vegetative state with no prospects of recovery.[16] The Re J Case concerned an infant with severe disabilities suffering constant pain from his condition, and whether or not invasive measures should be

[14] *Pretty v Director of Public Prosecutions and Secretary of State for the Home Department* [2001] UKHL 61, [2002] 1 AC 800.

[15] *Osman v the United Kingdom* App no 23452/94 ECHR 1998-VIII [115]. The case was about the applicant's husband, who was threatened and later shot and killed by their son's teacher. The applicant claimed a violation of Article 2, as the State had failed to protect her husband's life.

[16] *Airedale NHS Trust v Bland* [1993] UKHL 17, [1993] AC 789.

taken in order to resuscitate him, although there was little to no chance of survival.[17] In both cases, a distinction was made between death as a result of withholding or withdrawing treatment and death as a result of an action by a third party. In the Bland Case, it was held that 'the sanctity of life entails its inviolability by an outsider [. . .] even if the person in question has consented to its violation',[18] and the Re J Case had found it unacceptable to use treatment for the purpose of hastening death.[19]

The House later concluded that the Convention did not entail an obligation for the State to allow assisted suicide and that there was no contradiction between the State's refusal to permit assisted suicide and Article 2 of the Convention.[20]

This point was emphasized in the answer to Mrs Pretty's claim that denying her husband a guarantee not to be prosecuted was forcing her to continue her life in suffering and, by doing so, accumulated to a 'proscribed treatment' within the meaning of Article 3 of the Convention.[21] The House evaluated this claim from almost all aspects. First of all, Article 3 had to be taken in conjunction with Article 2. In some cases, the State could take action, which might amount to a violation under Article 3, to protect individuals' right to life. That meant, even if the refusal of the DPP to give a guarantee violated Mrs Pretty's Article 3 right, this would be justified by the State's obligation under Article 2. In addition, the term treatment could not have an 'unrestricted or extravagant meaning', and defining the DPP's refusal as proscribed treatment would be a far-reaching interpretation of Article 3.[22]

The House referred to the Rees Case, in which the Court had found a wide margin of appreciation in regard to a positive obligation in matters where no consensus among the member States existed and that were rather in a 'transitional stage'.[23] Under these circumstances, a positive obligation to accept a right to die would be 'more judgmental, more prone to variation from State to State, more dependent on the opinions and beliefs of the people and less susceptible to any universal injunction'.[24] For the House, this meant there was no such duty rising from the Convention to allow assistance in suicide for terminally ill patients. The House concluded that Article 3 had not been violated.

---

[17] Re J (A Minor) (Wardship: Medical Treatment) [1990] 3 AII ER 930.

[18] *Bland Case*, [831].

[19] *Re J Case*, [46].

[20] *Pretty Case-HL*, [9].

[21] ECHR Art 3(1) 'No one shall be subjected to torture or to inhuman or degrading treatment or punishment.'

[22] *Pretty Case-HL*, [13].

[23] *Rees v the United Kingdom* 17 October 1986 Ser A no 106, [37]. The applicant was born female but had gender reassignment surgery and claimed violation of Arts 8 and 12 of the Convention because the State refused to change his gender from female to male in his birth certificate. Although emphasizing the need for legislative development to meet the need of transgender people, The Court found no violation of the Convention rights based on the wide margin of appreciation enjoyed by the States on questions surrounding newly (at the time) developing legal issues.

[24] *Pretty Case-HL*, [15].

Mrs Pretty had claimed that her decision on how and when to end her life should be within her right to self-determination, protected under Article 8 of the Convention, as an aspect of the right to respect for private and family life. If and when there was an interference with an end-of-life decision, the State should justify the necessity of its interference. Mrs Pretty referred to the Canadian Rodriguez Case, in support of her Article 8 claims.[25]

In the Rodriguez Case, all except one of the SCC's judges had agreed that end-of-life decisions were within the ambit of personal autonomy. However, the ban on assisted suicide was found justified, considering the effective protection of life, especially the vulnerability of the group concerned. After analysing the SCC's reasoning, the House stated that there was 'no close analogy' in the Convention for the provisions relied on in the Rodriguez Case.[26] Only Article 5 of the Convention referred to the right to liberty and security, which was the basis of the Rodriguez Case. The protection assured by Article 8 was only applicable to the 'personal autonomy while individuals are living their lives' and did not include end-of-life decisions.[27]

On this point, Lord Hope made a separate statement and accepted that 'the way she [Mrs Pretty] chooses the closing moments of her life is a part of the act of living, and she has a right to ask that this too must be respected' under Article 8.[28] However, according to Lord Hope, it did not amount to a positive obligation on the State to make assisted suicide possible.[29]

Although it excluded end-of-life decisions from the ambit of Article 8, the House continued to present its justification in case interference was found.

Reference was made to the 1999 Council of Europe Recommendation 1418 on the Protection of the Human Rights and Dignity of the Terminally Ill and Dying.[30] Under paragraph 9(c), it is written:

> The Assembly therefore recommends that the Committee of Ministers encourage the member states of the Council of Europe to respect and protect the dignity of terminally ill or dying persons in all respects:

---

[25] *Pretty Case-HL*, [17].

[26] *Pretty Case-HL*, [23].

[27] *Pretty Case-HL*, [23]. Although the wording of the Convention might not directly state liberty and security under Article 8, a comparison with consideration of the contexts of both the Canadian provisions and the Convention would have more depth and better reflect the essence of the rights compared. The SCC described the right to make an end-of-life decision as a matter of personal autonomy, and the fact that one might not exercise this autonomy from fear of criminal prosecution would interfere with this right. The scope of this statement cannot be limited to Article 5 of the Convention. It is still a State action withholding the person from making an end-of-life decision as an expression of his personal autonomy, which is within the ambit of Article 8 of the Convention. See text to footnote 624 under Sect. 3.7.1.3 'Judgment of the Supreme Court of Canada'.

[28] *Pretty Case-HL*, [100].

[29] *Pretty Case-HL*, [100].

[30] Council of Europe, Recommendation 1418 on protection of the human rights and dignity of the terminally ill and dying (adopted by the Parliamentary Assembly on 25 June 1999 at the 24th sitting) 1999. http://assembly.coe.int/nw/xml/xref/xref-xml2html-en.asp?fileid=16722&lang=en.

[. . .]

(c) by upholding the prohibition against intentionally taking the life of terminally ill or dying persons, while;

(1) recognising that the right to life, especially with regard to a terminally ill or dying person, is guaranteed by the member States, in accordance with Article 2 of the European Convention on Human Rights which states that 'no one shall be deprived of his life intentionally;
(2) recognising that a terminally ill or dying person's wish to die never constitutes any legal claim to die at the hand of another person;
(3) recognising that a terminally ill or dying person's wish to die cannot of itself constitute a legal justification to carry out actions intended to bring about death.

According to the House, this paragraph indicated a consensus among the member States about the illegality of assisted suicide.[31] Although member States could make exceptional regulations to allow euthanasia or assisted suicide, for example, in the Netherlands, the practice was strictly regulated and never carried out by someone other than a medical professional. Paragraph 9(c)(3) of the Recommendation 1418 stated that the 'wish to die cannot *of itself* constitute a legal justification'.[32] If the State had not legalized euthanasia or assisted suicide through specific regulations, according to the Recommendation 1418, there was no obligation upon the State to grant a terminally ill patient's wish to die.

On the other hand, the prohibition of assisted suicide was justified by the fear of abuse in the House's opinion. The will to protect the elderly and 'undesirability of anything which could appear to encourage suicide' prevented the House from making any exceptions and justified the blanket ban on assisted suicide.[33]

Mrs Pretty had also claimed that the 1961 Act was discriminatory towards people with disabilities. Unlike physically-abled persons, Mrs Pretty could not carry out her end-of-life decision without assistance. However, the threat of prosecution her husband would face was depriving her of the possibility of exercising her decision. While someone physically capable of committing suicide autonomously would not face any legal obstacles, Mrs Pretty was being deprived of this option just because she did not have the physical ability. Mrs Pretty argued that this was a discriminatory differential treatment under Article 14 of the Convention.[34]

The House rejected the discrimination argument, as none of the prior articles were found applicable to the case. Even if the claims were within the scope of any other Convention right, the House stated that Article 14 still would not be applicable in Mrs Pretty's case, since the situation did not amount to discrimination. The decriminalization of suicide in the UK was not for the purpose of legalizing it.

The law confers no right to commit suicide. Suicide was always, as a crime, anomalous, since it was the only crime with which no defendant could ever be charged. The main effect

[31] *Pretty Case-HL*, [28].
[32] Emphasis added.
[33] *Pretty Case-HL*, [29].
[34] *Pretty Case-HL*, [32].

> of the criminalisation of suicide was to penalise those who attempted to take their own lives and failed, and secondary parties. Suicide itself (and with it attempted suicide) was decriminalised because recognition of the common law offence was not thought to act as a deterrent, because it cast an unwarranted stigma on innocent members of the suicide's family and because it led to the distasteful result that patients recovering in hospital from a failed suicide attempt were prosecuted, in effect, for their lack of success.[35]

Decriminalizing suicide was not an acknowledgment of it as a right but was instead a change because punishment was proven not to be the most beneficial approach. During the third and final reading of the amendment to the 1961 Act in the House of Commons, Mr Charles Fletcher-Cooke had emphasized this point. 'It must not be thought that because we are changing the method of treatment for those unfortunate people we seek to depreciate the gravity of the action of anyone who tries to commit suicide.'[36]

Another point the House gave importance to was the personal case-by-case character of criminal law. When deciding whether or not to prosecute or which penalty would be suitable for the offender, criminal law took into consideration the specific circumstances of each case. The DPP's discretion on prosecution or the court's deliberation over the necessity of a sentence were all considerations to make after the event had occurred and not before. As the House said, 'the broad policy of criminal law is to apply offence-creating provisions to all and to give weight to personal circumstances either at the stage of considering whether or not to prosecute or, in the event of conviction, when penalty is to be considered'.[37] Finally, the House clarified that it was not within the power of the DPP to grant any kind of guarantee in advance to Mrs Pretty's husband for his possible assistance in her suicide.

The House's reasoning shows a strict approach towards assisted dying. The UK accepted the right to refuse treatment. However, an action by a third person with the intention to cause death, even if it was upon the patient's request, was not acceptable and not protected as an expression of personal autonomy and the right to self-determination. The Bland Case had stated that 'the principle of sanctity of human life must yield to the principle of self-determination', but this approach was only limited to patients' right to refuse treatment.[38] The House did not extend it to end-of-life decisions, and sanctity of life was upheld over the wishes of the patient. The Re J Case had made a distinction regarding intentions, which meant any act with the intention to ease the patient's pain or suffering, even if this act happened to hasten the patient's death, was lawful as long as the primary intention was not to cause death.[39] The House did not deviate from this view in the case of Mrs Pretty. Although the patient's wishes and best interest were regarded highly, a wish to die did not generate any form of obligation upon the State.

---

[35] *Pretty Case-HL*, [35].

[36] HC Deb 28 July 1961 Vol 645 Col 823.

[37] *Pretty Case-HL*, [36].

[38] *Bland Case*, [864].

[39] *Re J Case*, [46].

4.1.3.3 Judgment of the ECtHR

In December 2001, Mrs Pretty brought her claims against the UK before the Court. The evaluation by the Court will be examined next.

4.1.3.3.1 On Article 2 of the Convention

The Court first commented on the scope of Article 2, which did not only require a State 'to refrain from the intentional and unlawful taking of life, but also to take appropriate steps to safeguard the lives of those within its jurisdiction.'[40] Emphasizing the nature of the right to life, the Court stated:

> Article 2 cannot, without distortion of language, be interpreted as conferring the diametrically opposite right, namely a right to die; nor can it create a right to self-determination in the sense of conferring on an individual the entitlement to choose death rather than life.[41]

4.1.3.3.2 On Article 3 of the Convention

The Court started by summarizing the case law development on Article 3. Initially, the wording of Article 3 referred to a negative obligation on the State not to inflict any inhuman or degrading treatment to people under its jurisdiction. Jurisprudence has not been limited to the wording of the article and previous case law has shown that Article 3 also included a positive obligation on the State, namely to take necessary measurements to prevent any sort of proscribed treatment that might be inflicted by its organs or private individuals. The A v UK Case, concerning ill-treatment of a child, was set as an example for the States' positive obligation.[42] The stepfather of the applicant was brought before the UK courts on charges of assault for beating his stepson with a garden cane in order to 'discipline' him. Acquitted by the British Courts, the stepfather's actions were found justifiable on the grounds of 'reasonable punishment' of a child.[43] The applicant had claimed that the law violated the Convention, as it did not protect him from his stepfather's assault.[44] The Court found a violation of Article 3 since it was the State's duty 'to take measures designed to ensure that individuals within their jurisdiction are not subjected to torture or inhuman or degrading treatment or punishment, including such ill-treatment administered by private individuals'.[45]

---

[40] *Pretty Case*, [38].

[41] *Pretty Case*, [39].

[42] *A v the United Kingdom* 23 September 1998 ECHR 1998-VI.

[43] *A v UK Case*, [10]-[11].

[44] *A v UK Case*, [8].

[45] *A v UK Case*, [22].

With the positive obligation on States in mind, the Court addressed what would be considered as proscribed treatment within the meaning of Article 3.

> As regards the types of 'treatment' which fall within the scope of Article 3 of the Convention, the Court's case-law refers to 'ill-treatment' that attains a minimum level of severity and involves actual bodily injury or intense physical or mental suffering. Where treatment humiliates or debases an individual, showing a lack of respect for, or diminishing, his or her human dignity, or arouses feelings of fear, anguish or inferiority capable of breaking an individual's moral and physical resistance, it may be characterised as degrading and also fall within the prohibition of Article. The suffering which flows from naturally occurring illness, physical or mental, may be covered by Article 3, where it is, or risks being, exacerbated by treatment, whether flowing from conditions of detention, expulsion or other measures, for which the authorities can be held responsible.[46]

Based on this description, one could argue that Mrs Pretty's situation could be interpreted as proscribed treatment. Her wish to end her life and her incapability to do so on her own were not being respected. Forcing her to go through a painful death, which she feared, and the fact that this fear had become a physical and mental burden was diminishing her dignity. Would the Court extend the scope of Article 3 to cover the failure of taking necessary measures in order to render it possible for Mrs Pretty to end her life on her terms without suffering a painful death?

Regarding illnesses, the Court referred to the D v UK Case.[47] The applicant, who was from St Kitts, was diagnosed with AIDS while he was in prison in the UK for his involvement with drugs. After a while, the authorities wanted to transfer him back to St Kitts, which the applicant claimed would violate his Convention rights since he could not receive adequate treatment or support in St Kitts as he did in the UK.[48] The UK responded that the applicant's removal would not amount to a violation of Article 3 as his illness and not the authorities in St Kitts caused the disadvantaged situation.[49] The Court held that in cases of deportation, States were obliged to take into account whether the deportee would face any kind of proscribed treatment that 'emanates from intentionally inflicted acts of the public authorities in the receiving country or from those of non-State bodies in that country when the authorities there are unable to afford him appropriate protection'.[50] In the D v UK Case, the Court extended this obligation also to possible proscribed treatments, where 'the source of the risk of proscribed treatment in the receiving country stems from factors which cannot engage either directly or indirectly the responsibility of the public authorities of that country, or which, taken alone, do not in themselves infringe the standards of that Article'.[51] In other words, D could not be deported to St Kitts, as he would not receive the equivalent medical care he was receiving in the UK. Even if there was no 'intentionally inflicted act' by the authorities in St Kitts and even if the UK was not

[46] *Pretty Case*, [52].

[47] *D v the United Kingdom* 2 May 1997 ECHR 1997-III.

[48] *D v UK Case*, [7]-[10], [40].

[49] *D v UK Case*, [42].

[50] *D v UK Case*, [49].

[51] *D v UK Case*, [49].

responsible for D's illness, the mere fact that D would not be able to receive the same standard of treatment made Article 3 applicable to the case.

Seeing how the Court can be liberal with its approach and does not hesitate to broaden the scope of a Convention right through its interpretation where it deems necessary, it would not be impossible to imagine a similar approach to Mrs Pretty's case. Even if the State had no involvement in her disease and the pain it has been causing her, could the refusal of granting her wish to receive assistance for her suicide be interpreted as a 'source' of proscribed treatment according to the Court's interpretation in the D v UK Case?

The response was negative. The Court did not find Mrs Pretty's situation comparable with the circumstances of the previous cases and set limits to its interpretational boundaries by stating:

> While the Court must take a dynamic and flexible approach to the interpretation of the Convention, which is a living instrument, any interpretation must also accord with the fundamental objectives of the Convention and its coherence as a system of human rights protection.[52]

The question in the A v UK Case was whether the law that allowed for the defence of 'reasonable punishment' provided adequate protection in accordance with Article 3. In the D v UK Case, it was not the applicant's illness that had engaged Article 3 but rather the medical care conditions imposed upon the applicant in case of deportation. The request of Mrs Pretty, on the other hand, was for the DPP to grant a guarantee to her husband in order for him to assist her with suicide without the threat of prosecution or for a legislative change in the 1961 Act. According to the Court, one would have to extend the meaning of Article 3 beyond its objectives to construe a positive obligation on the State under these circumstances.[53]

The Court found no violation, as a positive obligation for the State to allow assisted suicide could not be interpreted into Article 3.[54]

4.1.3.3.3 On Article 8 of the Convention

The Court's liberal approach in interpretation has, perhaps, shown itself the most on Article 8. Case law shows that Article 8 covers a wide range of aspects regarding human life and social interactions, and its ambit is not restricted.[55]

Even though a right to self-determination concerning the end of life had not been previously established under Article 8, the Court declared that it considered personal autonomy as 'an important principle underlying the interpretation of its

[52] *Pretty Case*, [54].

[53] *Pretty Case*, [54].

[54] *Pretty Case*, [55].

[55] ECHR (2021) Guide on Article 8 of the European Convention on Human Rights. https://www.echr.coe.int/documents/guide_art_8_eng.pdf.

guarantees'.[56] The Court agreed with Lord Hope's dissenting statement that one's decision on how to spend the final stages of life was closely related to one's person and must, therefore, be respected.[57]

The Court is usually cautious with cases concerning controversial issues. This caution is obvious in the Pretty Case as well with the delicate choice of words in the way the Court extended Article 8's ambit to include end-of-life decisions and expressed its view on the right to die.

> The applicant in this case is prevented by law from exercising her choice to avoid what she considers will be an undignified and distressing end to her life. The Court *is not prepared to exclude* that this constitutes an interference with her right to respect for private life as guaranteed under Article 8/1 of the Convention.[58]

Assuming and without definitely deciding there was an interference, the Court moved on to scrutinize whether it could be justified under Article 8(2).

For an interference with the right to respect for private life to be justified under Article 8(2), the interference should serve a 'legitimate aim', be 'in accordance with the law' and 'necessary in a democratic society'. When the Court evaluates the necessity of an interference, it takes into account whether the interference responds to a 'pressing social need' and the matter of the case to determine the margin of appreciation enjoyed by the member States, which was determined to be wide in the matter of assisted suicide.[59]

The Court agreed with Mrs Pretty that she was neither vulnerable nor in need of protection.[60] However, the State had an obligation to protect its citizens and an interest in regulating criminal law for their protection. It had to be examined if a justification was possible through the State's legitimate aim to ensure public health and safety, which had to be balanced against personal autonomy. The balance between the two depended on the severity of possible damage to either interest.

> The more serious the harm involved the more heavily will weigh in the balance considerations of public health and safety against the countervailing principle of personal autonomy. The law in issue of this case, section 2 of the 1961 Act, was designed to safeguard life by protecting the weak and vulnerable and especially those who are not in a condition to take informed decisions against acts intended to end life or to assist in ending life. Doubtless the conditions of terminally ill individuals will vary. But many will be vulnerable and it is the vulnerability of the class which provides the rationale for the law in question. It is primarily for States to assess the risk and the likely incidence of abuse if the general prohibitions on assisted suicides were relaxed or if exceptions were to be created. Clear risks of abuse do exist, notwithstanding arguments as to the possibility of safeguards and protective procedures.[61]

---

[56] *Pretty Case*, [61].

[57] *Pretty Case*, [64].

[58] *Pretty Case*, [67] (emphasis added).

[59] *Pretty Case*, [70]-[71].

[60] *Pretty Case*, [73].

[61] *Pretty Case*, [74].

Although Mrs Pretty was not in a vulnerable state herself and her wish to end her life was indeed an expression of her personal autonomy, the State's aim of 'protecting the weak and vulnerable' justified the interference with her personal autonomy, namely the blanket ban on assisted suicide. The Court pointed out the discretion of the State to determine the necessary measures for protection. Lacking any consensus among the member States, the national authorities enjoyed a broader margin of appreciation in assessing the risk of abuse and the appropriate measures against it.

The Court also drew attention to the flexibility applied in practice due to section 2(4) of the 1961 Act. Previous exemplary cases in the UK about 'mercy killings' demonstrated a level of consideration for the circumstances of each individual case and for the public interest in prosecuting such cases. The enforcement of the law showed that the situation of people like Mrs Pretty was not ignored. Since the ban on assisted suicide pursued a legitimate aim and did not entirely disregard the individual characteristics of each case, the Court found the interference justified.

> It does not appear to be arbitrary to the Court for the law to reflect the importance of the right to life, by prohibiting assisted suicide while providing a system of enforcement and adjudication which allows due regard to be given in each particular case to the public interest in bringing a prosecution, as well as to the fair and proper requirements of retribution and deterrence.[62]

There is some significance to the Court's reasoning on the justification under Article 8(2). It does not only consider the aspects of public health and safety, namely the protection of the vulnerable, but also factors in the fact that the special circumstances of these cases have not been ignored by the justice system in practice and that importance is given whether there is any public interest in prosecution. This reasoning might hint at a future positive obligation of the State to give particular regard to cases on assisted suicide when deciding on whether or not to prosecute. Criminal law and procedure law take into account the circumstances of each case, but perhaps someday failing to do so might be qualified as a violation of Article 8.

4.1.3.3.4 On Article 9 of the Convention

The Court did not accept a violation of Article 9, freedom of thought, conscience, and religion. No matter how strongly Mrs Pretty might have felt about assisted suicide, her strong beliefs could only be held as a 'commitment to the principle of personal autonomy' under Article 8. It could not be argued as a manifestation of a spiritual belief covered by Article 9.[63]

---

[62] *Pretty Case*, [76].

[63] *Pretty Case*, [82].

4.1.3.3.5 On Article 14 of the Convention

The Court disagreed with the House of Lords and, since it had found an initial violation of Article 8, assessed the claim of discrimination against physically incapable terminally ill patients in deciding when and how to die. The same reasoning justifying the interference with Article 8 applied here as well. Not providing an exception for people physically unable to end their lives without assistance in the law was justified through concerns of public safety and the protection of the vulnerable. States enjoyed a certain margin of appreciation to assess the risks. Therefore, no violation of Article 14 read together with Article 8 was found.[64]

4.1.4 The Haas Case

4.1.4.1 Circumstances of the Case

The applicant, Mr Haas, had been suffering from bipolar affective disorder for twenty years and had attempted suicide twice before. He became a member of the assisted suicide organization, Dignitas, and wanted to receive assistance to end his life because his illness was difficult to treat and 'made it impossible for him to live with dignity'.[65] Mr Haas had contacted several psychiatrists to obtain a prescription for NaP without any success. He then requested permission from the Swiss authorities to receive NaP without a prescription.

The Federal Department of Public Health and the Health Department of the Canton of Zürich had both refused Mr Haas's request on the grounds that the requirement for a prescription could not be waived and that Article 8 of the Convention did not oblige the State to 'create conditions for committing suicide without the risk of failure and without pain'.[66] Mr Haas appealed both refusals before the Federal Department of the Interior and the Administrative Court of the Canton of Zürich, respectively. Both appeals were dismissed. Claiming that obtaining the necessary prescription for NaP was almost impossible in practice and that the level of hardship amounted to an interference with his Article 8 right under the Convention, Mr Haas appealed to the Swiss Federal Supreme Court.

---

[64] *Pretty Case*, [87]-[88].

[65] *Haas v Switzerland* App no 31322/07 ECHR 2011 [7].

[66] *Haas Case*, [10].

4.1.4.2 Judgment of the Federal Supreme Court

After recognizing that end-of-life decisions of mentally competent patients were within the right to self-determination, the Federal Supreme Court stated that neither Article 10(2) of the Swiss Federal Constitution[67] nor Article 8 of the Convention constituted a right to receive assistance for committing suicide.[68]

The Federal Supreme Court referred to the previous R v UK and Pretty Cases, as well as the Canadian Rodriguez Case.[69] However, the case of Mr Haas was different from these cases in many respects. The question before the Federal Supreme Court was whether Article 8 of the Convention gave rise to a positive obligation on the State to make means available for a pain- and risk-free suicide, namely to enable Mr Haas to obtain NaP without a prescription.

Although recognizing the ECtHR's long-established principle of practical and effective rights,[70] the Federal Supreme Court disagreed with Mr Haas's claim that the NaP procedures made it impossible for him to obtain suicide assistance. Swiss law allowed for assisted suicide. However, considering Article 2 of the Convention and the State's duty to protect life, procedures set out by law such as the prescription requirement were justified in order to assure the authenticity of a patient's decision to end his or her life.

According to the Federal Supreme Court, procedures to receive suicide assistance in Switzerland were reasonably clear. A doctor must thoroughly examine the situation to make sure that all options have been exhausted and that the patient was fully competent to make an end-of-life decision. Putting these procedures in place ensured that patients had received every possible treatment, and the decision to end life was made after thorough consideration. These procedures aimed to protect public health and safety and prevent abuse. Despite the relatively liberal approach Switzerland had taken towards assisted suicide, it remained highly crucial to protect people from impulsive decisions and to control the risk of abuse. Assisting suicide was also not considered to be within the job description of a physician. However, physicians could decide to provide suicide assistance by prescribing NaP under reasonable circumstances with respect to the patients' wishes.

---

[67] 101 Federal Constitution of the Swiss Confederation of 18 April 1999 (1 January 2021). Art 10(2) 'Every person has the right to personal liberty and in particular to physical and mental integrity and to freedom of movement.'

[68] *Haas* [2006] BGer 2A.48/2006 & 2A.66/2006, BGE 133 58; Translation found under *Haas Case*, [16].

[69] In its decision, the Supreme Court does not refer to the R v UK Case, but rather to the Reed v UK Case with the application number of 7630/76. However, the date and the report information of the cited case by the Supreme Court are those of the R v UK Case. It is also obvious from the argumentation that reference was meant to be made to R v UK instead of Reed v UK.

[70] 'The Convention is intended to guarantee not rights that are theoretical or illusory but rights that are practical and effective.' *Case 'relating to certain aspects of the laws on the use of languages in education in Belgium' (merits)* 23 July 1968 Ser A no 6, 28; *Airey v Ireland* 9 October 1979 Ser A no 32, [24]; *Artico v Italy* 13 May 1980 Ser A no 37, [33].

The Federal Supreme Court referred to the SAMS Guideline'04 and repeated the three requirements for a prescription of NaP. First, the physician must confirm that the patient's illness would lead to death in a short manner of time. Second, all alternatives must be discussed with and made available to the patient. Finally, it must be confirmed that the patient has made an autonomous well-thought decision. The physician could only then decide to prescribe NaP if these conditions were met.

The Federal Supreme Court recognized the difficulty of cases involving mental illnesses, which could also cause severe suffering. However, the Federal Supreme Court also recognized that end-of-life decisions must be approached with more caution in cases involving a mental illness. The requirement for a prescription ensured that the patient's decision to end his or her life was not just a symptom of the mental illness that could be treated but a well-thought autonomous decision made by a competent person.

Mr Haas's appeal was dismissed in November 2006. The Federal Supreme Court found no violation of the Convention. The procedural requirements set out by law served the legitimate aim of balancing society's interests with the individual's personal autonomy. An exception from the prescription requirement could not be made for Mr Haas.[71]

After the Federal Supreme Court's decision, Mr Haas sent out letters to 170 psychiatrists in the Basel region requesting to be admitted as a patient for the purpose of an evaluation of his condition and assessment of his capability to make the decision to end his life. None of the psychiatrists he contacted agreed to take him as a patient. Some gave the reason that they did not have enough time, some refused on ethical grounds and some believed that Mr Haas could be treated.[72]

4.1.4.3 Judgment of the ECtHR

4.1.4.3.1 The Applicant's Submission

Mr Haas claimed that it was nearly impossible for him to obtain a prescription for NaP, and the 170 refusals were proof of his claim. Therefore, the right to decide when and how one would die was neither practical nor effective.[73] He mentioned previous incidents in which physicians had been investigated or prosecuted for prescribing NaP to patients with mental illness on the grounds that they had not exercised proper due diligence in carrying out a thorough psychiatric assessment. Psychiatrists were hesitant to prescribe NaP, and Dignitas was no longer in touch with any doctor who was willing to do so. According to Mr Haas, this simply made it impossible for him to exercise his right to decide when or how to end his life. He emphasized how long he had been suffering from his disorder. According to the right

[71] *Haas Case*, [16].
[72] *Haas Case*, [17].
[73] *Haas Case*, [33].

to self-determination, he could not be forced to any more additional treatment. His persistence to achieve his wish through legal means by obtaining a prescription should have been regarded as proof of his capacity to take this decision and how serious and genuine it was. He could not meet the conditions for obtaining a prescription, and this obstacle amounted to an interference that violated his Article 8 right under the Convention.

4.1.4.3.2 The Government's Submission

The Government argued that, unlike Mrs Pretty, Mr Haas was physically capable of acting autonomously. Agreeing with the Federal Supreme Court's decision, the Government stated that the right to self-determination did not generate a right to receive assistance for committing suicide, whether in the form of active or passive assistance. Even if the Court found an interference with Article 8, this should be deemed justified, considering its legal basis of protecting public health and safety.

The Government pointed out examples of patients with mental illness who had used assisted suicide to end their lives to demonstrate the availability of the process. The applicant's claim that physicians were hesitant to prescribe NaP for assisted suicide due to fear of prosecution was not realistic. Especially in Zürich, a new practice had been adapted to relieve doctors from such fear since 2006. If the applicant had shown willingness to follow the conditions, he would have very well been able to obtain the prescription, given that the requirements were fulfilled. However, in the Government's view, the applicant's conduct raised suspicion, especially the numerous of letters he had sent. Rather than psychiatrists in Zurich, he had chosen 170 psychiatrists in the Basle region. Apart from this, the wording of his letter was not encouraging for a psychiatrist to take him as a patient. Mr Haas was refusing any alternative treatment options in advance, although exhausting alternative methods was a prerequisite to consider assisted suicide. Furthermore, an association like Dignitas, where patients with mental illness have been provided with assistance before, should have knowledge of psychiatrists who are available for such an assessment.

Although the Swiss practice was quite liberal on the matter compared to other member States, this did not simplify the complex and delicate nature of assisted suicide. The case in hand did not concern a choice between a long-suffering painful death caused by a terminal disease and a painless way out; it concerned a choice between life and death, which raised additional ethical questions. The Government, here, underlined its obligation to protect individuals' lives, and sometimes even from the individuals themselves.[74] For the Government, it was crucial to distinguish when

[74] The Kılavuz Case concerned the applicant's son, who was in prison at the time of his death and had been suffering from psychological problems. Authorities were made aware of these problems after a physician's examination. The guardians could also observe the situation and have witnessed 'hysterical' behaviours. The applicant's son committed suicide in his prison cell and the Court found a violation of Article 2 of the Convention based on the fact that the domestic authorities had

dealing with mental illness whether the wish to die was a symptom of the disorder or an autonomous expression of free will. Only a specialist, namely a psychiatrist, could make this distinction after a thorough examination. The Government stated that this prerequisite was 'an appropriate and necessary means for protecting the lives of vulnerable persons whose decision to commit suicide could be based on a temporary crisis that altered their capacity for discernment.'[75]

4.1.4.3.3 Assessment of the Court

The Court repeated the broadness of the term 'private life' and stated;

> [A]n individual's right to decide by what means and at what point his or her life will end, provided he or she is capable of freely reaching a decision on this question and acting in consequence, is one of the aspects of the right for private life within the meaning of Article 8 of the Convention.[76]

What the Court was 'not prepared to exclude' in the Pretty Case was now positively included in the scope of the right to respect for private life.[77]

Distinguishing the situation of Mr Haas from Mrs Pretty's, the Court focused on the question of whether there was a positive obligation on the State to make NaP available to the applicant without a prescription as an exception to the practice of assisted suicide in order for the applicant to end his life in a dignified manner.[78]

This question would be answered through the balancing of interests. The Court reiterated that the Convention must be interpreted as a whole. The subject matter of the present case required Article 8 to be taken in conjunction with Article 2, while considering present-day conditions whether there was a consensus among member States and the level of the margin of appreciation attributed to them.

The Court found that Article 8, together with Article 2, obliged 'the national authorities to prevent an individual from taking his or her own life if the decision has not been taken freely and with full understanding of what is involved.'[79] It was clear to the Court that there was no consensus among the member States on the subject of the right to die, which called for a wider margin of appreciation. Adding these factors into the equation, the Court recognised the high sensitivity of the subject and the risk of abuse surrounding it. The Court considered that the Swiss regulations pursued, '*inter alia*, the legitimate aims of protecting everybody from hasty decisions and preventing abuse, and, in particular, ensuring that a patient lacking discernment does

failed to protect the deceased from himself, and even though they were aware of his problems, they had not taken the necessary measures to avoid the unfortunate outcome. *Kılavuz v Turkey* App no 8327/03, 21 October 2008.

[75] *Haas Case*, [48].

[76] *Haas Case*, [51].

[77] *Pretty Case*, [67].

[78] *Haas Case*, [53].

[79] *Haas Case*, [54].

not obtain a lethal dose of sodium pentobarbital.'[80] Article 2 entailed an obligation to make sure a patient's decision to die was made competently and with free will, and it was for this obligation that procedures were put in place. The procedures were not only necessary to prevent impulsive decisions, but considering the liberal approach of Switzerland, they were also paramount to make sure associations like Dignitas acted lawfully and transparently.

The Court accepted that the applicant's claim about physicians' fear of prosecution had a realistic basis. Nevertheless, the Court also agreed with the Swiss Government on the questionable nature of the applicant's letters to 170 psychiatrists. The Court was not convinced that it was impossible for the applicant to find a psychiatrist, who would be willing to follow the procedures and eventually assist him with his decision to end his life.

Accordingly, the Court found no violation of Article 8 of the Convention.

4.1.5 The Koch Case

4.1.5.1 Circumstances of the Case

The applicant, Mr Koch, who is a German citizen, applied to the Court claiming a violation of his and his late wife's right to respect for private and family life under Article 8 of the Convention.[81]

Mr Koch's wife had suffered an accident in 2002, leaving her paralysed, on artificial ventilation, and dependant on constant assistance. She was suffering from sensorimotor quadriplegia, which caused spasms and had a life expectancy of a minimum of fifteen years.[82] Finding her situation undignified, she wanted to end her life with Mr Koch's assistance. They had also contacted Dignitas in Switzerland.

Mrs Koch had requested authorisation to obtain NaP from the German Federal Institute for Drugs and Medical Devices (Federal Institute) in November 2004, which had been refused since the purpose of use was not compatible with the regulations. The couple appealed the decision together in January 2005. Before the Federal Institute could decide on the appeal, the applicant and his wife travelled to Zurich, where Mrs Koch ended her life in February 2005 with the assistance of Dignitas.

In March 2005, the Federal Institute ruled on the appeal, stating that Article 8 of the Convention did not entail a positive obligation on the State to make means possible for committing suicide. On the contrary, Article 2(2) of the German Basic Law obliged the State to protect life, which was the basis for refusing to grant a

[80] *Haas Case*, [56].

[81] *Koch v Germany* App no 497/09, 19 July 2012.

[82] Sensorimotor quadriplegia means spinal cord injury with the loss of sensory and motor functions in all four limbs and the torso. See footnote 7 under Sect. 4.1.2 'The Sanles Sanles Case'.

licence for NaP for assisted suicide. In addition, since Mrs Koch had already passed away, the applicant could not appeal the decision, as he was not the subject of the refusal by the Federal Institute.

4.1.5.2 Judgments of the Domestic Courts

Mr Koch challenged the Federal Institute's refusal before the Cologne Administrative Court in February 2006, before the North-Rhine Westphalia Administrative Court of Appeal in June 2007, and finally before the Federal Constitutional Court in November 2008, all of which gave an inadmissibility decision.

The common ground for all three decisions was the applicant's lack of locus standi. Rights under Article 6(1) of the Basic Law[83] and Article 8 of the Convention could not be transferred in order for the applicant to claim violations on behalf of his wife. The Cologne Administrative Court emphasized the wide margin of appreciation granted to the member States on the subject of the right to die and that any interference would have been in accordance with the Convention.[84] The North-Rhine Westphalia Administrative Court of Appeal stated that even if a right to die had existed, the applicant could not make a claim on behalf of his wife since this right would have been very personal and he did not have victim status.[85]

The Federal Constitutional Court also stated that this was not a case where the applicant could claim 'a posthumous right of his wife to human dignity' as it was 'not possible to lodge a constitutional complaint to assert another person's human dignity or other non-transferable rights',[86] and dismissed the application.[87] Mr Koch lodged an application to the ECtHR.

4.1.5.3 Judgment of the ECtHR

4.1.5.3.1 The Applicant's Submission

Mr Koch claimed that his own interests under Article 8 of the Convention had been affected by the obstacle to obtain the necessary drug for his wife to have a painless dignified death in their family house. Being the husband and sole caregiver to his

[83] Basic Law Art 6(1) 'Marriage and the family shall enjoy the special protection of the state.'

[84] *Koch Case*, [16]-[18].

[85] *Koch Case*, [19].

[86] The German understanding of human dignity protects the personality rights of deceased persons only in cases of defamation. Circumstances of each case would be evaluated in order to determine a violation of personality rights. However, the approach is important in understanding the meaning given to the concept of human dignity. It has also been established that successors to the deceased could be entitled to monetary damages if commercial profit had been made on the deceased by third parties. See Rösler (2008), pp. 175ff.

[87] *Koch* [2008] BVerfG 1 BvR 1832 [7].

wife, the suffering she had gone through and the fact that they were forced to travel to Switzerland had affected him just as well. In a marriage, the rights that were enjoyed jointly as a couple entitled Mr Koch to seek the protection of those rights, giving him the necessary victim status to bring an application before the Court. It was also against the spirit of human rights and the Convention to require his wife to remain alive in a state of suffering and pain, which she had found undignified, until the finalization of the proceedings. It did not satisfy the practicality and effectiveness of the Convention rights to force suffering patients, such as his wife, to postpone carrying out their wish to end their life in dignity. There could also be no obligation arising from Article 2 of the Convention to live life until its 'natural end'.

Mr Koch stated that there was no other option except for obtaining NaP that would allow for a dignified, painless death to his wife at their family house. Refusing life-sustaining treatment was not an option in his wife's situation since the death expectancy was not imminent in her case. Mr Koch also argued against the risk of abuse justification presented by the Government. Granting his wife's request would not have amounted to abuse, and there were no indications towards that end.[88]

4.1.5.3.2 The Government's Submission

The Government claimed that there was no violation of the applicant's right under Article 8 and that he did not have the necessary victim status within the meaning of Article 34 of the Convention to bring an application before the Court since he was not affected by the refusal of the Federal Institute. Mr Koch could not invoke public interest in his application either, as the Court had already ruled on the subject of assisted suicide in the previous Pretty Case. Although there were exceptional circumstances when an application could be pursued without the victim, this did not apply to the present case.[89] The applicant's wife could have requested an interim measure in order to accelerate the proceedings and waited for the result before she travelled to Switzerland. Although sympathising with the applicant's emotional distress, the Government believed that this was a natural outcome of his wife's circumstances and there was no involvement by the State.

Referring to the Pretty and Haas Cases, a right to die and a positive obligation upon the State to secure such a right had not been established, in the view of the Government. If the Court were to find an interference with Article 8, such an

[88] *Koch Case*, [39].

[89] In cases where the actual victim had died before having a chance to lodge an application, the Court accepts a close relative to apply, which is mostly in cases of death or disappearance of the actual victim and issues related to Art 2. Claims under other article rights, such as 3 or 5, have also been accepted as long as they were linked to a matter violating Art 2. Pursuing cases that do not involve the death or disappearance of the actual victim has been harder. The Court seeks whether the applicant's own interests have been affected. If not, the Court does not accept the locus standi of the applicant. ECHR (2020) Practical Guide on Admissibility Criteria. https://www.echr.coe.int/Documents/Admissibility_guide_ENG.pdf, pp. 10–17.

interference would nevertheless be justified under the second paragraph. The Government stated that the inadmissibility decisions by the domestic courts did not mean that there had not been a full evaluation of the merits of the case. The Government also referred to the importance given to human life and dignity, especially considering the historical background of euthanasia in Germany during the Nazi period, and stated that these concepts were essential in the German legal system. Together with the wide margin of appreciation enjoyed by the member States in the matter of assisted dying, any interference would be in accordance with Article 8(2).

According to the Government, granting a licence for NaP was not the only way for the applicant's wife to fulfil her wish to end her life. She could have refused treatment, particularly the respiratory support, and achieved the same objective.

Finally, the Government pointed out the risks of allowing unrestricted drug access. It could lead some patients, who considered themselves a burden to their family and society, to feel psychological pressure in deciding to end their lives. According to the Government, 'the overriding interest of protecting life justified the refusal to grant the applicant's wife the authorisation to obtain a lethal dose of pentobarbital of sodium'.[90]

4.1.5.3.3 Submissions by the Interveners

Dignitas and the Aktion Lebensrecht für Alle e. V.[91] gave their submissions as third-party interveners. Dignitas, parallel to its objective, reaffirmed that decisions concerning the end of life were within the right to self-determination, and the State should intervene only as far as to ensure the autonomous nature of these decisions.[92] ALfA, as an advocate for the unrestricted right to life for all, believed that the rights in question were non-transferable, and Mr Koch could not possibly rely on them to claim a violation.[93]

While Dignitas supported granting the licence for NaP, ALfA repeated the importance of protecting life and emphasized the usefulness of palliative care instead of allowing assisted suicide.[94]

---

[90] *Koch Case*, [56]-[59].

[91] Aktions Lebensrecht für Alle e. V. (ALfA) is a German civil organization that supports the right to life movement and believes that life must be protected at every stage. With a special focus on abortion, ALfA is also against euthanasia and assisted suicide. Instead, they advocate for better hospice care and provide assistance for pregnant women in need. ALfA, Die Aktion Lebensrecht für Alle. https://www.alfa-ev.de/ueber-uns/.

[92] *Koch Case*, [40].

[93] *Koch Case*, [41].

[94] *Koch Case*, [63]-[64].

4.1.5.3.4 Assessment of the Court

The Court rejected the applicant's violation claim of Article 8 on behalf of his wife. In the Sanles Sanles Case, the Court had ruled that Article 8 rights could not be transferred to relatives or successors of the victim. Although the applicant argued that he had a closer relationship with his wife than the one in Sanles Sanles, the Court did not find sufficient reason to deviate from its case law.[95] The applicant was, nevertheless, under the protection of the Convention regarding his own interests.

The Court focused on answering the question of whether the applicant, as the husband of Mrs Koch, did have viable interests of his own.

The Court started by examining the relationship between the applicant and his wife.[96] Considering their 25 years of marriage, their travel to Switzerland together, their joint application to appeal the Federal Institute's refusal, and the fact that Mr Koch had pursued the proceedings after his wife's death, the Court had no doubt as to the existence of close family ties and accepted Mr Koch's 'strong and persistent interest in the adjudication of the merits of the original motion'.[97] Furthermore, the present case concerned 'fundamental questions evolving around a patient's wish to self-determinedly end his or her life which are of general interest transcending the person and the interest both of the applicant and his late wife'.[98]

Considering the circumstances, the Court rejected the Government's claim that the wife could have requested an interim measure for a speedy proceeding. The Court did not find it upon itself to judge whether or not Mrs Koch should have waited.

Repeating what it had implied in the Pretty Case and expressly accepted in the Haas Case, the Court stated:

> an individual's right to decide in which way and at which time his or her life should end, provided that he or she was in a position freely to form her own will and to act accordingly, was one of the aspects of the right to respect for private life within the meaning of Article 8 of the Convention.[99]

Right to respect for private life was a non-exhaustive list of interests that could be subject to judicial review. All of this in mind, the Court found the Federal Institute's refusal and the inadmissibility decisions by the domestic courts based on the lack of locus standi to be a violation of the applicant's right under Article 8 and continued to discuss whether this violation was justified.

The Court did not find any legitimate aim in the domestic courts' refusal to examine the merits of the case. It found a violation of the applicant's right 'to see the

95 *Koch Case*, [79]-[81].

96 For a relative to claim interference to his/her own rights, the Court looks for three criteria; (a) 'the existence of close family ties', (b) 'a sufficient personal or legal interest in the outcome of the proceedings', (c) 'previously expressed interest in the case'. *Koch Case*, [44].

97 *Koch Case*, [45].

98 *Koch Case*, [46].

99 *Koch Case*, [52].

merits of his motion examined by the courts'.[100] However, given the principle of subsidiarity, the Court refrained from evaluating the substance of the case, which also further emphasized the domestic courts' obligation to examine the merits of the case brought to them.[101]

The Court did not find it necessary to assess the claims of violations of Article 6(1) and 13 since a violation of Article 8 had already been established.

4.1.6 The Gross Case

4.1.6.1 Circumstances of the Case

The applicant, Ms Gross, was born in 1931 and lived in Switzerland. She was not suffering from any illness except the inconveniences brought on by advanced age. She wanted to end her life, as she complained about the declining quality of her health and did not wish to endure the suffering caused by it. After a failed suicide attempt in 2005 and being admitted to a psychiatric hospital for six months, she contacted EXIT for suicide assistance to avoid any consequence of another failed attempt. EXIT had informed her that it would be hard to obtain a prescription from a physician for NaP in her case.

In 2008, a psychiatrist had given an expert opinion on Ms Gross's mental capacity to make an autonomous end-of-life decision. Although he had found Ms Gross capable of such a decision, he did not prescribe the necessary NaP in order to keep his role solely as a medical expert on the case. Ms Gross had contacted three other physicians for the prescription but without any success. Two of the contacted physicians feared that prescribing NaP would not be in line with the code of professional conduct since Ms Gross was not terminally ill.[102] Ms Gross had also requested permission from the Health Board of the Canton of Zurich to obtain NaP, which was also refused.[103]

4.1.6.2 Judgments of the Domestic Courts

Ms Gross had appealed against the Health Board's refusal before the Zurich Administrative Court, which dismissed the appeal on the grounds that the procedural requirements of assisted suicide were to ensure public safety and prevent abuse, and therefore, justified. The Administrative Court found the expert opinion from 2008 insufficient due to the lack of a thorough examination of the state of Ms Gross's

[100] *Koch Case*, [68].

[101] *Koch Case*, [71].

[102] In this case, the code of professional conduct refers to the SAMS Guideline'04.

[103] *Gross v Switzerland* App no 67810/10, 14 May 2013, [11].

health, whether she suffered any illness that suggested a near-death and whether her wish was a symptom of an illness. A mere confirmation of her autonomous decision could not be sufficient for the procurement of NaP.[104]

After the Administrative Court's dismissal, Ms Gross brought her appeal before the Swiss Federal Supreme Court, repeating her request and claiming that her right to choose when and how to die was left ineffective by the refusal of her request. She asked the Federal Supreme Court to rule in favour of prescribing NaP also to those who did not suffer from any illness.

Her appeal was, yet again, dismissed on 12 April 2010 for reasons that the State had no positive obligation to ensure access to a lethal drug for the realization of assisted suicide. Referring to the Haas Case, the Federal Supreme Court stated that it had already been established that the procedural requirements of assisted suicide pursued a legitimate aim and whether these requirements would be relaxed to give easier access to assisted suicide was within the margin of appreciation of the member State, namely within the competence of the legislator. As for Ms Gross's case, conditions in which a physician could prescribe NaP were clear under the SAMS Guidelines, and Ms Gross did not meet these conditions.[105]

Upon the Federal Supreme Court's dismissal of her appeal, Ms Gross lodged an application to the ECtHR on 10 November 2010, claiming a violation of her right to decide when and how to end her life under Article 8 of the Convention.

4.1.6.3 Judgment of the ECtHR

4.1.6.3.1 The Applicant's Submission

Claiming that NaP was the only pain-free method to end one's life in a dignified manner, the applicant found the refusal of her request to obtain NaP to violate her right to choose when and how to die that was protected under Article 8 of the Convention. The Swiss Government was obligated to give effect to the Convention rights. She also did not agree that there was a risk of abuse in her case. Since an association would be providing suicide assistance, there was no chance of the NaP falling into the hands of a third party.[106]

The applicant also claimed that her end-of-life decision did not have to be medically justified. The conditions laid out in the SAMS Guidelines were for terminal patients and did not apply to her case. Relying on these guidelines, which were not adopted as a legal instrument, contravened her right to choose when and how to die.[107]

---

[104] *Gross Case-Chamber*, [14]-[15].

[105] *Gross Case-Chamber*, [19]-[21].

[106] *Gross Case-Chamber*, [44].

[107] *Gross Case-Chamber*, [45].

4.1.6.3.2 The Government's Submission

The Government stated that the protection of public health and safety was among a State's duties, and the State could take any measures it deemed fit to achieve these objects. This reasoning would even justify a complete ban on assisted suicide. Given the fact that most suicide decisions were made in a depressive state of mind, it was within the State's competence to set out requirements for the application of assisted suicide to ensure the authenticity of a patient's end-of-life decision. The procedural requirements of the practice of assisted suicide in Switzerland served this legitimate aim, justifying them under Article 8(2) of the Convention. The Government also pointed out that the applicant had not shown much effort to meet these requirements. It was also not established that NaP was the most efficient and only way to ensure a dignified death.[108]

The Government repeated that Switzerland had liberal regulations on assisted suicide compared to those of other member States, which led to a new trend called 'suicide tourism' and Switzerland 'could not be blamed for seeking to put in place safeguards against the risk of floodgates being opened'.[109]

4.1.6.3.3 Submissions by the Interveners

Four parties had intervened in the proceedings and submitted opinions on the matter of the case. The first association, the Alliance Defending Freedom,[110] argued against assisted suicide by stating that personal autonomy could never prevail over public safety and the protection of the rights of others.[111] The European Centre for Law and Justice[112] criticized the Haas Case for tempering with the inviolability of human life and Article 2. There could be no right to assisted suicide derived from the Convention without jeopardizing its essence.[113] The Americans United for Life

[108] *Gross Case-Chamber*, [49]-[51].

[109] *Gross Case-Chamber*, [53].

[110] Alliance Defending Freedom is a Christian faith-based internationally active non-profit organization formed in 1994 with the goal to defend freedom of religion and the sanctity of life through legal means. They have been involved in several Supreme Court cases in the US and are known to have substantial influence. Alliance Defending Freedom, Who We Are. https://www.adflegal.org/about-us. ADF has been subject to controversies for being against same-sex marriage, for which it has been listed as a hate group by the Southern Poverty Law Center, another non-profit organization legally advocating for civil rights. Southern Poverty Law Center, Alliance Defending Freedom. https://www.splcenter.org/fighting-hate/extremist-files/group/alliance-defending-freedom.

[111] *Gross Case-Chamber*, [54].

[112] The European Centre for Law and Justice, based in Strasbourg and formed in 1998, is an international non-governmental 'Christian-inspired' organization, which advocates for 'religious freedoms and dignity of the person' through 'advocacy, education and litigation'. European Center for Law and Justice, About the ECLJ. https://eclj.org/about-us.

[113] *Gross Case-Chamber*, [55].

organization[114] also supported these opinions, stating that the right to privacy could not be broadened to overrule the interest of protecting life and ethics of medicine.[115]

Contrary to those opinions arguing against assisted suicide, Dignitas referred to the Swiss public's support to the right to decide the time and manner of one's own death. The Swiss public had accepted and supported assisted suicide as part of an expression of personal autonomy. Part of this acceptance was controlled, yet simple and effective access to the necessary drug.[116]

4.1.6.3.4 Assessment of the Chamber

The Court repeated its statement from the Pretty and Koch Cases:

> Without in any way negating the principle of the sanctity of life protected under the Convention, the Court has considered that, in an era of growing medical sophistication combined with longer life expectancies, many people are concerned that they should not be forced to linger on in old age or in states of advanced physical or mental decrepitude which conflict with the strongly held ideas of self and personal identity.[117]

As it was already expressly established in the Haas and Koch Cases, the Court repeated that the right to decide when and how to die was within the ambit of Article 8 of the Convention.[118] However, the right to die could be subject to limitation considering public interest and the wide margin of appreciation due to the lack of consensus among member States. Within this margin of appreciation, Switzerland does not criminalize suicide assistance, given that the motives are not selfish.

According to the Court, it was not always sufficient for the member States to refrain from intervening to ensure that the Convention rights were 'practical and effective'. For individuals to enjoy their rights, it might be necessary for member States to take certain measures, such as adopting a legislative framework.[119] With this in mind, the Court identified the question before it as to whether the State had sufficiently regulated assisted suicide and whether it was sufficiently clear under which circumstances physicians could prescribe NaP. In the Haas Case, the Court had focused on whether the prescription requirement to obtain NaP was justified and if this requirement obstructed the practicality and effectiveness of the right to decide when and how to die. However, in the present case, the Court examined if the Swiss practice on assisted suicide provided sufficient clarity.

[114] Americans United for Life is an internationally active organization formed as early as 1971 in the USA. Known as a 'pro-life' organization, it stands against abortion and assisted dying. Americans United for Life, About. https://aul.org/mission/.

[115] *Gross Case-Chamber*, [56].

[116] *Gross Case-Chamber*, [57].

[117] *Gross Case-Chamber*, [58]; *Pretty Case*, [65]; *Koch Case*, [51].

[118] *Gross Case-Chamber*, [59]; *Haas Case*, [51]; *Koch Case*, [52].

[119] *Gross Case-Chamber*, [62].

Although the Swiss Federal Supreme Court had referred to the SAMS Guidelines in the case law, these guidelines were not a legal instrument enacted by the legislature. Other than these medical ethics guidelines that only concerned terminally ill patients, there were no other provisions provided by the State that regulated under which circumstances physicians could prescribe NaP. The ambiguity led to the denial of Ms Gross's request for a prescription. By four votes to three, the Chamber decided that 'the absence of clear and comprehensive legal guidelines' outlining the extent of the right to decide the time and manner of one's own death violated Article 8 of the Convention. The Chamber limited its finding to the necessity of clarifying under which circumstances physicians could prescribe NaP for the purpose of assisted suicide and did not go further into the substance for the sake of the principle of subsidiarity.[120]

Judges of the dissenting opinion did not agree that there was a violation of Article 8. The SAMS Guidelines and the Swiss Federal Supreme Court's case law had already established a clear practice on assisted suicide. It was clear when a physician could prescribe NaP to a patient for suicide assistance. In its case law, the Court had already accepted the necessity of safeguards, especially in a member State with a more liberal approach towards assisted suicide. Since there was no consensus among member States regarding the right to die, there was a wide margin of appreciation. According to the dissenting opinion, the Court could not oblige Switzerland to regulate the practice of assisted suicide further, which was already clearly established by the jurisprudence of the Federal Supreme Court.[121]

4.1.6.3.5 Assessment of the Grand Chamber

The Government's request to refer the case to the Grand Chamber was granted on 7 October 2013. In an inquiry made on 7 January 2014, the Government discovered that Ms Gross had passed away. On 10 November 2011, before the Chamber had rendered its decision on the case, Ms Gross had finally obtained a prescription for NaP and ended her life with the assistance of EXIT. Based on this information, the Government requested an inadmissibility decision.[122]

The counsel for the applicant claimed that he was not aware of Ms Gross' death until 9 January 2014, after the Government's inquiry. The counsel did not have direct contact with Ms Gross since January 2010. Ms Gross had asked the counsel to maintain correspondence through her person of trust, Mr F, who was a retired pastor working for EXIT. Upon Ms Gross's request, Mr F had not disclosed the information on her death to the counsel. She wanted the procedures to continue, with the idea that it might help people like her. The counsel requested the Court to continue the

---

[120] *Gross Case-Chamber*, [65]-[69].

[121] *Gross Case-Chamber*, Joint Dissenting Opinion of Judges Raimondi, Jočienė and Karakaş [10].

[122] *Gross v Switzerland* [GC] App no 67810/10 ECHR 2014, [19]-[21].

proceedings in order to resolve a highly debated matter that concerned public interest.[123]

The Court recalled that it was necessary for the functioning of the Court and the distribution of justice that the parties to an application effectively participate in the proceedings,[124] do not give misleading information,[125] and disclose any changes to the circumstances relevant to the application.[126] Failure to do so could lead to an inadmissibility decision, but according to the Court's case law, 'the applicant's intention to mislead the Court must always be established with sufficient certainty'.[127]

The reason for Ms Gross's application was that she could not obtain a prescription for NaP due to the lack of sufficient guidelines on assisted suicide regarding people who did not suffer from a terminal illness. Yet, she had obtained a prescription before the Chamber had rendered its decision, dissolving the core of her application. Furthermore, she had given specific directives to Mr F not to inform her counsel and, by extension, the Court about her death. Ms Gross had taken intentional measures for her death to remain unknown, which was a fact highly likely to affect the case's outcome. The Grand Chamber, by nine votes to eight, decided that these circumstances amounted to 'an abuse of the right of individual application' under Article 35(3)(a) of the Convention.[128]

While voting with the majority, Judge Silvis made a note on the abuse of the right of individual application. He agreed that only dismissing the case would not have emphasized the importance of informing the Court about relevant developments to the case. However, he did not agree that 'the applicant's intention to mislead the Court must always be established with sufficient certainty' in order to amount to an abuse of the right of individual application. He found that the case law of the Court had set 'unnecessarily high' standards for finding abuse, and the Grand Chamber had 'forced itself to undertake the rather speculative exercise' of determining Ms Gross's intentions to give an inadmissibility decision based on Article 35(3)(c).[129]

The Grand Chamber decided with a very close vote. Eight judges disagreed with describing the situation as an abuse of the right of individual application. They argued that the intention to mislead the Court could not be attributed with 'sufficient certainty' to Ms Gross, and doing so had a 'stigmatizing effect' on her memory.[130] In addition, identifying an application as an abuse of the right of individual application

[123] *Gross Case-GC*, [22]-[26].

[124] ECHR (2021) Rules of Court. https://www.echr.coe.int/Documents/Rules_Court_ENG.pdf, Rules 44A, 44C (rules referred to in the Gross Case have not been subject to change since 2004).

[125] ECHR (2021) Rules of Court, Rule 44D.

[126] ECHR (2021) Rules of Court, Rule 47(7).

[127] *Gross Case-GC*, [28].

[128] *Gross Case-GC*, [35].

[129] *Gross Case-GC*, Concurring Opinion of Judge Silvis.

[130] *Gross Case-GC*, Joint Dissenting Opinion of Judges Spielman, Ziemele, Berro-Lefèvre, Zupančič, Hajiyev, Tsotsoria, Sicilianos, and Keller [6]-[7].

was limited to cases where the Court had wasted its time and effort on issues outside its scope. However, assisted suicide was currently being debated as people started travelling to Switzerland for services of organizations like EXIT or Dignitas, and it was highly likely that more applications related to this subject would come before the Court. According to the dissenting judges, it would have been more appropriate to dismiss the application under Article 37(1)(c) of the Convention without calling it an abuse.[131]

4.1.7 *The Lambert Case*

4.1.7.1 Circumstances of the Case

The Lambert Case concerned the withdrawal of life-sustaining treatment of a patient in an irreversible unconscious state.[132] Although it is not a case on the right to die within the context of this study, it provides a more comprehensive understanding of the Court's approach to the balance between Articles 2 and 8 of the Convention in end-of-life decisions.

Mr Vincent Lambert had suffered severe head injuries after a traffic accident in September 2008, leaving him with tetraplegia and a chronic vegetative state. He was treated in various French hospitals. The specialized Coma Science Group from Liège University Hospital assessed Mr Lambert's situation and concluded that he was in a 'minimally conscious state plus'.[133] From September 2011 until October 2012, Mr Vincent received regular physiotherapy with no successful results. Attempts to achieve communication were also unsuccessful. After observing signs of resistance to daily care and deliberations with Mr Lambert's wife, the medical team decided to withdraw nutrition and limit hydration as of 10 April 2013. On 11 May 2013, a court injunction ordered the hospital to resume artificial nutrition. The Court argued that due to the lack of an advance directive and the absence of an appointed trusted person, Mr Lambert's family had to be involved in the decision-making procedure, including his parents, who disagreed with the wife.

A new collective decision-making procedure was started in September 2013. Mr Lambert's physician, Dr Kariger, had consulted six other physicians, three of whom

---

[131] ECHR Art 37(1) 'The Court may at any stage of the proceedings decide to strike an application out of its list of cases where the circumstances lead to the conclusion that (c) for any other reason established by the Court, it is no longer justified to continue the examination of the application.'

[132] *Lambert and Others v France* [GC] App no 46043/14 ECHR 2015 (extracts).

[133] Minimally conscious state (MSC) is a term used to differentiate patients who retain 'limited but clearly-discernable behavioral signs of consciousness', while the added subdivision of plus (MSC+) refers to 'the presence of (a) command-following, (b) intelligible verbalization, or (c) gestural or verbal yes/no intentional communication'. Although the subdivision of plus is based on the presence of some sort of functional connectivity, there is no consensus in the literature on its exact definition or which specific criteria should it entail. Thibaut et al. (2020), p. 1245.

were chosen by Mr Lambert's parents and an expert from a specialized extended-care facility. Dr Kariger also held two meetings with the family, including Mr Lambert's wife, parents, and eight siblings. While his wife and six siblings favoured discontinuing treatment, his parents and other two siblings were opposed. In a final meeting with the medical team held on 9 December 2013, all physicians except one were in favour of withdrawing treatment. After a detailed report describing the irreversibility of Mr Lambert's situation and the futility of further medical treatment, Dr Kariger announced his intention to withdraw artificial nutrition and hydration on 11 January 2014.

Mr Lambert's parents and two siblings applied to the Châlons-en-Champagne Administrative Court, seeking an injunction to prohibit the hospital from withdrawing treatment and transferring Mr Lambert to another specialized facility. On 16 January 2014, the Administrative Court suspended Dr Kariger's decision while refusing the request for Mr Lambert's transfer. Although Mr Lambert had previously expressed to his wife and one brother that he would not wish to be kept alive in a highly dependent state, the Administrative Court did not accept these testimonies as a formal manifestation of an express wish in the absence of an advance directive drawn up by Mr Lambert. After the Administrative Court found a violation of Mr Lambert's right to life under Article 2 of the Convention due to Dr Kariger's incorrect assessment of Mr Lambert's wishes, the case was brought before the Conseil d'État by Mr Lambert's wife, his nephew, and the Reims University Hospital, where he was receiving medical care.[134]

4.1.7.2 Judgment of the Conseil d'État

Article L 1110-5 of the French Code of Public Health regulates the right to receive proper medical treatment.[135] It also prohibits treatment continued with 'unreasonable obstinacy', namely treatment that is 'futile or disproportionate or [has] no other effect than to sustain life artificially'.[136] Article L 1111-4 regulates personal autonomy in medical decision-making and the right to refuse treatment. For situations of unconsciousness, Article L 1111-4 further regulates:

---

[134] *Lambert Case*, [10]-[28].

[135] French Code of Public Health Art L 1110-5 (version in force from 23 April 2005 to 4 February 2016). The French Code of Public Health was amended by Act No 2005-370 of 22 April 2005 on patients' rights and end of life (the Leonetti Act, named after its rapporteur Mr Jean Leonetti), which brought new rights to patients, prohibited unreasonable obstinacy and allowed withholding or withdrawing medical treatment that was futile. In 2016, France enacted Act No 2016-87 of 2 February 2016, establishing new rights to patients and the terminally ill (the Claeys-Leonetti Act, named after its rapporteurs Mr Alain Claeys and Mr Jean Leonetti), which permits terminal sedation and strengthens advance directives. See Baumann et al. (2009); see also Van Zeebroeck (2019).

[136] Translation of the relevant Arts by the Court under *Lambert Cas*, [53].

> [...] Where the individual is unable to express his or her wishes, no intervention or examination may be carried out, except in cases of urgency or impossibility, without the person of trust referred to in Article L. 1111-6, the family or, failing this, a person close to the patient having been consulted.
>
> Where the individual is unable to express his or her wishes, no decision to limit or withdraw treatment, where such a measure would endanger the patient's life, may be taken without the collective procedure defined in the Code of Medical Ethics having been followed and without the person of trust referred to in Article L. 1111-6, the family or, failing this, a person close to the patient having been consulted, and without any advance directives issued by the patient having been examined. The decision to limit or withdraw treatment, together with the reasons for it, shall be recorded in the patient's file. [...][137]

Article R 4127-37, which forms Article 37 of the Code of Medical Ethics, describes the collective procedure as:

> [...] The decision to limit or withdraw treatment shall be taken by the doctor in charge of the patient, after consultation with the care team where this exists, and on the basis of the reasoned opinion of at least one doctor acting as a consultant. There must be no hierarchical link between the doctor in charge of the patient and the consultant. The reasoned opinion of a second consultant shall be sought by these doctors if either of them considers it necessary.
>
> The decision to limit or withdraw treatment shall take into account any wishes previously expressed by the patient, in particular in the form of advance directives, if drawn up, the views of the person of trust the patient may have designated and those of the family or, failing this, of another person close to the patient. [...]
>
> Reasons shall be given for any decision to limit or withdraw treatment. The opinions received, the nature and tenor of the consultations held within the care team and the reasons for the decision shall be recorded in the patient's file. The person of trust, if one has been designated, the family or, failing this, another person close to the patient, shall be informed of the nature of and the reasons for the decision to limit or withdraw treatment. [...][138]

Sitting as the full court, the Conseil d'État asked for a collective expert medical report to be prepared in order to make an informed assessment of whether the conditions to withdraw treatment that amounts to unreasonable obstinacy have been met. Additionally, the Conseil d'État requested general written observations from the National Medical Academy, the National Ethics Advisory Committee, the National Medical Council, and Mr Jean Leonetti.

After a thorough examination of Mr Lambert and his medical file and consultations with his family members, the experts concluded that Mr Lambert's consciousness had deteriorated since the assessment of the Coma Science Group, that there were no signals indicating a minimally conscious state, and that the brain damage was irreversible. The expert report also stated that it was not possible to establish functional communication with Mr Lambert and that his reactions were

[137] French Code of Public Health Art L 1111-4 (version in force from 23 April 2005 to 4 February 2016).

[138] ibid Art 4127-37 (version in force from 31 January 2010 to 6 August 2016), English translation by the Court under *Lambert Case*, [54].

non-conscious responses.[139] The National Medical Council and Mr Leonetti wrote that to withdraw treatment, which had 'no other effect than to sustain life artificially', there must be no recovery prospects of the cognitive and relational functions. While Mr Leonetti stated that the sole responsibility of making such a decision in cases of irreversible loss of consciousness was on the physician, the National Medical Academy reiterated that the Act applied in cases of minimal consciousness or chronic vegetative state. The National Ethics Advisory Committee emphasized the importance of a genuine collective decision-making process.[140]

After receiving the expert medical reports and observations from the relevant authorities, the Conseil d'État went on to examine whether the legal framework on withdrawal of treatment violated any of the Convention rights. The legal framework provided by the Code of Public Health was found compatible with Articles 2 and 8 of the Convention. While taking a decision to withdraw treatment in cases of patients who were not able to express their wishes, the physician should consider all medical and non-medical factors of the specific case. The assessment of all relevant factors, including the patient's prognosis, stage of suffering, and previously expressed wishes to family members or friends, should be guided by 'maximum beneficence towards the patient'. As to the case of Mr Lambert, the Conseil d'État found that Dr Kariger's actions were in accordance with the Code of Public Health. The findings of the expert medical report attested to the irreversible nature of Mr Lambert's situation. In addition, both Mr Lambert and his wife were nurses who had encountered similar situations in their line of work and had conversations about such topics. Mr Lambert had expressed his wish not to be kept artificially alive if he were ever in a highly dependent state, a statement that was found to be in line with Mr Lambert's character by other family members. Considering the thoroughness of the collective procedure carried out by Dr Kariger and the nature of Mr Lambert's prognosis, the Conseil d'État found the decision to withdraw treatment lawful and set aside the Administrative Court's judgment.[141]

4.1.7.3 Judgment of the ECtHR

4.1.7.3.1 On the Applicants' Locus Standi

Mr Lambert's parents, his half-brother, and his sister lodged an application with the Court, claiming that withdrawing artificial nutrition and hydration would constitute a violation of Mr Lambert's right under Article 2, 3, and 8 of the Convention, in addition to the violation of Article 3 that was already caused by the discontinuance of physiotherapy since October 2012. The Court accepted Mr Lambert's wife, nephew, and half-sister as third-party interveners. While the applicants relied on the sanctity

[139] *Lambert Case*, [38]-[43].

[140] *Lambert Case*, [44].

[141] *Lambert Case*, [48]-[51].

of life, which was stressed in the Pretty Case, the third-party interveners relied on personal autonomy and the right to decide the time and manner of one's own death, as stated in the Haas and Koch Cases.[142] Both sides wished to represent Mr Lambert's interests, albeit being opposed to each other.

The Court stated two criteria to accept a third party to raise a complaint on behalf of a vulnerable person: 'the risk that the direct victim will be deprived of effective protection of his or her rights, and the absence of a conflict of interests between the victim and the applicant'.[143] The Court did not find any risk to the protection of Mr Lambert's rights and no conflict of interests considering the previously expressed wishes by Mr Lambert.[144] The Court did not accept the applicants' locus standi to raise complaints on behalf of Mr Lambert. However, the victim' next-of-kin could claim a violation of Article 2 on their own behalf where the State's responsibility was engaged with the victims's death. Although Mr Lambert was still alive, it was certain that withdrawing artificial nutrition and hydration would lead to his death. Therefore, the Court went on to examine the issue of the case under Article 2 as if raised by the applicants on their own behalf.

4.1.7.3.2 On Articles 2 and 8 of the Convention

The applicants claimed that the discontinuation of artificial nutrition and hydration did not meet the criteria of withholding or withdrawing treatment that amounted to unreasonable obstinacy (therapeutic abstention). Hence, according to the applicants, withdrawal of treatment in Mr Lambert's case would amount to the intentional taking of life, namely euthanasia (or, more precisely, involuntary passive euthanasia). The Act of 22 April 2005 was unclear and resulted in Dr Kariger's decision to withdraw treatment, which amounted to the State's failure to protect life under Article 2. According to the applicants, the concept of unreasonable obstinacy and what constituted a medical treatment (whether artificial nutrition and hydration was treatment or care) were not sufficiently described; and the previous statements made by Mr Lambert to his wife should not have been taken into consideration.

The Court stressed the distinction between therapeutic abstention, which was the matter of the current case, and euthanasia, which was illegal under French Law. Reading the Convention as a whole, the Court stated that 'reference should be made, in examining a possible violation of Article 2, to Article 8 of the Convention and to the right to respect for private life and the notion of personal autonomy it encompasses'.[145] The existence of a legal framework compatible with Article 2, respect for the patient's previously expressed wishes, and the possibility of a judicial remedy in case of doubts about the patient's best interest were factors to be taken into

[142] *Lambert Case*, [98].

[143] *Lambert Case*, [102].

[144] *Lambert Case*, [104].

[145] *Lambert Case*, [142].

consideration.[146] Although the majority did, not all member States allowed withdrawing or withholding life-sustaining treatment. The lack of consensus justified a certain margin of appreciation. However, there was a consensus regarding the importance of the patient's wishes.[147]

The Court moved on to examine whether the legal framework provided sufficient clarity regarding its applicability, the definition of treatment, and what constituted unreasonable obstinacy. There had been no applications before the French Courts under the Act of 22 April 2005 until the proceedings regarding the Lambert Case. The Conseil d'État, in light of the parliamentary proceedings, had found that the Act applied to all patients whether or not at the end stages of life. It had also ruled that the concept of treatment included artificial nutrition and hydration. The Court referred to the Guide on the decision-making process regarding medical treatment in end-of-life situations.[148] According to the Guide, there was indeed no consensus among member States whether artificial nutrition and hydration were classified as a treatment or a form of care. However, the common point was the emphasis on the patient's wishes.

Regarding the concept of unreasonable obstinacy, the Conseil d'État had stated the medical and non-medical factors to consider. To that end, two safeguards were prescribed: first, the irreversible loss of consciousness did not, by itself, provide sufficient grounds for unreasonable obstinacy. Second, if the patient's wishes were unknown, it could not be assumed in favour of discontinuing treatment. Together with the Conseil d'État's interpretations, the Court found the Act of 22 April 2005 to be sufficiently clear and in accordance with Article 2 of the Convention. The Court also agreed with the Conseil d'État that Dr Kariger had satisfied the requirements of the collective decision-making procedure, details of which were within the margin of appreciation of the State. After finding the legal framework compatible with Article 2, the Court considered the possibility of a legal remedy. Convening as a full court with seventeen members for an injunction proceeding, the Conseil d'État had carried out a thorough examination of the matter by requesting an expert medical report from three specialists and observations from relevant authorities.[149]

The Court did not accept the applicant's claim that Mr Lambert's previously expressed wishes should not have been taken into consideration. When the patient

---

[146] *Lambert Case*, [143]; These three factors are also referred to as the 'Lambert criteria'. Sartori (2018), pp. 34–35.

[147] *Lambert Case*, [147].

[148] The 'Guide on the Decision-Making Process Regarding Medical Treatment in End-of-Life Situations' (2014) was drawn up by the Committee on Bioethics of the Council of Europe, and it facilitates the implementation and interpretation of the Oviedo Convention on Human Rights and Biomedicine (4 April 1997, ETS No 164). Committee on Bioethics of the Council of Europe (2014) Guide on the Decision-Making Process Regarding Medical Treatment in End-of-Life Situations. https://www.coe.int/en/web/bioethics/guide-on-the-decision-making-process-regarding-medical-treatment-in-end-of-life-situations.

[149] *Lambert Case*, [149]-[175].

was unconscious, and there were no advance directives, the patient's wishes could be ascertained from previous statements made to a family member or close friend.[150]

The Court ruled twelve votes to five that there would be no violation of Article 2 if Dr Kariger's decision to withdraw artificial nutrition and hydration was carried out and that it was not necessary to rule separately on the complaints under Article 8.[151]

In their dissenting opinion, five judges stated that the applicants did have locus standi and could bring claims before the Court on behalf of Mr Lambert. More importantly, they stated that there was, indeed, a violation of Article 2. Although Mr Lambert was in a vegetative state, he was not brain dead. The artificial feeding and hydration was not an intrusive measure that caused any pain to the patient. Moreover, there was no indication that Mr Lambert was in any kind of suffering. Lacking any advance directive or appointment of a person of trust, conversations he held with his wife were not sufficient to determine Mr Lambert's true wishes. A higher level of certainty should have been sought in such a sensitive matter, which was prone to abuse. Even if Mr Lambert had expressed his wish not to be kept alive artificially, that statement was only indicative for the physician in the decision-making process but not a decisive factor. Considering that Mr Lambert was not in a terminal stage, discontinuing artificial nutrition and hydration would result in death by starvation. Although member States might enjoy a margin of appreciation, this margin was not unlimited and had to be viewed under the Convention values. According to the dissenting opinion, the State should have given more weight to the protection of life and human dignity.[152]

The dissenting judges agreed with the applicants that concepts of ordinary and extraordinary treatments, unreasonable obstinacy, and artificial sustainment or prolongation of life were not sufficiently precise terms. Furthermore, the judges disagreed on the classification of the case insofar as applying the legal framework in Mr Lambert's case would result in euthanasia rather than therapeutic abstention. There was no reasonable justification for the State not to intervene for the protection of life.[153]

The Lambert criteria have been applied in two subsequent cases regarding the withdrawal of life-sustaining treatment of minor patients. The Gard Case concerned an infant with irreversible brain damage, and the Afiri and Biddarri Case was about a 14-year-old minor in a permanent vegetative state.[154] In both cases, the parents had opposed the physicians' decision to withdraw treatment. In both cases, considering

---

[150] *Lambert Case*, [177]-[180].

[151] *Lambert Case*, [182]-[184].

[152] *Lambert Case*, Joint Partly Dissenting Opinion of Judges Hajiyev, Šikuta, Tsotsoria, de Gaetano and Gritco [2]-[7].

[153] *Lambert Case*, Joint Partly Dissenting Opinion of Judges Hajiyev, Šikuta, Tsotsoria, de Gaetano and Gritco [8]-[10].

[154] *Gard and Others v the United Kingdom* (dec) App no 39793/17, 27 June 2017; *Afiri and Biddarri v France* (dec) App no 1828/18, 23 January 2018.

the margin of appreciation enjoyed by the States, the Court found that the domestic authorities had fulfilled their positive obligation under Article 2 by sufficiently considering all relevant aspects, including the parents' opinion.[155]

4.1.8 The Nicklinson Case

4.1.8.1 Circumstances of the Case

Mr Nicklinson had suffered a stroke in 2004 that had left him almost completely paralysed, in a situation called the locked-in syndrome. He was in constant physical and mental pain and had decided that he no longer wanted to live. To that end, he made a living will in 2007 that all treatments, except pain medication, would be withdrawn. He wanted a dignified death. But while refusing nutrition and hydration would cause too much distress to his family, euthanasia and assisted suicide were not legally available options in the UK.[156]

Mr Lamb had become paralysed after a car accident in 1991 and was bound to a wheelchair with complete immobility except for his right hand. His irreversible condition caused him severe pain. He wanted to end his life but that would not be possible without assistance.[157]

Mr Nicklinson went to the High Court for a declaration that medical assistance to end his life would be justified under the necessity defence or that the current law violated his Article 8 rights under the Convention. In the meantime, Mr Nicklinson's physician, Dr Nitschke, had developed a machine that would allow Mr Nicklinson to receive a lethal drug upon a command he could give by blinking a phrase. Using this machine would nevertheless constitute a crime under section 2(1) of the 1961 Act. The High Court refused Mr Nicklinson's arguments, stating that Article 8 of the Convention did not provide a justification for euthanasia, and even if the prohibition on assisted suicide interfered with Article 8, it was still justified within the margin of appreciation. After receiving the High Court's judgment on 16 August 2012, Mr Nicklinson refused medical treatment, nutrition and hydration. He died shortly after on 22 August 2012 from pneumonia.[158]

On behalf of Mr Nicklinson, his wife appealed the decision before the Court of Appeal. At this point, Mr Lamb joined the procedures as a claimant. The appeal was dismissed unanimously. The Court of Appeal rejected the notion that the common law defence of necessity could justify euthanasia and assisted suicide. Following the Pretty Case, the prohibition on euthanasia and assisted suicide did not violate the

---

[155] *Gard Case*, [89]-[98], [123]-[124]; *Afiri and Biddarri Case*, [28]-[47].

[156] *Nicklinson and Lamb v the United Kingdom* Apps No 2478/15 and 1787/15, 23 June 2015, [4]-[6].

[157] *Nicklinson Case*, [7]-[8].

[158] *Nicklinson Case*, [9]-[15].

applicants' interests under Article 8 of the Convention. The Court of Appeal further stated that such a sensitive and controversial topic that contained several moral and ethical considerations could not be resolved by judicial means, but it was upon the Parliament to change the law. Since the matter of assisted suicide has been discussed in Parliament without resulting in any legislative changes, the Court of Appeal would have to apply the existing law.[159]

4.1.8.2 Judgment of the Supreme Court

The case came before the Supreme Court (previously House of Lords).[160] The appeal focused on whether section 2(1) of the 1961 Act was compatible with Article 8 of the Convention and, if so, whether assisted suicide could be justified with the common law defence of necessity under certain circumstances. While a violation of Article 8 based on the lack of exceptions permitting voluntary euthanasia was claimed before the High Court and the Court of Appeal, the applicants chose not to pursue this claim before the Supreme Court but rather focus their arguments on assisted suicide.

The appeal was dismissed by seven votes to two. The Supreme Court decided unanimously that the question of the compatibility of section 2(1) of the 1961 Act with Article 8 of the Convention was for the UK to decide since the matter of assisted death was within the margin of appreciation. While four judges (Lords Clarke, Sumption, Reed, and Hughes) considered it would be institutionally inappropriate for the Supreme Court to assess the compatibility of section 2(1), five judges (Lords Neuberger, Mance, Wilson, Kerr, and Lady Hale) held that the Supreme Court was indeed constitutionally authorized to make a declaration of incompatibility. As Lord Neuberger stated:

> The interference with Applicants' article 8 rights is grave, the arguments in favour of the current law are by no means overwhelming, the present official attitude to assisted suicide seems in practice to come close to tolerating it in certain situations, the appeal raises issues similar to those which the courts have determined under the common law, the rational connection between the aim and effect of section 2 is fairly weak, and no compelling reason has been made out for the court simply ceding any jurisdiction to Parliament.[161]

Of those five Judges, three (Lords Neuberger, Mance, and Wilson) refused to give an incompatibility decision for the case at hand because while the Supreme Court could make a compatibility judgment, it was not appropriate to do so in the matter of assisted suicide in that particular time. Being a highly controversial and sensitive topic that carried the risk of abuse among many other uncertainties, allowing assisted suicide would require careful consideration, detailed provisions, and safeguards. The

[159] *Nicklinson Case*, [16]-[23].

[160] R (Nicklinson and another) v Ministry of Justice, R (AM) v Director of Public Prosecutions [2014] UKSC 38, [2015] AC 657.

[161] *Nicklinson Case-SC*, [111].

Parliament was discussing the matter of assisted suicide and considering the proposed Assisted Dying Bill. Therefore, it would be appropriate to wait for the outcome of the parliamentary deliberations. Nevertheless, the Supreme Court urged the Parliament to address the matter of assisted suicide and stated that if the Parliament did not adequately address this issue, the Supreme Court could intervene upon another similar application.[162]

Lord Neuberger held that it would be a 'revolutionary step' to extend the necessity defence to justify suicide assistance. It was clear to the Supreme Court that the legislatures of the 1961 Act did not intend for any exceptions, which was also clear from the recent amendment made in 2009.[163] Although successfully argued before the Dutch Courts, the necessity defence was not accepted in the UK.

Lady Hale and Lord Kerr on the other hand, held that section 2(1) of the 1961 Act was, in fact, incompatible with Article 8 of the Convention because it did not provide any exceptions and failed to strike a fair balance.[164]

4.1.8.3 Judgment of the ECtHR

Mrs Nicklinson, on her own and her husband's behalf, complained that there was a violation of Article 8 due to the domestic courts' failure to make a compatibility assessment of section 2(1) of the 1961 Act with Article 8 of the Convention. The ECtHR started by stating that Article 13 guaranteed everyone to seek an effective remedy before the domestic courts for violations of their rights and freedoms under the Convention, except for challenges against the member States' primary legislation. However, the Human Rights Act of 1998 had incorporated the Convention into the national law, and domestic courts were authorized to make an assessment of incompatibility against primary legislation if necessary.[165] Despite the existing legal basis for the Supreme Court to evaluate a challenge against primary legislation, the ECtHR considered it problematic to assess whether the domestic courts followed the procedural requirements in a case, in which the member State enjoyed a wide margin of appreciation. When issues within the margin of appreciation were brought before the ECtHR, the ECtHR usually referred to the Parliament's discretion to assess the appropriate way to address the matter. The ECtHR had also taken the same approach in the Pretty Case, where it had stated that it was 'primarily for States to assess the risk and likely incidence of abuse if the general prohibition on assisted suicides were

---

[162] *Nicklinson Case-SC*, [118] (Lord Neuberger), [293] (Lord Clarke).

[163] *Nicklinson Case-SC*, [130]. In the Purdy Case, Lord Brown had already signalled that a necessity defence would not be successful in the case of suicide assistance. *R (Purdy) v the Director of Public Prosecutions* [2009] UKHL 45, [2010] 1 AC 345, [83].

[164] *Nicklinson Case-SC*, [321] (Lady Hale), [361] (Lord Kerr).

[165] Art 4 '(1) Subsection (2) applies in any proceedings in which a court determines whether a provision of primary legislation is compatible with a Convention right. (2) If the court is satisfied that the provision is incompatible with a Convention right, it may make a declaration of that incompatibility.'

relaxed or if exceptions were to be created'.[166] Therefore, it would be inappropriate not to allow the domestic courts to make the same referral. Mrs Nicklinson's application was found manifestly ill-founded.[167]

The second applicant, Mr Lamb, complained that the lack of judicial procedures to enable voluntary euthanasia violated his rights under Articles 6, 8, 13, and 14. Both applicants were seeking the possibility of using Dr Nitschke's machine that would allow them the chance of assisted suicide by giving a command through blinking. If this alternative could not be realized, their only option would have been voluntary euthanasia. Therefore, their claims before the High Court and the Court of Appeal included both arguments for assisted suicide and euthanasia. However, they had decided to leave out euthanasia from their application before the Supreme Court. By doing so, they had not given the Supreme Court a chance to evaluate the subject matter of euthanasia and whether the law on murder constituted a violation of Article 8 by not allowing an exception. The ECtHR rejected the arguments that the Supreme Court's approach on assisted suicide could also be read to include euthanasia. These two methods of assisted dying had different legal bases, and the applicants had intentionally left euthanasia out of their claims before the Supreme Court. Since the domestic remedies had not been exhausted for the part concerning euthanasia, the ECtHR found Mr Lamb's application inadmissible.[168]

4.2 Analysis of the European Court of Human Rights' Case Law

The Court has dealt with assisted suicide and withdrawal of life-sustaining treatment, but not with euthanasia. There has been no case from the Netherlands, Belgium or Luxembourg, where euthanasia has been legalized. However, that will change soon. A case from Belgium regarding euthanasia is currently pending before the Court.[169] Mr Mortier's mother, who was suffering from chronic depression, ended her life through euthanasia, and the attending physician had not notified the applicant about the decision before euthanasia was performed.[170] The applicant claims that the State failed to fulfil its positive obligation to protect the life of his mother under Article

[166] *Pretty Case*, [74].

[167] *Nicklinson Case*, [79]-[86].

[168] *Nicklinson Case*, [87]-[95].

[169] *Mortier v Belgium* App no 78017/17 (pending case); ADF International is representing Mr Mortier and the application form to the Court can be found at ADF International, Mortier v Belgium. https://adfinternational.org/legal/mortier-v-belgium/.

[170] Beuselinck, who is an oncologist in Belgium, writes that he has seen some family members worry about the possibility of euthanasia being performed on their patient without their knowledge. The Mortier Case seems to support this claim. Beuselinck (2017), pp. 104–105.

2 of the Convention, and there was a violation of his rights under Article 8. It is yet to be seen how the Court will decide on its first euthanasia case.

So far, the Court's case law on the right to die has been limited to a procedural review with a 'flavour' of personal autonomy.[171] Initially, in the Pretty Case, the Court indirectly accepted that 'the choice to avoid what [one] considers will be an undignified and distressing end to [one's] life' (a choice that would have been realized through assisted suicide) was part of the right to respect for private life.[172] In the Haas Case, the Court rephrased this 'choice' as 'an individual's right to decide by what means and at what point his or her life will end'.[173] The Court also addressed the relationship between Articles 2 and 8, stating that 'the Convention must be read as a whole' when seeking a balance.[174] While expressly declaring it as a principle under Article 8 in the Pretty Case,[175] the Court implicitly addressed personal autonomy as an interest to be balanced against the State's positive obligation under Article 2 in the Haas Case.[176] This role of personal autonomy was expressly stated later in the Lambert Case.[177] However, the Court limited itself to a procedural approach, leaving the determination of how to strike this balance to the member States. In the Gross Case, although it had later been rendered ineffective by the Grand Chamber's judgment, the Chamber had found it necessary to establish 'comprehensive and clear guidelines' regarding the permissibility of physician-assisted suicide, but had not commented on the substance.[178] The same approach is apparent in the Koch and Nicklinson Cases, where the focus was on whether the German and British Courts, respectively, had adequately examined the applicants' claims.[179] This procedural approach is in line with the principle of subsidiarity since the 'better placed' national authorities have '*chronological* or *procedural* priority' over the Court to address conflicting interests, especially in matters that involve controversial moral issues upon which there is no consensus among member States.[180] This is also the approach the Court has taken on reproductive rights,

[171] Brems calls a procedural approach that has a certain substantive element that must be taken into consideration and that provides guidance to the member States a 'substance-flavoured procedural review'. Brems (2017), p. 35.

[172] *Pretty Case*, [67].

[173] *Haas Case*, [51].

[174] *Haas Case*, [54].

[175] *Pretty Case*, [61].

[176] 'For the Court, this latter Article (Article 2) obliges the national authorities to prevent an individual from taking his or her own life *if the decision has not been taken freely and with full understanding of what is involved.*' *Haas Case*, [54] (emphasis added).

[177] *Lambert Case*, [142].

[178] *Gross Case-Chamber*, [63], [69].

[179] *Koch Case*, [65]-[72]; *Nicklinson Case*, [84]-[85], [94].

[180] Letsas (2006), pp. 720–729.

such as access to abortion and medically assisted reproduction.[181] Just as in the right to die, the debate on these topics is also highly controversial surrounded with ethical concerns to which there is no consensus.

The principle of subsidiarity is a fundamental principle of the ECHR that serves the idea that national courts are in the best position to evaluate violations of Convention rights as they possess a more complete understanding of the circumstances. They are primarily responsible to prevent violations of the ECHR or provide redress for such violations. The ECtHR will only intervene where national courts have not adequately fulfilled their primary obligation. Protocol No 15 that amended the Convention makes a clear reference to the principle of subsidiarity, as well as the margin of appreciation.[182] Since the national courts are 'the first guarantors of the Convention',[183] they also carry the obligation to thoroughly evaluate such cases with their merits, as was pointed out by the ECtHR in the Koch Case.

It remains within the margin of appreciation of each member State to determine whether the weight given to personal autonomy will tip the balance in favour of the right to die. Despite their freedom to determine how much weight is given to which competing interests, member States must nevertheless provide a justification for restricting the right to decide on the time and manner of one's own death since the Court has explicitly included this right in Article 8 of the Convention.

4.3 Critical Remarks on Council of Europe Member States

In light of the analysis of the Court's case law, one more look at the previous chapter, 'Right to Die in Practice', is in order. Do the right to die practices in the member States comply with the Convention?

Switzerland does not have a legislation regulating its assisted suicide practice. The omission of Article 115 of the Swiss Criminal Code, which does not penalize selfless suicide assistance, is not a sufficiently strong foundation to carry the entire assisted suicide practice that it has evolved into today. The SAMS Guidelines, which

---

[181] Recent case law shows that the Court has become more direct in cases on access to abortion and no longer shys away from a substantial evaluation as it used to. ECHR (2021) Factsheet on Reproductive Rigths. https://www.echr.coe.int/documents/fs_reproductive_eng.pdf.

[182] Protocol No 15 amending the Convention for the Protection of Human Rights and Fundamental Freedoms, 24 June 2013, CETS No 213 (entered into force on 1 August 2021). In order to make the principle of subsidiarity more practical, Protocol No 16 introduced a procedure, which allows the highest courts or tribunals of a member State to request an advisory opinion from the ECtHR. Protocol No 16 to the Convention for the Protection of Human Rights and Fundamental Freedoms, 2 October 2013, CETS No 214 (in force since 1 August 2018 and ratifed only by 13 member States).

[183] Para 13 'A central element of the principle of subsidiarity, under which national authorities are the first guarantors of the Convention, is the right to an effective remedy under Article 13 of the Convention.' Council of Europe (2018) Copenhagen Declaration on the Reform of the European Convention on Human Rights System. https://www.echr.coe.int/Documents/Copenhagen_Declaration_ENG.pdf.

can be considered the only source for guidance, are neither legally binding nor sufficiently clear. The ambiguity of the Swiss practice of assisted suicide and its requirements interferes not only with Article 8 of the Convention, but also with the principles of accessibility and foreseeability under Article 7 of the Convention.[184] 'First the law must be sufficiently clear for individuals to conduct themselves in accordance with its commands and, secondly, where there is judicial development of the law, any changes must be predictable.'[185] Looking back at the Swiss case law on assisted suicide, it can be stated that the application of Article 115 of the Criminal Code is neither sufficiently clear nor predictable. The Chamber's decision agrees with this statement although it was rendered mute by the Grand Chamber for different reasons.

Furthermore, the supervisory mechanism of the Swiss assisted suicide practice is hardly adequate. The only method of control is the obligation to notify the authorities in cases of unnatural deaths, which includes assisted suicide. However, it is doubtful that this minimal method of supervision satisfies the State's positive obligation under Article 2 of the Convention. Considering the highly active and liberal role assisted suicide organizations play in the Swiss practice and their lack of transparency, their activities should be subject to stricter supervision. For example, the SAMS Guideline'18 requires a previously established relationship and repeated discussions between the physician and the patient that makes the request for assisted suicide understandable. However, most foreigners who travel to Switzerland for assisted suicide die shortly after their arrival, and usually meet with the prescribing physician only once. This situation obviously does not comply with Guideline'18. If the State shares the same opinion as SAMS, there should have been more actions taken against assisted suicide organizations and affiliated physicians. It is not consistent to refer to the SAMS Guidelines for clarity, but not to supervise the practice according to the requirements listed in them. Even if the SAMS Guideline'18 would not have required a previously established relationship, it is not realistically possible that the autonomous well-thought nature of the assisted suicide request in each case could be determined without a doubt after a single meeting. It does not satisfy the State's duty to protect life and especially the lives of those who are vulnerable to leave the control of the assisted suicide practice solely on the prescription requirement and a police investigation only after death has occurred, which is more often a mere formality.

---

[184]ECHR Art 7 '1. No one shall be held quilty of any criminal offence on account of any act or omission which did not constitute a criminal offence under national or international law at the time when it was committed. Nor shall a heavier penalty be imposed than the one that was applicable at the time the criminal offence was committed.

2. This article shall not prejudice the trial and punishment of any person for any act or omission which, at the time when it was committed, was criminal according to the general principles of law recognised by civilised nations.'

[185]ECHR (2019) Article 7: The "quality of law" requirements and the principle of (non-) retrospectiveness of the criminal law under Article 7 of the Convention. https://www.echr.coe.int/Documents/Research_report_quality_law_requirements_criminal_law_Art_7_ENG.PDF, p. 3.

The Netherlands and Belgium both have a detailed legal framework that should provide sufficient legal guidance, notwithstanding the subjective nature of several concepts within the practice such as unbearable suffering and the difficulties of generalizing medical situations into one common rule that apply for all cases. It should be added that the practice of assisted suicide in Belgium, despite not being covered by the Belgian Euthanasia Act, is peculiar. Although it has been established in practice that assisted suicide will be supervised under the same requirements of euthanasia, this clarification should have been done on a legislative level considering that the definition provided by the Euthanasia Act clearly excludes assisted suicide. Considering that the Euthanasia Act has been amended several times since 2002, the State had many chances to rectify this situation.

Regarding the State's positive obligation to adopt adequate safeguards to prevent abuses and protect the vulnerable under Article 2 of the Convention, the compatibility of the Dutch and Belgian practices are questionable. The analyses of the respective States have shown that the number of assisted dying cases has risen tremendously over the past two decades. Arguments such as increasing awareness of end-of-life options including euthanasia and assisted suicide, or decreasing fear from prosecution that subsequently leads to a higher percentage of notification by physicians are only theories that aim to explain the situation. There should be further research in order to satisfactorily rule out the existence of a slippery slope. This determination should be considered part of the State's duty under Article 2, and both the Netherlands and Belgium could be in violation of the Convention if they do not take the necessary steps. If research proves a slippery slope, namely an extension of the right to die practice beyond the limits of the respective legal framework due to generous interpretation or human error, Article 2 would require the State to adopt additional safeguard measures to reassure the balance between the right to die and the right to life.

What might be another concern under the Convention is section 14(4) of the Belgian Euthanasia Act that effectively prohibits healthcare institutions from adopting a non-euthanasia policy within their premises. If, for example, a Catholic hospital were to lose its 'Catholic' title because its healthcare professionals were practicing euthanasia and assisted suicide, this could raise a question of infringement of the healthcare institution's freedom of religion under Article 9.

Despite the German Federal Administrative Court's judgment that assited suicide could constitute necessary medical care in extreme cases, the German Federal Ministry of Health's effort to prevent access to NaP regardless of the circumstances were not compatible with Article 8 of the Convention. Applications to obtain NaP to the German Federal Institute for Drugs and Medical Devices have either been rejected or left unanswered. This interference could have also amounted to a prescribed treatment under Article 3 in cases of applicants who were suffering unbearably.

Although the UK did not legalize assisted dying, the DPP's discreationary power on whether to prosecute assisted suicide cases brings up concerns related to the principles of accessability and foreseeability under Article 7 of the Convention. The DPP's 'Policy for Prosecutors in Respect of Cases of Encouraging or Assisting

Suicide' is a non-exhaustive list of factors that might be considered in favour or against prosecution. The Parliament has thoroughly discussed and decided against providing an exception to the blanket ban on assisted suicide and the ECtHR will respect this approach due to the wide margin of appreciation. However, the DPP's discretionary power does introduce a sort of exception. Publishing a policy for the exercise of that power will most likely raise the demand for further clarity, as it has already been the case. But when the UK Supreme Court has left the matter to the Parliament, and the Parliament has discussed and decided not to provide any exceptions, how can the DPP be the appropriate authority to draw the lines of the exception to the blanket ban assisted suicide?

On an additional note, we have seen the engagement of the medical profession in all of the selected jurisdictions. While the medical profession's participation in the discussion on the right to die is highly necessary and appreciated, this does not relieve the parliament from its duties as the democratically legitimated legislature. Although the medical aspect of the right to die is highly essential, there are several other aspects that must be taken into consideration in the decision of if and how this right will be practiced. The burden of identifying the limits of the right to die cannot be solely left to the medical profession.

The right to die continues to be a subject of heated debate, and the ECtHR will most likely have to go beyond its procedural approach to ensure the compatibility of its practice with the Convention.

4.4 The Right to Die and the International Covenant on Civil and Political Rights

While this study focuses on the right to die under the ECHR, it is complementary to the general picture to take a brief look at the International Covenant on Civil and Political Rights (ICCPR)[186] and the Human Rights Committee's[187] documents. This is also relevant because all of the permissive jurisdictions analysed here are party to the ICCPR.

[186] International Covenant on Civil and Political Rights, 16 December 1966, United Nations, Treaty Series vol 999, 171.

[187] The United Nations Human Rights Committee, regulated by Arts 28 to 45 of the ICCPR, consists of independent experts who monitor the implementation of the ICCPR by its member States. Member States must submit periodical reports on their implementation of the ICCPR and which measures they have taken to that end, and the Human Rights Committee responds with its Concluding Observations. The Committee also publishes General Comments on human rights issues. OHCHR, Introduction of the Committee. https://www.ohchr.org/en/hrbodies/ccpr/pages/ccprintro.aspx.

Article 6(1) of the ICCPR protects the right to life and obliges States to protect life from any arbitrary deprivation.[188] Article 2 requires States to take necessary measures to respect and protect the rights recognized under the ICCPR and to provide effective remedy to those whose rights have been violated.[189] In its General Comment No 36, the Human Rights Committee reiterated the States' positive obligation to adopt measures for the protection of life,[190] and in relation to assisted dying, stated:

> While acknowledging the central importance to human dignity of personal autonomy, States should take adequate measures, without violating their other Covenant obligations, to prevent suicides, especially among individuals in particularly vulnerable situations, including individuals deprived of their liberty. States parties that allow medical professionals to provide medical treatment or the medical means in order to facilitate the termination of life of afflicted adults, such as the terminally ill, who experience severe physical or mental pain and suffering and wish to die with dignity, must ensure the existence of robust legal and institutional safeguards to verify that medical professionals are complying with the free, informed, explicit and, unambiguous decision of their patients, with a view to protecting patients from pressure and abuse.[191]

Although the Human Rights Committee does not acknowledge a right to die, it does not necessarily find it contrary to the ICCPR. According to the Committee, determining the autonomous nature of the request to die is an obligation stemming from the right to life under ICCPR. States are also obliged to make sure that patients are not subjected to unwarranted pressure and that the practice of assisted dying is protected from abuse. These positive obligations are in line with the ECtHR's approach and the duties upon Council of Europe member States under Article 2 of the ECHR.

---

[188] Art 6(1) 'Every human being has the inherent right to life. This right shall be protected by law. No one shall be arbitrarily deprived of his life.'

[189] Art 2 '1. Each State Party to the present Covenant undertakes to respect and to ensure to all individuals within its territory and subject to its jurisdiction the rights recognized in the present Covenant, without distinction of any kind, such as race, colour, sex, language, religion, political or other opinion, national or social origin, property, birth or other status.

2. Where not already provided for by existing legislative or other measures, each State Party to the present Covenant undertakes to take the necessary steps, in accordance with its constitutional processes and with the provisions of the present Covenant, to adopt such laws or other measures as may be necessary to give effect to the rights recognized in the present Covenant.

3. Each State Party to the present Covenant undertakes:

(a) To ensure that any person whose rights or freedoms as herein recognized are violated shall have an effective remedy, notwithstanding that the violation has been committed by persons acting in an official capacity;

(b) To ensure that any person claiming such a remedy shall have his right thereto determined by competent judicial, administrative or legislative authorities, or by any other competent authority provided for by the legal system of the State, and to develop the possibilities of judicial remedy;

(c) To ensure that the competent authorities shall enforce such remedies when granted.'

[190] UN Human Rights Committee (2019) General Comment No 36, Article 6 (right to life), CCPR/C/GC/36, para. 21.

[191] UN Human Rights Committee (2019) General Comment No 36, Article 6 (right to life), para. 9.

Regarding the specific practices in the selected permissive jurisdictions, the Human Rights Committee has already expressed concerns about Switzerland and the Netherlands.

In its Third Periodic Report on Switzerland, the Human Rights Committee briefly mentioned Article 115 of the Swiss Criminal Code, the 'liberal provision [that] has fostered the birth of many assisted-suicide organizations'.[192] Later in its Concluding Observations, the Committee expressed its concern 'about the lack of independent or judicial oversight to determine that a person seeking assistance to commit suicide is operating with full free and informed consent.'[193] In light of Article 6 of the ICCPR, the Committee urged Switzerland to consider a legislative amendment to ensure that the autonomous and well thought nature of the assisted suicide request.[194] Interestingly, assisted suicide was completely excluded from the Committee's Concluding Observations of 2017.[195] Although Switzerland has not taken any steps to adopt further safeguard measures, the Committee did not repeat its concerns.

The Committee had already voiced some concerns before the Dutch Euthanasia Act came into force in 2002. In its Concluding Observations from 2001, the Committee stated

> [W]here a State party seeks to relax legal protection with respect to an act deliberately intended to put an end to human life, the Committee believes that the Covenant obliges it to apply the most rigorous scrutiny to determine whether the State party's obligations to ensure the right to life are being complied with (articles 2 and 6 of the Covenant).[196]

The Committee was concerned that the requirements listed under the Euthanasia Act could be easily circumvented and 'with the passage of time, such a practice might lead to routinization and insensitivity to the strict application of requirements in a way not anticipated.'[197] The ex post facto supervision by the RTEs was not satisfactory as an adequate safeguard against abuse, and a stronger a priori control mechanism was suggested.[198] In 2009, the Committee repeated its dissatisfaction by the lack of an a priori review procedure to ensure that the request to die was not subject to undue influence, and urged the Netherlands to review its Euthanasia Act

---

[192] UN Human Rights Committee (2007) Third periodic report on Switzerland, CCPR/C/CHE/3, 17 December 2007, para. 6.3; all Human Rights Committee documents are available at https://www.ohchr.org/EN/HRBodies/CCPR/Pages/CCPRIndex.aspx.

[193] UN Human Rights Committee (2009) Concluding observations of the Human Rights Committee on Switzerland, CCPR/C/CHE/CO/3, 3 November 2009, para. 13.

[194] UN Human Rights Committee (2009) Concluding observations of the Human Rights Committee on Switzerland, para. 13.

[195] UN Human Rights Committee (2017) Concluding observations on the fourth periodic report of Switzerland, CCPR/C/CHE/CO/4, 22 August 2017.

[196] UN Human Rights Committee (2001) Concluding observations of the Human Rights Committee on the Netherlands, CCPR/CO/72/NET, 27 August 2001, para. 5(a).

[197] UN Human Rights Committee (2001) Concluding observations of the Human Rights Committee on the Netherlands, para. 5(b).

[198] UN Human Rights Committee (2001) Concluding observations of the Human Rights Committee on the Netherlands, para. 5(d).

under Article 6 of the ICCPR.[199] The importance of an a priori review procedure was repeated again in 2019.[200]

Surprisingly, the Committee has never commented on the Belgian assisted dying practice. It was neither raised as a question in any of the lists of issues to be considered nor mentioned in the concluding observations.[201] It is interesting that the Committee has commented on Switzerland and the Netherlands but ignored the Belgian practice. The last Concluding Observations on Canada were in 2015 before the MAID law entered into force.[202] However, the list of issues raised for the next Concluding Observations does not mention Canada's MAID practice either.[203]

Even though the Committee has refrained from elaborating on the right to die, it can be concluded that the ICCPR, like the ECHR, imposes a positive obligation upon permissive States to ensure their assisted dying practices are equipped with adequate safeguard measures. The wish to end one's own life must be autonomous, well thought and informed. According to the Committee, an a priori procedure is better suited for this purpose. The Committee also acknowledges the possibility of a slippery slope and worries about the normalization of assisted dying.

4.5 The Right to Die and the European Union Law

Although the right to die is not an aspect under the competence of the European Union, the permissive approach adopted by several of its member States raises a question in relation to the trend known as 'suicide tourism' or 'death tourism'. Switzerland, which is not a EU member, is not the only destination for people who wish to end their lives through the assistance of another. Belgian physicians

---

199 UN Human Rights Committee (2009) Concluding observations of the Human Rights Committee on the Netherlands, CCPR/C/NLD/CO/4, 25 August 2009, para. 7.

200 UN Human Rights Committee (2019) Concluding Observations on the fifth periodic report of the Netherlands, CCPR/C/NLD/CO/5, 22 August 2019, paras. 28–29.

201 UN Human Rights Committee (2003) List of issues to be taken up in connection with the consideration of the fourth periodic report of Belgium, CCPR/C/80/L/BEL, 28 November 2003; -- (2004) Concluding observations of the Human Rights Committee on Belgium, CCPR/CO/81/BEL, 12 August 2004; -- (2010) List of issues to be taken up in connection with the consideration of the fifth periodic report of Belgium, CCPR/C/BEL/Q/5, 13 April 2010; -- (2010) Draft concluding observations of the Human Rights Committee on Belgium, CCPR/C/BEL/CO/5, 16 November 2010; -- (2016) List of issues prior to submission of the sixth periodic report of Belgium, CCPR/C/BEL/QPR/6, 29 July 2016; -- (2019) Concluding observations on the sixth periodic report of Belgium, CCPR/C/BEL/CO/6, 6 December 2019.

202 UN Human Rights Committee (2015) Concluding observations on the sixth periodic report of Canada, CCPR/C/CAN/CO/6, 13 August 2015.

203 UN Human Rights Committee (2021) List of issues prior to submission of the seventh periodic report of Canada, CCPR/C/CAN/QPR/7, 24 August 2021.

report an increasing number of euthanasia requests from French citizens.[204] Although a long established physician-patient relationship is sought, neither the Belgian Euthanasia Act nor the Dutch Euthanasia Act prevent non-citizens or non-residents from receiving euthanasia or suicide assistance within their jurisdiction. This is the same situation in Luxembourg where euthanasia and assisted suicide are legal since 2009.[205] Therefore, citizens of other EU member States, where assisted dying is not a legal option, could realize their wish to end their lives in one of these permissive States. This raises a question about the relation between 'death tourism' and freedom to provide services under Article 56 of the Treaty on the Functioning of the European Union.[206]

EU citizens' freedom to travel to another EU member State to receive services is also protected under Article 56 TFEU. According to Article 57, there should be remuneration for the services provided. Although making profit is not the intention in cases of euthanasia or suicide assistance, the fee to cover the costs is sufficient to qualify it as services within the meaning of Article 56.[207] The European Court of Justice had already ruled that medical services that were carried out in accordance with the law of the member State were considered services under Article 56.[208]

On the other hand, Article 7 of the Charter of Fundamental Rights of the EU protects the right to private and family life,[209] and the interpretation of Article 7 of the Charter is parallel to its corresponding Article 8 of the ECHR.[210] Since the ECJ's case law foresees that the four fundamental freedoms of EU should be interpreted in light of European Fundamental rights, restricting a EU citizen to travel to a member State where assisted dying is legal would contradict with Article 56 TFEU and

---

[204] Warlop (2019) De plus en plus de Français demandent l'euthanasie en Belgique. In: RTBF. https://www.rtbf.be/info/monde/detail_de-plus-en-plus-de-francais-demandent-l-euthanasie-en-belgique?id=10226537.

[205] (2012) Information on requesting euthanasia or assisted suicide. In: Guichet.lu. https://guichet.public.lu/en/citoyens/famille/euthanasie-soins-palliatifs/fin-de-vie/euthanasie-assistance-suicide.html.

[206] Consolidated Version of the Treaty on the Functioning of the European Union (TFEU) 26 October 2012, OJ C 326/47, Art 56 'Within the framework of the provisions set out below, restrictions on freedom to provide services within the Union shall be prohibited in respect of nationals of Member States who are established in a Member State other than that of the person for whom the services are intended.'

[207] Barnard (2019), pp. 290–296; Woll (2018), p. 211.

[208] Case C-159/90 *The Society for the Protection of Unborn Children Ireland Ltd v Stephen Grogan and others* [1991] ECR I-04685, [16]-[21]; In this case, the question was whether the distribution of information on abortion services in the UK was protected under the freedom to provide services in Ireland where abortion was illegal.

[209] Charter of Fundamental Rights of the European Union, 26 October 2012, OJ C 326/391, Art 7 'Everyone has the right to respect for his or her private and family life, home and communications.'

[210] Charter Art 52(3) 'In so far as this Charter contains rights which correspond to rights guaranteed by the Convention for the Protection of Human Rights and Fundamental Freedoms, the meaning and scope of those rights shall be the same as those laid down by the said Convention. This provision shall not prevent Union law providing more extensive protection.'

Article 7 of the Charter.[211] Therefore, if member States, which are restrictive of the right to die, cannot prevent its citizens from travelling to another member State to receive assisted dying services. If a patient were not able to travel without assistance from another, would Article 56 protect the third-person assisting the patient against criminal liability in the home member State? If the third-person's assistance is absolutely necessary for the patient to exercise their freedom to receive services, discouraging the third-person with threat of prosecution should also be considered contradictory to Article 56 TFEU. However, the margin of appreciation attributed to States with regard to the right to die should not be disregarded. Any restriction on the freedom to receive right to die services in another member State would be subject to a proportionality test. In a field as controversial as the right to die where there is no consensus among member States, the ECJ is likely to adopt a cautious approach like the ECtHR.

References

(2012) Information on requesting euthanasia or assisted suicide. In: Guichet.lu. https://guichet.public.lu/en/citoyens/famille/euthanasie-soins-palliatifs/fin-de-vie/euthanasie-assistance-suicide.html

ADF International, Mortier v Belgium. https://adfinternational.org/legal/mortier-v-belgium/

ALfA, Die Aktion Lebensrecht für Alle. https://www.alfa-ev.de/ueber-uns/

Alliance Defending Freedom, Who We Are. https://www.adflegal.org/about-us

Americans United for Life, About. https://aul.org/mission/

Barnard C (2019) The substantive law of the EU: the four freedoms, 6th edn. Oxford University Press, Oxford

Baumann A, Audibert G, Claudot F, Puybasset L (2009) Ethics review: end of life legislation – the French model. Crit Care 13(1):204. https://doi.org/10.1186/cc7148

Beuselinck B (2017) 2002–2016: fourteen years of euthanasia in Belgium: first-line observations by an oncologist. In: Jones DA, Gastmans C, MacKeller C (eds) Euthanasia and assisted suicide: lessons from Belgium. Cambridge University Press, Cambridge, pp 101–113

Brems E (2017) The "logics" of procedural-type review by the European Court of Human Rights. In: Gerards J, Brems E (eds) Procedural review in European fundamental rights cases. Cambridge University Press, Cambridge

Committee on Bioethics of the Council of Europe (2014) Guide on the decision-making process regarding medical treatment in end-of-life situations. https://www.coe.int/en/web/bioethics/guide-on-the-decision-making-process-regarding-medical-treatment-in-end-of-life-situations

Council of Europe (2018) Copenhagen Declaration on the Reform of the European Convention on Human Rights System. https://www.echr.coe.int/Documents/Copenhagen_Declaration_ENG.pdf

Council of Europe, Parliamentary Assembly, Recommendation 1418 on protection of the human rights and dignity of the terminally ill and dying (adopted by the Parliamentary Assembly on 25 June 1999 at the 24th sitting) 1999. http://assembly.coe.int/nw/xml/xref/xref-xml2html-en.asp?fileid=16722&lang=en

ECHR (2019) Article 7: the "quality of law" requirements and the principle of (non-) retrospectiveness of the criminal law under Article 7 of the Convention. https://www.echr.

[211] Woll (2018), pp. 212–213.

coe.int/Documents/Research_report_quality_law_requirements_criminal_law_Art_7_ENG.PDF
ECHR (2020) Practical Guide on Admissibility Criteria. https://www.echr.coe.int/Documents/Admissibility_guide_ENG.pdf
ECHR (2021) Factsheet on Reproductive Rigths. https://www.echr.coe.int/documents/fs_reproductive_eng.pdf
ECHR (2021) Guide on Article 8 of the European Convention on Human Rights. https://www.echr.coe.int/documents/guide_art_8_eng.pdf
ECHR (2021) Rules of Court. https://www.echr.coe.int/Documents/Rules_Court_ENG.pdf
European Center for Law and Justice, About the ECLJ. https://eclj.org/about-us
HC Deb 28 July 1961 Vol 645 Col 823
Letsas G (2006) Two concepts of the margin of appreciation. Oxf J Leg Stud 26(4):705–732. https://doi.org/10.1093/ojls/gql030
Mayo Clinic (2019) Spinal Cord Injury. https://www.mayoclinic.org/diseases-conditions/spinal-cord-injury/symptoms-causes/syc-20377890
OHCHR, Introduction of the Committee. https://www.ohchr.org/en/hrbodies/ccpr/pages/ccprintro.aspx
Rösler H (2008) Dignitarian posthumous personality rights - an analysis of U.S. and German constitutional and tort law. Berk J Int L 26:153–205
Sartori D (2018) End-of-life issues and the European Court of Human Rights. The value of personal autonomy within a "proceduralized" review. QIL Zoom-in 52:23–43
Southern Poverty Law Center, Alliance Defending Freedom. https://www.splcenter.org/fighting-hate/extremist-files/group/alliance-defending-freedom
Thibaut A, Bodien YG, Laureys S, Giacino JT (2020) Minimally conscious state "plus": diagnostics criteria and relation to functional recovery. J Neurol 267(5):1245–1254. https://doi.org/10.1007/s00415-019-09628-y
UN Human Rights Committee (2019) General Comment No 36, Article 6 (right to life), CCPR/C/GC/36
UN Human Rights Committee (2001) Concluding observations of the Human Rights Committee on the Netherlands, CCPR/CO/72/NET, 27 August 2001
UN Human Rights Committee (2003) List of issues to be taken up in connection with the consideration of the fourth periodic report of Belgium, CCPR/C/80/L/BEL, 28 November 2003
UN Human Rights Committee (2004) Concluding observations of the Human Rights Committee on Belgium, CCPR/CO/81/BEL, 12 August 2004
UN Human Rights Committee (2007) Third periodic report on Switzerland, CCPR/C/CHE/3, 17 December 2007
UN Human Rights Committee (2009) Concluding observations of the Human Rights Committee on Switzerland, CCPR/C/CHE/CO/3, 3 November 2009
UN Human Rights Committee (2009) Concluding observations of the Human Rights Committee on the Netherlands, CCPR/C/NLD/CO/4, 25 August 2009
UN Human Rights Committee (2010) Draft concluding observations of the Human Rights Committee on Belgium, CCPR/C/BEL/CO/5, 16 November 2010
UN Human Rights Committee (2010) List of issues to be taken up in connection with the consideration of the fifth periodic report of Belgium, CCPR/C/BEL/Q/5, 13 April 2010
UN Human Rights Committee (2015) Concluding observations on the sixth periodic report of Canada, CCPR/C/CAN/CO/6, 13 August 2015
UN Human Rights Committee (2016) List of issues prior to submission of the sixth periodic report of Belgium, CCPR/C/BEL/QPR/6, 29 July 2016
UN Human Rights Committee (2017) Concluding observations on the fourth periodic report of Switzerland, CCPR/C/CHE/CO/4, 22 August 2017
UN Human Rights Committee (2019) Concluding observations on the sixth periodic report of Belgium, CCPR/C/BEL/CO/6, 6 December 2019

UN Human Rights Committee (2019) Concluding Observations on the fifth periodic report of the Netherlands, CCPR/C/NLD/CO/5, 22 August 2019
UN Human Rights Committee (2021) List of issues prior to submission of the seventh periodic report of Canada, CCPR/C/CAN/QPR/7, 24 August 2021
Van Zeebroeck S (2019) Patient's orders: patient's rights and the doctor's obligations under the Claeys-Leonetti law of 2016 in France. Statut Law Rev 40(3):266–272. https://doi.org/10.1093/slr/hmy004
Warlop Q (2019) De plus en plus de Français demandent l'euthanasie en Belgique. In: RTBF. https://www.rtbf.be/info/monde/detail_de-plus-en-plus-de-francais-demandent-l-euthanasie-en-belgique?id=10226537
Woll LK (2018) Sterben dürfen und sterben lassen? Die Herrschaft über den eigenen Tod im Lichte der EMRK, des deutschen Rechts und des Unionrechts. ZEuS 21(2):181–216
Zwart T (1994) The admissibility of human rights petitions - the case law of the European Commission of Human Rights and the Human Rights Committee. Martinus Nijhoff, Dordrecht

Chapter 5
Conclusion

The right to die debate raises the question of the limits of the respect for personal autonomy. These limits are determined by balancing that autonomy against the competing interests. Does personal autonomy not only outweigh the interests of others but extend far enough to justify helping someone to die?

As a first step, it is paramount to clarify what is meant by the right to die. Without establishing a consistent terminology, which lays a neutral foundation enabling a constructive debate, confusion will remain and prevent any progress. The discussion here has been limited to the right to decide the time and manner of one's own death, a decision that requires the active participation (euthanasia) or assistance (assisted suicide) of a third party. Other end-of-life decisions, whether made by the patient (refusal of treatment) or third parties (termination of life without request, withdrawing or withholding treatment, hastening death through pain medication, palliative sedation), should be kept separate and are beyond the scope of this thesis.

Whether the application of the right to die will lead the practice down a slippery slope is a crucial question within this debate that will determine the tipping point of the balancing scale, the answer to which relies heavily on the collection of extensive data from existing permissive jurisdictions. Such data, unfortunately, does not exist on a satisfactory level. Even if a slippery slope is detected in one of the permissive jurisdictions, this risk might not be equally fearsome for other States that have regulated or wish to regulate the right to die, since several other aspects, such as the respective medical, sociological, cultural, and historical backgrounds will play a substantial role in its application. This is evident in the examination of the selected jurisdictions that illustrate the different paths taken towards the right to die.

The Swiss model of assisted dying was born out of the respect for personal autonomy. The assisted suicide organizations have played a pioneering role in its development, while the medical profession has been cautiously keeping a distance as much as possible. Despite being unregulated and heavily reliant on customary rules set forth by the assisted suicide organizations, the Swiss model has cross-border influence that has undoubtedly heated up the international right-to-die debate.

D. N. Kayacan, *The Right to Die with Dignity*, European Union and its Neighbours in a Globalized World 6, https://doi.org/10.1007/978-3-031-04516-5_5

Meanwhile, the Dutch model of assisted dying is a fruit of the physician-patient relationship and has been developed hand in hand with the judicial system. After years of cooperation between the medical profession and the courts that have laid down the foundations, legislation finally caught up with the practice in 2002 when the Dutch Euthanasia Act came into force. Belgium followed the Netherlands and adopted its own Euthanasia Act. Different from its Dutch neighbour, there was neither an extensive case law leading up to the decriminalization of euthanasia nor explicit support from the medical profession in Belgium. The Dutch and Belgian practices of assisted dying are exemplary and should be continuously observed for possible indications of a slippery slope, which would necessitate counter measures. It is true that both practices have outgrown their initial limits since the respective acts were first adopted, and the numbers of people requesting an assisted death have increased. However, there is no consensus whether a slippery slope truly exists, and several other reasons have been presented that could explain the rise in numbers. It is necessary to conduct further empirical research on the assisted dying practices in the Netherlands and Belgium, as they are important examples to other jurisdictions that might consider legalizing assisted dying.

The UK Parliament has not yet been convinced to legalize assisted dying in the UK. However, there is a level of tolerance in practice towards people who help another to travel somewhere where they can legally receive assistance in dying. When assessing whether the prohibition on assisted suicide in the UK violated Article 8 of the Convention, the ECtHR not only relied on the margin of appreciation enjoyed by the member States in this regard but also attributed importance to the prosecutorial discretion that allowed the special circumstances of each case to be taken into account. While the medical profession in the UK remains cautious, assisted dying continues to be a subject of public debate.

Although assisting suicide is not a crime in Germany, a practice similar to the Swiss model has not developed. In 2015, the Parliament banned business-like acts of suicide assistance. However, the Constitutional Court found this prohibition in violation of the right to a self-determined death that was rooted in human dignity and personal freedom. It also stated that a regulation on assisted suicide could not set prerequisites other than ensuring the authenticity of the decision to end one's own life as an expression of personal autonomy. Therefore, any legal framework that will be adopted may not require a medical indication such as incurable illness or unbearable suffering. This judgment puts Germany in a much more liberal position than the permissive jurisdictions mentioned above, which do seek a medical indication as a prerequisite for assisted dying. However, how the judgment will be reflected in practice is yet to be seen.

The Rodriguez and Carter Cases from Canada, which are 22 years apart, have shown two different approaches in cases with very similar circumstances regarding the applicants. The comparison of these two cases is an excellent example on how the interpretations of the same values can change, and how the respect for personal autonomy has gained weight over time.

Within the context of the Convention, the right to die is a question of balance between the right to life enshrined in Article 2 the right to privacy enshrined in

Article 8. Whether the member States find it appropriate to submit to the expression of personal autonomy as the decision to end one's own life in light of their positive obligation to protect the vulnerable is within their margin of appreciation. Due to the highly sensitive nature of the matter, this margin of appreciation is considerably wide at the moment. What is clear from the ECtHR's case law is that the right to decide on the time and manner of one's own death is an aspect of Article 8, and any limitation thereupon must be justified, even if this justification can be achieved relatively easily due to the margin of appreciation. It is also clear that any member State that chooses to allow the practice of assisted dying must take the necessary steps and put adequate safeguards in place to ensure the safety of others as part of its positive obligation under Article 2 of the Convention. The States must also provide sufficient clarity as to the legal boundaries of their assisted dying practices.

Combining the analysis of permissive jurisdictions and the case law of the ECtHR, there are a few lessons, or in other words duties under the ECHR, one can deduct for the practice of assisted dying. Slippery slope

First, all relevant procedural aspects should be defined with clarity in order to provide sufficient guidance to both healthcare professionals and patients. While the legislators should set out the legal framework, the medical associations are better suited to draw up guidelines that deal with details requiring expert knowledge, ranging from what dosage of medication should be used for euthanasia to the determination of when an illness becomes terminal. The involvement of the medical associations in the Dutch practice is a good example of this. However, it should not be forgotten that medical associations are not legislators, and they should neither be left alone with the responsibility to determine the boundaries of assisted dying nor be tasked to be the guardians of the practice.

Second, psychiatric consultation should always take place. This is not only necessary to assess whether the patient has the decision-making capacity to make an end-of-life decision, but also to reveal any other reasons that could be motivating the request to die. For example, the main reason could be the fear of becoming a burden to one's family, and reassurance from a family member could perhaps change the situation. Care must be given to determine whether the request is truly authentic.

Third, there should be a palliative filter. Although patients cannot be forced to choose other alternatives, they must be nevertheless informed of all available options. In order to inform the patient properly, the physician should consult a palliative care specialist.[1]

[1] A research done in 2015 ranks countries according to a 'Quality of Death Index', which is a score given to the end-of-life care system with consideration to the 'palliative and healthcare environment', 'human resources', 'affordability of care', 'quality of care' and 'community engagement'. According to the Quality of Death Index, Belgium has ranked 5th, the Netherlands 8th and Switzerland 15th with their overall scores. While the Dutch healthcare system had a better capacity to deliver palliative care than the other two, Belgium had a perfect score in affordability. The Economist Intelligence Unit (2015) The 2015 Quality of Life Index. https://eiuperspectives.economist.com/healthcare/2015-quality-death-index.

Fourth, an effective supervisory system should be put in place. Transparency is an important principle, and non-transparent practices are usually perceived with a touch of scepticism. So far, an ex post facto supervision has been favoured by the permissive jurisdictions. An a priori supervision might provide more safety against any possible abuse and relieve the physician from solely carrying the role of gatekeeper. Additionally, an a priori supervision guarantees better compliance with the State's duty to protect the vulnerable.

Fifth, there should be regular research in order to collect data on the assisted dying practice and analyse the statistics to see if there is an increase in the number of people requesting to die with assistance. If that is the case, the reasons behind the increasing number should be investigated and thoroughly addressed in due time.

Furthermore, the patients' morale should be considered when setting procedural rules so as to not expose them to unnecessary stress and hardship. Additionally, psychological support should be made available, or in fact compulsory, to the healthcare personal participating in assisted dying procedures.

The interests that stand against the realization of personal autonomy in the context of the right to die must be identified accurately. As John Stuart Mill has so elegantly summarized, 'the only purpose for which power can be rightfully exercised over any member of a civilized community, against his will, is to prevent harm to others'.[2] Is there harm in allowing someone who is competent enough to assess his or her best interests, to choose what he or she considers to be a dignified end? The balance will shift in favour of the right to die as the respect for personal autonomy grows stronger. However, personal autonomy is not limitless, and especially in the matter of end-of-life decisions, there are several other aspects that must be considered. The intensity of the competing interests will not always be the same, for example, in the case of a patient who is in agony due to a severe somatic illness and in the case of a patient suffering from a psychiatric disorder. Psychiatric disorders can be challenging to diagnose, and the course of treatment will likely be unique for each patient, further complicating the prognosis. With the complex nature of psychiatric disorders in mind, establishing a general set of rules that are applicable to all circumstances is a highly troublesome task. Therefore, one must proceed with the utmost caution when arguing in favour of assisted dying in such cases. Moreover, assisted dying for those who are neither suffering from physical nor psychological problems but are merely tired of life presents additional difficulties. Even if the request for an assisted death is autonomous and well-considered, involving a physician in a person's death, whose request is based on non-medical reasons, is difficult to reconcile with the ethics of medicine.

At this point, it should be acknowledged that a purely legal approach falls short of providing satisfying answers to the right-to-die question. The most basic counterargument is the protection of life, or more concretely stated, the protection of the vulnerable. It is argued that no amount of safeguards could remedy the risk of abuse, which is also called the slippery slope, inherent in the practice of the right to

[2] Mill (2010, originally published in 1859), p. 27.

die. This argument is based on the fear that legalizing assisted dying will put the lives of those who do not really wish to die in danger. Whether someone has the capacity to make an end-of-life decision involves psychiatry. Whether this decision is taken freely and autonomously involves both psychiatry and psychology. An assisted death is most often requested in cases of terminal illness and unbearable pain that requires medical expertise. Whether there are alternatives that would improve the situation of the person wishing to die is a matter of palliative care. If purposefully causing a patient's death is compatible with a physician's role is a matter of medical ethics. The evaluation of whether there is a possibility that the practice of assisted dying would devalue life and normalize the killing of others requires both a psychological and sociological approach. While the protection of the vulnerable has been addressed here, arguments based on religious or spiritual beliefs on the value of life have been avoided since such beliefs cannot be imposed on others and, therefore, should not be listed as competing interests. However, it is also undeniable that religion plays a role in shaping societal views and, in turn, affecting the acceptability of the right to die. There are also highly controversial moral, ethical, and philosophical aspects. An interdisciplinary cooperation is the most favourable approach in identifying the extent to which personal autonomy can be exercised in the form of the right to die without harming others.

It is not likely that the ECtHR will deviate from its procedural approach in the near future and impose the implementation of the right to die on jurisdictions where it has not already been put into practice. Member States are far from reaching a consensus on the applicability of the right to die. However, it is a topic that receives ever-growing attention. Considering the ongoing debates in several Parliaments and the recent judgments from the Italian and Austrian Constitutional Courts on the matter, the right to die is certainly not losing momentum.

References

Mill JS (2010, originally published in 1859) On liberty. Penguin Books, London

The Economist Intelligence Unit (2015) The 2015 Quality of Life Index. https://eiuperspectives.economist.com/healthcare/2015-quality-death-index

Table of Cases

Austria

Austrian Case on Assisted Suicide [2020] VfGH G 139/2019-71

Belgium

Case on the 2014 Amendment [2015] Cour constitutionnelle Judgment No 153/2015

Canada

AB v Canada (Attorney General) 2017 ONSC 3759, 139 OR (3d) 139
AC v Manitoba (Director of Child and Family Services) 2009 SCC 30, [2009] 2 SCR 181
Andrews v Law Society of British Columbia (1989) 1 SCR 143 (SCC)
Burke v Prince Edwards Island (1991) 93 Nfld PEIR 356 (Supreme Court-Trial Division of Prince Edward Island)
Canada (Attorney General) v Bedford 2013 SCC 72, [2013] SCR 1101
Carter v Canada (Attorney General) [2012] BCSC 886 (BCSC)
Carter v Canada (Attorney General) [2013] BCCA 435 (BCCA)
Carter v Canada (Attorney General) 2015 SCC 5, [2015] 1 SCR 331
R v Morgentaler (1988) 1 SCR 30 (SCC)
R v Oakes (1986) 1 RCS 103 (SCC)
Rodriguez v British Columbia (Attorney General) [1992] 18 WCB (2d) 279, [1993] BCWLD 347
Rodriguez v British Columbia (Attorney General) (1993) CanLII 1191 (BCCA)
Rodriguez v British Columbia (Attorney General) (1993) 3 SCR 519 (SCC)
Truchon c Procureur général du Canada 2019 QCCS 3792

D. N. Kayacan, *The Right to Die with Dignity*, European Union and its Neighbours in a Globalized World 6, https://doi.org/10.1007/978-3-031-04516-5

Colombia

[1997] Colombian Constitutional Court Decision C-239/1997
[2014] Colombian Constitutional Court Decision T-970/2014
[2017] Colombian Constitutional Court Decision T-544/2017

European Court of Human Rights

A v the United Kingdom 23 September 1998 ECHR 1998-VI
Afiri and Biddarri v France (dec) App no 1828/18, 23 January 2018
Airey v Ireland 9 October 1979 Ser A no 32
Artico v Italy 13 May 1980 Ser A no 37
Calvelli and Ciglio v Italy [GC] App no 32967/96 ECHR 2002-I
Case 'relating to certain aspects of the laws on the use of languages in education in Belgium' (merits) 23 July 1968 Ser A no 6
Centre for Legal Resources on behalf of Valentin Câmpeanu v Romania [GC] App no 47848/08 ECHR 2014
D v the United Kingdom 2 May 1997 ECHR 1997-III
Gard and Others v the United Kingdom (dec) App no 39793/17, 27 June 2017
Gross v Switzerland App no 67810/10, 14 May 2013
Gross v Switzerland [GC] App no 67810/10 ECHR 2014
Haas v Switzerland App no 31322/07 ECHR 2011
Hasan and Chaush v Bulgaria [GC] App no 30985/96 ECHR 2000-XI
Kılavuz v Turkey App no 8327/03, 21 October 2008
Koch v Germany App no 497/09, 19 July 2012
Lambert and Others v France [GC] App no 46043/14 ECHR 2015 (extracts)
McCann and Others v the United Kingdom 27 September 1995 Ser A no 324
Mortier v Belgium App no 78017/17 (pending case)
Nicklinson and Lamb v the United Kingdom Apps No 2478/15 and 1787/15, 23 June 2015
Osman v the United Kingdom App no 23452/94 ECHR 1998-VIII
Pretty v the United Kingdom App no 2346/02 ECHR 2002-III
R v the United Kingdom (1983) 33 DR 270 (European Commission of Human Rights)
Rees v the United Kingdom 17 October 1986 Ser A no 106
Sanles Sanles v Spain (dec) App no 48335/99 ECHR 2000-XI

European Court of Justice

Case C-159/90 *The Society for the Protection of Unborn Children Ireland Ltd v Stephen Grogan and others* [1991] ECR I-04685

Germany

[2020] BVerfG 1 BvL 2/20
Against the Federal Institute [2019] BVerwG 3 C 6.17
Case on Sec 217 [2020] BVerfG 2 BvR 2347/15

Koch [2008] BVerfG 1 BvR 1832
Koch (2) [2017] BVerwG 3 C 19.15

Italy

[2019] Italian Constitutional Court Judgment No 242/2019

Switzerland

Aargau Case [2005] Verwaltungsgericht des Kantons Aargau BE 2003.00354-K3
Baumann [2009] BGer 6B_14/2009 & 6B_48/2009
Case on the Blue Oasis [2007] Verwaltungsgericht des Kantons Zürich VB.2007.00472
Dignitas v Swissmedic [2008] BGer 2C_839/2008
Dr X [2005] BGer 2P.310/2004
Dr Y [2008] BGer 2C_191/2008
ERAS and others [2018] BGer 2C_608/2017
Case on the EXIT Agreement [2010] BGer 1C_438/2009, BGE 136 II 415
Haas [2006] BGer 2A.48/2006 & 2A.66/2006, BGE 133 58
Zurich Case [1999] Verwaltungsgericht des Kantons Zürich VB.99.00145, (2000) AJP 474

The Netherlands

Brongersma-RB [2000] Rechtbank Haarlem ECLI:NL:RBHAA:2000:AA7926
Brongersma-GH [2001] Gerechtshof Amsterdam ECLI:NL:GHAMS:2001:AD6753
Brongersma-HR [2002] Hoge Raad ECLI:NL:HR:2002:AE8772
Case on Dementia-RB [2019] Rechtbank Den Haag ECLI:NL:RBDHA:2019:9506
Case on Dementia-HR [2020] Hoge Raad ECLI:NL:HR:2020:712
Chabot [1994] Hoge Raad ECLI:NL:HR:1994:AD2122
Pols [1984] Rechtbank Groningen ECLI:NL:RBGRO:1984:AB7546
Pols [1984] Gerechtshof Leeuwarden ECLI:NL:GHLEE:1984:AC2140
Pols [1986] Hoge Raad ECLI:NL:HR:1986:AC9531
Postma [1973] Rechtbank Leeuwarden ECLI:NL:RBLEE:1973:AB5464
Schoonheim [1984] Hoge Raad ECLI:NL:HR:1984:AC8615
Schoonheim [1986] Gerechtshof's-Gravenhage ECLI:NL:GHSGR:1986:AC8621
van Oijen [2003] Gerechtshof Amsterdam ECLI:NL:GHAMS:2003:AF9392
van Oijen [2004] Hoge Raad ECLI:NL:HR:2004:AP1493
Wertheim [1981] Rechtbank Rotterdam ECLI:NL:RBROT:1981:AB7817

The United Kingdom

Airedale NHS Trust v Bland [1993] UKHL 17, [1993] AC 789
Local Authority v Z [2004] EWHC 2817 (Fam)
Pretty v Director of Public Prosecutions and Secretary of State for the Home Department [2001] UKHL 61, [2002] 1 AC 800
R (AM) v General Medical Council (Martin v GMC) [2015] EWHC 2096 (Admin)

R (Conway) v Secretary of State for Justice [2017] EWHC 640 (Admin)
R (Conway) v Secretary of State for Justice [2018] EWCA Civ 1431
R (Conway) v Secretary of State for Justice [2018] UKSC B1
R (Newby) v Secretary of State for Justice [2019] EWHC 3118 (Admin)
R (Nicklinson and another) v Ministry of Justice, R (AM) v Director of Public Prosecutions [2013] EWCA Civ 961
R (Nicklinson and another) v Ministry of Justice, R (AM) v Director of Public Prosecutions [2014] UKSC 38, [2015] AC 657
R (Purdy) v the Director of Public Prosecutions [2009] UKHL 45, [2010] 1 AC 345
R (Purdy) v the Director of Public Prosecutions [2009] EWCA Civ 92
Re J (A Minor) (Wardship: Medical Treatment) [1990] 3 AII ER 930

Table of Legislation

United Nations

Convention on Psychotropic Substances of 1971, 9 December 1975, A/RES/3443, available at https://treaties.un.org/pages/ViewDetails.aspx?src=TREATY&mtdsg_no=VI-16&chapter=6

Convention on the Rights of the Child, 20 November 1989, United Nations, Treaty Series, vol 1577, 3, available at https://treaties.un.org/Pages/ViewDetails.aspx?src=TREATY&mtdsg_no=IV-11&chapter=4&clang=_en

International Covenant on Civil and Political Rights, 16 December 1966, United Nations, Treaty Series vol 999, 171, available at https://treaties.un.org/pages/ViewDetails.aspx?src=TREATY&mtdsg_no=IV-4&chapter=4&clang=_en

Council of Europe

Convention for the Protection of Human Rights and Dignity of the Human Being with regard to the Application of Biology and Medicine: Convention on Human Rights and Biomedicine, 4 April 1997, ETS No 164 (Oviedo Convention), available at https://www.coe.int/en/web/bioethics/oviedo-convention

European Convention for the Protection of Human Rights and Fundamental Freedoms, as amended by Protocols Nos 11 and 14, 4 November 1950, ETS 5, available at https://www.coe.int/en/web/conventions/full-list

Protocol No 15 amending the Convention for the Protection of Human Rights and Fundamental Freedoms, 24 June 2013, CETS No 213

Protocol No 16 to the Convention for the Protection of Human Rights and Fundamental Freedoms, 2 October 2013, CETS No 214

Resolution (96) 9 on Observor Status for Canada with the Council of Europe (adopted by the Committee of Ministers on 3 April 1996 at the 562nd meeting of the Ministers' Deputies) 1996, available at https://search.coe.int/cm/Pages/result_details.aspx?ObjectId=09000016804c8f65

D. N. Kayacan, *The Right to Die with Dignity*, European Union and its Neighbours in a Globalized World 6, https://doi.org/10.1007/978-3-031-04516-5

European Union

Charter of Fundamental Rights of the European Union, 26 October 2012, OJ C 326/391, available at https://eur-lex.europa.eu/legal-content/EN/TXT/?uri=celex%3A12012P%2FTXT

Consolidated Version of the Treaty on the Functioning of the European Union (TFEU) 26 October 2012, OJ C 326/47, available at https://eur-lex.europa.eu/legal-content/EN/TXT/?uri=celex%3A12012E%2FTXT

Australia

Victoria, Voluntary Assisted Dying Act 2017, No 61 of 2017 (19 June 2020) available at https://www.legislation.vic.gov.au/in-force/acts/voluntary-assisted-dying-act-2017/004

Western Australia, Voluntary Assisted Dying Act 2019, No 027 of 2019 (19 December 2019) available at https://www.legislation.wa.gov.au/legislation/statutes.nsf/law_a147242.html

Austria

Federal Act on the Establishment of Dying Wills (*Bundesgesetz über die Errichtung von Sterbeverfügungen – Sterbeverfügungsgesetz, StVfG*) BGBI. I Nr. 242/2021, 31 December 2021 available in German at https://www.parlament.gv.at/PAKT/VHG/XXVII/I/I_01177/index.shtml

Belgium

1994021048 Belgian Constitution of 17 February 1994 (17 March 2021) (*De gecoördineerde Grondwet, La Constitution coordonnée*) English translation available at https://www.dekamer.be/kvvcr/showpage.cfm?section=/publications/constitution&language=nl&story=constitution.xml

1867060850 Criminal Code of 8 June 1867 (4 May 2020) (*Strafwetboek, Code Penal*) available in French at http://www.ejustice.just.fgov.be/eli/loi/1867/06/08/1867060850/justel

2002009590 Act on Euthanasia of 28 May 2002 (23 March 2020) (*Wet betreffende de euthanasia, Loi relative à l'euthanasie*) available in French at http://www.ejustice.just.fgov.be/eli/loi/2002/05/28/2002009590/justel

2002022737 Act on Patients' Rights of 22 August 2002 (31 December 2018) (*Wet betreffende de rechten van de patient, Loi relative aux droits du patient*) available in French at http://www.ejustice.just.fgov.be/eli/loi/2002/08/22/2002022737/justel

2002022868 Act on Palliative Care of 14 June 2002 (21 March 2018) (*Wet betreffende de palliatieve zorg, Loi relative aux soins palliatifs*) available in French at http://www.ejustice.just.fgov.be/eli/loi/2002/06/14/2002022868/justel

2020040680 Act amending the Belgian legislation on euthanasia of 15 March 2020 (*Wet tot wijziging van de wetgeving betreffende de euthanasia*) available in

French at https://www.ejustice.just.fgov.be/cgi_loi/change_lg.pl?language=fr&la=F&table_name=loi&cn=2020031502

Canada

Canadian Charter of Rights and Freedoms, Part I of the Constitution Act, 1982, Schedule B to the Canada Act 1982 (UK), 1982, c 11, available at https://laws-lois.justice.gc.ca/eng/Const/page-15.html

Canadian Criminal Code, RSC 1985, c C-46 (before the amendment of 16 June 2016, after the amendments of 16 June 2016 and 17 March 2021) all versions available at https://laws-lois.justice.gc.ca/eng/acts/c-46/

An Act to amend the Criminal Code and to make related amendments to other Acts (medical assistance in dying) SC 2016, c 3 (17 June 2016) available at https://laws-lois.justice.gc.ca/eng/annualstatutes/2016_3/fulltext.html

An Act to amend the Criminal Code (medical assistance in dying) SC 2021, c 2 (17 March 2021) available at https://laws-lois.justice.gc.ca/eng/AnnualStatutes/2021_2/page-1.html

Regulations for the Monitoring of Medical Assistance in Dying, SOR/2018-166 (1 November 2019) available at https://laws-lois.justice.gc.ca/eng/regulations/SOR-2018-166/index.html

France

Code of Public Health (*Code de la santé publique*) available in French at https://www.legifrance.gouv.fr/codes/texte_lc/LEGITEXT000006072665/?isSuggest=true

Act No 2005-370 of 22 April 2005 on patients' rights and end of life (*Loi relative aux droits des malades et à la fin de vie*) available in French at https://www.legifrance.gouv.fr/jorf/id/JORFTEXT000000446240/

Act No 2016-87 of 2 February 2016 establishing new rights to patients and the terminally ill (*Loi créant de nouveaux droits en faveur des malades et des personnes en fin de vie*) available in French at https://www.legifrance.gouv.fr/loda/id/JORFTEXT000031970253/2016-02-04#JORFTEXT000031970253

Germany

Basic Law of the Federal Republic of Germany of 23 May 1949 (1 January 2021) (*Grundgesetz für die Bundesrepublik Deutschland*) available in German at https://www.bundestag.de/gg, English translation available at https://www.gesetze-im-internet.de/englisch_gg/index.html

Criminal Code of 13 November 1998 (19 October 2021) (*Strafgesetzbuch*) available in German at https://dejure.org/gesetze/StGB, English translation of the 28 June 2019 version available at https://www.gesetze-im-internet.de/englisch_stgb/index.html

Act on the Trade of Narcotic Drugs of 28 July 1981 (9 June 2021) (*Betäubungsmittelgesetz*) available in German at https://dejure.org/gesetze/

BtMG, English translation of the 22 January 2010 version available at https://www.bundesgesundheitsministerium.de/fileadmin/Dateien/3_Downloads/Gesetze_und_Verordnungen/GuV/N/Narcotic_Drugs_18_12_2009.pdf

New Zealand

End of Life Choice Act 2019, 2019 No 67 (7 November 2020) available at https://www.legislation.govt.nz/act/public/2019/0067/latest/DLM7285905.html

Spain

The Organic Law for the Regulation of Euthanasia (*Ley Orgánica 3/2021, de 24 de marzo, de regulación de la eutanasia*) BOE no 72, 25 March 2021, 34037-34049 available in Spanish at https://www.boe.es/diario_boe/txt.php?id=BOE-A-2021-4628

Switzerland

101 Federal Constitution of the Swiss Confederation of 18 April 1999, SR 101 (1 January 2021) (*Bundesverfassung der Schweizerischen Eidgenossenschaft*) available at https://www.fedlex.admin.ch/eli/cc/1999/404/en

301.100 Aargau Cantonal Health Act of 10 November 1987 (before the amendment of 20 January 2009) (*Gesundheitsgesetz Kanton Aargau*) available in German at https://www.lexfind.ch/fe/de/tol/121/versions/542/de

311.0 Swiss Criminal Code of 21 December 1937 (1 July 2020) (*Schweizerisches Strafgesetzbuch*) available at https://www.fedlex.admin.ch/eli/cc/54/757_781_799/en

810.1 Zurich Cantonal Health Act of 4 November 1962 (before the amendment of 2 April 2007) (*Gesundheitsgesetz Kanton Zürich*) available in German at http://www.zhlex.zh.ch/Erlass.html?Open&Ordnr=810.1,04.11.1962,20.11.1962,055

812.21 Federal Act on Medicinal Products and Medical Devices of 15 December 2000 (1 August 2020) (*Bundesgesetz über Arzneimittel und Medizinprodukte*) available at https://www.fedlex.admin.ch/eli/cc/2001/422/en

812.121 Federal Act on Narcotics and Psychotropic Substances of 3 October 1951 (1 February 2020) (*Bundesgesetz über die Betäubungsmittel und die psychotropen Stoffe*) available at https://www.fedlex.admin.ch/eli/cc/1952/241_241_245/en

812.121.1 Ordinance on Narcotics Control of 25 May 2011 (1 January 2013) (*Verordnung über die Betäubungsmittelkontrolle*) available in German at https://www.fedlex.admin.ch/eli/cc/2011/362/de

812.121.11 Ordinance of the FDHA on the Lists of Narcotics, Psychotropic Substances, Precursors and Auxiliary Chemicals of 30 May 2011 (15 December 2020) (*Verordnung des EDI über die Verzeichnisse der Betäubungsmittel, psychotropen Stoffe, Vorläuferstoffe und Hilfschemikalien*) available in German at https://www.fedlex.admin.ch/eli/cc/2011/363/de#fn-d14668e237

The Netherlands

BWBR0001854 Criminal Code of 3 March 1881 (1 August 2021) (*Wetboek van Strafrecht*) available in Dutch at https://wetten.overheid.nl/BWBR0001854/2021-07-01, English translation of the 1 October 2012 version available at https://www.legislationline.org/documents/section/criminal-codes/country/12/Netherlands/show

BWBR0005009 Burial Act of 7 March 1991 (*Wet op de lijkbezorging*) available in Dutch at https://wetten.overheid.nl/BWBR0005009/2018-08-01

BWBR0012410 Termination of Life on Request and Assistance with Suicide (Review Procedures) Act of 10 April 2001 (19 March 2020) (*Wet toetsing levensbeëindiging op verzoek en hulp bij zelfdoding*) available in Dutch at https://wetten.overheid.nl/BWBR0012410/2020-03-19, English translation of the 1 April 2002 version available at https://www.ieb-eib.org/ancien-site/pdf/loi-euthanasie-pays-bas-en-eng.pdf

The United Kingdom

Suicide Act 1961 (1 February 2010) available at https://www.legislation.gov.uk/ukpga/Eliz2/9-10/60

Coroners and Justice Act (1 February 2010) 2009 available at https://www.legislation.gov.uk/ukpga/2009/25/contents

The manufacturer's authorised representative in the EU is Springer Nature Customer Service Centre GmbH, Europaplatz 3, 69115 Heidelberg, Germany. If you have any concerns regarding our products, please contact ProductSafety@springernature.com

Printed and bound by CPI Group (UK) Ltd, Croydon, CR0 4YY
30/09/2026
02225497-0009